# Contents

**Working Together to Safeguard Children: Executive Summary**    7
    Introduction    7
    Part 1: Statutory guidance    8
    Part 2: Non-statutory practice guidance    18

**Preface**    22
    Introduction    22
    Purpose of the document and who should read it    22
    Content of this guidance    24
    Other related guidance    24
    Status of the document as statutory guidance    25
    When does the guidance apply?    26

**Glossary**    27

**Part 1: Statutory Guidance**    28

**Chapter 1 – Introduction: working together to safeguard and promote the welfare of children and families**    29
    Supporting children and families    29
    Parenting, family life and services    29
    Lord Laming's progress report    30
    The Government's response    30
    An integrated approach    31
    A shared responsibility    31
    The child in focus    32
    Key definitions    34

**Chapter 2 – Roles and responsibilities**    40
    Introduction    40
    The statutory framework within which organisations operate    40
    Infrastructure and governance to deliver safeguarding responsibilities    42
    Information sharing    43
    ContactPoint    44
    Common Assessment Framework (CAF)    44
    Local authorities that are children's services authorities    45
    Other local authority roles    48
    Health services    51

Health organisations                                                                52
Roles of different health services                                                  60
Health professionals                                                                67
Criminal justice organisations                                                      70
Schools and further education institutions                                          78
Early years services                                                                80
Children and Family Court Advisory and Support Service (Cafcass)                    81
The armed services                                                                  82
The voluntary and private sectors                                                   84
Faith communities                                                                   86

## Chapter 3 – Local Safeguarding Children Boards                                   88
LSCB role                                                                           88
Scope of the LSCB                                                                    89
LSCB functions                                                                      90
Other policies and procedures                                                       93
LSCB governance and operational arrangements                                        99
Membership of an LSCB                                                               102

## Chapter 4 – Training, development and supervision for inter-agency working       113
Introduction and definitions                                                       113
Purpose                                                                            114
Roles and responsibilities                                                         114
Content, audiences and values                                                      118
Planning, organisation, delivery and evaluation                                    121
Effective support and supervision                                                  123
Table 1: Suggested training for different target groups                            126

## Chapter 5 – Managing individual cases where there are concerns about a child's safety and welfare    133
Introduction                                                                       133
Working with children when there are concerns about their
safety and welfare                                                                 133
Principles underpinning work to safeguard and promote
the welfare of children                                                            134
The processes for safeguarding and promoting the welfare of children               137
The welfare of unborn children                                                     140
Referrals to local authority children's social care where there are
concerns about a child's safety or welfare                                         140
Response of local authority children's social care to a referral                   144
Initial assessment                                                                 146

HM Government

# Working Together to Safeguard Children

## A guide to inter-agency working to safeguard and promote the welfare of children

**March 2010**

Next steps – child in need but no suspected actual or likely significant harm    150
Next steps – suspicion that a child is suffering, or is likely to suffer,
significant harm    151
Immediate protection    152
Strategy discussion    153
Section 47 enquiries and core assessment    155
Child Assessment Orders    158
The impact of section 47 enquiries on the family and child    159
The outcome of section 47 enquiries    159
Concerns are not substantiated    160
Concerns are substantiated, but the child is not judged
to be continuing to, or be likely to, suffer significant harm    160
Concerns are substantiated and the child is judged to be
continuing to, or be likely to, suffer significant harm    162
The initial child protection conference    162
Action following the initial child protection conference    172
Completion of the core assessment    174
The child protection plan    175
Intervention    176
The child protection review conference    179
Discontinuing the child protection plan    180
Children looked after by the local authority    181
Pre-birth child protection conferences and reviews    182
Recording that a child is the subject of a child protection plan    182
Managing and providing information about a child    183
Recording in individual case records    184
Request for a change of worker    185

**Chapter 6 – Supplementary guidance on safeguarding
and promoting the welfare of children    191**
Introduction    191
Sexually exploited children    191
Children affected by gang activity    192
Fabricated or induced illness (FII)    192
Investigating complex (organised or multiple) abuse    194
Female genital mutilation    195
Forced marriage and honour-based violence    196
Allegations of abuse made against a person who works with children    199
Abuse of disabled children    201
Child abuse linked to belief in 'spirit possession'    204
Child victims of trafficking    204

## Chapter 7 – Child death review processes    208

Introduction    208
Overall principles    209
Involvement of parents and family members (for all child deaths)    209
The Regulations relating to child deaths    210
Supply of information about child deaths by registrars    211
Duty and powers of coroners to share information    212
Duty and powers of Medical Examiners (MEs) to share information    212
Definition of an unexpected death of a child    212
Definition of preventable child deaths    213
LSCB responsibilities for the child death review processes    213
Procedures to be followed by the local Child Death Overview Panel
(for all child deaths)    215
The process to be followed by Child Death Overview Panels
(for all child deaths)    217
Roles and responsibilities when responding rapidly to an
unexpected death of a child    220
Other related processes    221
Processes for a rapid response from professionals to all
unexpected deaths of children (0–18 years)    223
Use of child death information to prevent future deaths    231

## Chapter 8 – Serious case reviews    233

Reviewing and investigative functions of Local Safeguarding Children Boards    233
The purposes of Serious Case Reviews    234
Safeguarding siblings or other children    234
When should a LSCB undertake a Serious Case Review?    235
When should a LSCB consider undertaking a Serious Case Review?    235
Which LSCB should take lead responsibility?    237
Membership of SCR sub-committees and SCR Panels    237
Instigating a Serious Case Review    238
Timescales for initiating and undertaking a Serious Case Review    241
Who should be involved in the Serious Case Review?    242
Individual management reviews – general principles    243
The Serious Case Review overview report    247
SCR Panel responsibilities for the overview report    248
The executive summary    249
LSCB action on receiving the Serious Case Review report    251
Reviewing institutional abuse    252
Accountability and disclosure    253
Learning lessons locally    254
Learning lessons nationally    255

## Part 2: Non-statutory practice guidance                                    257

## Chapter 9 – Lessons from research                                          258

Introduction                                                                  258
The impact of maltreatment on children                                        258
Physical abuse                                                                259
Emotional abuse                                                               260
Sexual abuse                                                                  260
Neglect                                                                       260
Sources of stress for children and families                                  261
Social exclusion                                                              262
Domestic violence                                                             262
Mental illness of a parent or carer                                          265
Parental problem drug use                                                     269
Parental problem alcohol use                                                  274
Parents with a Learning Disability                                            278

## Chapter 10 – Implementing the principles on working with children and their families     284

Introduction                                                                  284
Family group conferences                                                      284
Support, advice and advocacy to children and families                         285
Communication and information                                                 286
Race, ethnicity and culture                                                   286
Children in 'Families at risk' having very poor outcomes                      287
Think Family practice                                                         288
Effectiveness of parenting and family interventions                           289
Working with fathers                                                          290
Family Intervention Projects                                                  290
Family Nurse Partnership                                                      291

## Chapter 11 – Safeguarding and promoting the welfare of children who may be particularly vulnerable     292

Introduction                                                                  292
Children living away from home                                                292
Abuse by children and young people                                            302
Children whose behaviour indicates a lack of parental control                 307
Race and racism                                                               308
Violent extremism                                                             309
Domestic violence                                                             310
Child abuse and information communication technology (ICT)                    315
Children with families whose whereabouts are unknown                          316

Children who go missing                                                      316
Children who go missing from education                                       317
Children of families living in temporary accommodation                       319
Migrant children                                                             319
Unaccompanied asylum-seeking children (UASC)                                 319

## Chapter 12 – Managing individuals who pose a risk of harm to children                                                            322

Introduction                                                                322
Collaborative working                                                       322
Use of the term 'Schedule One offender'                                     322
New offences targeted at those who sexually exploit children and young people 324
Multi-Agency Public Protection Arrangements (MAPPA)                         324
Other processes and mechanisms                                              328

## Appendices

Appendix 1 – Statutory framework                                            336
Appendix 2 – Framework for the Assessment of Children in Need               344
Appendix 3 – Using standardised assessment tools to evidence assessment
                  and decision making                                       350
Appendix 4 – MOD child protection contacts                                  353
Appendix 5 – Procedures for managing allegations against people
                  who work with children                                    356
Appendix 6 – Faith community contacts and resources                         366
Appendix 7 – A guide to acronyms in the document                            368
References and internet links                                               371

# Working Together to Safeguard Children: Executive Summary

## Introduction

Working Together sets out how organisations and individuals should work together to safeguard and promote the welfare of children and young people in accordance with the Children Act 1989 and the Children Act 2004. It is important that all practitioners working to safeguard children and young people understand fully their responsibilities and duties as set out in primary legislation and associated regulations and guidance.

This guidance was most recently updated in 2006. This latest revision follows the publication of Lord Laming's report, *The Protection of Children in England: A Progress Report*, in March 2009, the acceptance by the Government of all of his recommendations and the Government's detailed response and action plan published in May 2009. Many of Lord Laming's recommendations are reflected in or given effect by this revised guidance. It has also been updated to reflect developments in legislation, policy and practice relating to safeguarding children.

Working Together is addressed to practitioners and frontline managers who have particular responsibilities for safeguarding and promoting the welfare of children, and to senior and operational managers in:

- organisations that are responsible for commissioning or providing services to children, young people, and adults who are parents/carers; and

- organisations that have a particular responsibility for safeguarding and promoting the welfare of children and young people.

Part 1 of the document comprises Chapters 1 to 8, which are issued as statutory guidance. Practitioners and agencies will have different responsibilities that apply to different areas of the guidance and should consult the preface for a fuller explanation of their statutory duties. Part 2 of the document incorporates Chapters 9 to 12 and is issued as non-statutory practice guidance.

This executive summary is not guidance in itself. It aims to help readers gain an overview of the document, and of main changes made to the 2006 version.

Over time Working Together has become a lengthy document containing a good deal of material in addition to the core statutory guidance. The Department for Children, Schools and Families will:

- produce an easily navigable web-based version of this document, with hyperlinks to relevant supporting guidance;

- produce in partnership with stakeholders a short practitioner guide; and

- work with stakeholders to identify what might be done to present the document more effectively to ensure that the statutory requirements to safeguard and promote the welfare of children and young people are not inadvertently obscured by non-statutory guidance.

# Part 1: Statutory guidance

## Chapter 1 – Introduction: working together to safeguard and promote the welfare of children and families

Chapter 1 sets the context for the revised guidance by discussing the reasons for the changes in safeguarding policy and practice since 2006. It also outlines the key definitions and concepts used in the guidance.

The publication of the *Every Child Matters* Green Paper in 2003 alongside the formal response to the Inquiry into the death of Victoria Climbié, and followed by the Children Act 2004, set out 'being safe' as one of five important outcomes for children and young people. In this context, three key provisions were:

- the creation of Children's Trusts under the duty to co-operate[1];

- the setting up of Local Safeguarding Children Boards (LSCBs); and

- the duty on all agencies to make arrangements to safeguard and promote the welfare of children.

Lord Laming's progress report, *The Protection of Children in England: A Progress Report*, made 58 recommendations relating to: leadership and accountability, support for children, inter-agency working, children's workforce, improvement and challenge, organisation and finance and the legal framework. The Government's detailed response to Lord Laming's recommendations was published in May 2009. Twenty-three of these recommendations have been addressed by this revised guidance.

Protecting children from harm and promoting their welfare depends on a shared responsibility and effective joint working between different agencies. This in turn relies on constructive relationships between individual practitioners, promoted and supported by:

- the commitment of senior managers to safeguard and promote the welfare of children; and

- clear lines of accountability.

---

1　This has now been strengthened by placing Children's Trust Boards on a statutory footing from 1 April 2010.

## Chapter 2 – Roles and responsibilities

Chapter 2 explains the roles, responsibilities and duties of the different people and organisations that work directly with, and whose work affects, children and young people. It states that all organisations that provide services or work with children and young people should:

- have senior managers who are committed to children's and young people's welfare and safety;

- be clear about people's responsibilities to safeguard and promote children's and young people's welfare;

- check that there are no known reasons or information available that would prevent staff and volunteers from working with children and young people;

- have procedures for dealing with allegations of abuse against members of staff and volunteers;

- make sure staff get training that helps them do their job well;

- have procedures about how to safeguard and promote the welfare of young people; and

- have agreements about working with other organisations.

Section 11 of the Children Act 2004, section 175 of the Education Act 2002 and section 55 of the Borders, Citizenship and Immigration Act 2009 place duties on organisations and individuals to ensure that their functions are discharged with regard to the need to safeguard and promote the welfare of children. An overview of these duties and the structure of children's services under the Children Act 2004 are set out in the preface to this guidance and in Appendix 1.

Safeguarding and promoting the welfare of children is the responsibility of the local authority, working in partnership with other public organisations, the voluntary sector, children and young people, parents and carers, and the wider community. A key objective for local authorities is to ensure that children are protected from harm. Other functions of local authorities that make an important contribution to safeguarding are housing, sport, culture and leisure services, and youth services.

Health professionals and organisations have a key role to play in safeguarding and promoting the welfare of children. The general principles they should apply are:

- to aim to ensure that all affected children receive appropriate and timely preventative and therapeutic interventions;

- those professionals who work directly with children should ensure that safeguarding and promoting their welfare forms an integral part of all stages of the care they offer;

- those professionals who come into contact with children, parents and carers in the course of their work also need to be aware of their safeguarding responsibilities; and

- ensuring that all health professionals can recognise risk factors and contribute to reviews, enquiries and child protection plans, as well as planning support for children and providing ongoing promotional and preventative support through proactive work.

All health professionals working directly with children and young people should ensure that safeguarding and promoting their welfare forms an integral part of all elements of the care they offer.

The police also have a key role in safeguarding children. They recognise the fundamental importance of inter-agency working in combating child abuse, as illustrated by well-established arrangements for joint training involving police and social work colleagues. All forces have child abuse investigation units and while they normally take responsibility for investigating such cases, safeguarding children is a fundamental part of the duties of all police officers.

The police are committed to sharing information and intelligence with other organisations and should be notified as soon as possible where a criminal offence has been, or is suspected of, being committed. LSCBs should have in place a protocol agreed between the local authority and the police, to guide both organisations in deciding how section 47 enquiries should be conducted, and in which circumstances joint enquiries are appropriate.

Probation services supervise offenders with the aim of reducing re-offending and protecting the public. By working with offenders who are parents/carers, Offender Managers can safeguard and promote the welfare of children. Probation areas/Trusts will also:

- provide a statutory victim contact scheme to the victims of violent and sexual offences;

- deliver unpaid work requirements to 16- and 17-year olds;

- fulfil their role as statutory partner of YOTs; and

- ensure support for victims, and indirectly children in the family, of convicted perpetrators of domestic abuse participating in accredited domestic abuse programmes.

Offender Managers should also ensure there is clarity and communication between risk management processes; these are described in greater detail in Chapter 12.

Governors/Directors of all prison establishments should have in place arrangements that protect the public from prisoners in their care. All prisoners who have been identified as presenting a risk of harm to children will not be allowed contact with them unless a favourable risk assessment has been undertaken by the police, probation, prison and children's social care services. Governors/Directors of women's establishments with Mother and Baby Units need to ensure that staff working on duty are prioritised for child protection training.

Governors/Directors of Young Offender Institutions (YOIs) are required to adhere to the policies, agreed by the Prison Service and the Youth Justice Board, for safeguarding and promoting the welfare of children held in custody.

Secure Training Centres (STCs) house vulnerable, sentenced and remanded young people aged between 12 and 17 years. Each STC has a duty to safeguard and promote the welfare of the children in its custody.

Youth Offending Teams are responsible for the supervision of children and young people subject to pre-court interventions and statutory court disposals. YOTs have a duty to make arrangements to ensure that their functions are discharged with regard to the need to safeguard and promote the welfare of children.

Schools (including independent and non-maintained schools) and further education institutions have a duty to safeguard and promote the welfare of pupils under the Education Act 2002. They should create and maintain a safe learning environment for children and young people, and identify where there are child welfare concerns and take action to address them, in partnership with other organisations where appropriate.

Early years services – children's centres, nurseries, childminders, pre-schools, playgroups, and holiday and out-of-school schemes – all play an important part in the lives of large numbers of children. Everyone working in early years services should know how to recognise and respond to the possible abuse and neglect of a child. The Early Years Foundation Stage makes it clear that all registered providers, except childminders, must have a practitioner who is designated to take lead responsibility for safeguarding children within each early years setting and who should liaise with local statutory children's services agencies as appropriate.

In care and related proceedings under the Children Act 1989, the responsibility of the Children and Family Court Advisory and Support Service (Cafcass) is to safeguard and promote the welfare of individual children who are the subject of family proceedings by providing independent social work advice to the court.

Under section 55 of the Borders, Citizenship and Immigration Act 2009 the UKBA has a duty to ensure that its functions are discharged with regard to the need to safeguard and promote the welfare of children.

Looking after under 18 year olds in the armed forces comes under the Ministry of Defence's comprehensive welfare arrangements, which apply to all members of the armed forces. There is already a responsibility on children's social care services to monitor the welfare of care leavers, and those joining the armed forces have unrestricted access to local authority social care services staff.

The voluntary sector is active in working to safeguard the children and young people with whom they work, and plays a key role in providing information and resources to the wider public about the needs of children.

Faith communities provide a wide range of activities for children and, as such, should have appropriate arrangements in place to safeguard and promote their welfare.

## Chapter 3 – Local Safeguarding Children Boards

Chapter 3 explains the role, functions, governance and operation of Local Safeguarding Children Boards.

The LSCB is the key statutory mechanism for agreeing how the relevant organisations in each local area will co-operate to safeguard and promote the welfare of children, and for ensuring the effectiveness of what they do.

The scope of the LSCB role falls into three categories: firstly, they engage in activities that safeguard all children and aim to identify and prevent maltreatment, or impairment of health or development, and to ensure that children are growing up in circumstances consistent with safe and effective care; secondly, they lead and co-ordinate proactive work that aims to target particular groups; and thirdly, they lead and co-ordinate arrangements for responsive work to protect children who are suffering, or likely to suffer, significant harm.

The core functions of an LSCB are set out in regulations and are:

- developing policies and procedures including those on:
  - action taken where there are concerns about the safety and welfare of a child, including thresholds for intervention;
  - training of people who work with children or in services affecting the safety and welfare of children;
  - recruitment and supervision of people who work with children;

- investigation of allegations concerning people who work with children;

- safety and welfare of children who are privately fostered; and

- co-operation with neighbouring children's services authorities (i.e. local authorities) and their LSCB partners.

- communicating and raising awareness;

- monitoring and evaluation;

- participating in planning and commissioning;

- reviewing the deaths of all children in their areas; and

- undertaking Serious Case Reviews.

County-level and unitary local authorities are responsible for establishing an LSCB in their area and ensuring that it is run effectively. LSCBs should have a clear and distinct identity within local Children's Trust governance arrangements. It is the responsibility of the local authority, after consultation with Board partners, to appoint the Chair of the LSCB.

Membership of the LSCB is made up of senior managers from different services and agencies in a local area, including the independent and voluntary sector. In addition, the Board receives input from experts – for example, the designated nurse or doctor.

To function effectively, LSCBs need to be supported by their member organisations with adequate and reliable resources. The budget for each LSCB and the contribution made by each member organisation should be agreed locally.

LSCBs should ensure the effectiveness of work undertaken by member organisations through a variety of mechanisms including peer review, self-evaluation, performance indicators and joint audit.

Key changes to Chapter 3 since 2006 include the requirement for LSCBs to produce and publish an annual report on the effectiveness of safeguarding in the local area, the appointment of two representatives of the local community to each LSCB, statutory representation on the LSCB of schools and, subject to the passage of the Children Schools and Families Bill, a provision to ensure appropriate information is disclosed to the LSCB in order to assist it in the exercise of its functions.

The revised chapter also provides further clarity over the complementary roles of the LSCB and the Children's Trust Board and makes clear that the Chair of the LSCB should be someone independent of the local agencies. Taken together, these changes aim to strengthen transparency and accountability of LSCBs.

## Chapter 4 – Training, development and supervision for inter-agency working

Chapter 4 covers training, development and supervision to enable those working with children to develop the necessary skills, judgement and confidence. Training for multi- and inter-agency working means training that will equip people to work effectively with those from other professions and agencies.

Employers are responsible for ensuring their employees are confident and competent in carrying out their responsibilities, and for ensuring employees are aware of how to recognise and respond to safeguarding concerns. Employers should also identify adequate resources and support for inter-agency training.

Through their work on the local Children and Young People's Plan, Children's Trust Boards are responsible for ensuring that workforce strategies are developed in their local areas. An LSCB should contribute to, and work within, the framework of the local workforce strategy. The LSCB is responsible for developing local policies for the training of people who work with children or in services affecting the safety and welfare of children. This includes training in relation to child death review processes and Serious Case Reviews. LSCBs should review and evaluate the provision and availability of single and inter-agency training to ensure training reaches all relevant staff.

All training in safeguarding and promoting the welfare of children should create an ethos that:

- is child-centred;

- promotes the participation of children and families in the processes;

- values working collaboratively;

- respects diversity; and

- promotes equality.

*The Common Core of Skills and Knowledge for the Children's Workforce* (2010)[2] sets out the six areas of expertise that everyone working with children, young people and families should be able to demonstrate. These include safeguarding and promoting the welfare of children.

Training and development for inter-agency work at the appropriate level should be targeted at practitioners in voluntary, statutory and independent agencies who:

- are in regular contact with children and young people;

---

2        www.dcsf.gov.uk/everychildmatters/strategy/deliveringservices1/commoncore/
         commoncoreofskillsandknowledge/

- work regularly with children and young people, and with adults who are parents or carers, and who may be asked to contribute to assessments of children in need; or

- have particular responsibility for safeguarding children.

Training and development is also relevant to operational managers and those with strategic responsibility for services, in particular LSCB members.

Effective supervision is important in promoting good standards of practice, and supervisors should be available to practitioners as an important source of advice and expertise.

## Chapter 5 – Managing individual cases where there are concerns about a child's safety and welfare

Chapter 5 provides guidance on what should happen if somebody has concerns about the welfare of a child (including those living away from home) and, in particular, concerns that a child may be suffering, or likely to suffer, significant harm. It also sets out the principles underpinning work to safeguard and promote the welfare of children.

The chapter is structured according to the four key processes that underpin work with children and families: assessment, planning, intervention and reviewing. The *Framework for the Assessment of Children in Need and their Families* (2000) should be followed when undertaking assessments of children in need and their families.

The chapter sets out in detail the processes to be followed when safeguarding and promoting the welfare of children. These include:

- responding to concerns about the welfare of a child and making a referral to a statutory organisation (children's social care, the police or the NSPCC) that can take action to safeguard and promote the welfare of children;

- undertaking an initial assessment of the child's situation and deciding what to do next;

- taking urgent action to protect the child from harm, if necessary;

- holding a strategy discussion where there are suspicions that a child may be suffering significant harm and, where appropriate, convening a child protection conference; and

- undertaking a core assessment as part of the section 47 enquiries to decide whether a child is continuing to be likely to suffer significant harm and therefore should be the subject of a child protection plan, implementing the plan and reviewing it at regular intervals.

The key changes to Chapter 5 include emphasising the importance of keeping the focus on the child and his or her safety and welfare, understanding the daily life experience of the child, seeing the child alone where appropriate and using information about the family's history and functioning to inform decision making. It also stresses the importance of analysing the inter-relationships between strengths and protective factors and vulnerabilities and risk factors when deciding whether a child is suffering or likely to suffer significant harm, and of the accurate recording of actions.

The chapter clarifies the relationship between the common assessment, referral to children's social care and an initial assessment. It also sets out that a referrer should be able to discuss their concerns with a qualified social worker.

The guidance extends the timescale for the completion of an initial assessment from seven to ten working days with effect from 1 April 2010. It makes it clear that the planning and reviewing processes for looked after children who are also the subject of a child protection plan should be integrated into one process during the coming year. This change is also reflected in the Care Planning, Placement and Case Review (England) Regulations 2010 and accompanying statutory guidance *Putting Care into Practice*.

## Chapter 6 – Supplementary guidance on safeguarding and promoting the welfare of children

Chapter 6 summarises the supplementary guidance to Working Together. This guidance includes:

- Home Office, Department of Health (2002). Complex Child Abuse Investigations: Inter-agency issues;

- Home Office (2004). Home Office Circular 10/2004 on The Female Genital Mutilation Act 2003;

- DCSF (2007). Safeguarding Children for Abuse Linked to a Belief in Spirit Possession;

- DCSF and Home Office (2007). Safeguarding Children who may have been trafficked;

- HM Government (2008). Safeguarding Children in whom Illness is Fabricated or Induced;

- DCSF (2009). Safeguarding Disabled Children – Practice Guidance;

- HM Government (2009). The Right to Choose: Multi-agency statutory guidance for dealing with Forced Marriage, and HM Government (2009) Multi-agency practice guidelines: handling cases of forced marriage;

- HM Government (2009). Safeguarding Children and Young People from Sexual Exploitation;

- HM Government (2010). Safeguarding Children and Young People who may be affected by Gang Activity; and

- Guidance on allegations of abuse made against a person who works with children, which can be found in Appendix 5 of this document.

This chapter has been updated to reflect new or revised guidance which relates to Working Together and has been issued since 2006.

## Chapter 7 – Child death review processes

Chapter 7 sets out the processes to be followed when a child dies in the LSCB area(s) covered by a Child Death Overview Panel.

There are two inter-related processes for reviewing child deaths:

- a rapid response by a group of key professionals who come together for the purpose of enquiring into and evaluating each unexpected death of a child; and

- an overview of all child deaths in the area, undertaken by a panel.

Either of these processes can identify cases requiring a Serious Case Review (covered in Chapter 8).

The key changes to Chapter 7 include revised definitions of preventable child deaths and unexpected deaths, and clarity on the roles of coroners and registrars and on how to respond appropriately to the deaths of children with life limiting illnesses. An additional section has been included on parents and family members which clarifies the level of involvement parents and family members should have and the type of support they will need.

## Chapter 8 – Serious Case Reviews

Chapter 8 sets out the processes LSCBs should follow when undertaking a Serious Case Review (SCR). The purposes of SCRs are to:

- establish what lessons are to be learned from the case about the way in which local professionals and organisations work individually and together to safeguard and promote the welfare of children;

- identify clearly what those lessons are both within and between agencies, how and within what timescales they will be acted on, and what is expected to change as a result; and

- improve intra- and inter-agency working and better safeguard and promote the welfare of children.

When a child dies (including death by suspected suicide), and abuse or neglect are known or suspected to be a factor in the death, the LSCB should always conduct a SCR. A SCR should also always be carried out when a child dies in custody, either in police custody, on remand or following sentencing, in a YOI, a STC, or a secure children's home or where the child was detained under the Mental Health Act 2005. LSCBs should always consider whether a SCR should be conducted in other circumstances where a child has been harmed. These circumstances are set out in the guidance.

The SCR should look into the involvement of organisations and professionals in the lives of the child and family, irrespective of whether local authority children's social care is, or has been, involved with the child or family As the prime purpose of SCRs is to learn lessons for improving both individual agency and inter-agency working, it is important that their recommendations are acted on promptly and effectively.

A revised version of Chapter 8 was published in December 2009. It made clear that the prime purpose of a SCR is to learn lessons both at an individual and inter-agency/LSCB level; extended the time scale for completing a SCR from four to six months; strengthened the requirements in relation to executive summaries, and made clear that the Chair of the SCR Panel should be independent.

Further changes have now been incorporated, in particular the inclusion of a template for SCR executive summaries and a flow chart providing an overview of the SCR process. In parallel, Chapter 3 makes clear that LSCBs will need to include in their annual reports progress updates on the actions that have been taken in response to current and recent SCRs.

## Part 2: Non-statutory practice guidance

### Chapter 9 – Lessons from research

Chapter 9 summarises the impact of maltreatment on children's health and developmental progress, and sets out some of the key messages from research and inspection that have informed this guidance.

The maltreatment of children – physically, emotionally, sexually or through neglect – can have major long-term effects on all aspects of a child's health, development and wellbeing.

Professionals must take special care to help safeguard and promote the welfare of children and young people who may be living in particularly stressful circumstances. These include families:

- living in poverty;

- where there is domestic violence;

- where a parent has a mental illness;

- where a parent is misusing drugs or alcohol;

- where a parent has a learning disability;

- that face racism and other forms of social isolation; and

- living in areas with a lot of crime, poor housing and high unemployment.

The research evidence in Chapter 9 has been updated since the 2006 edition.

## Chapter 10 – Implementing the principles on working with children and their families

Chapter 10 sets out in more detail specific aspects of working with children, young people and families.

Family Group Conferences (FGCs) may be appropriate in a number of contexts where there is a plan or decision to be made. The family is the primary planning group in the process. Where there are plans to use FGCs in situations where there are concerns about possible harm to a child, they should be developed and implemented under the auspices of LSCB. FGCs should not replace or remove the need for child protection conferences.

Children and families may be supported through their involvement in safeguarding processes by advice and advocacy services, and they should always be informed of services that exist locally and nationally.

Local authorities have a responsibility to ensure that children and adults understand the processes that will be followed when there are concerns about the child. Information should be made available in the family's preferred language.

Children from all cultures may be subject to abuse and neglect, and while professionals should be sensitive to differing family patterns and lifestyles, they must be clear that child abuse cannot be condoned for religious or cultural reasons.

## Chapter 11 – Safeguarding and promoting the welfare of children who may be particularly vulnerable

This chapter outlines the circumstances of children who may be particularly vulnerable. It is intended to help inform the practice that underpins the procedures in Chapter 5, which set out the basic framework within which action should be taken when a parent, professional or any other person has concerns about the welfare of a child.

The chapter gives advice to organisations and individuals on safeguarding in the context of:

- children living away from home;

- abuse by children and young people;

- bullying;

- children whose behaviour indicates a lack of parental control;

- race and racism;

- violent extremism;

- domestic violence;

- child abuse and information communication technology (ICT);

- children with families whose whereabouts are unknown;

- children who go missing;

- children who go missing from education;

- children of families living in temporary accommodation;

- migrant children; and

- unaccompanied asylum-seeking children (UASC).

## Chapter 12 – Managing individuals who pose a risk of harm to children

Chapter 12 provides practice guidance and information about a range of mechanisms that are available when managing people who have been identified as presenting a risk, or potential risk, of harm to children.

The Children Act 1989 recognised that the identification and investigation of child abuse, together with the protection and support of victims and their families, requires multi-agency collaboration. As part of that protection, action has been taken, usually by the police and social services, to prosecute known offenders or control their access to vulnerable children. The Sexual Offences Act 2003 introduced a number of new offences to deal with those who abuse and exploit children in this way.

The term 'Schedule One offender' should no longer be used for anyone convicted of a crime against a child. The focus should be on whether the individual poses a 'risk of harm to children'. Home Office guidance explains how these people who present a potential risk of harm to children should be identified. Practitioners should use the new list of offences as a 'trigger' to further assessments.

Where the offender is given a community sentence, Offender Managers monitor their risk to others and liaise with partner agencies. Prison establishments undertake a similar responsibility where the offender has been sentenced to a period of custody.

The Multi-Agency Public Protection Arrangements (MAPPA) provide a national framework for the assessment and management of risks posed by serious and violent offenders. The Responsible Authorities need to ensure that strategies to address risk are identified, and plans developed, implemented and reviewed on a regular basis. The MAPPA framework identifies three separate but connected levels at which risk is managed:

- ordinary risk management;

- local inter-agency risk management; and

- Multi Agency Public Protection Panels (MAPPP).

There are other processes and mechanisms for working with and monitoring people who may present a risk to children. For example, the Vetting and Barring Scheme (VBS) aims to ensure that unsuitable people do not work with children, whether in paid employment or on a voluntary basis. Since October 2009, the duties to refer concerns regarding individuals under List 99 and the Protection of Children Act 1999 have been replaced with a duty to provide information to the Independent Safeguarding Authority. As another example, people placed on the sex offender list are served with a notification that ensures the police are informed of their whereabouts in the community.

# Preface

## Introduction

*Working Together to Safeguard Children* has evolved through several revisions. It contains detailed procedural guidance on safeguarding and promoting the welfare of children and families. The parts of the document that are statutory guidance for particular organisations are set out below. It is not necessary for all practitioners to read every part of Working Together to understand the principles and perform their roles effectively; Table 1 sets out for reference which parts of the document are particularly relevant to different roles. But the rest of the document contains information that may also be useful.

Over time, Working Together has become a lengthy document containing a good deal of material on the roles of different organisations and how to safeguard children in different situations. The Department for Children, Schools and Families (DCSF) will be working with stakeholders on what might be done to present the document more effectively to ensure that the statutory requirements on safeguarding and promoting the welfare of children are not inadvertently obscured by non-statutory guidance. It will also work in partnership with stakeholders to produce a short practitioner guide. In the shorter term, the Department intends to produce an easily navigable web-based version of this document, with hyperlinks to relevant supporting guidance.

This revision of Working Together is being published at around the same time as new guidance on *Children's Trusts: Statutory guidance on co-operation arrangements, including the Children's Trust Board and the Children and Young People's Plan*. The purpose of the Children's Trust Board is to bring all partners with a role in improving outcomes for children together to agree a common strategy on how they will co-operate to improve children's wellbeing and to help embed partnership in partners' routine delivery of their own functions. It is therefore essential that Children's Trust Boards and Local Safeguarding Children Boards – the latter responsible for co-ordinating work to safeguard and promote the welfare of children – work closely together. This is addressed in Chapter 3 of this guidance.

## Purpose of the document and who should read it

This document sets out how organisations and individuals should work together to safeguard and promote the welfare of children.

It is addressed to practitioners and front line managers who have particular responsibilities for safeguarding and promoting the welfare of children, and to senior and operational managers, in organisations that:

- are responsible for commissioning or providing services to children, young people, and adults who are parents/carers; or

- have a particular responsibility for safeguarding and promoting the welfare of children.

Table 1 can be used as a guide to navigate the document. All practitioners and managers may be required to read chapters that are not listed as necessary under their job function in particular circumstances.

*Table 1: How to use this document*

| Practitioners | Chapters it is necessary to read | Chapters it is advisable to read |
|---|---|---|
| Those with a strategic and managerial responsibility for commissioning and delivering services for children and families | 1, 2, 3, 4, 5 | 6, 9, 10 |
| Operational managers within organisations employing staff to work with children and families, or with responsibility for commissioning and delivering services | 1, 2 (relevant section), 5 | 3, 4, 6, 9, 10, 11, 12 |
| Those with a particular responsibility for safeguarding children, such as designated health and education professionals, police, social workers | 1, 2, 3, 4, 5, 7, 8, 10, 11 | 6, 9, 12 |
| Those who work regularly with children and young people and adults who are carers and who may be asked to contribute to assessments of children in need | 1, 2 (relevant section), 5, 11 | 6, 8, 9, 10, 12 |
| Others in contact with children and young people and parents who are carers | It is not necessary for others to read this document. Instead read the summary guide *What to do if you're worried a child is being abused* | 1, 2 (relevant section), 5, 10 |

For more detail on which practitioners come under which group, see paragraph 4.30.

## Content of this guidance

This guidance reflects the principles contained within the United Nations Convention on the Rights of the Child, ratified by the UK Government in 1991. It takes into account the European Convention of Human Rights, in particular Articles 6 and 8. It also takes account of other relevant legislation at the time of publication. It is particularly informed by the requirements of the Children Act 1989, which provides a comprehensive framework for the care and protection of children, and the Children Act 2004, which underpins the *Every Child Matters* reforms and includes the provisions on Local Safeguarding Children Boards.

## Other related guidance

This document is one of a suite of documents that gives guidance on the governance, strategic planning and delivery of children's services, and on the cross-cutting issue of safeguarding and promoting the welfare of children[3].

The documents support provisions in the Children Act 2004, which underpin *Every Child Matters*. These include the creation of duties on local agencies in relation to children and young people's 'wellbeing' and 'welfare'.

- *Children's Trusts: Statutory guidance on co-operation arrangements, including the Children's Trust Board and the Children and Young People's Plan* brings together statutory guidance on Children's Trust co-operation arrangements, and the procedures and functions of the Children's Trust Board, including the Board's role in preparing, reviewing and monitoring the local Children and Young People's Plan. It replaces *Children's Trusts: statutory guidance on inter-agency co-operation to improve well-being of children, young people and their families* (2008) and *Children and Young People's Plan Guidance* (2009).

- *Statutory guidance on the Duty to Make arrangements to Safeguard and Promote the Welfare of Children* sets out the key arrangements agencies should make to safeguard and promote the welfare of children in the course of discharging their normal functions.

- Guidance on the governance, leadership and structures required within the new strategic framework is provided in *The Roles and Responsibilities of the Director of Children's Services and the Lead Member for Children's Services* and the chapter on Local Safeguarding Children Boards within this revised version of *Working Together to Safeguard Children*.

---

3    All documents referred to are available at: www.dcsf.gov.uk/everychildmatters/

These core documents should be used alongside other key policy and planning documents relating to *Every Child Matters*. These include:

- *The National Service Framework for Children, Young People and Maternity Services*, which sets out a 10-year programme to stimulate long-term and sustained improvement in children's health and wellbeing. This guidance will help health and social care organisations to meet Standard Five on safeguarding and promoting the welfare of children and young people.

- The revised Care Planning, Placement and Case Review Regulations (England) 2010 and accompanying statutory guidance *Putting Care into Practice*, which describe how local authorities should exercise these functions for looked after children.

- *Information Sharing: Guidance for practitioners and managers* and the supporting materials, which are for everyone who works with children and young people, and explain when and how information can be shared legally and professionally.

- The *Common Assessment Framework (CAF) guides for managers and practitioners,* which are for all strategic and operational managers across all children's services who have responsibility for implementing the CAF and for all practitioners who want to know about the CAF and how to use it.

A number of other documents focus directly on integrated front line delivery and the processes that support it[4]. Appendix 1 sets out the statutory framework for safeguarding and promoting children's welfare.

## Status of the document as statutory guidance

This document is intended to provide a national framework within which agencies and professionals at local level – individually and jointly – draw up and agree on their own ways of working together to safeguard and promote the welfare of children. It applies to England.

This guidance replaces the previous version of *Working Together to Safeguard Children*, which was published in 2006. Chapter 8 of this guidance replaces the previous version of Chapter 8 that was published in December 2009.

Part 1 of this document is statutory guidance. Part 2 is non-statutory practice guidance.

The whole of Part 1 is issued as guidance under **section 7 of the Local Authority Social Services Act 1970**, which requires local authorities in their social services functions to act under the general guidance of the Secretary of State. It should be complied with by local

---

4    These can be found at: www.dcsf.gov.uk/everychildmatters/

authorities carrying out their social services functions, unless local circumstances indicate exceptional reasons that justify a variation.

Chapters 3, 4, 7 and 8 are issued under **section 16 of the Children Act 2004**, which states that Children's Services Authorities (county-level and unitary local authorities) and each of the statutory partners must, in exercising their functions relating to a Local Safeguarding Children Board (LSCB), have regard to any guidance given to them for the purpose by the Secretary of State. This means that they must take the guidance into account and, if they decide to depart from it, have clear reasons for doing so. A full list of statutory LSCB partners is given in Chapter 3 and summarised in Table A in Appendix 1.

Where this document is not statutory guidance for a particular organisation, it still represents a standard of good practice and will help organisations fulfil other duties in co-operation with partners. For example, managers and staff with a particular responsibility in the organisations covered by the duty to safeguard and promote the welfare of children in section 11 of the Children Act 2004 are encouraged to read this document and follow it in conjunction with the guidance on that duty.

The same principle applies to educational institutions with duties in this area under the Education Act 2002, sections 157 and 175, early years providers with a duty in this area under section 40 of the Childcare Act 2006, the Children and Family Court Advisory and Support Service (Cafcass) which has a duty in this area under section 12(1) of the Criminal Justice and Court Services Act 2000, and the UK Border Agency which has a duty under section 55 of the Borders, Citizenship and Immigration Act 2009.

## When does the guidance apply?

The guidance comes into force upon publication with two exceptions. The timescale for initial assessments being undertaken within 10 working days comes into force on 1 April 2010.

Where a looked after child is also the subject of a child protection plan, this guidance sets out that the child protection plan should be reviewed as part of the overarching care plan. The revised Care Planning, Placement and Case Review Regulations (England) 2010 and accompanying statutory guidance *Putting Care into Practice* will come into force on 1 April 2011. Local authorities will wish to use the intervening period between the issuing of this guidance and 1 April 2011 to integrate the two reviewing systems appropriately.

# Glossary

Terminology in this area is complex, and changes as services are reshaped. This glossary sets out what is meant in the document by some key terms.

| Term used in this document | Meaning |
|---|---|
| Abuse and neglect | Forms of maltreatment of a child – see paragraph 1.32 for details |
| Child | Anyone who has not yet reached their 18th birthday – see paragraph 1.19 |
| Child protection | Process of protecting individual children identified as either suffering, or likely to suffer, significant harm as a result of abuse or neglect – see paragraphs 1.23, 1.24 and Chapter 5 |
| 'Children's social care' or 'local authority children's social care' | The work of local authorities exercising their social services functions with regard to children. This is not meant to imply a separate 'children's social services' department |
| Local authorities | In this guidance, this generally means top tier local authorities. These local authorities are responsible for social services and education. In England these authorities are defined as: a county council; a metropolitan district council; a non-metropolitan district council for an area where there is no county council; a London borough council; the Common Council of the City of London and the Council of the Isles of Scilly |
| Safeguarding and promoting the welfare of children | The process of protecting children from abuse or neglect, preventing impairment of their health and development, and ensuring they are growing up in circumstances consistent with the provision of safe and effective care that enables children to have optimum life chances and enter adulthood successfully. See paragraphs 1.20–1.22 |
| Wellbeing | Section 10 of the Children Act 2004 requires local authorities and other specified agencies to co-operate with a view to improving the wellbeing of children in relation to the five outcomes first set out in *Every Child Matters* – see paragraph 1.1 |

# Part 1: Statutory Guidance

# Chapter 1 – Introduction: working together to safeguard and promote the welfare of children and families

## Supporting children and families

1.1    All children deserve the opportunity to achieve their full potential. In 2003, the Government published the *Every Child Matters* Green Paper alongside the formal response to the report into the death of Victoria Climbié. The Green Paper set out five outcomes that are key to children and young people's wellbeing:

- be healthy;

- stay safe;

- enjoy and achieve;

- make a positive contribution; and

- achieve economic wellbeing.

1.2    The Children Act 2004 subsequently became law and set out these outcomes in statute. The publication of the Children's Plan in 2007, which was developed having regard to the principles and articles of the UN Convention on the Rights of the Child, further set out the role of Government and a wide range of agencies and professionals in improving children's lives.

1.3    To achieve the five *Every Child Matters* outcomes, children need to feel loved and valued, and be supported by a network of reliable and affectionate relationships. They need to feel they are respected and understood as individual people and to have their wishes and feelings consistently taken into account. If they are denied the opportunity and support they need to achieve these outcomes, children are at increased risk not only of an impoverished childhood, but also of disadvantage and social exclusion in adulthood. Abuse and neglect pose particular problems.

## Parenting, family life and services

1.4    Patterns of family life vary and there is no single, perfect way to bring up children. Good parenting involves caring for children's basic needs, keeping them safe and protected, being attentive and showing them warmth and love, encouraging them to express their views and consistently taking these views into account, and providing the stimulation needed for their development and to help them achieve their potential, within a stable environment where they experience consistent guidance and boundaries.

1.5     Parenting can be challenging. Parents themselves require and deserve support. Asking for help should be seen as a sign of responsibility rather than as a parenting failure.

1.6     A wide range of services and professionals provide support to families in bringing up children. Sometimes children will seek out and ask for help and advice themselves. However, in the great majority of cases, it will be the decision of parents when to ask for help and advice on their children's care and upbringing. As well as being responsive to children's direct requests for help and advice, professionals also need to engage with parents at the earliest opportunity when doing so may prevent problems or difficulties becoming worse. Only in exceptional cases should there be compulsory intervention in family life – for example, where this is necessary to safeguard a child from significant harm. Such intervention should – provided this is consistent with the safety and welfare of the child – support families in making their own plans for the welfare and protection of their children.

## Lord Laming's progress report

1.7     On 12 November 2008 the Secretary of State for Children, Schools and Families asked Lord Laming to provide an urgent report on the progress being made across the country to implement effective arrangements for safeguarding children. Lord Laming published *The Protection of Children in England: A Progress Report*[5] on 12 March 2009. He confirmed that robust legislative, structural and policy foundations are in place but commented that although 'a great deal of progress has been made' in protecting children from harm, 'much more needs to be done to ensure that … services are as effective as possible at working together to achieve positive outcomes for children'.

1.8     Lord Laming made 58 recommendations relating to: leadership and accountability, support for children, inter-agency working, children's workforce, improvement and challenge, organisation and finance and the legal framework.

## The Government's response

1.9     The Government immediately accepted all of Lord Laming's recommendations and, in May 2009 published *The Protection of Children in England: Action Plan*[6]. This set out

---

5       http://publications.everychildmatters.gov.uk/eOrderingDownload/HC-330.pdf
6       http://publications.dcsf.gov.uk/eOrderingDownload/DCSF-Laming.pdf

the Government's detailed response to Lord Laming's recommendations and made a number of commitments for future action. Progress has already been made to address a number of the recommendations and to fulfil many of the commitments made in the Government's action plan. The publication of this updated and revised version of *Working Together to Safeguard Children* guidance addresses a further 23 of Lord Laming's recommendations.

## An integrated approach

1.10    Children have varying needs that change over time. Judgements on how best to intervene when there are concerns about harm to a child will often, and unavoidably, entail an element of risk – at the extreme, of leaving a child for too long in a dangerous situation or of removing a child unnecessarily from his or her family. The way to proceed in the face of uncertainty is through competent professional judgements, based on a sound assessment of the child's needs and the parents' capacity to respond to these – including their capacity to keep the child safe from significant harm – and the wider family circumstances.

1.11    Effective measures to safeguard children are those that also promote their welfare. They should not be seen in isolation from the wider range of support and services already provided and available to meet the needs of children and families:

- enquiries under section 47 of the Children Act 1989 may reveal significant unmet needs for support and services among children and families. These should always be explicitly considered, even where concerns are not substantiated about significant harm to a child, if the child and/or their family so wishes; and

- if processes for managing concerns about individual children are to result in improved outcomes for children, then effective plans for safeguarding and promoting children's welfare should be based on a wide-ranging assessment of the needs of the child, including the child's wishes and feelings, whether they are suffering or likely to suffer significant harm, parental capacity and their family circumstances.

## A shared responsibility

1.12    Safeguarding and promoting the welfare of children – and in particular protecting them from significant harm – depends on effective joint working between agencies and professionals that have different roles and expertise. Individual children, especially some of the most vulnerable children and those at greatest risk of suffering harm and social exclusion, will need co-ordinated help from health, education, early years, children's social care, the voluntary sector and other agencies, including youth justice services.

1.13   In order to achieve this joint working, there needs to be constructive relationships between individual workers, promoted and supported by:

- a strong lead from elected or appointed authority members, and the commitment of chief officers in all agencies – in particular, the Director of Children's Services and Lead Member for Children's Services[7] in each local authority; and

- effective local co-ordination by the Local Safeguarding Children Board in each area.

1.14   For those children who are suffering, or likely to suffer, significant harm, joint working is essential to safeguard and promote their welfare and, where necessary, to help bring to justice the perpetrators of crimes against children. All agencies and professionals should:

- be alert to potential indicators of abuse or neglect;

- be alert to the risks of harm that individual abusers, or potential abusers, may pose to children;

- prioritise direct communication and positive and respectful relationships with children, ensuring the child's wishes and feelings underpin assessments and any safeguarding activities;

- share and help to analyse information so that an assessment can be made of whether the child is suffering or is likely to suffer harm, their needs and circumstances;

- contribute to whatever actions are needed to safeguard and promote the child's welfare;

- take part in regularly reviewing the outcomes for the child against specific plans; and

- work co-operatively with parents, unless this is inconsistent with ensuring the child's safety.

## The child in focus

1.15   Lord Laming reiterated the importance of frontline professionals getting to know children as individual people and, as a matter of routine, considering how their situation feels to them. Ofsted's evaluation of 50 Serious Case Reviews conducted

---

between 1 April 2007 and 31 March 2008 highlighted 'the failure of all professionals to see the situation from the child's perspective and experience; to see and speak to the children; to listen to what they said, to observe how they were and to take serious account of their views in supporting their needs as probably the single most consistent failure in safeguarding work with children.'

1.16    Since 2005, local authorities have been under a duty under the Children Act 1989 (as amended by section 53 of the Children Act 2004) to ascertain the child's wishes and feelings and give due regard to their age and understanding when determining what (if any) services to provide under section 17 of the Children Act 1989, and before making decisions about action to be taken to protect individual children under section 47 of the Children Act 1989. These duties complemented existing requirements relating to the wishes and feelings of children who are, or may be, looked after (section 22(4) Children Act 1989), those being provided accommodation (section 20(6) Children Act 1989) and children taken into police protection (section 46(3)(d)).

1.17    In discharging their duties under these sections, the local authority must give due consideration to the child's 'wishes and feelings' so far as is reasonably practicable and consistent with the child's welfare and giving due regard to the child's age and understanding. There will be occasions when it is not possible to ascertain the child's wishes and feelings. In these circumstances, professionals should record in writing why it was not reasonably practicable or consistent with the child's welfare to elicit his or her wishes and feelings.

1.18    Effective ongoing action to keep the child in focus includes:

- developing a direct relationship with the child;

- obtaining information from the child about his or her situation and needs;

- eliciting the child's wishes and feelings – about their situation now as well as plans and hopes for the future;

- providing children with honest and accurate information about the current situation, as seen by professionals, and future possible actions and interventions;

- involving the child in key decision-making;

- providing appropriate information to the child about his or her right to protection and assistance;

- inviting children to make recommendations about the services and assistance they need and/or are available to them;

- ensuring children have access to independent advice and support (for example, through advocates or children's rights officers) to be able to express their views and influence decision-making; and

- the importance of eliciting and responding to the views and experiences of children is a defining feature of staff recruitment, professional supervision, performance management and the organisation's broader aims and development.

## Key definitions

### Children

1.19   In this document, as in the Children Acts 1989 and 2004 respectively, **a child** is anyone who has not yet reached their 18th birthday. 'Children' therefore means 'children and young people' throughout. The fact that a child has reached 16 years of age, is living independently or is in further education, is a member of the armed forces, is in hospital or in custody in the secure estate for children and young people, does not change his or her status or entitlement to services or protection under the Children Act 1989.

### Safeguarding and promoting welfare and child protection

1.20   **Safeguarding and promoting the welfare of children** is defined for the purposes of this guidance as:

- protecting children from maltreatment;

- preventing impairment of children's health or development;

- ensuring that children are growing up in circumstances consistent with the provision of safe and effective care;

and undertaking that role so as to enable those children to have optimum life chances and to enter adulthood successfully.

1.21   Protecting children from maltreatment is important in preventing the impairment of health or development though that in itself may be insufficient to ensure that children are growing up in circumstances consistent with the provision of safe and effective care. These aspects of safeguarding and promoting welfare are cumulative, and all contribute to the outcomes set out in paragraph 1.1.

1.22   Young people at serious risk of harm from community based violence such as gang, group and knife crime are likely to have significant needs. Agencies and professionals need to ensure that the safeguarding process responds effectively to the needs of children at risk of suffering violence within the community. This may involve both the perpetrators and victims of violent activity.

1.23    **Child protection** is a part of safeguarding and promoting welfare. This refers to the activity that is undertaken to protect specific children who are suffering, or are likely to suffer, significant harm.

1.24    Effective child protection is essential as part of wider work to safeguard and promote the welfare of children. However, all agencies and individuals should aim to proactively safeguard and promote the welfare of children so that the need for action to protect children from harm is reduced.

## Children in need

1.25    Children who are defined as being 'in need', under section 17 of the Children Act 1989, are those whose vulnerability is such that they are unlikely to reach or maintain a satisfactory level of health or development, or their health and development will be significantly impaired, without the provision of services (section 17(10) of the Children Act 1989), plus those who are disabled. The critical factors to be taken into account in deciding whether a child is in need under the Children Act 1989 are:

- what will happen to a child's health or development without services being provided; and

- the likely effect the services will have on the child's standard of health and development.

Local authorities have a duty to safeguard and promote the welfare of children in need.

## The concept of significant harm

1.26    Some children are in need because they are suffering, or likely to suffer, significant harm. The Children Act 1989 introduced the concept of significant harm as the threshold that justifies compulsory intervention in family life in the best interests of children, and gives local authorities a duty to make enquiries to decide whether they should take action to safeguard or promote the welfare of a child who is suffering, or likely to suffer, significant harm.

1.27    A court may make a care order (committing the child to the care of the local authority) or supervision order (putting the child under the supervision of a social worker or a probation officer) in respect of a child if it is satisfied that:

- the child is suffering, or is likely to suffer, significant harm; and

- the harm, or likelihood of harm, is attributable to a lack of adequate parental care or control (section 31).

1.28 There are no absolute criteria on which to rely when judging what constitutes significant harm. Consideration of the severity of ill-treatment may include the degree and the extent of physical harm, the duration and frequency of abuse and neglect, the extent of premeditation, and the presence or degree of threat, coercion, sadism and bizarre or unusual elements. Each of these elements has been associated with more severe effects on the child, and/or relatively greater difficulty in helping the child overcome the adverse impact of the maltreatment. Sometimes, a single traumatic event may constitute significant harm, for example, a violent assault, suffocation or poisoning. More often, significant harm is a compilation of significant events, both acute and long-standing, which interrupt, change or damage the child's physical and psychological development. Some children live in family and social circumstances where their health and development are neglected. For them, it is the corrosiveness of long-term emotional, physical or sexual abuse that causes impairment to the extent of constituting significant harm. In each case, it is necessary to consider any maltreatment alongside the child's own assessment of his or her safety and welfare, the family's strengths and supports[8], as well as an assessment of the likelihood and capacity for change and improvements in parenting and the care of children and young people.

> **Under section 31(9) of the Children Act 1989 as amended by the Adoption and Children Act 2002:**
>
> 'harm' means ill-treatment or the impairment of health or development, including, for example, impairment suffered from seeing or hearing the ill-treatment of another;
>
> 'development' means physical, intellectual, emotional, social or behavioural development;
>
> 'health' means physical or mental health; and
>
> 'ill treatment' includes sexual abuse and forms of ill-treatment which are not physical.
>
> **Under section 31(10) of the Act:**
>
> Where the question of whether harm suffered by a child is significant turns on the child's health and development, his health or development shall be compared with that which could reasonably be expected of a similar child.

---

8      For more details see Adcock, M. and White, R. (1998). *Significant Harm: its management and outcome.* Surrey: Significant Publications.

1.29    To understand and identify significant harm, it is necessary to consider:

- the nature of harm, in terms of maltreatment or failure to provide adequate care;

- the impact on the child's health and development;

- the child's development within the context of their family and wider environment;

- any special needs, such as a medical condition, communication impairment or disability, that may affect the child's development and care within the family;

- the capacity of parents to meet adequately the child's needs; and

- the wider and environmental family context.

1.30    The child's reactions, his or her perceptions, and wishes and feelings should be ascertained and the local authority should give them due consideration, so far as is reasonably practicable and consistent with the child's welfare and having regard to the child's age and understanding[9].

1.31    To do this depends on communicating effectively with children and young people, including those who find it difficult to do so because of their age, an impairment, or their particular psychological or social situation. This may involve using interpreters and drawing upon the expertise of early years workers or those working with disabled children. It is necessary to create the right atmosphere when meeting and communicating with children, to help them feel at ease and reduce any pressure from parents, carers or others. Children will need reassurance that they will not be victimised for sharing information or asking for help or protection; this applies to children living in families as well as those in institutional settings, including custody. It is essential that any accounts of adverse experiences coming from children are as accurate and complete as possible. Accuracy is key, for without it effective decisions cannot be made and, equally, inaccurate accounts can lead to children remaining unsafe, or to the possibility of wrongful actions being taken that affect children and adults[10].

## What is abuse and neglect?

1.32    Abuse and neglect are forms of maltreatment of a child. Somebody may abuse or neglect a child by inflicting harm, or by failing to act to prevent harm. Children may

---

9       Section 53 of the Children Act 2004 amended section 17 and section 47 of the Children Act 1989, so that before determining what, if any, services to provide to a child in need under section 17, or action to take with respect to a child under section 47, the wishes and feelings of the child should be ascertained as far as is reasonable and given due consideration.

10      Jones, D. P. H. (2003). *Communicating with Vulnerable Children: a Guide for Practitioners*, pp.1-2. London: Gaskell.

be abused in a family or in an institutional or community setting, by those known to them or, more rarely, by a stranger for example, via the internet. They may be abused by an adult or adults, or another child or children.

## Physical abuse

1.33  Physical abuse may involve hitting, shaking, throwing, poisoning, burning or scalding, drowning, suffocating, or otherwise causing physical harm to a child. Physical harm may also be caused when a parent or carer fabricates the symptoms of, or deliberately induces, illness in a child.

## Emotional abuse

1.34  Emotional abuse is the persistent emotional maltreatment of a child such as to cause severe and persistent adverse effects on the child's emotional development. It may involve conveying to children that they are worthless or unloved, inadequate, or valued only insofar as they meet the needs of another person. It may include not giving the child opportunities to express their views, deliberately silencing them or 'making fun' of what they say or how they communicate. It may feature age or developmentally inappropriate expectations being imposed on children. These may include interactions that are beyond the child's developmental capability, as well as overprotection and limitation of exploration and learning, or preventing the child participating in normal social interaction. It may involve seeing or hearing the ill-treatment of another. It may involve serious bullying (including cyberbullying), causing children frequently to feel frightened or in danger, or the exploitation or corruption of children. Some level of emotional abuse is involved in all types of maltreatment of a child, though it may occur alone.

## Sexual abuse

1.35  Sexual abuse involves forcing or enticing a child or young person to take part in sexual activities, not necessarily involving a high level of violence, whether or not the child is aware of what is happening. The activities may involve physical contact, including assault by penetration (for example, rape or oral sex) or non-penetrative acts such as masturbation, kissing, rubbing and touching outside of clothing. They may also include non-contact activities, such as involving children in looking at, or in the production of, sexual images, watching sexual activities, encouraging children to behave in sexually inappropriate ways, or grooming a child in preparation for abuse (including via the internet). Sexual abuse is not solely perpetrated by adult males. Women can also commit acts of sexual abuse, as can other children.

## Neglect

1.36  Neglect is the persistent failure to meet a child's basic physical and/or psychological needs, likely to result in the serious impairment of the child's health or development. Neglect may occur during pregnancy as a result of maternal substance abuse. Once a child is born, neglect may involve a parent or carer failing to:

- provide adequate food, clothing and shelter (including exclusion from home or abandonment);

- protect a child from physical and emotional harm or danger;

- ensure adequate supervision (including the use of inadequate care-givers); or

- ensure access to appropriate medical care or treatment.

It may also include neglect of, or unresponsiveness to, a child's basic emotional needs.

# Chapter 2 – Roles and responsibilities

## Introduction

2.1     Everyone shares responsibility for safeguarding and promoting the welfare of children and young people, irrespective of individual roles. Nevertheless, in order that organisations and practitioners collaborate effectively, it is vital that all partners who work with children – including local authorities, the police, the health service, the courts, professionals, the voluntary sector and individual members of local communities – are aware of, and appreciate, the role that each of them play in this area.

## The statutory framework within which organisations operate

2.2     Although all organisations that work with children and young people share a commitment to safeguard and promote their welfare, many organisations have specific roles and responsibilities to do so that are underpinned by a statutory duty or duties.

2.3     Local authorities that are children's services authorities[11] have a number of specific duties to organise and plan services and to safeguard and promote the welfare of children. These duties fall within the remit of the Director of Children's Services (DCS) under section 18 of the Children Act 2004. It is essential that the DCS, or senior managers reporting to the DCS, have relevant skills and experience in, and knowledge of, safeguarding and child protection, and that they provide high quality leadership in this area as part of the delivery of effective children's social care services as a whole.

2.4     Local authorities – along with district councils, NHS bodies (Strategic Health Authorities (SHAs), designated Special Health Authorities, Primary Care Trusts (PCTs), NHS trusts, and NHS foundation trusts), the Police (including the British Transport Police), probation and prison services (under the National Offender Management Service (NOMS) structure), Youth Offending Teams (YOTs), secure training centres and Connexions – also have a duty under section 11 of the Children Act 2004 to ensure that their functions are discharged with regard to the need to safeguard and promote the welfare of children. Guidance for these organisations

---

11     These are top tier local authorities, defined in England as a county council; a metropolitan district council; a non-metropolitan district council for areas for which there is no county council; a London borough council; the Common Council of the City of London; and the Council of the Isles of Scilly. See Glossary.

about their duty under section 11 is contained in *Making Arrangements to Safeguard and Promote the Welfare of Children* (HM Government, 2007)[12].

2.5    Local authorities in the exercise of their education functions also have a duty under section 175 of the Education Act 2002 to carry out those functions with a view to safeguarding and promoting the welfare of children. In addition, maintained (state) schools and Further Education (FE) institutions, including sixth-form colleges, have a duty under section 175 to exercise their functions with a view to safeguarding and promoting the welfare of their pupils (students under 18 years of age in the case of FE institutions). The statutory guidance to local authorities, maintained schools, and FE institutions about these duties is in *Safeguarding Children and Safer Recruitment in Education*[13], which is due to be updated and reissued in 2010. Regulations under section 157 of the Education Act 2002 prescribe as a standard for independent schools, including academies and technology colleges, that they should draw up and implement effectively a written policy to safeguard and promote the welfare of children who are pupils at the school which complies with *Safeguarding Children and Safer Recruitment in Education*. In addition, under section 87 of the Children Act 1989, independent schools that provide accommodation for children also have a duty to safeguard and promote the welfare of those pupils. Boarding schools, residential special schools, and FE institutions that provide accommodation for children under 18 must have regard to the respective National Minimum Standards[14] for their establishment.

2.6    Early years providers have a duty under section 40 of the Childcare Act 2006 to comply with the welfare requirements of the Early Years Foundation Stage, under which providers are required to take necessary steps to safeguard and promote the welfare of young children.

2.7    Safeguarding is a key function of the Children and Family Court Advisory and Support Service (Cafcass). Section 12(1) of the Criminal Justice and Court Services Act 2000 sets out Cafcass's duty to safeguard and promote the welfare of children involved in family proceedings in which their welfare is, or may be, in question.

2.8    The United Kingdom Border Agency (UKBA) is required under section 55 of the Borders, Citizenship and Immigration Act 2009 to carry out its functions having regard to the need to safeguard and promote the welfare of children who are in the UK. The UKBA instruction *Arrangements to Safeguard and Promote Children's Welfare in the United Kingdom Border Agency*[15] sets out the key principles to be taken into account in all Agency activities. Section 55 is intended to have the same effect as

12    www.everychildmatters.gov.uk/resources-and-practice/IG00042/
13    www.dcsf.gov.uk/everychildmatters/resources-and-practice/IG00175/
14    www.dh.gov.uk/en/PublicationsAndStatistics/Legislation/ActsAndBills/DH_4001911
15    www.ukba.homeoffice.gov.uk/sitecontent/documents/policyandlaw/legislation/bci-act1/

section 11 of the Children Act 2004. Statutory guidance on this duty, which mirrors the statutory guidance to other agencies, has been issued to the UKBA jointly by the Home Office and the DCSF[16].

2.9  All organisations must ensure they have in place safe recruitment policies and practices, including enhanced Criminal Records Bureau (CRB) checks for all staff, including agency staff, students and volunteers, working with children. It is an offence knowingly to employ a person who has been barred by the Independent Safeguarding Authority (ISA) from working in posts which involve caring for or treating children. Information about whether a person is barred will be given on an enhanced CRB check. From 26 July 2010, staff can register under the new Vetting and Barring Scheme[17] and from November 2010 registration will be compulsory for new entrants to the workforce.

2.10  An overview of the duties mentioned above and the structure of children's services under the Children Act 2004 are set out in the Preface to this guidance and Appendix 1.

## Infrastructure and governance to deliver safeguarding responsibilities

2.11  To fulfil their commitment to safeguard and promote the welfare of children and young people all organisations that provide services for children, parents or families, or work with children, should have in place:

- clear priorities for safeguarding and promoting the welfare of children explicitly stated in key policy documents and commissioning strategies;

- a clear commitment by senior management to the importance of safeguarding and promoting children's welfare through both the commissioning and the provision of services;

- a culture of listening to and engaging in dialogue with children – seeking their views in ways appropriate to their age and understanding, and taking account of those both in individual decisions and the establishment or development and improvement of services;

- a clear line of accountability and governance within and across organisations for the commissioning and provision of services designed to safeguard and promote the welfare of children and young people;

- recruitment and human resources management procedures and commissioning processes, including contractual arrangements, that take account of the need to

16   www.dcsf.gov.uk/everychildmatters/12870
17   For more information on the Vetting and Barring Scheme see: www.isa-gov.org.uk

safeguard and promote the welfare of children and young people, including arrangements for appropriate checks on new staff and volunteers and adoption of best practice in the recruitment of new staff and volunteers;

- a clear understanding of how to work together to help keep children and young people safe online by being adequately equipped to understand, identify and mitigate the risks of new technology;

- procedures for dealing with allegations of abuse against members of staff and volunteers (see paragraphs 6.32–6.42) or, for commissioners, contractual arrangements with providers that ensure these procedures are in place;

- arrangements to ensure that all staff undertake appropriate training to equip them to carry out their responsibilities effectively, and keep this up to date by refresher training at regular intervals; and that all staff, including temporary staff and volunteers who work with children, are made aware of both the establishment's arrangements and their responsibilities for safeguarding and promoting the welfare of children;

- policies for safeguarding and promoting the welfare of children (for example, pupils/students), including a child protection policy, effective complaints procedures and procedures that are in accordance with guidance from the local authority and locally agreed inter-agency procedures;

- arrangements to work effectively with other organisations to safeguard and promote the welfare of children, including arrangements for sharing information (see paragraph 2.12); and

- appropriate whistle blowing procedures and a culture that enables issues about safeguarding and promoting the welfare of children to be addressed.

## Information sharing

2.12    Effective information sharing underpins integrated working and is a vital element of both early intervention and safeguarding. The cross-government guidance *Information Sharing: Guidance for practitioners and managers* and associated training materials[18] provides advice on when and how frontline practitioners can share information legally and professionally. The guidance also covers how organisations can support practitioners and build their confidence in making information sharing decisions. It is intended for practitioners and managers who have to make decisions about sharing personal information on a case by case basis in all services and sectors, whether they are working with children, young people, adults or families. It is also for those who support these practitioners and managers and for others with

---

18    See www.dcsf.gov.uk/ecm/informationsharing

responsibility of information governance. It should be read in conjunction with any specific organisational or professional guidance.

2.13   Every Children's Trust Board should assure themselves that all partners consistently apply the Information Sharing Guidance. This should mean that:

- all practitioners are aware of, and have access to, the information sharing guidance and training, and are confident in making decisions about information sharing; and

- the organisational and cultural aspects that are required to embed information sharing have been, or are being, addressed.

2.14   The *Embedding information sharing toolkit*[19] focuses on the organisation and cultural aspects of information sharing. It describes activities that are specifically designed to address the key barriers and drivers of effective information sharing and presents real examples of these activities from local areas.

## ContactPoint

2.15   ContactPoint[20] provides a quick way for people working with children to find out who else is working with the same child. It includes basic information[21] about every child in England from birth to their 18th birthday (over 18 in certain circumstances) and contact details for parents or carers and practitioners or other services working with that child. ContactPoint is subject to stringent security controls with access limited only to people with the appropriate training who have undergone security checks and who need to use it professionally.

## Common Assessment Framework (CAF)

2.16   The CAF is a tool to enable early and effective assessment of children and young people who need additional services or support from more than one agency. It is a holistic consent-based needs assessment framework which records, in a single place and in a structured and consistent way, every aspect of a child's life, family and environment. National eCAF[22], still being developed, will be a secure IT system for storing and accessing information captured through the CAF process. Practitioners will only be given access to information on national eCAF for a child or young

---

19      Available at: www.dcsf.gov.uk/ecm/informationsharing

20      Information on ContactPoint is available at: www.dcsf.gov.uk/ecm/Contactpoint

21      The Children Act 2004 Information Database (England) Regulations 2007 available at www.opsi.gov.uk/si/si2007/uksi_20072182_en_1

22      Information on National eCAF is available at: www.dcsf.gov.uk/everychildmatters/strategy/deliveringservices1/caf/ecaf/ecaf/

person with whom they are working and then only with the specific consent of the child or young person (or parent/carer as appropriate).

2.17   The Children's Trust Board should have clear arrangements in place for implementing the CAF locally. This includes ensuring that the whole children and young people's workforce are aware of it and how it is used, and that there are enough people in the local area with the necessary skills, training and support to undertake a CAF. These arrangements should reflect that **the CAF form is not a referral form, although it may be used to support a referral or specialist assessment**. The absence of a CAF should not be a barrier to accessing services.

## Local authorities that are children's services authorities

2.18   The safety and welfare of children and young people is the responsibility of the local authority, working in partnership with other public organisations, the private and third sector, and service users and carers. Integrating the delivery of these services at the frontline can help to maximise their effectiveness. An integrated and preferably co-located workforce that includes active partners from the police, health visiting services and other relevant health services, can enable these services to be provided both more effectively and more efficiently. Local authorities should work with partners to ensure that all services are working together effectively at an operational level, for example by meeting regularly to help build and develop positive professional relationships, share information, discuss issues and improve working practices. Local authorities, together with their Children's Trust partners, should look closely at any opportunity to integrate and co-locate services, taking into account specific local needs and circumstances.

2.19   As part of exercising statutory responsibilities, and in order to ensure that specialist services are commissioned effectively, it is important that local authorities work through the Children's Trust Board and wider co-operation arrangements to agree, in consultation with the LSCB:

- governance arrangements and systems to support commissioning of specialist services between relevant partners;

- a strategic approach to understanding needs, including a sophisticated analysis of data and effective engagement with children, young people and families;

- a strategic approach to understanding the effectiveness of current services, and identifying priorities for change – including where services need to be improved, reshaped or developed;

- integrated and effective arrangements for ensuring that priorities for change are delivered through the Children and Young People's Plan by the Children's Trust partners; and

- integrated and effective approaches to understanding the impact of specialist services on outcomes for children, young people and families, and using this understanding to constructively challenge progress and drive further improvement.

2.20 All services that are commissioned and/or delivered by the local authority will have an impact on the lives of children and families, and local authorities have a particular responsibility towards those children and families most at risk of social exclusion.

2.21 Local authorities have responsibilities for ensuring appropriate arrangements to safeguard and promote the welfare of children are in place for all children residing within their area, including:

- children excluded from school/receiving alternative provision;

- home educated children; and

- those placed in custody[23].

2.22 In order to ensure that children are protected from harm, local authorities commission, and may themselves provide a wide range of care and support for:

- adults, who may in turn be parents or carers of children and young people;

- children and families, including those groups whose needs may not be immediately obvious such as disabled children, children involved in gangs, unaccompanied asylum-seeking children and children within the immigration system;

- older people;

- people with physical or learning disabilities;

- people with mental health problems;

- people with substance misuse problems;

- ex-offenders and young offenders, including those in custody and their families;

- families, especially where children have special needs, and/or where children are growing up in special circumstances as set out in the National Service Framework for Children Young People and Maternity Services[24] and families experiencing multiple and complex problems;

---

23 The home local authority of a child or young person in custody retains continuing responsibility for safeguarding them and promoting their welfare.

24 www.dh.gov.uk/en/Publicationsandstatistics/Publications/PublicationsPolicyAndGuidance/ DH_4089101

- adults and children affected by domestic violence;

- children who need to be looked after by the local authority, through fostering or residential care; and

- children who are placed for adoption.

Local authorities also have a duty under section 17 of the Crime and Disorder Act 1998 to do all they reasonably can to prevent crime and disorder in the exercise of their functions.

2.23    Local authorities have specific duties in respect of children under the Children Acts 1989 and 2004. They have a general duty to safeguard and promote the welfare of children in need in their area and, provided that this is consistent with the child's safety and welfare, to promote the upbringing of such children by their families by providing services appropriate to the child's needs. They should do this in partnership with parents, in a way that is sensitive to the child's race, religion, culture and language and that takes account of the child's wishes and feelings. Services might include childcare for young children, after-school care for school children, counselling, short breaks, family centre services, practical help in the home or targeted parenting and family support.

2.24    Within local authorities, children's social care staff act as the principal point of contact for children about whom there are welfare concerns. They may be contacted directly by children, parents or family members seeking help, by concerned friends and neighbours, or by professionals and others from statutory and voluntary organisations. The need for family support should be considered at the first sign of difficulties, as early support can prevent more serious problems developing. Contact details need to be clearly signposted, including on local authority websites, on notice boards in schools, health centres, public libraries and leisure centres, and in telephone directories. Specific consideration should be given as to how children and young people will be made aware of whom they can contact if they require advice and/or support: this includes children living away from home in educational, health or custodial settings, for example. Good practice in information sharing and processes such as the CAF and the lead professional role should be fully embedded throughout the Children's Trust co-operation arrangements.

2.25    Local authorities, with the help of other organisations as appropriate, also have a duty to make enquiries if they have reason to suspect that a child in their area is suffering, or likely to suffer, significant harm, to enable them to decide whether they should take any action to safeguard and promote the child's welfare (see Chapter 5).

2.26    Where a child or young person is suffering or likely to suffer significant harm, children's social care staff have lead responsibility for undertaking an assessment of the child's needs, the parents' capacity to meet these needs and to keep the child safe and promote his or her welfare, and of the wider family and environmental circumstances. The child's own account of their needs, concerns, the capacity of their parents to protect them and promote their welfare, as well as other factors, should be taken into account as part of the assessment and subsequent interventions.

2.27    A well-supported workforce is essential to the effective and safe delivery of these functions. It is important that local authorities ensure that high quality, experienced social workers undertake key management and supervisory roles in intake/duty teams and receive high quality, specialist training in these roles.

## Other local authority roles

### Adult social services

2.28    Local authorities are also the lead agency for safeguarding adults. Services do not always neatly divide into those for adults and those for children, and there will be circumstances when adult services can make a contribution to the safeguarding of children, and circumstances when staff in adult services may become aware of risks of harm to children which should be disclosed, and vice versa. There will also be circumstances when safeguarding children and adults can and should be done jointly. For all these reasons children and adult services should be aware of each other's roles and responsibilities, and service and workforce planning should take account of the family and neighbourhood context in which safeguarding work is carried out.

### Housing authorities and registered social landlords

2.29    As outlined in the section 11 guidance[25], housing and homelessness staff in local authorities, and others with a front line role such as environmental health officers, can play an important role in safeguarding and promoting the welfare of children as part of their day-to-day work – recognising child welfare issues, sharing information, making referrals and subsequently managing or reducing risks of harm.

2.30    In many areas, local authorities do not directly own and manage housing, having transferred these responsibilities to one or more registered social landlords (RSLs). Housing authorities remain responsible for assessing the needs of families, under homelessness legislation, and for managing nominations to RSLs who provide housing in their area. They continue to have an important role in safeguarding

---

25    www.everychildmatters.gov.uk/resources-and-practice/IG00042/

children because of their contact with families as part of the assessment of need, and because of the influence they have designing and managing prioritisation, assessment and allocation of housing.

2.31    From 1 April 2010, the Tenant Services Authority (TSA) will regulate the whole social housing sector using its new regulatory framework[26]. The TSA has been consulting tenants and landlords on proposed regulatory standards for social landlords; the final standards will be issued shortly. Under the TSA's proposals, all social housing providers would be expected to understand and respond to the particular needs of their tenants and co-operate with other partners at a local level, including local authorities, to promote social, environmental and economic wellbeing in those areas.

2.32    A number of RSLs across the country provide specialist supported housing schemes specifically for young people at risk and/or young people leaving care and pregnant teenagers. These schemes cater for 16- and 17-year-olds. Housing authorities and children's services should refer to the forthcoming joint DCSF and CLG guidance about their duties under Part III of the Children Act 1989 and Part 7 of the Housing act 1996 to secure or provide accommodation for homeless 16- and 17-year-old children.

## Sport, culture and leisure services

2.33    Sport and cultural services designed for children and families – such as libraries, play schemes and play facilities, parks and gardens, sport and leisure centres, events and attractions, museums and arts centres – are directly provided, purchased or grant-aided by local authorities, the commercial sector, and by community and voluntary organisations. Staff, volunteers and contractors who provide these services have various degrees of contact with children who use them, and appropriate arrangements need to be in place. These should include:

- procedures for staff and others to report concerns they may have, about the children they meet, which are in line with *What to do if you're worried a child is being abused*[27] and LSCB procedures, as well as arrangements such as those described above; and

- appropriate codes of practice for staff, particularly sports coaches, such as the codes of practice issued by national governing bodies of sport, the Health and Safety Executive or the local authority.

---

26    Expected to be published in March 2010

27    www.dcsf.gov.uk/everychildmatters/resources-and-practice/IG00182/

Sports organisations can also seek advice on child protection issues from the Child Protection in Sport Unit (CPSU), while third sector organisations can also seek advice from the Safe Network (see paragraph 2.188).

## Youth services

2.34 Youth and community workers (YCWs) have close contact with children and young people and should be alert to signs of abuse and neglect, and know how to act on concerns about a child's welfare. Increasingly, Youth Services form part of targeted rather than universal services and thus are dealing with a higher proportion of vulnerable young people. Local authority youth services (LAYS) should give written instructions, consistent with *What to do if you're worried a child is being abused* and LSCB procedures, on when YCWs should consult colleagues, line managers and other statutory authorities about concerns they may have about a child or young person. The LAYS instructions should emphasise the importance of safeguarding the welfare of children and young people, should make the YCW aware of Working Together guidance and should assist the YCW in balancing the desire to maintain confidentiality between the young person and the YCW and the duty to safeguard and promote the welfare of the young person and others. Volunteers within the youth service are subject to the same requirement.

2.35 Where the local authority commissions local voluntary youth organisations or other providers through grant or contract arrangements, the authority should ensure that proper arrangements to safeguard children and young people are in place (for example, this might form part of the agreement for the grant or contract). The organisations might get advice on how to do so from their national bodies or the LSCB.

## Services provided under s114 of the Learning and Skills Act 2000 (The Connexions Service)

2.36 In April 2008 local authorities were given responsibility for Connexions and the ability to decide how best information, advice and guidance services should be delivered. Connexions has a substantial workforce working directly with young people including professionally qualified personal advisers and other delivery staff working under their supervision. Connexions is centred on young people and, as such, safeguarding and promoting the welfare of young people is a primary concern. Connexions staff should take account of and respond to behaviour that is likely to damage the overall wellbeing of young people and should address their welfare and safety needs in a holistic manner.

2.37 Local authorities should ensure that their Connexions service:

- identifies, keeps in touch with and provides the necessary support to young people in their geographical area. The needs of young people from vulnerable groups such as teenage mothers, care leavers, young people supervised by YOTs, young people in custody and young people with learning difficulties and/ or disabilities are a particular priority as is ensuring support and planning for young people in custody and their resettlement back into the community;

- identifies young people who may be being abused or neglected and, in these cases, alerts the appropriate authority. Staff should be aware of the agencies and contacts to use to refer young people whom they suspect are suffering harm, and should be aware of the way in which these concerns will be followed up;

- minimises risk to the safety of young people on premises for which they are responsible and maintains the necessary capacity to carry out relevant risk assessments;

- minimises the risk that organisations to which they signpost young people, such as those providing employment and training opportunities, pose a threat to the moral development and physical and psychological wellbeing of young people;

- complies with current vetting regulations in the recruitment of all staff (including volunteers); and

- makes staff aware of risks to the welfare of young people so that they can exercise their legal, ethical, operational and professional obligations to safeguard them from these risks.

2.38    Connexions should work closely with other agencies concerned with child safety and welfare to analyse rigorously the nature and distribution of risk within the cohort of young people, and to use this information to design services, allocate resources and otherwise take action to address both cause and effect.

## Health services

### General principles for all health services

2.39    The safety and the health of a child are intertwined aspects of their wellbeing. Many 'health' interventions also equip a child to 'stay safe'[28].

2.40    All organisations commissioning or providing healthcare, whether in the NHS or third sector, independent healthcare sector or social enterprises, should ensure there is board level focus on the needs of children and that safeguarding children is an integral part of their governance systems.

---

28      'Staying safe' is a key outcome of *Every Child Matters*

2.41 All healthcare staff involved in working with children should attend training in safeguarding and promoting the welfare of children, and have regular updates as part of continuing professional development. See Chapter 4 for details of inter-agency training.

## Health organisations

### The Care Quality Commission and registration requirements

2.42 The Care Quality Commission (CQC) is the independent regulator of safety and quality for all health services. From April 2010, NHS trusts and NHS foundation trusts need to be registered with the CQC[29]. The Commission has a range of statutory independent enforcement actions to use where care does not meet the essential levels of safety and quality that users are entitled to expect.

2.43 GP practices and high street dental practices will be required to register with the CQC, regardless of whether they provide wholly private or wholly NHS services, or a mix of both and will be subject to a consistent set of quality standards. Registration of primary dental care providers will start from 2011 and primary medical care providers from 2012.

2.44 Any enforcement action being considered by the CQC, including possible deregistration, should include, where appropriate, arrangements in partnership with the relevant PCT to re-provide services for children as quickly and safely as possible.

### Monitor

2.45 NHS foundation trusts are regulated by Monitor, an independent regulator, which has authority to hold them to account for meeting their responsibilities under the Children Acts. This is unlike NHS trusts, which are overseen by Strategic Health Authorities. However, NHS foundation trusts are assessed by the CQC in the same way as other providers.

### Strategic Health Authorities

2.46 SHAs are the regional headquarters of the NHS. Each SHA is responsible for ensuring that patients have access to high-quality services in its area. SHAs oversee the performance of PCTs and NHS trusts and hold PCTs to account, including for safeguarding and promoting the welfare of children. SHAs are themselves directly accountable to the Department of Health and safeguarding is considered by the Department of Health as part of their SHA assurance process.

2.47    SHAs should consider individual organisations' arrangements for, and contribution to, safeguarding children as an integral part of their governance system. Their performance and management of the healthcare system should be informed by information such as existing national data collections, LSCB audit, progress against action plans and/or child death and Serious Case Review recommendations and regulatory/inspection findings where appropriate. Bespoke local surveys and data gathering should be avoided unless there is a clear business need in order to minimise duplication and burden of reporting.

2.48    SHAs membership of LSCBs (see paragraph 3.70) will enable them to oversee the health contribution to safeguarding children at local level. Further advice on how SHAs should engage with LSCBs is set out in Annex D of the *Local Safeguarding Children Boards: A Review of Progress* report[30].

## Primary Care Trust commissioners

2.49    PCTs are responsible for improving the health and wellbeing of their local population, including children and young people. To achieve this, they are under a legal duty to work with the local authority to assess what kind of health services people need.

2.50    PCTs can commission services from a range of different organisations and generally hold the providers of these services to account via contracts. PCTs can ask the regulators to step in if the providers are not meeting the expected standards. PCTs should have a collaborative, multi-agency approach to commissioning and should work with local authorities to commission and provide co-ordinated and, wherever possible, integrated services, in particular through Children's Trust co-operation arrangements.

2.51    PCTs should identify a senior lead for children and young people[31] to ensure that their needs are at the forefront of local planning and service delivery. PCTs should also identify a board executive lead for safeguarding children who takes responsibility for governance, systems and organisational focus on safeguarding children. This might be the same person.

2.52    Designated professionals should work closely with, and be performance managed and supported in their role by, this board executive lead as part of the board lead's portfolio of responsibilities. If this person is not the board level lead for clinical governance and clinical professional leadership, the designated professional will also need to work closely with this lead person (see paragraphs 2.109–2.123).

---

30    www.dcsf.gov.uk/everychildmatters/_download/?id=3082
31    NSF Core Standards 3 – Markers of good practice

2.53   There should be a named public health professional who addresses issues related to children in need as well as children in need of protection. The Joint Strategic Needs Assessment should include these needs which in turn should inform the Children and Young People's Plan and the LSCB business plan. When considering commissioning services for the health and wellbeing of children in need in their area, PCTs should ensure this includes those who are temporarily resident in the area, such as children held in secure settings.

2.54   PCT Chief Executives have responsibility for ensuring that the health contribution to safeguarding and promoting the welfare of children is discharged effectively across the whole local health economy through the PCTs' commissioning arrangements. PCTs should ensure that all their staff are alert to the need to safeguard and promote the welfare of children. Each PCT is responsible for identifying a senior paediatrician and senior nurse to undertake the role of designated professionals for safeguarding children in commissioning services across the health economy (see paragraphs 2.109–2.123).

2.55   PCTs should ensure that all providers from whom they commission services – including organisations in the public sector, independent sector, third sector and social enterprises – have comprehensive and effective single and multi-agency policies and procedures to safeguard and promote the welfare of children. These should be in line with, and informed by, LSCB procedures, and easily accessible for staff at all levels within each organisation.

2.56   PCTs are expected to ensure that safeguarding and promoting the welfare of children are integral to clinical governance and audit arrangements. Service specifications drawn up by PCT commissioners should include clear service standards for safeguarding and promoting the welfare of children, consistent with LSCB procedures. Section 4A and schedule 11 part 5 of the national contracts provide the means to prescribe the requirements for safeguarding children. By monitoring the service standards of all providers, PCTs will assure themselves that the required safeguarding standards are being met. Where practice-based commissioners undertake commissioning of services, this should be done in partnership with PCTs, who need to ensure their safeguarding duties are fulfilled.

2.57   PCTs should ensure GP practices and staff have robust systems and practices in place to ensure they can fulfil their role in safeguarding and promoting the welfare of children. PCTs will wish to consider how they support GP practices, for instance by assistance with protected time for, and access to, training in child protection.

2.58   PCTs are responsible for planning integrated GP out-of-hours services in their local area, and staff working within these services should know how to access advice from designated and named professionals within the PCT and LSCB. Each GP and member of the Primary Health Care Team should have access to a copy of the LSCB's procedures.

2.59    PCTs are encouraged to bring together commissioning expertise on sexual violence services, to form a local Sexual Assault Referral Services (SARS) care pathway for children and young people. All SARS for children and young people, including services provided through Sexual Assault Referral Centres (SARCs), should comply with the standards for paediatric forensic medical services *Service Specification for the Clinical Evaluation of Children and Young People who may have been sexually abused* (RCPCH, 2009), the *Children's NSF*[32] and the *You're Welcome quality criteria: Making health services young people friendly*[33]. PCTs should ensure that staff know their local services and be clear about the different agencies' roles and responsibilities, so that they are not hesitant about responding appropriately. *A Resource for Developing Sexual Assault Referral Centres*[34], jointly published by the Department of Health, Home Office and the Association of Chief Police Officers (ACPO) in October 2009, sets out the minimum elements essential for providing high quality SARCs services for adults and children who are victims of sexual assault.

2.60    PCTs must co-operate with the local authority in the establishment and operation of the LSCB and, as partners, must share responsibility for the effective discharge of its functions in safeguarding and promoting the welfare of children. Representation on the Board should be at an appropriate level of seniority. PCTs are also responsible for providing and/or ensuring the availability of appropriate expertise and advice and support to the LSCB, in respect of a range of specialist health functions – for example, primary care, mental health (adult, adolescent and child) and sexual health – and for co-ordinating the health component of Serious Case Reviews (see Chapter 8). They should notify the SHA and the CQC of all Serious Case Reviews. The PCT must also ensure that all health organisations, including those in the third sector, independent healthcare sector and social enterprises with whom they have commissioning arrangements, have links with a specific LSCB and are aware of LSCB policies and procedures. This is particularly important where providers' boundaries/ catchment areas (including Ambulance Trusts and NHS Direct services[35]) are different from those of LSCBs. The PCT should also ensure that health agencies work in partnership in accordance with their agreed LSCB plan, including in secure settings such as Young Offenders Institutions, Secure Children's Homes/Training Centres (where relevant) and Youth Offending Teams in the community.

---

32    www.dh.gov.uk/en/Healthcare/Children/DH_4089111

33    www.dh.gov.uk/prod_consum_dh/groups/dh_digitalassets/@dh/@en/documents/digitalasset/ dh_4121564.pdf

34    www.dh.gov.uk/prod_consum_dh/groups/dh_digitalassets/@dh/@en/@ps/@sta/@perf/documents/ digitalasset/dh_108350.pdf

35    NHS Direct is a national service staffed by nurses and health advisors providing 24 hour health advice and information through a national telephone number (0845 46 47), the NHS Choices website (www. nhs.uk) and a digital TV service

## General principles for all provider services

2.61    These principles apply to all NHS health services and health service providers in both the NHS and independent healthcare settings. The aim is to ensure that all children and young people receive appropriate and timely early intervention and therapeutic interventions.

2.62    All health professionals working directly with children and young people should ensure that safeguarding and promoting their welfare forms an integral part of all elements of the care they offer. Other health professionals who come into contact with children, parents and carers in the course of their work also need to be fully informed about their responsibility to safeguard and promote the welfare of children and young people. This is important as even though a health professional may not be working directly with a child, they may be seeing their parent, carer or other significant adult and have knowledge which is relevant to a child's safety and welfare. A National Institute for Health and Clinical Excellence (NICE) clinical guideline, *When to suspect child maltreatment*[36], is a resource to help healthcare practitioners who are not specialists in child protection.

2.63    All health professionals who work with children, young people and families should be able to:

- understand risk factors and recognise children and young people in need of support and/or safeguarding;

- recognise the needs of parents who may need extra help in bringing up their children, and know where to refer for help and use the CAF to access support as appropriate for them;

- recognise the risks of abuse or neglect to an unborn child;

- communicate effectively with children and young people and stay focused on the child's safety and welfare;

- liaise closely with other agencies, including other health professionals, and share information as appropriate;

- assess the needs of children and the capacity of parents/carers to meet their children's needs, including the needs of children who display sexually harmful behaviours;

- plan and respond to the needs of children and their families, particularly those who are vulnerable;

---

36    www.nice.org.uk/nicemedia/pdf/CG89FullGuideline.pdf

- contribute to child protection conferences, family group conferences and strategy discussions;

- contribute to planning and commissioning support for children who are suffering, or likely to suffer, significant harm, for example, children living in households with domestic violence or parental substance misuse;

- help ensure that children who have been abused or neglected and parents under stress have access to services to support them;

- be alert to the strong links between adult domestic violence and substance misuse and child abuse and recognise when a child is in need of help, services or at potential risk of suffering significant harm;

- where appropriate, play an active part, through the child protection plan, in keeping the child safe;

- as part of generally safeguarding children and young people, provide ongoing promotional and preventative support, through proactive work with children, families and expectant parents; and

- contribute to child death and Serious Case Reviews and implementation of the lessons learned (see Chapters 7 and 8).

2.64   The above should all be undertaken with reference to the core processes set out in this document (summarised in *What to do if you're worried a child is being abused*), *Responding to domestic abuse: A handbook for health professionals*[37], *Improving safety, Reducing Harm: Children, young people and domestic violence; a practical toolkit for front line practitioners*[38] and LSCB procedures. It is essential that all health professionals and their teams have access to advice and support from named and designated child safeguarding professionals, clinical supervision and undertake regular safeguarding training and updating (see paragraphs 2.109–2.123).

2.65   All health professionals working with children will commonly complete CAFs, which should be the responsibility of all concerned with child welfare. This includes GPs, health visitors, school nurses and other community health professionals and should not be dependent on grade or position, but rather on competence and degree of involvement with, and knowledge of, the child or young person.

2.66   The cross-government guidance *Information Sharing: Guidance for practitioners and managers* and associated training materials provides advice on when and how

---

37   www.dh.gov.uk/prod_consum_dh/groups/dh_digitalassets/@dh/@en/documents/digitalasset/ dh_4126619.pdf

38   www.dh.gov.uk/en/Publicationsandstatistics/Publications/PublicationsPolicyAndGuidance/ DH_108697

practitioners can share information legally and professionally (see paragraphs 2.12–2.14).

## NHS trusts, NHS foundation trusts and PCT provider services

2.67 NHS trusts, NHS foundation trusts and PCT provider services are responsible for providing health services in hospital and community settings. They must co-operate with the local authority in the establishment and operation of the LSCB and, as statutory partners, share responsibility for the effective discharge of its functions in safeguarding and promoting the welfare of children. They should have a board executive lead for safeguarding children who takes responsibility for governance, systems and organisational focus on safeguarding children and works closely with the named health professionals.

2.68 Representation on the LSCB should be at an appropriate level of seniority. A wide range of their staff will come into contact with children and parents in the course of their normal duties. All these staff should be trained in how to safeguard and promote the welfare of children, be alert to potential indicators of abuse or neglect in children, and know how to act on their concerns in line with LSCB procedures.

2.69 All NHS trusts, NHS foundation trusts and PCT provider services should identify a named doctor and a named nurse – and a named midwife where they provide maternity services – for child protection (see paragraph 2.109).

2.70 Staff working in urgent care settings should be able to recognise abuse or neglect and have a thorough knowledge of local procedures for making enquiries to find out whether a child is the subject of a child protection plan. Staff in urgent care settings should also be alert to the need to safeguard the welfare of children when treating parents or carers of children, and be alert to parents and carers who seek medical care from a number of sources in order to conceal the repeated nature of a child's injuries. Specialist paediatric advice should be available at all times to A&E departments and all units where children receive care. If a child – or children from the same household – presents repeatedly, even with slight injuries, in a way that doctors, nurses or other staff find worrying, they should act upon their concerns in accordance with Chapter 5 of this guidance (the key processes are summarised in *What to do if you're worried a child is being abused*). Children and families should be actively and appropriately involved in these processes, unless this could result in an increased risk of harm to the child.

2.71 In most circumstances, the relevant child's GP should be notified of visits by children to all urgent care settings. Children and young people or, where they lack competency, their parents, should be informed about this information sharing; where they object, and clinicians agree that it would not be in their best interests for information to be shared with their GP (for example, where a young person is seeking contraceptives) then a disclosure should not take place.

2.72    Where the child or young person is not registered with a GP, the appropriate contact in the PCT is to be notified for arranging registration. Consent should be sought from the child, young person or their family, as appropriate, for relevant information to be disclosed to the PCT, health visitor, school nurse or other health professional. It is important to strike an appropriate balance between protecting the confidentiality of individuals and allowing appropriate information sharing between professionals; any decision to share information without seeking consent or to override a refusal to provide consent should therefore only take place when it is in the public interest to do so. Where there is a clear risk either of a child suffering significant harm, or serious harm to an adult, the public interest test will almost certainly be satisfied. There will be other cases where practitioners will be justified in sharing some confidential information in order to make decisions on sharing further information or taking action. In these cases the information shared should be proportionate. All decisions to share or not share information about a child or young person should be fully documented, and information sharing should be explained to the child, young person or family, as appropriate, unless this could increase the risk of harm to the child.

2.73    In addition to the accountability arrangements for NHS foundation trusts set out in paragraph 2.46, NHS foundation trusts are accountable to the PCTs that commission services from them and to their local populations through a board of governors. National standards and the legal framework for the NHS apply to NHS foundation trusts just as they do to other parts of the NHS.

## Ambulance trusts and NHS Direct sites

2.74    The staff working in these health services will have access (by phone or in person) to family homes and be involved with individuals in a time of crisis. They may therefore be in a position to identify initial concerns regarding a child's welfare and be able to alert children's social care, the GP or other appropriate health professional in line with locally agreed procedures. Ambulance trusts and NHS Direct sites should have a named professional for safeguarding children (see paragraph 2.109 for more detail). All staff should be aware of local procedures in line with LSCB policies and be appropriately trained.

## Independent sector, third sector and social enterprises

2.75    Independent sector, third sector and social enterprise providers contracted to provide NHS services should comply with the requirements in this document with respect to safeguarding and promoting the welfare of children, including the requirement to notify the local authority of children who are, or are likely to be, accommodated for at least three months (see paragraph 11.30)[39]. This will be included in their contract with the commissioning PCT, and PCTs should ensure that they apply the same standards and requirements as for NHS providers.

2.76 All providers of healthcare, whether operating in the NHS or independently are subject to registration requirements set out under the Health and Social Care Act 2008 and administered by the CQC. Independent, third sector and social enterprise providers should enable access for staff to regular safeguarding training and supervision as appropriate, and should have proportionate coverage of named professionals (see paragraphs 2.109–2.123), and access to designated professionals for complex issues or where concerns may have to be escalated and involve social services. Clinical networks[40] can provide a further opportunity for sharing highly specialised resources across teams and geographical areas and PCTs should facilitate these where appropriate.

## GP practices

2.77 The family doctor or general practitioner (GP) is the first point of contact with the health service for most people. Most people are registered with a GP practice and have an ongoing relationship with that practice. In addition to maintaining their own professional skills in safeguarding and promoting the welfare of children, GPs have an important role to play as employers in ensuring staff whom they employ are trained in safeguarding and promoting the welfare of children (see Chapter 4).

## Roles of different health services

### Universal services

2.78 Universal child and family health services are provided by a range of professionals and their teams working within general practice or other provider organisations. There are many common responsibilities although specific arrangements may be different within community health services to those within general practice. While GPs and other health practitioners have responsibilities to all their patients, children may be particularly vulnerable and their welfare is paramount.

2.79 The Healthy Child Programme[41], 0-5 years and 5-19 years, provides a framework to ensure the promotion of the health and wellbeing of children and young people.

---

39    Section 85, Children Act 1989
40    A Guide to Promote a Shared Understanding of the Benefits of Managed Local Networks (Department of Health, 2005)
41    www.dh.gov.uk/en/Healthcare/Children/Maternity/index.htm

It is delivered by multi-agency support services involved with children and young people.

2.80    As part of the Programme, regular health reviews are undertaken which provide the opportunity to identify risk factors that make children more likely to experience poorer outcomes later in life, including family and environmental factors. This enables professionals to put together a package of support or referral to specialist services to address the issues raised. All professionals need to be alert to concerns and the requirements to safeguard children. More support should be targeted to children and families who are vulnerable or those with complex needs.

2.81    If concerns arise during an assessment that may require support from another agency it will be important for the professionals involved to work in partnership and share relevant information as required, in accordance with the Government's information sharing guidance.

2.82    All professionals delivering universal services have key roles to play both in the identification of children who may have been abused or neglected and those who are likely to be; and in subsequent intervention and protection from harm. Surgery consultations, home visits, treatment room sessions, child health clinic attendance, drop-in centres and information from staff such as health visitors, midwives, children's centre staff, school health team staff and practice nurses may all help to build up a picture of the child's situation and can alert the appropriate professional if there is a concern.

2.83    All professionals delivering primary care should know when it is appropriate to refer a child or young person to children's social care for help as a 'child in need', and know how to act on concerns that a child may be suffering, or likely to suffer, significant harm through abuse or neglect.

2.84    GPs, their staff and community health practitioners such as health visitors and school nurses are also well placed to recognise when a parent or other adult has problems that may affect their capacity as a parent or carer, or that may mean they pose a risk of harm to a child. When GPs and other health professionals have concerns that an adult's illness or behaviour may be causing, or putting a child at risk of, suffering significant harm, they should follow the procedures set out in Chapter 5 of this guidance (summarised in *What to do if you're worried a child is being abused*).

2.85    GPs, practice staff, and other community health practitioners have an important role in all stages of the child protection process and should have a clear means of identifying in records those children (together with their parents and siblings) who are the subject of a child protection plan. This will enable them to be recognised by the partners of the practice and any other doctor, nurse or health visitor who may be involved in the care of those children. There should be good communication between GPs, health visitors, school nurses (and the wider School Health Team), practice nurses and midwives in respect of all children and their families about whom there are concerns.

2.86   GPs and other community health practitioners, such as health visitors and school nurses, have key roles in appropriate information sharing with children's social care when enquiries are being made about a child. They will also contribute to assessments and be involved in a child protection plan, as appropriate. GPs, community health practitioners, other primary care professionals and practice staff should make available to child protection conferences relevant information about a child and family, whether or not they are able to attend.

*General practitioners*

2.87   All GPs have a duty to maintain their skills in the recognition of abuse and neglect, and to be familiar with the procedures to be followed if abuse or neglect is suspected. GPs should take part in training about safeguarding and promoting the welfare of children, and have regular updates as part of their post-graduate educational programme[42].

*Health visitors*

2.88   The specialist skills of the health visitor are crucially important in protecting children. Health visitors contribute to all stages of the child protection process, including Serious Case Reviews. They support the work of the LSCB through the delivery of multi-agency training programmes and membership of working and task sub-groups.

2.89   Health visitors are trained to recognise risk factors, triggers of concern and signs of abuse and neglect. Through their preventative work, they are frequently the first to recognise children who are being or are likely to be abused or neglected and therefore when safeguarding procedures need to be initiated. Knowledge of the family and their circumstances, as well as the child, probably gathered during home visits, enables the health visitor to recognise signs and symptoms of a worsening environment, lack of progress to improve the child's circumstances, or actual harm being suffered by the child.

2.90   Health visitors must have time to maintain effective contact with the child and family, to establish and develop a successful working relationship so they can

---

42     Good Medical Practice (GMC).
       www.gmc-uk.org/GMC_Good_Medical_Practise_1209.pdf_30373048.pdf

consider the situation objectively. Where formal safeguarding procedures are in place, health visitors need ongoing contact with families so that they continue to receive preventative health interventions both during the crisis, and in the future.

2.91 Health visitors should liaise with other professionals and agencies so that a full picture of risk factors and progress is obtained. A recurring theme in Serious Case Reviews has been inadequate sharing of information about vulnerable children. Health visitors should use professional judgement about what, and when, information is shared with others such as children's social care services, police and children's centres.

2.92 Health visitors should also consider the competence of those in their team, guiding them and ensuring they understand their own roles, responsibilities and relevant policies and procedures, as well as the legislative framework for safeguarding and promoting the welfare of children. Health visitors must have access to regular proactive child protection supervision to ensure good practice (see Chapter 4).

*School nurses[43]*

2.93 School nurses have a crucial role to play in safeguarding. They have regular contact with children aged 5-19 who spend a significant proportion of their time in school and are commonly the lead professional for CAFs. School nurses are educated in child health and development and have a prominent role in delivering the Healthy Child Programme. They have opportunities for periodic, anticipatory health assessments of this group of children as part of universal services. They lead public health actions, implement health education programmes and deliver enhanced services according to assessment of individual or group needs. They may be the first to identify the needs of specific children and instigate preventative interventions, and/or safeguarding procedures.

2.94 In their care and treatment of vulnerable children, school nurses may work with parents or carers, referring to, and liaising with specialists and can be instrumental in securing extra resources or support for families to increase their capacity for appropriate parenting.

2.95 The position of school nurses at the heart of caring about health and wellbeing within the school environment, alongside the personal care they offer, enables them to establish trusting relationships with children so they are the frequent recipient of confidences, which can lead to earlier intervention.

---

43    Nurses working in schools are often called 'school health advisers' or 'health advisers'

## Maternity services

2.96    The Healthy Child Programme starts in pregnancy. Midwives are the primary health professionals likely to be working with and supporting women and their families throughout pregnancy. However, other health professionals – including maternity support workers, health visitors and, where applicable, specialist key workers – may also be directly engaged in providing support. The close relationship they foster with their clients provides an opportunity to observe attitudes towards the developing baby and identify potential problems during pregnancy, birth and the child's early care.

2.97    It is estimated that a third of domestic violence starts or escalates during pregnancy (see paragraphs 11.79–11.92). All health professionals working with pregnant women should understand that vulnerable women are more likely to delay seeking care, to fail to attend antenatal clinics regularly and to deny and minimise abuse. It is important to provide a supportive and enabling environment, where the issue of abuse is raised with every pregnant woman, with the provision of information about specialist agencies, thus enabling disclosure should a woman so choose (Maternity Section Children's NSF, 2004). The Department of Health issued revised guidance, *Responding to Domestic Violence: a Handbook for Health Professionals*[44], in 2006.

## Child and Adolescent Mental Health Services (CAMHS)

2.98    Standard 9 of the NSF is devoted to the 'Mental Health and Psychological Wellbeing of Children and Young People'. The importance of effective partnership working is emphasised, and this is especially applicable to children and young people who have mental health problems as a result of abuse and/or neglect. Some forms of emotional distress may, however, fall short of being an identifiable mental health issue. It is also important that the more general need to promote emotional wellbeing among children and young people is not neglected as an essential component of safeguarding.

2.99    In the course of their work, child and adolescent mental health professionals will therefore want to identify as part of assessment and care planning whether child abuse or neglect, or domestic violence, are factors in a child's mental health problems, and ensure that this is addressed appropriately in their treatment and care. If they think a child is currently affected, they should follow local child protection procedures. Consultation, supervision and training resources should be available and accessible in each service (see Chapter 4).

2.100   Child and adolescent mental health professionals have a role in the initial assessment process in circumstances where their specific skills and knowledge are

---

44      www.dh.gov.uk/en/publicationsandstatistics/publications/publicationspolicyandguidance/DH_4126161

helpful. In addition, assessment and treatment services may need to be provided to young people with mental health problems or with other emotional difficulties who offend. The assessment of children with significant learning difficulties, a disability or sensory and communication difficulties may require the expertise of a specialist learning disability service or CAMHS.

2.101    CAMHS also have a role in the provision of a range of psychiatric and psychological assessment and treatment services for children and families. Services that may be provided, in liaison with local authority children's social care services, include the provision of reports for court, and direct work with children, parents and families. Services may be provided either within general or specialist multi-disciplinary teams, depending on the severity and complexity of the problem. In addition, consultation and training may be offered to services in the community – including, for example, social care schools, primary healthcare professionals and nurseries.

## Adult Mental Health Services

2.102    Adult mental health services – including those providing general adult and community, forensic, psychotherapy, alcohol and substance misuse and learning disability services – have a responsibility in safeguarding children when they become aware of, or identify, a child suffering or likely to suffer significant harm. This may be as a result of a service's direct work with those who may be mentally ill, a parent, a parent-to-be, or a non-related abuser, or in response to a request for the assessment of an adult perceived to represent a potential or actual risk to a child or young person. Adult mental health staff need to be especially aware of the risk of neglect, emotional abuse and domestic abuse to children. Staff should be able to consider the needs of any child in the family of their patient or client and to refer to other services or support for the family as necessary and appropriate, in line with local child protection procedures. Consultation, supervision and training resources should be available and accessible in each service.

2.103    In order to safeguard children of patients, mental health practitioners should routinely record details of patients' responsibilities in relation to children, and consider the support needs of patients who are parents and of their children, in all aspects of their work, using the Care Programme Approach. Mental health practitioners should refer to Royal College of Psychiatrists policy documents, including *Patients as Parents*[45] and *Child Abuse and Neglect: the Role of Mental Health Services*[46] and SCIE Guide 30[47].

---

45    www.rcpsych.ac.uk/files/pdfversion/cr105.pdf
46    www.rcpsych.ac.uk/files/pdfversion/cr120.pdf
47    Think child, think parent, think family: a guide to parental mental health and child welfare, 2009 SCIE Guide 30. www.scie.org.uk/publications/guides/guide30/index.asp

2.104 Close collaboration and liaison between adult mental health services and children's social care services are essential in the interests of children. It is similarly important that adult mental health liaise with other health providers, such as health visitors and general practitioners. This may require sharing information to safeguard and promote the welfare of children or to protect a child from significant harm. The expertise of substance misuse services and learning disability services may also be required. The assessment of parents with significant learning difficulties, a disability, or sensory and communication difficulties, may require the expertise of a specialist psychiatrist or clinical psychologist from a learning disability service or adult mental health service.

2.105 From April 2010, under section 131A of the Mental Health Act 1983, there is a duty on hospital managers to ensure that if a child or young person under the age of 18 is admitted to hospital for mental health treatment, the environment in the hospital is suitable having regard to their age. Managers of adult services must consult with a person who can provide appropriate advice on CAMHS who would need to be involved in decisions about accommodation, care and facilities for education in hospital.

## Visiting of psychiatric patients by children

2.106 All inpatient mental health services must have policies and procedures relating to children visiting inpatients, as set out in the *Guidance on the Visiting of Psychiatric Patients by Children* to NHS trusts[48]. Additional guidance has been provided for high-security hospitals. Mental health practitioners must consider the needs of children whose parent or relative is an inpatient – whether formal or informal – in a mental health unit, and make appropriate arrangements for them to visit if this is in the child's best interests.

## Alcohol and drug services

2.107 A range of services are provided, in particular by health and voluntary organisations, to respond to the needs of adults (who may have parental or caring responsibilities) and children who misuse drugs and alcohol. These services are linked to the relevant agencies at local level through Drug Action Teams, which comprise, as a minimum, health, social care, education and police representatives. It is important that arrangements are in place to enable children's social care services and substance misuse (including alcohol) services referrals to be made in relevant cases. Where children may be suffering significant harm because of their own substance misuse, or where parental substance misuse may be causing such harm, referrals need to be made by Drug Action Teams or alcohol services, in accordance with LSCB

---

48    www.dh.gov.uk/prod_consum_dh/groups/dh_digitalassets/@dh/@en/documents/digitalasset/ dh_4012658.pdf

procedures. Where children are not suffering significant harm, referral arrangements also need to be in place to enable children's broader needs to be assessed and responded to. Further information can be found in the DCSF/DH Joint Guidance on *Development of Local Protocols between Drug and Alcohol Treatment Services and Local Safeguarding and Family Services*[49].

## Health professionals

### Designated and named professionals

2.108   The terms 'designated professionals' and 'named professionals' denote professionals with specific roles and responsibilities for safeguarding children. As commissioners, all PCTs should have a designated doctor and nurse to take a strategic, professional lead on all aspects of the health service contribution to safeguarding children across the PCT area, which includes all providers. PCTs should ensure establishment levels of designated and named professionals are proportionate to the local resident populations and to the complexity of provider arrangements. For large PCTs, NHS trusts and foundation trusts which may have a number of sites, a team approach can enhance the ability to provide 24-hour advice and provide mutual support for those carrying out the designated and named professional role. If this approach is taken, it is important to ensure that the leadership and accountability arrangements are clear.

2.109   Designated and named professional roles should always be explicitly defined in job descriptions, and sufficient time, funding, supervision and support should be allowed to fulfil their child safeguarding responsibilities effectively. Further information can be found in the intercollegiate document *Safeguarding Children and Young People: Roles and Competencies for Health Care Staff*[50].

*Designated professionals*

2.110   Designated professionals are a vital source of professional advice on safeguarding children matters to the PCT, health professionals, particularly named safeguarding health professionals, local authority children's services departments and the LSCB. Appointment as a designated professional may be a full-time role employed as part of the PCT commissioning arm or the person may be employed by a provider organisation with certain time dedicated to the designated role. If the person is not employed by the PCT commissioning arm a clear service level agreement should be in place.

---

49      www.nta.nhs.uk/publications/documents/yp_drug_alcohol_treatment_protocol_1109.pdf

50      www.rcpch.ac.uk/doc.aspx?id_Resource=1535. This document is currently being updated

2.111 Designated professionals:

- provide advice to ensure the range of services commissioned by the PCT take account of the need to safeguard and promote the welfare of children;

- provide advice on the monitoring of the safeguarding aspects of PCT contracts;

- provide advice, support and clinical supervision to the named professionals in each provider organisation;

- provide skilled advice to the LSCB on health issues;

- play an important role in promoting, influencing and developing relevant training, on both a single and inter-agency basis, to ensure the training needs of health staff are addressed;

- provide skilled professional involvement in child safeguarding processes in line with LSCB procedures; and

- review and evaluate the practice and learning from all involved health professionals and providers commissioned by the PCT, as part of Serious Case Reviews (see paragraph 8.30).

*Named professionals*

2.112 All NHS trusts, NHS foundation trusts, and public, third sector, independent sector, social enterprises and PCTs providing services for children should identify a named doctor and a named nurse – and a named midwife if the organisation provides maternity services – for safeguarding. In the case of NHS Direct, Ambulance trusts and independent providers, this should be a named professional. The focus for the named professional's role is safeguarding children within their own organisation and they should work closely with the board safeguarding children lead to ensure all services are aware of their responsibilities (see paragraphs 2.61–2.65).

2.113 Named professionals have a key role in promoting good professional practice within their organisation, and provide advice and expertise for fellow professionals. They should have specific expertise in children's health and development, child maltreatment and local arrangements for safeguarding and promoting the welfare of children.

2.114 Named professionals should support the organisation in its clinical governance role, by ensuring that audits on safeguarding are undertaken and that safeguarding issues are part of the Trust's clinical governance system. They also have a key role in ensuring a safeguarding training strategy is in place and is delivered within their organisation.

2.115   Named professionals are usually responsible for conducting the organisation's internal management reviews, except when they have had personal involvement in the case when it will be more appropriate for the designated professional to conduct the review. Named professionals should be of sufficient standing and seniority in the organisation to ensure that the resulting action plan is followed up.

## Paediatricians

2.116   Paediatricians, wherever they work, will come into contact with child abuse or neglect in the course of their work. All paediatricians need to maintain their skills in the recognition of abuse, and be familiar with the procedures to be followed if abuse and neglect is suspected. Consultant paediatricians, in particular, may be involved in difficult diagnostic situations, differentiating those where abnormalities may have been caused by abuse from those that have a medical cause. In their contacts with children and families, they should be sensitive to clues suggesting the need for additional support or enquiries.

2.117   Where paediatricians undertake forensic medical examination, they must ensure they are competent to do so, or work together with a colleague, such as a forensic medical examiner, who has the necessary complementary skills[51].

2.118   Paediatricians are sometimes required to provide reports for child protection investigations, civil and criminal proceedings, and to appear as witnesses to give oral evidence. They must always act in accordance with guidance from the General Medical Council (GMC)[52] and professional bodies, ensuring their evidence is accurate. The Academy of Royal Colleges also issued guidance for those undertaking expert witness work in 2005[53].

## Dental practitioners and dental care professionals (DCPs)

2.119   Dental practitioners and dental care professionals (dental therapists, dental hygienists, dental nurses, etc.) may see vulnerable children, both within healthcare settings and when undertaking domiciliary visits. They are likely to identify injuries to the head, neck, face, mouth and teeth, as well as potentially identifying other child welfare concerns. From April 2011, primary dental practitioners will be required to register with the CQC and comply with the regulations for safeguarding.

---

51   The core and case-dependent skills required are outlined in detail in Guidance on Paediatric Forensic Examinations in Relation to Possible Child Sexual Abuse (2004), produced by the Royal College of Paediatrics and Child Health and the Association of Forensic Physicians. See: www.rcpch.ac.uk/doc.aspx?id_Resource=1750

52   Acting as an expert witness. See: www.gmc-uk.org/guidance/ethical_guidance/expert_witness_guidance.asp. This guidance also lists other sources of information and advice.

53   Medical Expert Witness: Guidance from the Academy of Medical Royal Colleges (2005) www.aomrc.org.uk

2.120   The dental team, irrespective of the healthcare setting in which they work, should therefore be included within the child protection systems and training within the local trust. *Child protection and the Dental Team – an introduction to safeguarding children in dental practice* is available[54] as guidance for all dental practice staff. Dentists should have access to a copy of the LSCB's procedures.

2.121   The dental team should have the knowledge and skills to identify concerns regarding a child's welfare. They should know how to refer to children's social care and who to contact for further advice, including the local named and designated professionals.

## Other health professionals

2.122   All other health professionals, including those not specifically covered in the preceding sections, and staff who provide help and support to promote children's health and development should have knowledge of the LSCB procedures and how to contact named professionals for advice and support. They should receive the training and supervision they need to recognise and act on child welfare concerns and to respond to the needs of children.

## Criminal justice organisations

## The police

2.123   The main roles of the police are to uphold the law, prevent crime and disorder and protect citizens. Children, like all citizens, have the right to the full protection offered by the criminal law. Under section 11 of the Children Act 2004, the police authority and chief officer of police for a police area in England must ensure that their functions are discharged having regard to the need to safeguard and promote the welfare of children. Offences committed against children can be particularly sensitive, and often require the police to work with other organisations, such as children's social care, in the conduct of any investigation.

2.124   The police recognise the fundamental importance of inter-agency working in combating child abuse, as illustrated by well-established arrangements for joint training involving police and social care colleagues. The police also have specialist training in investigating child abuse cases. The second edition of *Investigating Child Abuse and Safeguarding Children* was published by ACPO and the National Police Improvement Agency in 2009[55]. This sets out the investigative doctrine, training courses and terms of reference for police forces' child abuse investigation units (CAIUs).

---

54    www.cpdt.org.uk/
55    www.npia.police.uk/en/docs/Investigating_Child_Abuse_WEBSITE.pdf

2.125   All police forces have CAIUs and, despite variations in their structures and staffing levels, they normally take primary responsibility for investigating child abuse cases. All CAIUs have access to the national IMPACT Nominal Index (INI) which enables them to quickly check which forces hold information on a particular individual. The INI capability draws on a number of police databases, including child protection, domestic violence, crime, custody and intelligence. Police forces are in the process of migrating to the Police National Database (PND) which will continue to provide and enhance this facility.

2.126   Safeguarding children is not solely the role of CAIU officers – it is a fundamental part of the duties of all police officers. Patrol officers attending domestic violence incidents, for example, should be aware of the effect of such violence on any children normally resident within the household. The police also maintain relevant UK-wide databases such as VISOR – a database for the management of individuals who pose a serious risk of harm to the public[56]. Through the Safeguarding Vulnerable Groups Act 2006, the Government has established a new integrated Vetting and Barring Scheme, regulating all those who work with children (and vulnerable adults), which relies on regularly updated police information. Separate guidance is available to help the police carry out this responsibility, and officers engaged in, for example, community safety partnerships, Drug Action Teams, Multi Agency Risk Assessment Conference (MARAC) and Multi Agency Public Protection Arrangements (MAPPA) must keep in mind the needs of children in their area.

2.127   Children and young people also come into contact with the police as part of the criminal justice process, when arrested or taken to a police station for questioning or when asked to give evidence as a witness. The police have a duty to safeguard and promote the welfare of children in their care/custody at all stages of the process and ensure full compliance with the requirements of the Police and Criminal Evidence Act (PACE). Criminal and youth justice agencies and local authority children's services should have protocols in place to ensure that young people are not detained in police cells overnight and to ensure adequate safeguarding of young people in court settings and during escort to the secure estate.

2.128   The police hold important information about children who may be suffering, or likely to suffer significant harm, as well as those who cause such harm, which they should share with other organisations where this is necessary to protect children for example, the family court. This includes a responsibility to ensure that those officers representing the police at a child protection conference are fully informed about the case, as well as being trained and experienced in risk assessment and the decision-making process. Similarly, they can expect other organisations to share

---

56      VISOR has been developed jointly between the police and the probation service to assist management of offenders in the community

with them information and intelligence they hold to enable the police to carry out their duties.

2.129 Any evidence gathered by the police or other agencies in criminal investigations may be of use to local authority solicitors who are preparing for civil proceedings to protect the victim. The Crown Prosecution Service (CPS) should be consulted, so that they may decide on the issue of sharing evidence in the best interests of the child and in the interests of justice.

2.130 The police must be notified as soon as possible by local authority children's social care whenever a case referred to them involves a criminal offence committed, or suspected of having been committed, against a child. Other agencies should also consider sharing such information (see paragraphs 5.20 onwards). This does not mean that in all such cases a full investigation is required, or that there will necessarily be any further police involvement. It is important, however, that the police retain the opportunity to be informed and consulted, to ensure all relevant information can be taken into account before a final decision is made.

2.131 LSCBs should have in place a protocol, agreed between the local authority and the police, to guide both organisations in deciding how section 47 enquiries should be conducted and, in particular, the circumstances in which joint enquiries are appropriate.

2.132 In addition to their duty to investigate criminal offences, the police have emergency powers to enter premises and ensure the immediate protection of children believed to be suffering, or likely to suffer, significant harm. In such circumstances, the police should inform the child (if he or she appears competent to understand) and take such steps as are reasonably practicable to ascertain the child's wishes and feelings. Police emergency powers should be used only when necessary, the principle being that, wherever possible, the decision to remove a child from a parent or carer should be made by a court. Home Office Circular 017/2008[57] gives detailed guidance on this.

## Probation

2.133 The Probation Service supervises offenders with the aim of reducing re-offending and protecting the public. As part of their main responsibility to supervise offenders in the community, offender managers are in contact with, or supervising, a number of offenders who have been identified as presenting a risk, or potential risk, of harm to children. They also supervise offenders who are parents or carers of children and these children may be at heightened risk of involvement in (or exposure to) criminal or anti-social behaviour and of other poor outcomes. By working with these offenders to change their lifestyles and to enable them to change their behaviour,

---

57   www.homeoffice.gov.uk/about-us/publications/home-office-circulars/circulars-2008/017-2008/

offender managers safeguard and promote the welfare of offenders' children. In addition, Probation Areas/Trusts provide a direct service to children by:

- providing a statutory victim contact scheme to the victims of violent and sexual offences, including children and young people (where the victim is aged under 17, their parent or guardian is also entitled to services);

- delivering unpaid work requirements to 16- and 17-year-olds;

- fulfilling their role as statutory partner of YOTs; and

- ensuring support for victims, and indirectly children in the family, of convicted perpetrators of domestic abuse participating in accredited domestic abuse programmes.

2.134  Offender managers should also ensure that there is clarity and communication between MAPPA and other risk management processes – for example, in the case of safeguarding children, procedures covering registered sex offenders, domestic abuse management meetings, child protection procedures and procedures for the assessment of people identified as presenting a risk or potential risk of harm to children. See Chapter 12 for further information.

## Prisons

2.135  Governors of prisons (or, in the case of contracted prisons, their Directors) also have a duty to make arrangements to ensure that their functions are discharged with regard to the need to safeguard and promote the welfare of children and young people, not least those who have been committed to their custody by the courts.

2.136  In particular, Governors/Directors of women's establishments that have Mother and Baby Units must ensure that staff working on the units are prioritised for child protection training, and that there is always a member of staff on duty in the unit who is proficient in child protection, health and safety and first aid/child resuscitation. Each baby must have a childcare plan, setting out how the best interests of the child will be maintained and promoted during the child's time of residence on the unit.

2.137  Governors/Directors of all prison establishments must have in place arrangements that protect the public from prisoners in their care. This includes having effective processes in place to ensure prisoners are not able to cause harm to the public, particularly children. Restrictions are placed on prisoner communications (visits, telephone and correspondence) that are proportionate to the risk they present. As a response to incidents where prisoners have attempted to 'condition and groom' future victims, all prisoners who have been identified as presenting a continued risk of harm to children are not allowed contact with children, unless a favourable risk assessment has been undertaken. This assessment takes into consideration information held by the police, probation, prison and children's social care services.

2.138 The wishes and feelings of the child or young person are an important element of the assessment. When seeking the views of the parent or carer (person with parental responsibility) regarding contact, it is important that the child's wishes and feelings are sought. In the letter to the child's parent or carer, it should be emphasised that the child's wishes and feelings should be taken into account. If a child or young person is able to make an informed choice, these wishes and feelings must be given due consideration. Local authority children's social care services will ascertain the views of the child or young person during the home visit.

2.139 Governors should ensure that any staff working directly with the children of offenders are trained in child protection.

## The secure estate for children and young people

2.140 The Children Act 1989 applies to children and young people in the secure estate and the local authority continues to have responsibilities towards them in the same way as they do for other children in need. LSCBs will have oversight of the safeguarding arrangements within secure settings in their area.

2.141 The Youth Justice Board (YJB) has a statutory responsibility for the commissioning and purchasing of all secure accommodation for children and young people who are sentenced or remanded by the courts. It does not deliver services directly to young people but is responsible for setting standards for the delivery of those services.

2.142 There are three types of secure accommodation in which a young person can be placed, which together make up the secure estate for children and young people:

- *Young Offender Institutions (YOIs)* – YOIs are facilities run by both the Prison Service and the private sector and accommodate 15 to 17 year olds. Young people serving Detention and Training Orders can be accommodated beyond the age of 17 subject to child protection considerations. The majority of YOIs accommodate male young people, although there are four dedicated female units;

- *Secure Training Centres (STCs)* – STCs are purpose-built centres for young offenders up to the age of 17. STCs can accommodate both male and female young people who are held separately. They are run by private operators under contracts, which set out detailed operational requirements. There are four STCs in England; and

- *Secure Children's Homes (SCHs)* – Most SCHs are run by local authority children's social care. They can also be run by private or voluntary organisations. They accommodate children and young people who are placed there on a secure welfare order for the protection of themselves or others, and for those placed under criminal justice legislation. SCHs are generally used to accommodate young offenders aged 12 to 14, girls up to the age of 16, and 15 to 16 year old boys who are assessed as vulnerable.

2.143   All these establishments have a duty to effectively safeguard and promote the welfare of children and young people, which should include:

- protection of harm from self;

- protection of harm from adults; and

- protection of harm from peers.

Local authorities, LSCBs, YOTs and secure establishments should have agreed protocols setting out how they will work together and share information to safeguard and promote the welfare of children and young people in secure establishments.

2.144   All members of staff working in secure establishments have a duty to promote the welfare of children and young people and ensure that they are safeguarded effectively. In addition, Governors, Directors and senior managers have a duty to ensure that appropriate procedures are in place to enable them to fulfil their safeguarding responsibilities. These procedures should include, but not be limited to, arrangements to respond to:

- child protection allegations;

- incidents of self-harm and suicide; and

- incidents of violence and bullying.

2.145   All staff working within secure establishments should understand their individual safeguarding responsibilities and should receive appropriate training to enable them to fulfil these duties. Appropriate recruitment and selection processes should be in place to ensure staff's suitability to work with children and young people. These procedures should cover any adult working within the establishment, whether or not they are directly employed by the Governor/Director.

## Youth Offending Teams

2.146   The principal aim of the youth justice system is to prevent offending by children and young people. YOTs have a key role. YOTs are multi-agency teams that must include a probation officer, a police officer, a representative of the PCT, someone with experience in education, and someone with experience of social work relating to children. YOTs are responsible for the supervision of children and young people subject to pre-court interventions and statutory court disposals.

2.147 YOTs are well placed to identify those children and young people known to relevant organisations as being most at risk of offending, and to undertake work to prevent them offending. A significant number of the children who are supervised by the YOTs will also be children in need, and some of their needs will require safeguarding. It is necessary, therefore, for there to be clear links between youth justice and local authority children's social care, both at a strategic level and at an operational level for individual children and young people. YOT Management Boards are made up of statutory and other YOT partners at a senior level and provide strategic direction and oversight to YOTs at a local level.

2.148 YOTs, in partnership with these wider statutory partners, have a mutual duty to make effective local arrangements to ensure that their functions are discharged with regard to the need to safeguard and promote the welfare of children known to the youth justice system.

## The UK Border Agency

2.149 The primary duties of the UKBA are to maintain a secure border, to detect and prevent border tax fraud, smuggling and immigration crime, and to ensure controlled, fair migration that protects the public and that contributes to economic growth and benefits the country. The UKBA also has a role in granting protection to those who need it according to international conventions and the laws of the UK. It is also required to enforce immigration legislation and this will at times mean removing from the UK persons who have no legal entitlement to remain in the UK, which may include the short-term detention of individuals and families in Immigration Removal Centres.

2.150 The UKBA does not directly provide services to children and young people but it does play a part in identifying and acting upon concerns about the welfare of children with whom it comes into contact. Under section 55 of the Borders, Citizenship and Immigration Act 2009 the UKBA has a duty to ensure that its functions are discharged with regard to the need to safeguard and promote the welfare of children. Its main contributions to safeguarding and promoting the welfare of children include:

- ensuring good treatment and good interactions with children throughout the immigration, detention (where appropriate) and customs process;

- applying laws and policies that prevent the exploitation of children throughout and following facilitated illegal entry and trafficking; and

- detecting at the border any material linked to child exploitation through pornography.

2.151  Other elements of the UKBA's contribution include:

- exercising vigilance when dealing with children with whom staff come into contact and identifying children who may be likely to suffer harm; and

- making timely and appropriate referrals to agencies that provide ongoing care and support to children.

2.152  The UKBA makes referrals to the statutory agencies responsible for child protection or child welfare such as the police or local authority children's social care services. Wherever it is appropriate the UKBA will seek to establish national, regional and local protocols for joint working with these bodies.

*The UKBA and trafficking of persons, including children*

2.153  Since 1 April 2009, the UK has been bound by the Council of Europe Convention on Action against Trafficking in Human Beings. All UKBA staff at operational and case working grades complete training on how to identify potential victims of trafficking, and this includes specific sections on the features of child trafficking. Where a child is identified as vulnerable as a result of a suspicion of trafficking, details of the case are referred simultaneously to the relevant local authority and to specially trained 'competent authority' teams based in the UKBA and the UK Human Trafficking Centre.

2.154  These 'competent authority' teams consider all relevant information, including any provided by local authority children social care services, in determining whether a case meets the thresholds for trafficking set out in the Convention. A positive decision will lead to an extendable 45-day reflection period during which the victim will have access to support and will not be removed from the UK. Following this they may be eligible for a residence permit under current immigration policy. This is a significant safeguarding role for all UKBA staff and a major contribution by the Agency to the wider safeguarding of children.

## Schools and further education institutions

2.155  Schools (including independent schools and non-maintained special schools) and FE institutions should give effect to their duty to safeguard and promote the welfare of their pupils (students under 18 years of age in the case of FE institutions) under the Education Act 2002 and, where appropriate, under the Children Act 1989 (see paragraph 2.5) by:

- creating and maintaining a safe learning environment for children and young people; and

- identifying where there are child welfare concerns and taking action to address them, in partnership with other organisations where appropriate.

Schools also contribute through the curriculum by developing children's understanding, awareness and resilience. Ofsted inspect against the extent to which schools and colleges fulfil their safeguarding responsibilities. In Schools and FE colleges, how effectively the safeguarding of learners is promoted, is a limiting grade on overall effectiveness.

2.156 Creating a safe learning environment means having effective arrangements in place to address a range of issues. These include child protection arrangements, pupil health and safety, and bullying (including cyberbullying). Others include arrangements for meeting the health needs of children with medical conditions, providing first aid, school security, tackling drugs and substance misuse, having arrangements in place to safeguard and promote the welfare of children on extended vocational placements and ensuring support and planning for young people in custody and their resettlement back into the community.

2.157 Education staff have a crucial role to play in helping identify welfare concerns, and indicators of possible abuse or neglect, at an early stage. They should refer those concerns to the appropriate organisation, normally local authority children's social care, contributing to the assessment of a child's needs and, where appropriate, to ongoing action to meet those needs. When a child has special educational needs or is disabled, the school will have important information about the child's level of understanding and the most effective means of communicating with the child. The school will also be well placed to give a view on the impact of treatment or intervention on the child's care or behaviour. As the numbers of 14-16s in FE colleges for at least part of the week has increased, staff in this sector will need to be part of the arrangements for providing support for their role on safeguarding.

2.158 In addition to the features common to organisations working with children listed in paragraph 2.11, schools and FE institutions should have a senior member of staff who is designated to take lead responsibility for dealing with child protection issues, providing advice and support to other staff, liaising with the authority, and working with other organisations as necessary. A school or FE institution should remedy without delay any deficiencies or weaknesses in its arrangements for safeguarding and promoting welfare that are brought to its attention.

2.159    Staff in schools and FE institutions should not themselves investigate possible abuse or neglect. They have a key role to play by referring concerns about those issues to local authority children's social care, providing information for police investigations and/or enquiries under section 47 of the Children Act 1989, and by contributing to assessments.

2.160    Where a child of school age, including those attending FE institutions, is the subject of an inter-agency child protection plan, the school or FE institution should be involved in the preparation of the plan. The school's role and responsibilities in contributing to actions to safeguard the child, and promote his or her welfare, should be clearly identified.

2.161    Special schools, including non-maintained special schools and independent schools, that provide medical and/or nursing care should ensure that their medical and nursing staff have appropriate training and access to advice on child protection and on safeguarding and promoting the welfare of children.

2.162    Schools play an important role in making children and young people aware both of behaviour towards them that is not acceptable, and of how they can help keep themselves safe. The non-statutory framework for personal, social and health education (PSHE) provides opportunities for children and young people to learn about keeping safe. For example, pupils should be given information about:

- the availability of advice and support in their local area and online;

- recognising and managing risks in different situations, including on the internet, and then deciding how to respond;

- judging what kind of physical contact is acceptable and unacceptable; and

- recognising when pressure from others (including people they know) threatens their personal safety and wellbeing and develop effective ways of resisting pressure.

2.163    PSHE curriculum materials provide resources that enable schools to tackle issues regarding healthy relationships, including domestic violence, bullying and abuse. Discussions about personal safety and keeping safe can reinforce the message that any kind of violence is unacceptable, let children and young people know that it is acceptable to talk about their own problems, and signpost sources of help.

2.164    Corporal punishment is outlawed for all pupils in all schools, including independent schools, and FE institutions. The law forbids a teacher or other member of staff from using any degree of physical contact that is deliberately intended to punish a pupil, or that is primarily intended to cause pain or injury or humiliation.

2.165  Teachers at a school are allowed to use reasonable force to control or restrain pupils under certain circumstances. Other staff may also do so, in the same way as teachers, provided they have been authorised by the head teacher to have control or charge of pupils. All schools should have a policy about the use of force to control or restrain pupils. See *The Use of Force to Control or Restrain Pupils*[58] for further guidance.

## Early years services

2.166  Early years services – children's centres, nurseries, childminders, preschools, playgroups, and holiday and out-of-school schemes – all play an important part in the lives of large numbers of children. Many childcare providers have considerable experience of working with families where a child needs to be safeguarded from harm, and many local authorities provide, commission or sponsor specific services, including childminders, to work with children in need and their families.

2.167  All early years providers, regardless of type, size or funding of the setting, must:

- take necessary steps to safeguard and promote the welfare of children;

- promote the good health of children, take necessary steps to prevent the spread of infection, and take appropriate action when they are ill;

- manage children's behaviour effectively and in a manner appropriately for their stage of development and particular individual needs; and

- ensure that adults looking after children, or having unsupervised access to them, are suitable to do so.

2.168  These general welfare requirements are set out in detail in the *Statutory Framework for the Early Years Foundation Stage (EYFS)*[59].

2.169  Millions of families use early years services on an annual basis, meaning that early years services are a key route through which welfare concerns can be identified early in a child's life. The EYFS makes clear that all registered providers, excepting childminders, must have a practitioner who is designated to take lead responsibility for safeguarding children within each early years setting and who should liaise with local statutory children's services agencies as appropriate. This lead must also attend a child protection course. In addition, all early years settings must implement an effective safeguarding children policy and procedure.

2.170  It is expected that every person working in the early years sector should have an up-to-date knowledge of safeguarding children issues and be able to implement

---

58    www.teachernet.gov.uk/_doc/12187/ACFD89B.pdf

59    Available at: http://nationalstrategies.standards.dcsf.gov.uk/earlyyears

their setting's safeguarding children policy and procedures appropriately. These policies should be in line with LSCB guidance and procedures.

2.171   The EYFS also makes clear that registered early years providers should follow the guidance *What to do if you're worried a child is being abused*. Such providers must notify local child protection agencies of any suspected child abuse or neglect in line with LSCB local guidance and procedures.

## Children and Family Court Advisory and Support Service (Cafcass)

2.172   Cafcass's functions are to:

- safeguard and promote the welfare of children who are the subject of family proceedings;

- give advice to any court about any application made to it in such proceedings;

- make provision for children to be represented in such proceedings;

- provide information, advice and other support for children and their families; and

- assess risk.

2.173   Cafcass Officers have different roles in private and public law proceedings. These roles are denoted by different titles:

- Children's Guardians, who are appointed to safeguard the interests of a child who is the subject of specified proceedings under the Children Act 1989, or who is the subject of adoption proceedings;

- Parental Order Reporters, who are appointed to investigate and report to the court on circumstances relevant under the Human Fertilisation and Embryology Act 1990; and

- Children and Family Reporters, who prepare welfare reports for the court in relation to applications under section 8 of the Children Act 1989 (private law proceedings, including applications for residence and contact). Increasingly they also work with families at the stage of their initial application to the court.

Cafcass Officers can also be appointed to provide support under a Family Assistance Order under the Children Act 1989 (local authority officers can also be appointed for this purpose).

2.174   The Cafcass Officer has a statutory right in public law cases to access and take copies of local authority records relating to the child concerned and any application under the Children Act 1989. That power also extends to other records that relate to the child and the wider functions of the local authority, or records held by an authorised body (for example, the NSPCC) that relate to that child.

2.175   Where a Cafcass Officer has been appointed by the court as Children's Guardian and the matter before the court relates to specified proceedings (specified proceedings include public law proceedings; applications for contact; residence, specific issue and prohibited steps orders that have become particularly difficult can also be specified proceedings) they should be invited to all formal planning meetings convened by the local authority in respect of the child. This includes statutory reviews of children who are accommodated or looked after, child protection conferences, and relevant Adoption Panel meetings. The conference chair should ensure that all those attending such meetings, including the child and any family members, understand the role of the Cafcass Officer.

## The armed services

2.176   Young people under 18 may be in the armed forces as recruits or trainees, or may be dependants of a service family. The life of a service family differs in many respects from that of a family in civilian life, particularly for those stationed overseas, or on bases and garrisons in the UK. The services support the movement of the family in response to service commitments. The frequency and location of such moves make it essential that the service authorities are aware of any concerns regarding safeguarding and promoting the welfare of a child from a military family. The armed forces are fully committed to co-operating with statutory and other agencies in supporting families in this situation, and have procedures to help safeguard and promote the welfare of children. In areas of high concentration of service families, the armed forces seek particularly to work alongside local authority children's social care, including through representation on LSCBs and at child protection conferences and reviews.

2.177   Looking after under-18s in the armed forces comes under the MoD's comprehensive welfare arrangements, which apply to all members of the armed forces. Commanding Officers are well aware of the particular welfare needs of younger recruits and trainees and, as stated above, are fully committed to co-operating with statutory and other agencies in safeguarding and promoting the welfare of under-18s. Local authority children's social care already has a responsibility to monitor the wellbeing of care leavers, and those joining the armed forces should have unrestricted access to local authority social care workers.

2.178   Local authorities have the statutory responsibility for safeguarding and promoting the welfare of the children of service families in the UK. All three services provide professional welfare support, including 'special to type' social work services to augment those provided by local authorities. In the Royal Navy (RN) this is provided by the Naval Personal and Family Service (NPFS) and the Royal Marines Welfare Service; within the army this is provided by the Army Welfare Service (AWS); and in the Royal Air Force by the Soldiers Sailors Airmen and Families Association-Forces Help (SSAFA-FH). Further details of these services and contact numbers are given in Appendix 4.

2.179    When service families or civilians working with the armed forces are based overseas, the responsibility for safeguarding and promoting the welfare of their children is vested with the MoD, who fund the British Forces Social Work Service (Overseas). This service is contracted to SSAFA-FH, who provide a fully qualified Social Work and Community Health service in major overseas locations (for example, in Germany and Cyprus). Instructions for the protection of children overseas, which reflect the principles of the Children Act 2004 and the philosophy of inter-agency co-operation, are issued by the MoD as a Joint Service Publication (JSP) 834 *Safeguarding Children*. Larger overseas commands issue local child protection procedures, hold a Command list of children who are the subject of a child protection plan and have a Command Safeguarding Children Board, which operates in a similar way to those set up under this guidance, in upholding standards and making sure that best practice is reflected in procedures and observed in practice.

## Movement of children between the United Kingdom and Overseas

2.180    Local authorities should ensure that SSAFA-FH, the British Forces Social Work Service (Overseas), or the NPFS for RN families is made aware of any service child who is the subject of a child protection plan and whose family is about to move overseas. In the interests of the child, SSAFA-FH, the British Forces Social Work Service (Overseas) or NPFS can confirm that appropriate resources exist in the proposed location to meet identified needs. Full documentation should be provided and forwarded to the relevant overseas command. All referrals should be made to the Director of Social Work, HQ SSAFA FH or Area Officer, NPFS (East) as appropriate, at the addresses given in Appendix 4. Comprehensive reciprocal arrangements exist for the referral of child protection cases to appropriate UK authorities, relating to the temporary or permanent relocation of such children to the UK from overseas.

## United States Forces stationed in the United Kingdom

2.181    Each local authority with a United States (US) base in its area should establish liaison arrangements with the base commander and relevant staff. The requirements of English child welfare legislation should be explained clearly to the US authorities, so that local authorities can fulfil their statutory duties.

### Enquiries about children of ex-service families

2.182   Where a local authority believes that a child who is the subject of current child protection processes is from an ex-service family, NPFS, AWS or SSAFA-FH can be contacted to establish whether there is existing information that might help with enquiries. Such enquiries should be addressed to NPFS, AWS or the Director of Social Work, SSAFA-FH, at the address given in Appendix 4.

## The voluntary and private sectors

2.183   Voluntary organisations, both local and national, and private sector providers play an important role in delivering services for children and young people, including in early years provision, family support services, youth work and children's social care and healthcare. Many voluntary organisations are skilled in preventative work and may be well placed to reach the most vulnerable children, young people and families. The vast majority work in partnership and will play an important part in protecting and supporting a child and their family.

2.184   Voluntary organisations offer, for example:

- therapeutic work with children, young people and families, particularly in relation to child sexual abuse;

- specialist support and services for children and young people with disabilities or health problems;

- services for children and young people who are being sexually exploited and for children who abuse other children; and

- advocacy for looked after children and young people, and for parents and children who are the subject of section 47 enquiries and child protection conferences.

2.185   Voluntary organisations play a key role in providing information and resources to the wider public about the needs of children and young people, and resources to help families. Many campaign on specific issues on behalf of groups.

2.186   The NSPCC is the only voluntary organisation authorised to initiate proceedings to protect children under the terms of the Children Act 1989 and offers a number of services to children, adults and practitioners. It operates a helpline service advising adults and professionals on safeguarding matters and where necessary liaises with local statutory agencies to refer children at risk of abuse. The NSPCC also operates ChildLine which provides a telephone helpline across the UK for all children and young people who need advice about abuse, bullying, and other concerns. These services, along with other helplines such as Stop it Now! (which specialises in child sexual abuse prevention) and Parentline Plus (which offers support to anyone parenting a child), provide information, advice and support as well as important routes into statutory and voluntary services.

2.187    The voluntary sector is active in working to safeguard the children and young people with whom it works. A range of umbrella and specialist organisations, including the national governing bodies for sports, offer standards, guidance, training and advice for voluntary organisations on keeping children and young people safe from harm. In conjunction with other bodies, the NSPCC provides child protection advice; for example the Child Protection in Sport Unit, established in partnership with Sport England, provides advice and assistance on developing codes of practice and child protection procedures to sporting organisations. The Safe Network, jointly managed by the NSPCC and Children England, provides advice for the third sector and is working to create safeguarding standards for voluntary/ non-profit sector organisations.

2.188    Organisations in the voluntary and private sectors that work with children need to have the arrangements described in paragraph 2.11 in place in the same way as organisations in the public sector, and need to work effectively with LSCBs. Paid and volunteer staff need to be aware of their responsibilities for safeguarding and promoting the welfare of children, and of how they should respond to child protection concerns in line with this guidance (see *What to do if you're worried a child is being abused*). There should be clear and published local guidance for the voluntary sector on access pathways to services and how thresholds are applied when making a referral to social care.

## Faith communities

2.189    Churches, other places of worship and faith-based organisations provide a wide range of activities for children and young people. They are some of the largest providers of children and youth work, and have an important role in safeguarding children and supporting families. Religious leaders, staff and volunteers who provide services in places of worship and in faith-based organisations will have various degrees of contact with children.

2.190    Like other organisations that work with children, churches, other places of worship and faith-based organisations need to have appropriate arrangements in place for safeguarding and promoting the welfare of children, as described in paragraph 2.11. In particular, these arrangements should include:

- procedures for staff and others to report concerns that they may have about the children they meet that are in line with *What to do if you're worried a child is being* _abused_ and LSCB procedures, as well as arrangements such as those described above;

- appropriate codes of practice for staff, particularly those working directly with children, such as those issued by the Churches' Child Protection Advisory Service (CCPAS), the Catholic Safeguarding Advisory Service (CSAS) or other denomination or faith groups; and

- recruitment procedures in accordance with safer recruitment guidance[60] and LSCB procedures, alongside training and supervision of staff (paid or voluntary).

2.191    Where the police or local authority children's social care services wish to contact specific faith communities they should make contact with the relevant organisation listed at appendix 6, who will assist in speaking to the appropriate person.

## Specific considerations

2.192    As appropriate, churches, other places of worship and faith organisations should report all allegations against people who work with children to the local authority Designated Officer (LADO), and notify the Independent Safeguarding Authority (ISA) of any relevant information so that those who pose a risk to vulnerable groups can be identified and barred. In addition where they are a charity all serious incidents need reporting to the Charity Commission.

2.193    It is essential that faith communities have in place effective arrangements for working with sexual and violent offenders who wish to worship and be part of their religious community. This should include a contract of behaviour stipulating the boundaries an offender would be expected to keep. Faith communities should consult the MAPPA Guidance (2009) issued by the National Offender Management Service Public Protection Unit which specifically addresses 'Offenders and Worship'. Other resources are briefly outlined in appendix 6.

---

60    Recruiting safely: Safer recruitment guidance helping to keep children and young people safe and associated materials. www.cwdcouncil.org.uk/safeguarding/safer-recruitment/resources

# Chapter 3 – Local Safeguarding Children Boards

3.1    Safeguarding and promoting the welfare of children requires effective co-ordination in every local area. The Children Act 2004 required each local authority to establish a Local Safeguarding Children Board (LSCB) by 1 April 2006.

3.2    The LSCB is the key statutory mechanism for agreeing how the relevant organisations in each local area will co-operate to safeguard and promote the welfare of children in that locality, and for ensuring the effectiveness of what they do.

## LSCB role

### Objectives of the LSCB

3.3    The functions of an LSCB are set out in primary legislation[61] and regulations[62]. The core objectives of the LSCB are as follows:

a.    to co-ordinate what is done by each person or body represented on the Board for the purposes of safeguarding and promoting the welfare of children in the area of the authority; and

b.    to ensure the effectiveness of what is done by each such person or body for that purpose.

3.4    As explained in Chapter 1, safeguarding and promoting the welfare of children is defined for the purposes of this guidance as:

- protecting children from maltreatment;

- preventing impairment of children's health or development;

- ensuring that children are growing up in circumstances consistent with the provision of safe and effective care;

and undertaking that role so as to enable those children to have optimum life chances and enter adulthood successfully.

---

61    Sections 14 and 14 A of the Children Act 2004.
62    Local Safeguarding Children Regulations 2006, SI 2006/90.

3.5    The LSCB will therefore ensure that the duty to safeguard and promote the welfare of children is carried out in such a way as to contribute to improving all five *Every Child Matters* outcomes.

3.6    Safeguarding and promoting the welfare of children includes protecting children from harm. Ensuring that work to protect children is properly co-ordinated and effective remains a primary goal of LSCBs. When this core business is secure, however, LSCBs should go beyond it to work to their wider remit, which includes preventative work to avoid harm being suffered. This will help ensure a long-term impact on the safety of children.

## Scope of the LSCB

3.7    The scope of the LSCB includes safeguarding and promoting the welfare of children in three broad areas of activity.

3.8    First, activity that affects all children and aims to identify and prevent maltreatment, or impairment of health or development, and ensure children are growing up in circumstances consistent with safe and effective care. For example:

- mechanisms to identify abuse and neglect wherever they may occur;

- work to increase understanding of safeguarding children issues in the professional and wider community, promoting the message that safeguarding is everybody's responsibility;

- work to ensure that organisations working or in contact with children, operate recruitment and human resources practices that take account of the need to safeguard and promote the welfare of children;

- monitoring the effectiveness of organisations' implementation of their duties under section 11 of the Children Act 2004;

- ensuring children know who they can contact when they have concerns about their own or others' safety and welfare;

- ensuring that adults (including those who are harming children) know who they can contact if they have a concern about a child or young person;

- work to prevent accidents and other injures and, where possible, deaths; and

- work to prevent and respond effectively to bullying.

3.9     Second, proactive work that aims to target particular groups. For example:

- developing/evaluating thresholds and procedures for work with children and families where a child has been identified as 'in need' under the Children Act 1989, but where the child is not suffering or likely to suffer significant harm; and

- work to safeguard and promote the welfare of groups of children who are potentially more vulnerable than the general population, for example children living away from home, children who have run away from home, children missing from school or childcare, children in the youth justice system, including custody, disabled children and children and young people affected by gangs.

3.10    Thirdly, responsive work to protect children who are suffering, or are likely to suffer significant harm, including:

- children abused and neglected within families, including those harmed:

  - in the context of domestic violence; and

  - as a consequence of the impact of substance misuse, or of parental mental ill health;

- children abused outside families by adults known to them;

- children abused and neglected by professional carers, within institutional settings, or anywhere else where children are cared for away from home;

- children abused by strangers;

- children abused by other young people;

- young perpetrators of abuse;

- children abused through sexual exploitation; and

- young victims of crime.

3.11    Where particular children are the subject of interventions then that safeguarding work should aim to help them to achieve the planned developmental outcomes (see paragraphs 5.128–5.135) and to have optimum life chances. It is within the remit of LSCBs to check the extent to which this has been achieved as part of their monitoring and evaluation work.

## LSCB functions

3.12    The core functions of an LSCB are set out in primary legislation and regulations. This guidance gives further detail on what is required as well as examples of how the functions can be carried out. In all their activities, LSCBs should take account of the need to promote equality of opportunity and to meet the diverse needs of children.

## Thresholds, policies and procedures function

3.13 This general function has a number of specific applications set out in primary legislation and regulations.

   a) *Developing policies and procedures for safeguarding and promoting the welfare of children in the area of the authority, including policies and procedures in relation to:*

   i) *The action to be taken where there are concerns about a child's safety or welfare, including thresholds for intervention*

3.14 This includes concerns under both section 17 and section 47 of the Children Act 1989. It may mean for example:

- setting out thresholds for referrals to children's social care of children who may be in need, and processes for robust multi-agency assessment of children in need;

- agreeing inter-agency procedures for section 47 enquiries and developing local protocols on key issues of concern such as:

  – children abused through sexual exploitation;

  – children living with domestic violence, substance abuse, or parental mental ill health;

  – female genital mutilation;

  – forced marriage;

  – children missing from school;

  – children who may have been trafficked; and

  – safeguarding looked after children who are away from home.

- setting out how section 47 enquiries and associated police investigations should be conducted, and in particular, in what circumstances joint enquiries are necessary and/or appropriate.

3.15 Chapter 5 includes some further key points on which LSCBs should ensure that they have policies and procedures in place.

3.16 Clear thresholds and processes and a common understanding of them across local partners should help ensure that appropriate referrals are made and improve the effectiveness of joint work, leading to a more efficient use of resources. In developing these thresholds and processes the LSCB should work with the Children's Trust Board.

3.17    The Children's Trust Board working with the LSCB should ensure that the local arrangements for undertaking a common assessment are clear about when it is appropriate to use the Common Assessment Framework (CAF) and when it is appropriate to refer a possible child in need to children's social care services:

> *ii)   Training of persons who work with children or in services affecting the safety and welfare of children*

3.18    It is the responsibility of the LSCB to ensure that single agency and inter-agency training on safeguarding and promoting welfare is provided in order to meet local needs. This covers both the training provided by single agencies to their own staff, and multi-agency training where staff from more than one agency train together.

3.19    LSCBs may decide to carry out their function by taking a view as to the priorities for inter-agency and single-agency child protection training in the local area and feeding those priorities into the local workforce strategy. LSCBs will also want to evaluate the quality of this training, ensuring that relevant training is provided by individual organisations, and checking that the training is reaching the relevant staff within organisations.

3.20    In some areas it may be decided that the LSCB should also organise or deliver inter-agency training. As explained in Chapter 4, this is not part of the core requirement for LSCBs.

> *iii)  Recruitment and supervision of persons who work with children*

3.21    For example, by establishing effective policies and procedures, based on national guidance, for checking the suitability of people applying for work with children and ensuring that the children's workforce is properly supervised, with any concerns acted on appropriately. LSCBs should ensure that robust quality assurance processes are in place to monitor compliance by relevant agencies within their area with requirements to support safe practices. These processes should include audits of vetting practice and sampling of compliance with checks with Criminal Records Bureau and, once it is introduced, Independent Safeguarding Authority registration.

> *iv)  Investigation of allegations concerning persons working with children*

3.22    For example policies and procedures, based on national guidance (see paragraphs 6.32 to 6.42 and Appendix 5), to ensure that allegations are dealt with properly and quickly.

*v)  Safety and welfare of children who are privately fostered*

3.23   For example, by ensuring the co-ordination and effective implementation of measures designed to strengthen private fostering notification arrangements including: raising awareness of private fostering across partner agencies, third sector organisations and commissioned services; ensuring that relevant training practices are developed and followed up at multi-agency level; reviewing and responding to the findings of the annual private fostering report submitted by the local authority to the Chair of the LSCB; acting upon the findings of Ofsted inspections and research evidence on effective practice; providing effective leadership and challenge in this area; and reporting on private fostering in their own annual report as appropriate.

3.24   The requirements and expectations of local authorities are set out in amendments to the Children Act 1989 made by section 44 of the Children Act 2004, the Children (Private Arrangements for Fostering) Regulations 2005, and National Minimum Standards for private fostering.

*vi)  Co-operation with neighbouring children's services authorities (i.e. local authorities) and their Board partners*

3.25   For example, by establishing procedures to safeguard and promote the welfare of children who move between local authority areas, including as a result of out of area placements, in line with the requirements in Chapters 5, 7 and 8. This might include harmonising procedures, where appropriate, to bring coherence to liaison with an organisation (such as a police force) which spans more than one LSCB area. This could be relevant to geographically mobile families such as: asylum seeking children, traveller children, children in migrant families and children of families in temporary accommodation.

## Other policies and procedures

3.26   LSCBs should consider the need for other local protocols under this function, beyond those specifically set out in regulations, including:

- quick and straightforward means of resolving professional differences of view in a specific case, for example, on whether a child protection conference should be convened;

- attendance at child protection conferences, including quora;

- attendance at family group conferences;

- involving children and family members in child protection conferences, the role of advocates, criteria for excluding parents in exceptional circumstances;

- a decision-making process for the need for a child protection plan based upon the views of the agencies present at the child protection conference;

- handling complaints from families about the functioning of child protection conferences; and

- a procedure for handling complaints regarding requests to share information.

## Communicating and raising awareness function

b) *Communicating to persons and bodies in the area of the authority the need to safeguard and promote the welfare of children, raising their awareness of how this can best be done, and encouraging them to do so*

3.27  For example, by contributing to public campaigns to raise awareness in the wider community, including faith and minority communities and among statutory and independent agencies, including employers, about how everybody can contribute to safeguarding and promoting the welfare of children. This should involve listening to and consulting children and young people and ensuring that their views and opinions are taken into account in planning and delivering safeguarding and promoting welfare services.

## Monitoring and evaluation function

c) *Monitor and evaluate the effectiveness of what is done by the local authority and Board partners individually and collectively to safeguard and promote the welfare of children and advise them on ways to improve*

3.28  The LSCB has a key role in achieving high standards in safeguarding and promoting welfare, not just through co-ordinating but by evaluation and continuous improvement. For example, by asking individual organisations to self-evaluate under an agreed framework of benchmarks or indicators and then sharing results with the Board. It might also involve leading multi-agency arrangements to contribute to self-evaluation reports.

3.29  To evaluate multi-agency working the LSCB could perform joint audits of case files, looking at the involvement of the different agencies, and identifying the quality of practice and lessons to be learned in terms of both multi-agency and multi-disciplinary practice.

3.30  The LSCB should have a particular focus on ensuring that those key people and organisations that have a duty under section 11 of the Children Act 2004 or section 175 or 157 of the Education Act 2002 are fulfilling their statutory obligations about safeguarding and promoting the welfare of children.

3.31 LSCBs should ensure appropriate links with any secure setting in its area and be able to scrutinise restraint techniques, the policies and protocols which surround the use of restraint, and incidences and injuries. LSCBs with a secure establishment(s) in its areas should report annually to the Youth Justice Board on how effectively the establishment(s) is managing use of restraint. LSCBs should report more frequently if there are concerns on the use of restraint. Consideration should be given to sharing the information with relevant inspectorates (HMIP and Ofsted). Where appropriate, members of LSCBs (with secure establishments in its area) should be given demonstrations in the techniques accredited for use to assist their consideration of any child protection or safeguarding issue that might arise in relation to restraint. See paragraph 2.141 for more detail about the role of the secure estate.

3.32 All incidents when restraint is used in custodial settings and which results in an injury to a young person should be notified to, and subsequent action monitored by, the LSCB.

3.33 The function of an LSCB also includes advising the local authority and Board partners on ways to improve. The LSCB might do this by making recommendations (such as the need for further resources), by helping organisations to develop new procedures, by spreading best practice, by bringing together expertise in different bodies, or by supporting capacity building and training. Where there are concerns about the work of partners and these cannot be addressed locally, the LSCB should raise these concerns with others, as explained further in paragraph 3.109.

*d) Produce and publish an annual report on the effectiveness of safeguarding in the local area*

3.34 The Apprenticeships, Skills, Children and Learning Act 2009 introduces a requirement for LSCBs to produce and publish an annual report on the effectiveness of safeguarding in the local area. This report should provide an assessment of the effectiveness of local arrangements to safeguard and promote the welfare of children, set against a comprehensive analysis of the local area safeguarding context. It should recognise achievements and the progress that has been made in the local authority area as well as providing a realistic assessment of the challenges that still remain.

3.35 The report should demonstrate the extent to which the functions of the LSCB as set out in Working Together are being effectively discharged. This should include assessments of policies and procedures to keep children safe, including:

- the policies and procedures for the safe recruitment of frontline staff;

- an assessment of single and inter-agency training on safeguarding and promoting the welfare of children to meet the local needs;

- lessons learnt about the prevention of future child deaths which have been identified by the Child Death Overview Panel; and

- progress on priority issues (for example, child trafficking, sexual exploitation and domestic violence).

3.36    Annual reports should also include a clear account of progress that has been made in implementing actions from individual Serious Case Reviews (SCRs) completed during the year in question, plans to evaluate the impact of these actions and to monitor how these improvements are being sustained over time. This also applies to SCRs commissioned in previous years where any actions remained outstanding at the start of the reporting year. Where SCRs have been commissioned but not completed the annual report should note action already taken to learn lessons arising from the relevant cases. Common themes and recurring recommendations may be addressed together but the report must be clear on action taken in response to individual SCRs.

3.37    The report should provide robust challenge to the work of the Children's Trust Board in driving improvements in the safeguarding of children and young people and in promoting their welfare.

3.38    The LSCB must send a copy of the annual report to the Children's Trust Board. The Children's Trust Board in turn will be expected to respond to reports through the local Children and Young People's Plan. In preparing the Children and Young People's Plan, Children's Trust Boards will be expected to draw upon the advice from and the findings in the LSCB annual report, and show how they intend to respond to the issues raised.

3.39    This requirement will come into force from 1 April 2010. This will mean that a LSCB must publish its first report by 1 April 2011. Children's Trust Boards must produce a Children and Young People's Plan by 1 April 2011. The LSCB and the Children's Trust Board, within the parameters set by legislation, should work together to ensure that the LSCB annual report is developed in time so that it can be properly considered and effectively utilised by the Children's Trust Board.

## Function of participating in planning and commissioning

> e) *Participating in the local planning and commissioning of children's services to ensure that they take safeguarding and promoting the welfare of children into account*

3.40 This will be achieved to a large extent by contributing to the Children and Young People's Plan, and ensuring in discussion with the Children's Trust partners that planning and commissioning of services for children within the local authority area takes account of their responsibility to safeguard and promote children's welfare.

3.41 Where it is agreed locally that the LSCB is the 'responsible authority' for 'matters relating to the protection of children from harm' under the Licensing Act 2003, it must be notified of all licence variations and new applications for the sale and supply of alcohol and public entertainment.

## Functions relating to child deaths

3.42 From 1 April 2008, each LSCB acquired the compulsory functions set out in regulations relating to child deaths.

> f) *Collecting and analysing information about the deaths of all children in their area with a view to identifying:*
>
> i) *any matters of concern affecting the safety and welfare of children in the area of the authority, including any case giving rise to the need for a Serious Case Review;*
>
> ii) *any general public health or safety concerns arising from deaths of children.*

> g) *Putting in place procedures for ensuring that there is a co-ordinated response by the authority, their Board partners and other relevant persons to an unexpected death of a child.*

3.43 Chapter 7 explains how these functions should be implemented.

## Serious Case Review function

> h) *Undertaking reviews of cases where abuse or neglect of a child is known or suspected, a child has died or a child has been seriously harmed, and there is cause for concern as to the way in which the authority, their Board partners or other relevant persons have worked together to safeguard the child.*

3.44    By developing procedures and the detail of organisations' and individuals' roles, in accordance with Chapter 8, and ensuring that organisations undertake those roles. All relevant staff should be aware of when SCRs are required or should be considered.

## Other activities

3.45    The regulations make clear that in addition to the functions set out above, a LSCB may also engage in any other activity that facilitates, or is conducive to, the achievement of its objectives.

3.46    These further activities should be discussed and agreed as part of wider Children's Trust planning and the preparation of the Children and Young People's Plan.

3.47    For example, the LSCB could agree to take the lead within the Children's Trust partnership on work to tackle bullying, or could lead an initiative on domestic violence.

3.48    The LSCB will not in general be an operational body or one which delivers services to children, young people and their families. Its role is co-ordinating and ensuring the effectiveness of what its member organisations do, and contributing to broader planning, commissioning and delivery. It may however take on operational and delivery roles under this part of the regulations.

## Accountability for operational work

3.49    Whilst the LSCB has a role in co-ordinating and ensuring the effectiveness of local individuals' and organisations' work to safeguard and promote the welfare of children, it is not accountable for their operational work. Each Board partner retains their own existing lines of accountability for safeguarding and promoting the welfare of children by their services. The LSCB does not have a power to direct other organisations.

## LSCB governance and operational arrangements

3.50    County level and unitary local authorities are responsible for establishing an LSCB in their area and ensuring that it is run effectively.

3.51    An LSCB can cover more than one local authority area. Local authorities and their partners will wish to consider whether this is desirable, perhaps to ensure a better fit with the areas covered by other bodies, or because issues are common to different areas.

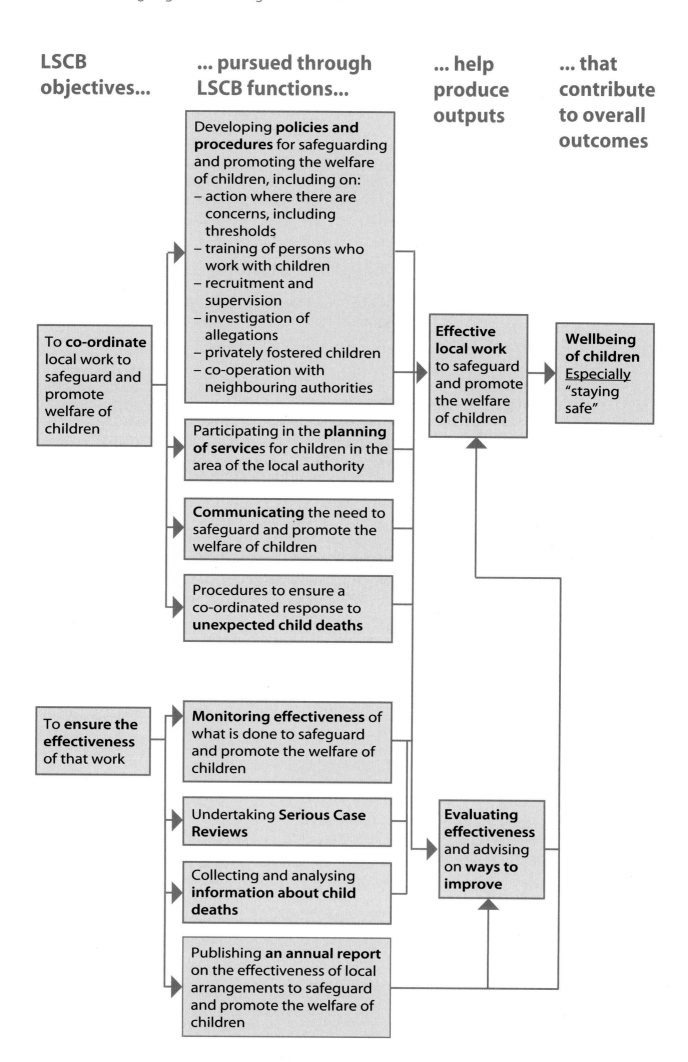

**LSCB objectives...**

**... pursued through LSCB functions...**

**... help produce outputs**

**... that contribute to overall outcomes**

To **co-ordinate** local work to safeguard and promote welfare of children

Developing **policies and procedures** for safeguarding and promoting the welfare of children, including on:
– action where there are concerns, including thresholds
– training of persons who work with children
– recruitment and supervision
– investigation of allegations
– privately fostered children
– co-operation with neighbouring authorities

Participating in the **planning of services** for children in the area of the local authority

**Communicating** the need to safeguard and promote the welfare of children

Procedures to ensure a co-ordinated response to **unexpected child deaths**

To **ensure the effectiveness** of that work

**Monitoring effectiveness** of what is done to safeguard and promote the welfare of children

Undertaking **Serious Case Reviews**

Collecting and analysing **information about child deaths**

Publishing **an annual report** on the effectiveness of local arrangements to safeguard and promote the welfare of children

**Effective local work** to safeguard and promote the welfare of children

**Evaluating effectiveness** and advising on **ways to improve**

**Wellbeing of children** Especially "staying safe"

## Chair

3.52   It is the responsibility of the local authority, after consultation with the LSCB partners, to appoint the LSCB chair. It is important that the chair, who must be of sufficient stature and authority, is selected with the agreement of a group of partners representing the key services involved in safeguarding children locally and should have access to training to support them in their role. There should be a presumption that the chair will be someone independent of the local agencies so that the LSCB can exercise its local challenge function effectively. It may take time to develop sufficient availability of suitable independent chairs but it is expected that LSCBs will work towards this over time.

3.53   The chair will have a crucial role in making certain that the Board operates effectively and secures an independent voice for the LSCB. He or she should be of sufficient standing and expertise to command the respect and support of all partners. The chair should act objectively and distinguish their role as LSCB chair from any day-to-day role.

## Relationship between the LSCB and the Children's Trust Board

3.54   The responsibilities of the LSCB are complementary to those of the Children's Trust – to promote co-operation to improve the wellbeing of children in the local area across all five *Every Child Matters* outcomes. The LSCB's role is:

- to ensure the effectiveness of the arrangements made by wider partnership and individual agencies to safeguard and promote the welfare of children.

3.55   An LSCB is not an operational sub-committee of the Children's Trust Board. Whilst the work of the LSCB contributes to the wider goals of improving the wellbeing of all children, it has a narrower focus on safeguarding and promoting welfare.

- The LSCB should not be subordinate to nor subsumed within the Children's Trust Board structures in a way that might compromise its separate identity and independent voice.

3.56   There must be a clear distinction between the roles and responsibilities of the LSCB and the Children's Trust Board. There should be:

- agreed local protocols between the LSCB and the Children's Trust Board in place to ensure that the LSCB is able to challenge and scrutinise effectively the work of the Children's Trust Board and partners.

3.57    The LSCB must be able to form a view of the quality of local activity, to challenge organisations as necessary, and to speak with an independent voice.

●   For that reason the LSCB and Children's Trust Board should be chaired by different people.

3.58    The Children's Trust Board should work with the LSCB to agree:

●   a strategic approach to understanding needs, including a sophisticated analysis of data and effective engagement with children, young people and families;

●   a clear approach to understanding the effectiveness of current services, and identifying priorities for change – including where services need to be improved, reshaped or developed;

●   integrated and effective arrangements for ensuring that priorities for change are delivered in practice through the Children and Young People's Plan; and

●   effective approaches to understand the impact of specialist services on outcomes for children, young people and families, and using this understanding constructively to challenge lack of progress and drive further improvement.

3.59    The Children's Trust Board – drawing on support and challenge from the LSCB – will ensure that the Children and Young People's Plan reflects the strengths and weaknesses of safeguarding arrangements and practices in the area and what more needs to be done by each partner to improve safeguarding and promotion of welfare. The LSCB is a formal consultee during the development of the Children and Young People's Plan.

●   Through the LSCB annual report, the LSCB will provide a comprehensive analysis of safeguarding in the local area. The report should challenge the work of the Children's Trust Board and its partners to ensure that necessary overarching structures, processes and culture are put in place to ensure that children are fully safeguarded.

●   The Children's Trust Board will draw on the advice and evidence in the annual report to inform the development and review of the local Children and Young People's Plan, and should show in the Plan how they intend to respond to issues raised by the LSCB.

3.60    Regulations make clear that there is flexibility for a local area to decide that an LSCB should have an extended role in addition its core functions. Those must of course still be related to its objectives.

●   In general the LSCB is not a body that commissions or delivers services to children, young people and their families. Where the LSCB has an extended role beyond its core functions, for example undertaking research or delivering training on safeguarding issues, there is scope for confusion between the respective roles of the LSCB and the Children's Trust Board. These additional activities should be discussed and agreed as part of the wider Children's Trust planning arrangements and in the preparation of the Children and Young People's Plan. In such cases, the LSCB as a body should be represented on the Children's Trust Board so that the Children's Trust Board can call the LSCB to account for the extent to which it has acted in accordance with the Children and Young People's Plan.

3.61   As set out in paragraph 3.68, the local authority Chief Executives and Council Leaders should satisfy themselves that the Directors of Children's Services are fulfilling their managerial responsibilities for safeguarding and promoting the welfare of children and young people, including in particular by ensuring that the relationship between the Children's Trust Board and the LSCB is working effectively.

## Membership of an LSCB

### The nature of members

3.62   As far as possible, organisations should designate particular, named people as their representative on the LSCB, so that there is consistency and continuity in the membership of the LSCB.

3.63   Members should be people with a strategic role in relation to safeguarding and promoting the welfare of children within their organisation. They should be able to:

- speak for their organisation with authority;
- commit their organisation on policy and practice matters; and
- hold their organisation to account.

*Role of Elected Members and Directors of Children's Services*

3.64   Local authority Elected Members and non-executive directors of other board partners should through their membership of governance bodies such as the cabinet of the local authority or a scrutiny committee or a governance board, hold their organisation and its officers to account for their contribution to the effective functioning of the LSCB.

3.65   Directors of Children's Services and Lead Members for Children's Services have central and complementary roles. Directors of Children's Services have responsibility for improving outcomes for all children and young people in their area. Lead Members for Children's Services have delegated responsibility from the Council for children, local young people and families and are politically accountable for ensuring that the local authority fulfils its legal responsibilities for safeguarding and promoting the welfare of children and young people. The Lead Member should provide the political leadership needed for the effective co-ordination of work with other relevant agencies with safeguarding responsibilities (such as the police and the health service). Lead Members should also take steps to assure themselves that effective quality assurance systems for safeguarding are in place and functioning effectively.

3.66 The Lead Member should be a 'participating observer' of the LSCB. In practice this means routinely attending meetings as an observer and receiving all its written reports. Lead Members should engage in discussions, ask questions and seek clarity, but not be part of the decision making process. This will enable the Lead Member to challenge, when necessary, from a well informed position.

3.67 Directors of Children's Services should ensure that all appropriate local authority services engage effectively with the LSCB. The Directors of Children's Services will be held to account for the effective working of the LSCB by their Chief Executive and challenged where appropriate by their Lead Member.

*Role of local authority Chief Executives and Council Leaders*

3.68 Local authority Chief Executives and Council Leaders also have critical roles to play. Chief Executives are responsible for satisfying themselves that the Directors of Children's Services are fulfilling their managerial responsibilities for safeguarding and promoting the welfare of children and young people, including in particular by ensuring that the relationship between the Children's Trust Board and the LSCB is working effectively; that clear responsibility has been assigned within the local authority and among Children's Trust partners for improving services and outcomes; and that targets for improving safeguarding and progress against them are reported to the Local Strategic Partnership.

3.69 Every year, as part of the Children's Trust annual report, the Chief Executive and the Leader of the Council should make an assessment of the effectiveness of local governance and partnership arrangements for improving outcomes for children and supporting the best possible standards for safeguarding children.

*Statutory members*

3.70 The LSCB should include representatives of the local authority and its Board partners, the statutory organisations which are required to co-operate with the local authority in the establishment and operation of the board and have shared responsibility for the effective discharge of its functions. These are the Board partners set out in section 13(3) of the Children Act (2004):

- District Councils in local government areas which have them;

- the Chief Officer of Police for a police area any part of which falls within the area of the local authority;

- the Local Probation Trust for an area any part of which falls within the area of the local authority;

- the Youth Offending Team for an area any part of which falls within the area of the local authority;

- Strategic Health Authorities (SHAs) and Primary Care Trusts (PCTs) for an area any part of which falls within the area of the local authority;

- NHS Trusts and NHS Foundation Trusts all or most of whose hospitals, establishments and facilities are situated in the local authority area;

- the Connexions Service providing services in any part of the area of the local authority;

- Cafcass (Children and Family Courts Advisory and Support Service);

- the Governor or Director of any Secure Training Centre in the area of the local authority; and

- the Governor or Director of any prison in the local authority area which ordinarily detains children.

3.71   The local authority should ensure that those responsible for adult social services functions are represented on the LSCB, given the importance of adult social care in the context of safeguarding and promoting the welfare of children. Similarly health organisations should ensure that adult health services and in particular adult mental health, adult drug and alcohol services and adult disability services are represented on the LSCB.

3.72   It will also be important to ensure that the LSCB has access to appropriate expertise and advice from all the relevant sectors, including a designated doctor and nurse.

3.73   The Children Act 2004 sets out that the local authority and its partners must co-operate in the establishment and operation of an LSCB. This places an obligation on local authorities and statutory LSCB partners to support the operation of the LSCB.

*Lay members*

3.74   The Apprenticeships, Skills, Children and Learning Act 2009 amends sections 13 and 14 of the Children Act 2004 (c.31) and provides for the appointment of two representatives of the local community to each LSCB in England.

3.75   The local authority must take reasonable steps to ensure that the LSCB includes two lay members from the local community. The role for lay members should in particular relate to:

● supporting stronger public engagement in local child safety issues and contributing to an improved understanding of the LSCB's child protection work in the wider community;

● challenging the LSCB on the accessibility by the public and children and young people of its plans and procedures; and

● helping to make links between the LSCB and community groups.

3.76   Lay members should operate as full members of the LSCB, participating on the Board itself and on relevant committees. LSCBs will need to think carefully about the type of training they will need to provide for lay members to ensure they are able to bring the most value to its work.

3.77   The local authority should set out its expectations of the role of the lay member within the LSCB, the length of appointment, the expected code of conduct of any lay member and the amount they will recompense them as appropriate for their time and contribution.

*Representation from schools*

3.78   From 1 April 2010, local authorities must take all reasonable steps to ensure schools are represented on the LSCB. This means taking steps to ensure that the following are represented: the governing body of a maintained school; the proprietor of a non-maintained special school; the proprietor of a city technology college, a city college for the technology of the arts or an Academy; and the governing body of a further education institution the main site of which is situated in the authority's area[63]. The local authority should also include independent schools as appropriate.

3.79   It would clearly be impractical for every school to attend the LSCB so a robust and fair system of representation needs to be identified to enable all schools to receive information and feed back comments to their representatives on the LSCB.

---

[63]   The Local Safeguarding Children Boards (Amendment) Regulations 2010, S.I. 2010/622, made under section 13(4) of the Children Act 2004 (c. 31).

3.80   Each LSCB should establish with the schools in its area a system that takes account of local circumstances, and the diverse range of schools should be represented. Where appropriate the LSCB should build on existing arrangements and avoid duplication. It would also need to consider the relationship with the school representatives who sit on the Children's Trust Board. School representatives need to speak for, and on behalf of, the body of schools they represent. This will require an efficient and effective means to communicate with all schools both to seek their views on issues and to feed information back.

*Other members*

3.81   The local authority should also secure the involvement of the NSPCC and other relevant national and local organisations. The knowledge and experience of the NSPCC and other large voluntary sector providers is an important national resource on which LSCBs should draw. At a minimum local organisations should include faith groups, children's centres, GPs, independent healthcare organisations, and voluntary and community sector organisations including bodies providing specialist care to children with severe disabilities and complex health needs. In areas where they have significant local activity, the armed forces (in relation both to the families of service men and women and those personnel that are under the age of 18), should also be included. In areas where there is an airport or seaport, an asylum screening unit or a number of asylum seeking families or unaccompanied asylum seeking children or a number of migrants with children, arrangements should be made to include the UK Border Agency and to ensure that the issues are dealt with in a strategic way as well as at the level of individual cases.

3.82   Where the number or size of similar organisations precludes individual representation on the LSCB, for example in the case of voluntary youth bodies, the local authority should seek to involve them through existing networks or forums, or by encouraging and developing suitable networks or forums to facilitate communication between organisations and with the LSCB.

*Involvement of other agencies and groups*

3.83   The LSCB should make appropriate arrangements at a strategic management level to involve others in its work as necessary. For example, there may be some organisations or individuals which are in theory represented by the statutory board partners but which should be engaged because of their particular role in service provision to children and families or in public protection. There will be other organisations and processes which the LSCB needs to link to, either through inviting them to join the LSCB, or through some other mechanism. For example:

   ● the coronial service;

- dental health services;

- domestic violence forums;

- drug and alcohol misuse services;

- Drug Action and Alcohol Teams;

- housing, culture and leisure services;

- housing providers;

- local authority legal services;

- local Multi-Agency Public Protection Arrangements (MAPPA);

- local sports bodies and services;

- local Family Justice Council;

- Local Criminal Justice Board;

- other health providers such as pharmacists;

- representatives of service users;

- sexual health services;

- the Crown Prosecution Service;

- witness support services;

- Family Intervention Projects; and

- Multi Agency Risk Assessment Conferences (MARACs).

3.84 LSCBs will also need to draw on the work of key national organisations and liaise with them when necessary, for example, the Child Exploitation and Online Protection Centre (CEOP).

*The role of members*

3.85 The individual members of LSCBs have a duty as members to contribute to the effective work of the LSCB, for example, in making the LSCB's assessment of performance as objective as possible, and in recommending or deciding upon the necessary steps to put right any problems. This should take precedence, if necessary, over their role as a representative of their organisation. Members of each LSCB should have a clear written statement of their roles and responsibilities.

Further advice on how SHAs should engage with LSCBs is set out in Annex D of the *Local Safeguarding Children Boards: A Review of Progress* report[64].

## Ways of working

3.86    The working practices of LSCB members need to be considered locally with a view to securing effective operation of LSCB functions and ensuring that all member organisations are effectively engaged.

3.87    Where there are multiple organisations of a particular kind in the local authority area, for example NHS Trusts or District Councils, they may decide to share attendance at meetings. Organisations pooling representation in this way need to agree how they will be consulted and how their views will be fed in to Board discussions.

3.88    It may be appropriate for the LSCB to set up working groups or sub-groups, on a short-term or a standing basis to:

● carry out specific tasks, for example: maintaining and updating procedures and protocols; reviewing serious cases; and identifying inter-agency training needs;

● provide specialist advice, for example: in respect of working with specific ethnic and cultural groups, or with disabled children and/or parents;

● bring together representatives of a sector to discuss relevant issues and to provide a contribution from that sector to LSCB work, for example: schools, the voluntary and community sector, faith groups; and

● focus on defined geographical areas within the LSCB's boundaries.

3.89    It is possible to form a 'core group' or 'executive group' of LSCB members to carry out some of the day-to-day business by local agreement.

3.90    In undertaking the child death review processes set out in Chapter 7, LSCBs should set up a Child Death Overview Panel which has a standing membership and whose Chair is a member of the LSCB. Two or more LSCBs can set up a panel to cover their combined area.

3.91    All groups working under the LSCB should be established by the LSCB, and should work to agreed terms of reference, with explicit lines of reporting, communication and accountability to the LSCB. This may take the form of a written constitution detailing a job description for all members and service level agreements between the LSCB, agencies and other partnerships. Chairs of sub-groups should be LSCB members.

---

64    www.dcsf.gov.uk/everychildmatters/_download/?id=3082

3.92    Where boundaries between LSCBs and their partner organisations such as the health service and the police are not co-terminous, there can be challenges for some member organisations in having to work to different procedures and protocols according to the area involved, or having to participate in several LSCBs. It may be helpful in these circumstances for adjoining LSCBs to collaborate as far as possible on establishing common policies and procedures, and joint ways of working, under the function *'Co-operation with neighbouring children's services authorities and their Board partners'*.

3.93    LSCBs should consider how to put in place arrangements to ascertain the views of parents and carers and the wishes and feelings of children (including children who might not ordinarily be heard) about the priorities and the effectiveness of local safeguarding work, including issues of access to services and contact points for children to safeguard and promote welfare. LSCBs should also consider how children, parents and carers can be given a measure of choice and control in the development of services.

*Information sharing for the purpose of LSCB functions*

3.94    The Children, Schools and Families Bill currently before Parliament includes provision requiring compliance with a request from a LSCB for appropriate information to be disclosed to it in order to assist it in the exercise of its functions. Subject to the passage of the Bill this provision will help remove uncertainty and give greater confidence to practitioners to share **appropriate** information with a LSCB. This could include confidential personal information about children who are the subject of reviews and about third parties who have a relationship with those children (for example, parents and siblings).

3.95    Where the LSCB requests personal information, the request should be for appropriate information that is relevant and proportionate to the purpose for which the information is sought. The LSCB should be able to explain that purpose to record holders, and why the information sought is appropriate, relevant and proportionate should the record holder require any justification of the need for the information or of the overriding public interest served by the disclosure of personal information in each case. No request should require a record holder to breach data protection principles, or other protections of confidential or personal information (for example, under the Human Rights Act) in a manner which cannot be justified; the 'golden rules' set out in *Information Sharing: Guidance for practitioners and managers* will help record holders observe these protections and principles.

## Financing and staffing

3.96   To function effectively LSCBs have to be supported by their member organisations with adequate and reliable resources.

3.97   Section 15 of the Children Act 2004 sets out that statutory board partners (or in the case of prisons, either the Secretary of State or the contractor) may:

- make payments towards expenditure incurred by, or for purposes connected with, an LSCB, either directly, or by contributing to a fund out of which payments may be made; and

- provide staff, goods, services, accommodation or other resources for purposes connected with an LSCB.

3.98   The budget for each LSCB and the contribution made by each member organisation should be agreed locally. The member organisations' shared responsibility for the discharge of the LSCB's functions includes shared responsibility for determining how the necessary resources are to be provided to support it.

3.99   The core contributions should be provided by the responsible local authority, the PCTs, and the police. Other organisations' contributions will vary to reflect their resources and local circumstances. For some, taking part in LSCB work may be the appropriate extent of their contribution. Other organisations may wish to contribute by committing resources in kind, rather than funds, as provided for in the legislation.

3.100  Where an LSCB member organisation provides funding, this should be committed in advance, usually into a pooled budget.

3.101  The board may choose to use some of its funding to support the participation of some organisations, such as local voluntary or community sector groups, for example, if they cannot otherwise afford to take part.

3.102  The funding requirement of the LSCB will depend on its circumstances and the work which it plans to undertake (which will in turn depend on the division of responsibilities between the LSCB and other parts of the wider Children's Trust partnership). However, each LSCB will have a core minimum of work.

3.103  The LSCB's resources will need to enable it to have staff to take forward its business, whether those are paid for from a common fund, or seconded as part of a contribution in kind. The particular staffing of each LSCB should be agreed locally by the Board partners. An effective LSCB needs to be staffed so that it has the capacity to:

- drive forward the LSCB's day to day business in achieving its objectives, including its co-ordination and monitoring/evaluating work;

- take forward any training and staff development work carried out by the LSCB, in the context of the local workforce strategy; and

- provide administrative and organisational support for the Board and its sub-committees, and those involved in policy and training.

## Planning

3.104 From 1 April 2010, under the Apprenticeships, Skills, Children and Learning Act 2009, Children's Trust Boards are responsible for a joint strategy which sets out how the Children's Trust partners will co-operate to improve children's wellbeing in the local area. Every area must publish a new joint Children and Young People's Plan on or before 1 April 2011.

3.105 In preparing the Children and Young People's Plan, the Children's Trust Board will conduct a comprehensive needs assessment following an extensive consultation to agree their priorities and set out how the partners will work together and align or pool their budgets to address those priorities. The Board should also identify the resources available across the partner agencies and the contribution each will make. LSCBs should contribute to, and work within, the framework established by the Children and Young People's Plan.

3.106 It is expected that all local areas should investigate the possibilities of integrating frontline delivery of services such that staff from children's social care services work in active partnership with the police, paediatric and relevant health services to maximise effectiveness. This, however, is a matter for local determination.

3.107 The LSCB's own activities should fit clearly within the framework of the Children and Young People's Plan. The voice and experiences of young people should strongly inform the LSCB's work programme. The LSCB should have a clear work programme, including measurable objectives; and a budget.

## Monitoring and inspection

3.108 The LSCB's role in ensuring the effectiveness of work to safeguard and promote the welfare of children by member organisations will be a peer review process based on self evaluation. This will be achieved to a large extent through performance indicators and joint audits. Its aim is to promote high standards of safeguarding work and to foster a culture of continuous improvement. It will also identify and act on identified weaknesses in services. To avoid unnecessary duplication of work the LSCB should ensure that its monitoring role complements and contributes to the work of both the Children's Trust Board and the inspectorates.

3.109   Where it is found that a Children's Trust partner is not performing effectively in safeguarding and promoting the welfare of children, and the LSCB is not convinced that any planned action to improve performance will be adequate, the LSCB chair or a member or employee designated by the chair should explain these concerns to those individuals and organisations that need to be aware of the failing and may be able to take action. For example, to the most senior individual(s) in the partner organisation, to relevant monitoring bodies such as Government Offices or SHAs, to the relevant inspectorate, and, if necessary, to the relevant government department.

3.110   The local inspection framework will play an important role in reinforcing the ongoing monitoring work of the LSCB. Individual services will be assessed through their own quality regimes. Part of the established inspection arrangements – led by Ofsted but involving other inspectorates – includes (1) annual unannounced inspections on safeguarding and services for looked after children under section 138 of the Education and Inspections Act 2006, and (2) a full inspection under section 20 of the Children Act 2004 of safeguarding and services for looked after children in each local authority area at least once every three years. The LSCB should draw on these.

3.111   The LSCB will be able to feed its views about the quality of work to safeguard and promote the welfare of children into these processes.

3.112   The effectiveness of the LSCB itself should also form part of the judgement of the Inspectorates, particularly through the Comprehensive Area Assessment. This may be done, for example, by examining the quality of the LSCB's planning and determining whether key objectives have been met. It will be for the local authority to lead in taking action, if intervention in the LSCB's own processes is necessary.

# Chapter 4 – Training, development and supervision for inter-agency working

## Introduction and definitions

4.1 This chapter provides guidance for employers, LSCBs and Children's Trust Boards and their constituent members on the training and development of staff and volunteers necessary for them to effectively safeguard and promote the welfare of children. This includes being able to recognise when a child may require protection, taking account of their age and ability and knowing what to do in response to concerns about the safety and welfare of a child. Practitioners and managers must also be able to work effectively with others, both within their own agency and across organisational boundaries and this can be achieved by a combination of single-agency and inter-agency training.

4.2 Particular terms are used to describe different types and aspects of training and development. **Training for inter- and multi-agency work** means training and education that equips people to work effectively with those from other agencies to safeguard and promote the welfare of children. This training typically takes place in two ways:

- **single-agency training**, which is training carried out by a particular agency for its own staff; and

- **inter- (or multi-) agency training**, which is for employees of different agencies who either work together formally or come together for training or development.

4.3 Research for the Department of Children, Schools and Families and the Department of Health[65] has shown that inter-agency training is highly effective in helping professionals understand their respective roles and responsibilities, the procedures of each agency involved in safeguarding children and in developing a shared understanding of assessment and decision-making practices. Further, the opportunity to learn together is greatly valued; participants report increased confidence in working with colleagues from other agencies and greater mutual respect.

---

65    Carpenter et al (2009) *The Organisation, Outcomes and Costs of Inter-agency Training to safeguard and promote the welfare of children*. London: Department for Children, Schools and Families

## Purpose

4.4   The purpose of training for inter-agency work at both strategic and operational levels is to achieve better outcomes for children and young people by fostering:

- a shared understanding of the tasks, processes, principles, roles and responsibilities outlined in national guidance and local arrangements for safeguarding children and promoting their welfare;

- more effective and integrated services at both the strategic and individual case level;

- improved communication and information sharing between professionals, including a common understanding of key terms, definitions and thresholds for action;

- effective working relationships, including an ability to work in multi-disciplinary groups or teams;

- sound child focused assessments and decision-making; and

- learning from Serious Case Reviews (SCRs) and reviews of child deaths.

## Roles and responsibilities

### Employers

4.5   Employers are responsible for ensuring that their staff are competent and confident in carrying out their responsibilities for safeguarding and promoting children's and young people's welfare.

4.6   It is the responsibility of employers to recognise that in order for staff to fulfil their duties in line with Working Together, they will have different training needs which are dependent on their degree of contact with children and young people and/or with adults who are parents or carers, their level of responsibility and independence of decision-making. A number of competency frameworks have been published by professional bodies to assist employers in identifying training needs (for example, *Safeguarding Children and Young People: Roles and Competences for Health Care Staff (2006); Roles, Skills, Knowledge and competencies for Safeguarding Children in the Sports Sector (2007)*).

4.7   Employers should ensure that all those in contact or working with children and young people and/or with adults who are parents or carers have a mandatory induction, which includes familiarisation with their child protection responsibilities and the policies and procedures to be followed if they have concerns about a child's safety or welfare. The Children's Workforce Development Council provides induction guidance[66] and supporting materials. Induction should be completed within the first six months of employment and before individuals take part in inter-agency training. Regular refresher training should also be provided at least every three years.

4.8 Employers should ensure that their employees who work or have contact with children are appropriately trained in child development and in how to recognise and act on potential signs of child abuse and neglect. Training should also include associated vulnerability and risk factors and resilience and protective factors, identifying potential violent behaviour and assessing the capacity of a parent or carer to meet a child's needs, taking into account their own needs/circumstances/ history/illness/addiction. Increasingly, professional bodies are requiring their members to demonstrate relevant education and training as part of revalidation.

4.9 Employers should ensure that appropriately qualified staff undertaking specialist roles in both children's and adults' services receive the necessary specialist training. For those experienced social workers undertaking key management and supervisory roles in duty or intake teams this should include training on managing referrals where there are concerns about the safety and welfare of a child or children.

4.10 Employers also have a responsibility to identify adequate resources and support for inter-agency training by:

- committing resources for inter-agency training, for example through funding, providing venues, providing staff who contribute to the planning, delivery and/ or evaluation of inter-agency training;

- providing staff who have the relevant expertise to support the LSCB (for example, by actively contributing to the LSCB training sub-group);

- releasing staff to attend the appropriate inter-agency training courses and ensuring the time for them to complete inter-agency training tasks and apply their learning in practice; and

- ensuring that staff receive relevant single-agency training that enables them to maximise the learning derived from inter-agency training.

4.11 In advance of the roll out of a clear national standard for the support social workers should expect from their employers, the Social Work Task Force has developed an initial framework to help employers and practitioners to assess the 'health' of their organisation on a range of issues affecting workload. This is published in their final report[67]. It is recommended that all employers of social workers make use of this tool to assess and improve the support they provide to frontline staff in managing their workload.

4.12   Employers have a responsibility to ensure that all staff, including administrative staff, are given opportunities to attend local courses in safeguarding and promoting the welfare of children, or ensure that safeguarding training is provided within the team. As employers, GPs have an important role to play in ensuring staff whom they employ are trained and should ensure that practice nurses, practice managers, receptionists and any other staff whom they employ are given the opportunity to attend local courses in safeguarding and promoting the welfare of children.

## Children's Trust Board

4.13   Through their work on the local Children and Young People's Plan (CYPP), Children's Trust Boards are responsible for ensuring that workforce strategies are developed in their local area. This includes making sure that training opportunities to meet priority needs identified by the LSCBs are available, and that all staff who work or have contact with children are appropriately trained in child development, recognise potential signs of abuse and neglect and know how to respond if they have concerns about a child's welfare.

4.14   Children's Trust Boards should ensure that systems are in place to deliver both single-agency and inter-agency training on safeguarding and promoting the welfare of children. They should consider, in discussion with the LSCB, which bodies should commission or deliver single and inter-agency training.

## The LSCB

4.15   The LSCB is responsible for developing local policies for safeguarding and promoting the welfare of children, in relation to the training of people who work with children or in services affecting the safety and welfare of children (see paragraphs 3.18–3.20). This includes training in relation to the child death review processes[68] and Serious Case Reviews.

4.16   LSCBs should contribute to, and work within, the framework of the local workforce strategy. They may decide to identify training needs and priorities and feed this information into the local workforce strategy to inform the planning and commissioning of training. LSCBs will want to review and evaluate the provision and

---

67      See *Building a safe, confident future: the final report of the Social Work Task Force* and the Government response, which can be found at www.dcsf.gov.uk/swtf

68      See http://childdeath.ocbmedia.com/

availability of single and inter-agency training and to check that the training is reaching all relevant staff within organisations.

4.17 As set out in 3.45, regulations make clear that there is flexibility for a local area to decide that an LSCB should have an extended role in addition to its core functions. Those must, of course, still be related to its objectives. The LSCB and Children's Trust Board may wish to make arrangements in their local area for the LSCB to manage the delivery of the inter-agency safeguarding training – research[69] indicates that where this currently happens the resulting training is highly effective.

4.18 If a LSCB provides such services there must be an agreed protocol in place between the Boards to enable the LSCB to be treated in the same way as other partners making a contribution to delivering the CYPP. Specifically the Children's Trust Board would need to be able to call the LSCB to account for the extent to which it acted in accordance with the CYPP.

4.19 The LSCB should ensure that all staff who work or have contact with children are appropriately trained to understand normal child development and to recognise and act on potential signs of abuse and neglect.

4.20 LSCBs should review and evaluate the quality, scope and effectiveness of single and inter-agency training to ensure it is meeting local needs and should report on this annually to the Children's Trust Board. LSCBs should include in their annual report an assessment of their progress in ensuring that all staff who work with or have contact with children are appropriately trained.

4.21 Where LSCBs have the responsibility for delivering or commissioning training, they should ensure adequate funding arrangements are in place to meet the priority needs identified and to achieve appropriate reach and scope of the training to meet the LSCB's strategic objectives.

4.22 LSCBs should ensure that they are appropriately staffed and have sufficient capacity to take forward any training and development work they carry out. This includes having the necessary administrative support and having adequate resources both to contribute to the planning and delivery or commissioning of training and its evaluation. Research[70] suggests over-reliance on a single inter-agency training co-ordinator makes LSCB training programmes vulnerable.

---

69 Carpenter et al (2009) *The Organisation, Outcomes and Costs of Inter-Agency Training to Safeguard and Promote the Welfare of Children.* London: Department for Children, Schools and Families

70 Ibid.

4.23   Induction and training for LSCB members, including lay members, independent chairs and any employees of the LSCB should be provided to support them to fulfil their responsibilities effectively.

## Content, audiences and values

4.24   This section provides further guidance for employers, LSCBs, Children's Trust Boards and their constituent partners on the content, audiences and values of training for working together to safeguard and protect children and to promote their welfare.

### Values

4.25   All training should place the child at the centre and promote the importance of understanding the child's daily life experiences, ascertaining their wishes and feelings, listening to the child and never losing sight of his or her needs.

4.26   All training should create an ethos that values working collaboratively with others (valuing different roles, knowledge and skills), respects diversity (including culture, race, religion and disability), promotes equality and encourages the participation of children and families in the safeguarding processes.

### Content and Audiences

4.27   Given that safeguarding children is everybody's responsibility, audiences for training are vast and diverse. This includes the whole of the children and young people's workforce and those working with adults who are parents or carers (for example, adult psychiatrists and probation staff). It includes paid staff and volunteers working in the statutory, voluntary, community and independent sectors.

4.28   *The Common Core of Skills and Knowledge for the Children's Workforce*[71] sets out six areas of expertise that **everyone** working with children, young people and families – including those who work as volunteers – should be able to demonstrate. These are:

- effective communication and engagement with children, young people and their families and carers;

- child and young person development;

- safeguarding and promoting the welfare of the child;

---

71      www.dcsf.gov.uk/everychildmatters/strategy/deliveringservices1/commoncore/
commoncoreofskillsandknowledge/

- supporting transitions;

- multi-agency working; and

- sharing information.

4.29 While it may not be practical for everyone to participate in inter-agency training, working together is an essential feature of all training in safeguarding and promoting the welfare of children. Single-agency training, and training provided in professional settings, should always equip staff for working with, communicating and sharing information with others. All safeguarding training should be consistent with *The Common Core of Skills and Knowledge*.

4.30 Table 1 at the end of this chapter groups audiences together based on their degree of contact with children and/or parents/carers and their levels of responsibility, in order to assist with the identification of training and development needs. The groups are as follows:

- those who have **occasional contact** with children, young people and/or parents/carers;

- those in **regular or in intensive but irregular contact** with children, young people and/or parents/carers;

- those who **work predominantly** with children, young people and/or parents/carers;

- those who have particular **specialist** child protection responsibilities;

- professional advisers and **designated** leads for child protection;

- **operational managers** of services for children, young people and/or parents/carers;

- **senior managers** responsible for strategic management of services for children, young people and/or parents/carers; and

- members of LSCBs.

4.31 Training should be available at a number of levels to address the learning needs of these staff. The table at the end of the chapter outlines responsibilities and suggests possible methods of delivery. Decisions should be made locally about how the levels are most appropriately delivered, as part of the planning of training.

4.32 Whilst the detailed content of training at each level of the framework should be specified locally, programmes should usually include the following:

- recognising and responding to safeguarding and child protection concerns;

- working together;

- completing child in need assessments;

- safeguarding disabled children;

- safeguarding children when there are concerns about domestic violence, parental mental health; and

- substance misuse.

4.33   Where national guidance and competence frameworks have been developed by professional bodies, these should be reflected in the content. The content should also reflect the principles, values and processes set out in this guidance on work with children and families. Steps should be taken to ensure the relevance of the content and delivery methods to different groups from the statutory, voluntary and independent sectors who will have different professional needs. The content of training programmes should be regularly reviewed and updated in the light of changing policy and legislation, research, learning from SCRs, child death reviews and practice experience, and should always reinforce the centrality of the child's daily life experience.

4.34   All healthcare staff involved in working with children should attend training in safeguarding and promoting the welfare of children and have regular updates as part of continuing professional development. Advice regarding the competencies required of staff can be found in the intercollegiate document *Safeguarding Children and Young People: Roles and competencies for Health Care Staff*[72].

4.35   The National Police Improvement Agency (NPIA) has responsibility for the development of special training for child abuse investigation officers. In addition to this, Child Exploitation and On-Line Protection Centre (CEOP) provides a range of specialist courses to both police officers and colleagues in the wider child protection and safeguarding community. These have been developed through the CEOP Academy to support those working to protect children and students have the opportunity to attend individual courses or study for a Postgraduate Certificate in Behavioural Forensic Psychology.

4.36   It is important to ensure that training involves and is available to all people who work with children and young people. Some agencies involved in safeguarding and promoting the welfare of children may not be formally part of the local Children's Trust Board. LSCBs should ensure that the needs of all staff are included when setting up training arrangements.

---

72   www.rcpch.ac.uk/doc.aspx?id_Resource=1535

## Planning, organisation, delivery and evaluation

### Planning, organisation and delivery

4.37    Training on safeguarding children and young people should be embedded within a wider framework of commitment to inter and multi-agency working at strategic and operational levels underpinned by shared goals, planning processes and values. It is most likely to be effective if it is delivered within a framework that includes:

- a training strategy mandated by the LSCB and endorsed by member agencies, that makes clear the difference between single-agency and inter-agency training and which partnerships or agencies are responsible for commissioning and delivering training;

- adequate resources and capacity to deliver or commission training;

- policies, procedures and practice guidelines to inform and support training delivery in line with the strategy;

- identification and periodic review of local training needs, taking into account research, national developments, learning from SCRs and child death reviews (not only those carried out locally), followed by decisions about priorities;

- robust arrangements for organising and co-ordinating delivery;

- structures and processes for the delivery of inter-agency training that are not unduly dependent on a single individual; and

- quality assurance processes (for example, as part of evaluation processes put in place by the LSCB).

4.38    All training to support inter- and multi-agency work should:

- be delivered by trainers who are knowledgeable about safeguarding (which includes child protection) and promoting the welfare of children. When delivering training on complex areas of work, trainers should have the relevant specialist knowledge and skills;

- be delivered by trainers who have completed a training for trainers programme or professional equivalent;

- be informed by current research evidence, lessons from serious case and child death reviews, and local and national policy and practice developments;

- be consistent with the values outlined in paragraphs 4.25 and 4.26;

- reflect an understanding of the rights of the child, and be informed by an active respect for diversity and the experience of service users and a commitment to ensuring equality of opportunity;

- involve children, young people and their parents/carers in the design, delivery and/or evaluation; and

- be regularly reviewed and evaluated to ensure that it meets the agreed learning outcomes and has a positive impact in practice.

4.39   Research[73] has shown that effective training on safeguarding and promoting the welfare of children is most likely to be achieved if there is a member of the Board with lead responsibility for training, a training sub-group for which this Board member is responsible, and a designated and suitably skilled training co-ordinator to manage the training and development work of the LSCB.

4.40   To be effective, a training sub-group should include people with sufficient knowledge of training needs and processes to enable them to make informed contributions to the development and evaluation of a training strategy.

4.41   Many areas maintain an inter-agency training panel (also known as training pool) of suitably skilled and experienced practitioners and managers from LSCB member agencies, who work together to design, deliver and evaluate inter-agency training. The effectiveness of this approach relies on having a skilled person to co-ordinate and develop the panel, and on the allocation of time to enable panel members to undertake this work.

4.42   In some areas, training may be delivered more efficiently and effectively if there is collaboration across local areas, especially where police or health boundaries embrace more than one local authority area.

## Quality assurance and evaluation of training

4.43   The LSCB, or the training sub-group acting on its behalf, has a responsibility to ensure that both single and inter-agency training is delivered to a consistently high standard, and that a process exists for evaluating the effectiveness of training.

4.44   Monitoring arrangements should be in place to ensure that:

- training is available for the target groups identified above;

- opportunities for refresher training are available and utilised; and

---

73   Carpenter et al (2009) *The Organisation, Outcomes and Costs of Inter-Agency Training to Safeguard and Promote the Welfare of Children*. London: Department for Children, Schools and Families.

- regular review and updating of training programmes takes place in line with the training strategy and local and national developments.

4.45 The LSCB should agree an evaluation strategy and determine the appropriate level at which evaluation of training courses should take place. The focus of the evaluation should be on the extent to which training is contributing to improving the knowledge and skills of the workforce with regard to working together to safeguard and promote the welfare of children. Evaluation should include the following:

- relevance, currency and accuracy of course content;

- quality of training delivery;

- short and longer term outcomes; and

- impact on working together and inter-professional relationships.

4.46 The LSCB should ensure that outcomes from an evaluation of training courses or programmes inform the planning of future training. In its annual report to the Children's Trust Board a review of the quality, scope, reach and effectiveness of both single and inter-agency training should be provided.

4.47 The Government has developed and disseminated a range of multi-disciplinary training resources[74]. These include materials on child development (*The Developing World of the Child (2006)*), assessing children in need (*The Child's World. Second Edition* (2009, 2010)) what to do if you are concerned that a child is being abused or neglected (*Safeguarding Children – a shared responsibility (2007)*) and fabricated or induced illness (*Incredibly Caring* (2008)) which help to support the provision of good quality training. The National Institute for Health and Clinical Excellence (NICE) published guidance on *When to suspect child maltreatment*[75]. *Guidance on Investigating Child Abuse and Safeguarding Children*[76] was published by the Association of Chief Police Officers and the National Policing Improvement Agency in 2009. In addition the Department for Children, Schools and Families publishes national overviews of SCRs and LSCBs publish executive summaries of individual SCRs, all of which should be used to inform the content of training.

## Effective support and supervision

4.48 Working to ensure children are protected from harm requires sound professional judgements to be made. It is demanding work that can be distressing and stressful. All of those involved should have access to advice and support from, for example,

---

74 www.everychildmatters.gov.uk/workingtogether
75 www.nice.org.uk/nicemedia/pdf/CG89FullGuideline.pdf
76 www.npia.police.uk/en/14532.htm

peers, managers, named and designated professionals. Those providing supervision should be trained in supervision skills and have an up to date knowledge of the legislation, policy and research relevant to safeguarding and promoting the welfare of children. Supervision can be defined as:

"an accountable process which supports assures and develops the knowledge, skills and values of an individual, group or team. The purpose is to improve the quality of their work to achieve agreed outcomes."

*Providing Effective Supervision (Skills for Care and CWDC 2007, page 5)*

4.49   The key functions of supervision are:

- management (ensuring competent and accountable performance/practice);

- development (continuing professional development);

- support (supportive/restorative function); and

- engagement/mediation (engaging the individual with the organisation)[77].

4.50   For many practitioners involved in day-to-day work with children and families, effective supervision is important to promote good standards of practice and to supporting individual staff members. The arrangements for organising how supervision is delivered will vary from agency to agency but there are some key essential elements. It should:

- help to ensure that practice is soundly based and consistent with LSCB and organisational procedures;

- ensure that practitioners fully understand their roles, responsibilities and the scope of their professional discretion and authority; and

- help identify the training and development needs of practitioners, so that each has the skills to provide an effective service.

4.51   Good quality supervision can help to:

- keep a focus on the child;

- avoid drift;

- maintain a degree of objectivity and challenge fixed views;

- test and assess the evidence base for assessment and decisions; and

- address the emotional impact of work.

---

77      Morrison, T. (2005) *Staff Supervision in Social Care. Third edition*. Brighton: Pavilion.

4.52    Supervision should enable both supervisor and supervisee to reflect on, scrutinise and evaluate the work carried out, assessing the strengths and weaknesses of the practitioner and providing coaching development and pastoral support. Supervisors should be available to practitioners as an important source of advice and expertise and may be required to endorse judgements at certain key points in time. Supervisors should also record key decisions within the child's case records.

4.53    Supervision will be both educative and supportive and facilitate the supervisee to explore their feelings about the work and the family. Effective safeguarding supervision needs to be regular and provide continuity, so that the relationship between supervisor and supervisee develops. Each session should include agreeing the agenda, reviewing actions from previous supervision, listening, exploring and reflecting, agreeing actions and reviewing the supervision process itself.

4.54    It is particularly important that social workers have appropriate supervision. The recent report *Building a safe, confident future: the final report of the Social Work Task Force*[78] emphasised that supervision is a critical aspect of the support that employers should provide to social workers. It identified three specific functions of the supervision which must be in place to support effective practice: line management; professional (or case) supervision; and continuing professional development.

4.55    In line with the Task Force's recommendations, a national standard for supervision will be developed for social workers, as part of the comprehensive reform programme which the Government has committed to taking forward with the profession and employers. Whilst this is developed, it is strongly recommended that employers comply with existing guidance on the features of good supervision for social workers, for example *Providing Effective Supervision*[79] (Skills for Care/CWDC 2007).

---

78    www.dcsf.gov.uk/swtf
79    www.cwdcouncil.org.uk/providing-effective-supervision

## Table 1: Suggested training for different target groups

| Target groups to include members of statutory, voluntary, independent and community organisations | Suggested training content | Suggested training methods | Employer, LSCB and CT responsibilities |
|---|---|---|---|
| **Group 1**<br>Staff in infrequent contact with children, young people and/or parents/carers who may become aware of possible abuse or neglect.<br>For example, librarians, GP receptionists, community advice centre staff, groundsmen, recreation assistants, environmental health officers. | • What is child abuse and neglect?<br>• Signs and indicators of abuse and neglect.<br>• Normal child development.<br>• Maintaining a child focus.<br>• What to do in response to concerns. | Integral part of agency induction.<br>Refresher training at least every 3 years.<br>For induction materials see CWDC website.<br>Could be delivered through e-learning. | The employer is responsible for organisation and delivery.<br>The LSCB is responsible for ensuring that single and inter-agency training is provided and that it is reaching relevant staff within organisations.<br>The LSCB is responsible for quality assurance. |
| **Group 2**<br>Those in regular contact or have a period of intense but irregular contact, with children, young people and/or parents/carers including all health clinical staff[80], who may be in a position to identify concerns about maltreatment, including those that may arise from the use of CAF.<br>For example, housing, hospital staff, YOT staff and staff in secure settings, the police other than those in specialist child protection roles, sports development officers, disability specialists, faith groups, community youth groups, play scheme volunteers. | The above plus:<br>• Documentation and sharing of information regarding concerns.<br>• Using the *Framework for the Assessment of Children in Need and their Families*: Own safeguarding roles and responsibilities. | Single-agency training<br>Refresher training at least every 3 years.<br>Could be delivered by workshops or e-learning or combination. | The employer is responsible for organisation and delivery.<br>The LSCB is responsible for ensuring that single and inter-agency training is provided and that it is reaching relevant staff within organisations.<br>The LSCB is responsible for quality assurance. |

| Target groups to include members of statutory, voluntary, independent and community organisations | Suggested training content | Suggested training methods | Employer, LSCB and CT responsibilities |
|---|---|---|---|
| Group 3<br>Members of the workforce who work predominantly with children, young people and/or their parents/carers and who could potentially contribute to assessing, planning, intervening and reviewing the needs of a child and parenting capacity where there are safeguarding concerns.<br>For example, paediatricians, GPs, youth workers, those working in the early years sector, residential staff, midwives, school nurses, health visitors, sexual health staff, teachers, probation staff, sports club welfare officers, those working with adults in, for example, learning disability, mental health, alcohol and drug misuse services, those working in community play schemes. | The above plus:<br>● Working together to identify, assess and meet the needs of children where there are safeguarding concerns.<br>● The impact of parenting issues, such as domestic abuse, substance misuse on parenting capacity.<br>● Recognising the importance of family history and functioning.<br>● Working with children and family members, including addressing lack of co-operation and superficial compliance within the context of role. | Inter-agency training.<br>In addition single-agency training and professional development related to specific role.<br>Refresher training at least every 3 years. | The employer is responsible for organisation and delivery.<br>The LSCB is responsible for ensuring that single and inter-agency training is provided and that it is reaching relevant staff within organisations.<br>The LSCB is also responsible for quality assurance.<br>Depending on local arrangements, the LSCB or Children's Trust partners may take responsibility for the delivery of inter-agency training.<br>The Children's Trust Board is responsible for ensuring training is available to met identified needs. |

| Target groups to include members of statutory, voluntary, independent and community organisations | Suggested training content | Suggested training methods | Employer, LSCB and CT responsibilities |
|---|---|---|---|
| **Group 4**<br>Members of the workforce who have particular responsibilities in relation to undertaking section 47 enquiries, including professionals from health, education, police and children's social care; those who work with complex cases and social work staff responsible for co-ordinating assessments of children in need. | The above plus:<br>● Section 47 enquiries, roles, responsibilities and collaborative practice.<br>● Using professional judgements to make decisions as to whether a child is suffering, or is likely to suffer, significant harm.<br>● Taking emergency action.<br>● Working with complexity.<br>● Communicating with children in line with interviewing vulnerable witness guidance. | Inter-agency training.<br>In addition single-agency training and professional development related to specific role.<br>Refresher training at least every 3 years. | The employer is responsible for organisation and delivery.<br>The LSCB is responsible for ensuring that single and inter-agency training is provided and that it is reaching relevant staff within organisations.<br>The LSCB is responsible for quality assurance.<br>Depending on local arrangements, the LSCB or Children's Trust partners may take responsibility for the delivery of inter-agency training.<br>The Children's Trust Board is responsible for ensuring training is available to met identified needs. |

| Target groups to include members of statutory, voluntary, independent and community organisations | Suggested training content | Suggested training methods | Employer, LSCB and CT responsibilities |
|---|---|---|---|
| **Group 5**<br>Professional advisors, named and designated lead professionals. | • Content as for groups 1, 2 and 3 and 4 if advising staff in that group.<br>• Promoting effective professional practice.<br>• Advising others. | Inter-agency training.<br>In addition single-agency training and professional development related to specific role.<br>Refresher training at least every 3 years. | The employer is responsible for organisation and delivery.<br>The LSCB is responsible for ensuring that single and inter-agency training is provided and that it is reaching relevant staff within organisations.<br>The LSCB is responsible for quality assurance.<br>Depending on local arrangements, the LSCB or Children's Trust partners may take responsibility for the delivery of inter-agency training.<br>The Children's Trust Board is responsible for ensuring training is available to met identified needs. |

| Target groups to include members of statutory, voluntary, independent and community organisations | Suggested training content | Suggested training methods | Employer, LSCB and CT responsibilities |
|---|---|---|---|
| Group 6<br>Operational managers at all levels including: practice supervisors; front line managers and managers of child protection units. | • Content as for groups 1, 2 and 3 and 4 if supervising staff in that group.<br>• Supervising child protection cases.<br>• Managing performance to promote effective inter-agency practice. Specialist training to undertake key management and/or supervisory roles in, for example, intake/duty teams. | Inter-agency training. In addition single-agency training and professional development related to specific role. Refresher training at least every 3 years. | The employer is responsible for organisation and delivery.<br>The LSCB is responsible for ensuring that single and inter-agency training is provided and that it is reaching relevant staff within organisations.<br>The LSCB is responsible for quality assurance.<br>Depending on local arrangements the LSCB or Children's Trust partners may take responsibility for the delivery of inter-agency training.<br>The Children's Trust Board is responsible for ensuring training is available to met identified needs. |

| Target groups to include members of statutory, voluntary, independent and community organisations | Suggested training content | Suggested training methods | Employer, LSCB and CT responsibilities |
|---|---|---|---|
| Group 7<br>Senior managers responsible for the strategic management of services; NHS board members. | • Content as for groups 1, 2 and 3 and section 11 expectations, roles and responsibilities. | In-house and LSCB induction programme.<br>National and local leadership programmes.<br>Refresher training every 3 years. | The employer is responsible for organisation and delivery.<br>The LSCB is responsible for ensuring that single and inter-agency training is provided and that it is reaching relevant staff within organisations.<br>The LSCB is responsible for quality assurance.<br>Depending on local arrangements, the LSCB or Children's Trust partners may take responsibility for the delivery of inter-agency training.<br>The Children's Trust Board is responsible for ensuring training is available to met identified needs. |

| Target groups to include members of statutory, voluntary, independent and community organisations | Suggested training content | Suggested training methods | Employer, LSCB and CT responsibilities |
|---|---|---|---|
| **Group 8** Members of the LSCB including: Board members Independent chair Directors of Children's Services Elected member Lay members Members of executive and sub/task groups Business support team Inter-agency trainers. | ● Content as for groups 1, 2 and 3 and roles, responsibilities and accountabilities. ● Expectations on members in order to promote effective co-operation that improves effectiveness. ● Current policy, research and practice developments. ● Lessons from Serious Case Reviews. ● Specialist training to undertake specific roles, for example independent chair; business manager. | LSCB induction programme. LSCB development days. Refresher training at least every 3 years. CWDC support materials? National Leadership Programme. | The employer in collaboration with the LSCB is responsible for organisation and delivery. The LSCB is responsible for ensuring that single and inter-agency training is provided and that it is reaching relevant staff within organisations. Depending on local arrangements, the LSCB or Children's Trust partners may take responsibility for the delivery of inter-agency training. The Children's Trust Board is responsible for ensuring that training is available to met identified needs. |

N.B these are illustrative examples of the audiences for each target group

# Chapter 5 – Managing individual cases where there are concerns about a child's safety and welfare

## Introduction

5.1    This chapter provides guidance on what should happen if somebody has concerns about the safety and welfare of a child (including those living away from home) and in particular, concerns that a child may be suffering, or is likely to suffer, significant harm. It incorporates the guidance on information sharing and sets out the principles which underpin work to safeguard and promote the welfare of children. Fundamental to safeguarding and promoting the welfare of each child is having a child centred approach. This means seeing the child and keeping the child in focus throughout assessments, while working with the child and family, and when reviewing whether the child is safe and his or her needs are being met. Undertaking direct work with the child is key: seeing the child alone when appropriate, ascertaining the child's wishes and feelings and understanding the meaning of their daily life experiences to them. Throughout this process, the safety of the child should be ensured.

5.2    This chapter is not intended as a detailed practice guide but it sets out clear expectations about the ways in which agencies and professionals should work together to safeguard and promote the welfare of children. In addition, the related practice guidance *What to do if you're worried a child is being abused*[81] is intended to be an accessible resource for practitioners and first line managers to use in their every day work.

## Working with children when there are concerns about their safety and welfare

5.3    Achieving good outcomes for children requires all those with responsibility for assessment and the provision of services to work together according to an agreed plan of action. Effective collaboration requires organisations and people to be clear about:

---

- their roles and responsibilities for safeguarding and promoting the welfare of children (see the *Statutory guidance on making arrangements to safeguard and promote the welfare of children under section 11 of the Children Act 2004* (2007) and Chapter 2);

- the purpose of their activity, the decisions required at each stage of the process and the planned outcomes for the child and family members;

- the legislative basis for the work;

- the policies and procedures to be followed, including the way in which information will be shared across professional boundaries and within agencies, and recorded for each child;

- which organisation, team or professional has lead responsibility and the precise roles of everyone else who is involved, including the way in which children and family members will be involved; and

- any timescales set down in regulations or guidance which govern the completion of assessments, making of plans and timing of reviews.

## Principles underpinning work to safeguard and promote the welfare of children

5.4    The following principles, which draw on findings from research, underpin work with children and their families to safeguard and promote the welfare of children (see also paragraph 2.18 in the guidance issued under section 11 of the Children Act 2004). These principles should be followed when implementing the guidance set out in this chapter. They will be relevant to varying degrees depending on the functions and level of involvement of the organisation and the individual practitioner concerned.

5.5    Work to safeguard and promote the welfare of children should be:

- **Child centred**
  The child should be seen (alone when appropriate) by the lead social worker[82] in addition to all other professionals who have a responsibility for the child's welfare. His or her welfare should be kept sharply in focus in all work with the child and family. The significance of seeing and observing the child cannot be overstated. The child should be spoken and listened to, and their wishes and feelings ascertained, taken into account (having regard to their age and

---

82    Local authority children's social care is required by the Children Act 1989 (as amended by section 53 of the Children Act 2004) to ascertain the child's wishes and feelings and to give due consideration to the child's wishes and feelings having regard to their age and understanding, when determining what (if any) services to provide.

understanding) and recorded when making decisions about the provision of services. Some of the worst failures of the system have occurred when professionals have lost sight of the child and concentrated instead on their relationship with the adults.

- **Rooted in child development**
  Those working with children should have a detailed understanding of child development and how the quality of the care they are receiving can have an impact on their health and development. They should recognise that as children grow, they continue to develop their skills and abilities. Each stage, from infancy through middle years to adolescence, lays the foundation for more complex development. Plans and interventions to safeguard and promote the child's welfare should be based on a clear assessment of the child's developmental progress and the difficulties the child may be experiencing. Planned action should also be timely and appropriate for the child's age and stage of development.

- **Focused on outcomes for children**
  When working directly with a child, any plan developed for the child and their family or caregiver should be based on an assessment of the child's developmental needs and the parents/caregivers' capacity to respond to these needs within their family and environmental context. The plan should set out the planned outcomes for the child; progress against these should be regularly reviewed and the actual outcomes should be recorded. The purpose of all interventions should be to achieve the best possible outcomes for each child, recognising that each child is unique. These outcomes should contribute to the key outcomes set out for all children in the Children Act 2004 (see paragraph 1.1).

- **Holistic in approach**
  Having a holistic approach means having an understanding of a child within the context of their family (parents or caregivers and the wider family) and of the educational setting, community and culture in which he or she is growing up. The interaction between the developmental needs of children, the capacities of parents or caregivers to respond appropriately to those needs, the impact of wider family and environmental factors on children and on parenting capacity, requires careful exploration during an assessment. The ultimate aim is to understand the child's developmental needs and the capacity of the parents or caregivers to meet them and to provide services to the child and to the family members that respond to these needs. The child's context will be even more complex when they are living away from home and looked after by adults who do not have parental responsibility for them.

- **Ensuring equality of opportunity**
  Equality of opportunity means that all children have the opportunity to achieve

the best possible developmental outcomes, regardless of their gender, ability, race, ethnicity, circumstances or age. Some vulnerable children may have been particularly disadvantaged in their access to important opportunities and their health and educational needs will require particular attention in order to optimise their current welfare as well as their long-term outcomes into adulthood.

- **Involving children and families**
  In the process of finding out what is happening to a child it is important to listen to the child, develop a therapeutic relationship with the child and through this gain an understanding of his or her wishes and feelings.

  The importance of developing a co-operative working relationship is emphasised so that parents or caregivers feel respected and informed; they believe staff are being open and honest with them and in turn they are confident about providing vital information about their child, themselves and their circumstances. The consent of children or their parents/caregivers, where appropriate, should be obtained for sharing information unless to do so would place a child at risk of suffering significant harm. Similarly, decisions should also be made with their agreement, whenever possible, unless to do so would place the child at risk of suffering significant harm.

- **Building on strengths as well as identifying difficulties**
  Identifying both strengths (including resilience and protective factors) and difficulties (including vulnerabilities and risk factors) within the child, his or her family and the context in which they are living is important, as is considering how these factors are having an impact on the child's health and development. Too often it has been found that a deficit model of working with families predominates in practice and ignores crucial areas of success and effectiveness within the family on which to base interventions. Working with a child or family's strengths becomes an important part of a plan to resolve difficulties.

- **Integrated in approach**
  From birth there will be a variety of different agencies and services in the community involved with children and their development, particularly in relation to their health and education. Multi- and inter-agency work to safeguard and promote children's welfare starts as soon as it has been identified that the child or the family members have additional needs requiring support/services beyond universal services, not just when there are questions about possible harm.

- **A continuing process not an event**
  Understanding what is happening to a vulnerable child within the context of his or her family and the local community and taking appropriate action are continuing and interactive processes, and not single events. Assessment should

continue throughout a period of intervention and intervention may start at the beginning of an assessment.

- **Providing and reviewing services**
  Action and services should be provided according to the identified needs of the child and family in parallel with assessment where necessary. It is not necessary to await completion of the assessment process. Immediate and practical needs should be addressed alongside more complex and longer term ones. The impact of service provision on a child's developmental progress should be reviewed at regular intervals.

- **Informed by evidence**
  Effective practice with children and families requires sound professional judgements which are underpinned by a rigorous evidence base, and draw on the practitioner's knowledge and experience. Decisions based on these judgements should be kept under review, and take full account of any new information obtained during the course of work with the child and family.

## The processes for safeguarding and promoting the welfare of children

5.6    Four key processes underpin work with children and families, each of which has to be carried out effectively in order to achieve improvements in the lives of children in need. They are assessment, planning, intervention and reviewing.

5.7    The flow charts at the end of this chapter illustrate the processes for safeguarding and promoting the welfare of children:

- from the point that concerns are raised about a child and are referred to a statutory organisation that can take action to safeguard and promote the welfare of children (Flow chart 1);

- through an initial assessment of the child's situation and what happens after that (Flow chart 2);

- taking urgent action, if necessary (Flow chart 3);

- to the strategy discussion, where there are concerns about a child's safety, and beyond that to the child protection conference (Flow chart 4); and

- what happens after the child protection conference, and the review process (Flow chart 5).

## Being alert to children's safety and welfare

5.8    Everybody who works or has contact with children, parents and other adults in contact with children should be able to recognise, and know how to act upon, evidence that a child's health or development is or may be being impaired – especially when they are suffering, or likely to suffer, significant harm. Practitioners, foster carers, and managers should be mindful always of the safety and welfare of children – including unborn children, older children and children living away from home or looked after by the local authority – in their work:

*With children*

5.9    *For example:* early years staff, teachers, school nurses, health visitors, GPs, Accident and Emergency and all other hospital staff, and staff, in the youth justice system, including the secure estate, should be able to recognise situations where a child requires extra support to prevent impairment to his or her health or development or possible signs or symptoms of abuse or neglect in children. All professionals working with children, and especially those in health and social care, should be familiar with the core standards set out in the *National Service Framework for Children, Young People and Maternity Services Core Standards* and in particular, Standard 5, *Safeguarding and Promoting the Welfare of Children and Young People.* Those working with children living away from home should also be familiar with the relevant statutory Regulations and National Minimum Standards[83]. Children living in custodial settings should be assessed as potential children in need under section 17 of the Children Act 1989 and all children subject to a court ordered secure remand (COSR) automatically acquire the status of a looked after child.

*With parents or caregivers who may need help in promoting and safeguarding their children's welfare*

5.10   *For example:* adult mental health, substance misuse services and criminal justice agencies should always consider the implications for children of patients' or users' behaviours and the impact these may have on their parenting capacity. Day nurseries and children's and family centres should keep the interests of children uppermost in their minds when working with parents, work in ways intended to bring about better outcomes for children and be alert to possible signs or symptoms of abuse or neglect. When dealing with cases of domestic violence, the police and other involved agencies should consider the impact that this behaviour has on children, in particular their emotional development, and the victim's capacity to protect a child from harm and meet their identified needs.

---

83     www.dcsf.gov.uk/everychildmatters/safeguardingandsocialcare/childrenincare/childrenincare/

*With family members, employees, or others who have contact with children*

5.11    *For example:* the police, probation and prison services, mental health services and housing authorities should be alert to the possibility that an individual may pose a risk of causing harm to a particular child, or to children in a local community. Employers of staff or volunteers who have substantial unsupervised access to children should guard against the potential for abuse or neglect, through rigorous selection processes, appropriate supervision and by taking steps to maintain a safe environment for children. For further details on this matter see Chapter 12.

## Use of the Common Assessment Framework

5.12    The Common Assessment Framework (CAF) offers a basis for early identification of children's additional needs, sharing of this information between organisations and the co-ordination of service provision. Where it is considered a child may have additional needs, with the consent of the child, young person or parents/carers, practitioners may undertake a common assessment in accordance with the national practice guidance[84] to assess these needs and to decide how best to support them. The findings from the common assessment may however give rise to concerns about a child's safety and welfare. Practitioners should be particularly concerned regarding children whose parents or caregivers are experiencing difficulties in meeting their needs as a result of domestic violence, substance misuse, mental illness and/or learning disability (see paragraphs 9.13–9.66). All staff members who have or become aware of concerns about the safety or welfare of a child or children should know:

●    who to contact in what circumstances, and how; and

●    when and how to make a referral to local authority children's social care services or the police.

## Discussion of concerns about a child's safety and welfare

5.13    Irrespective of whether a common assessment has been undertaken, where there are concerns that a child may be a possible child in need, and in particular where there are concerns about a child being harmed, relevant information about the child and family should be discussed with a manager, or a named or designated health professional or a designated member of staff depending on the organisational setting. Concerns can also be discussed, without necessarily identifying the child in question, with senior colleagues in another agency, (for example, children's social care services) in order to develop an understanding of the child's needs and circumstances.

---

84    See www.dcsf.gov.uk/everychildmatters/strategy/deliveringservices1/caf/cafframework

5.14   Where a child is not considered to be a possible child in need under section 17 of the Children Act 1989 the practitioner should consider what other types of services, including possibly a common assessment, should be offered. If it is agreed that the child may be a child in need under the Children Act 1989 (see paragraph 1.25), then a referral to children's social care should be discussed with the child and parents. If they consent, then the child should be referred to local authority children's social care and the processes set out in this chapter followed. If the child is believed or suspected to be suffering significant harm a referral should always be made to children's social care (see paragraph 5.17 below). If concerns arise about a child who is already known to local authority children's social care the allocated social worker should be informed immediately of these concerns.

5.15   There should always be the opportunity to discuss concerns about a child's safety and welfare with, and seek advice from, colleagues, managers, a designated or named professional, or other agencies but:

- never delay emergency action to protect a child from harm;

- always record in writing concerns about a child's welfare, including whether or not further action is taken; and

- always record in writing discussions about a child's welfare in the child's file. At the close of a discussion, always reach a clear and explicit recorded agreement about who will be taking what action or that no further action will be taken.

## The welfare of unborn children

5.16   The procedures and time scales set out in this chapter should also be followed when there are concerns about the welfare of an unborn child.

## Referrals to local authority children's social care where there are concerns about a child's safety or welfare

5.17   Local authorities with children's social services functions have particular responsibilities towards all children whose health or development may be impaired without the provision of services, or who are disabled (defined in the Children Act 1989 as 'children in need'). Where a child is considered to be a possible child in need a referral to children's social care should be made in accordance with the agreed LSCB procedures and formats. Where a common assessment has already been undertaken it should be used to support a referral to children's social care: however undertaking a CAF is not a prerequisite for making a referral.

5.18   If somebody believes or suspects that a child may be suffering, or is likely to suffer, significant harm then s/he should always refer his or her concerns to the local authority children's social care services. In addition to social care, the police and the NSPCC have powers to intervene in these circumstances. Sometimes concerns will arise within local authority children's social care itself, as new information comes to light about a child and family with whom staff are already in contact. While professionals should seek, in general, to discuss any concerns with the child and family and, where possible, seek their agreement to making referrals to local authority children's social care, **this should only be done where such discussion and agreement-seeking will not place a child at increased risk of suffering significant harm**.

## Responding to child welfare concerns where there is or may be an alleged crime

5.19   Whenever local authority children's social care has a case referred to it which constitutes, or may constitute, a criminal offence against a child it should always discuss the case with the police at the earliest opportunity.

5.20   Whenever other agencies or the local authority in its other roles encounter concerns about a child's welfare which constitute, or may constitute, a criminal offence against a child they must always consider sharing that information with local authority children's social care or the police in order to protect the child or other children from suffering significant harm. If a decision is taken not to share information the reasons must be recorded.

5.21   Sharing of information in cases of concern about children's welfare will enable professionals to consider jointly how to proceed in the best interests of the child and to safeguard children more generally (see paragraph 5.3).

5.22   In dealing with alleged offences involving a child victim the police should normally work in partnership with children's social care and/or other agencies. In circumstances where it is suspected that the child may have been conceived as the result of an incestuous relationship or interfamilial abuse, consideration should be given to the use of DNA testing and the role of genetics and geneticists. Whilst the responsibility to instigate a criminal investigation rests with the police they should consider the views expressed by other agencies. There will be less serious cases where, after discussion, it is agreed that the best interests of the child are served by a children's social care led intervention rather than a full police investigation.

5.23   In deciding whether there is a need to share information professionals should consider their legal obligations, including whether they have a duty of confidentiality to the child. Where there is such a duty, the professional may lawfully share information if the child consents or if there is a public interest of sufficient force. This must be judged by the professional on the facts of each case. Where there is a clear likelihood of a child suffering significant harm, or an adult suffering serious harm, the public interest test will almost certainly be satisfied. However, there will be other cases where practitioners will be justified in sharing some confidential information in order to make decisions on sharing further information or taking action – the information shared should be proportionate.

5.24    The child's best interests must be the overriding consideration in making any such decision, including in the cases of underage sexual activity on which detailed guidance is given below. The cross-government guidance, *Information Sharing: Guidance for practitioners and managers* (2008) provides advice on these issues[85]. Any decision on whether or not to share information must be properly documented. Decisions in this area should be made by, or with the advice of, people with suitable competence in child protection work such as named or designated professionals or senior managers.

*Allegations of harm arising from underage sexual activity*

5.25    Cases of underage sexual activity which present cause for concern are likely to raise difficult issues and should be handled particularly sensitively[86]. This includes situations where girls aged under 16 years present at a termination of pregnancy clinic.

5.26    A child under 13 years is not legally capable of consenting to sexual activity. Any offence under the Sexual Offences Act 2003 involving a child aged under 13 years is very serious and should be taken to indicate that the child is suffering, or is likely to suffer, significant harm.

5.27    Cases involving children aged under 13 years should always be discussed with a nominated child protection lead in the organisation. Under the Sexual Offences Act, penetrative sex with a child under 13 years old is classed as rape. Where the allegation concerns penetrative sex, or other intimate sexual activity occurs, there would always be reasonable cause to suspect that a child, whether girl or boy, is suffering, or is likely to suffer, significant harm. There should be a presumption that the case will be reported to children's social care and that a strategy discussion will be held in accordance with the guidance set out in paragraph 5.56 below. This should involve children's social care, police, health and other relevant agencies in discussing appropriate next steps with the professional. All cases involving under 13s should be fully documented including detailed reasons where a decision is taken not to share

---

85    See www.dcsf.gov.uk/informationsharing

86    Further guidance is provided by the Department of Health best practice guidance for doctors and other health professionals on the provision of advice and treatment to young people under 16 on contraception, reproductive and sexual health.

information. These decisions should be exceptional and only made with the documented approval of a senior manager.

5.28    Sexual activity with a child aged under 16 years is also an offence. Where it is consensual it may be less serious than if the child were aged under 13 years but may, nevertheless, have serious consequences for the welfare of the young person. Consideration should be given in every case of sexual activity involving a child aged 13–15 as to whether there should be a discussion with other agencies and whether a referral should be made to children's social care. The professional should make this assessment using the considerations below. Within this age range the younger the child the stronger the presumption must be that sexual activity will be a matter of concern. Cases of concern should be discussed with the nominated child protection lead and subsequently with other agencies if required. Where confidentiality needs to be preserved a discussion can still take place as long as it does not identify the child (directly or indirectly). Where there is reasonable cause to suspect that significant harm to a child has occurred, or is likely to occur, there should be a presumption that the case is reported to children's social care and a strategy discussion should be held to discuss appropriate next steps. Again, all cases should be carefully documented including where a decision is taken not to share information.

5.29    The considerations in the following checklist should be taken into account when assessing the extent to which a child (or other children) is suffering, or is likely to suffer, significant harm and therefore whether a strategy discussion should be held in order to share information:

- the age of the child. Sexual activity at a young age is a very strong indicator that there are risks to the welfare of the child (whether boy or girl) and, possibly, others;

- the level of maturity and understanding of the child;

- what is known about the child's living circumstances or background;

- age imbalance, in particular where there is a significant age difference;

- overt aggression or power imbalance;

- coercion or bribery;

- familial child sex offences;

- behaviour of the child i.e. withdrawn, anxious;

- the misuse of substances as a disinhibitor;

- whether the child's own behaviour because of the misuse of substances places him/her at risk of suffering harm so that he/she is unable to make an informed choice about any activity;

- whether any attempts to secure secrecy have been made by the sexual partner beyond what would be considered usual in a teenage relationship;

- whether the child denies, minimises or accepts concerns;

- whether the methods used are consistent with grooming; and

- whether the sexual partner/s is known by one of the agencies.

5.30   In cases of concern when sufficient information is known about the sexual partner/s, the agency concerned should check with other agencies, including the police, to establish whatever information is known about that person/s. In appropriate cases the police may share the required information without beginning a full investigation if the agency making the check requests this.

5.31   Sexual activity involving a 16 or 17 year old, even if it does not involve an offence, may still involve harm or the likelihood of harm being suffered. Professionals should still bear in mind the considerations and processes outlined in this guidance in assessing whether harm is being suffered, and should share information as appropriate. It is an offence for a person to have a sexual relationship with a 16 or 17 year old if they hold a position of trust or authority in relation to them.

## Response of local authority children's social care to a referral

5.32   When a parent, professional, or another person contacts local authority children's social care with concerns about a child's welfare, it is the responsibility of local authority children's social care to clarify with the referrer (including self-referrals from children and families):

- the nature of concerns;

- how and why they have arisen;

- what appear to be the needs of the child and family; and

- what involvement they are having or have had with the child and/or family members.

The referrer should have the opportunity to discuss their concerns with a qualified social worker. The process of clarifying the nature of the referral should always identify clearly whether there are concerns about maltreatment and the associated risk factors, the evidence for these concerns and whether it may be necessary to consider taking urgent action to ensure the child(ren) are safe from harm. Local authority children's social care should specifically ask the referrer if they hold any information about difficulties being experienced in the family/household due to domestic violence, mental illness, substance misuse and/or learning disability in order to inform its decision making.

5.33 Professionals who phone local authority children's social care should confirm their referrals in writing within 48 hours. The CAF provides a structure for the written referral but prior completion of a CAF should not be a pre-requisite for a referral being accepted by the local authority. At the end of any discussion about a child, the referrer (whether a professional or a member of the public or family) and local authority children's social care should be clear about the local authority's proposed course of action in response to the referral, timescales and who will be taking this action, or if no further action will be taken. The decision should be recorded by local authority children's social care in the child's case file and by the referrer (if a professional in another service). Local authority children's social care should acknowledge a written referral within one working day of receiving it. If the referrer has not received an acknowledgement within three working days they should contact local authority children's social care again.

5.34 **Local authority children's social care should decide how they will respond to the referral and record next steps of action within one working day.** This information should be consistent with the information set out in the Referral and Information Record (Department of Health, 2002). This decision should normally follow discussion with any referring professional/service, consideration of information held in any existing records and involve discussion with other professionals and services as necessary[87] (including the police, where a criminal offence may have been committed against a child). An initial consideration of the case should address – on the basis of the available evidence – whether there are concerns about impairment to the child's health and development or the child suffering harm which justifies an initial assessment to establish whether this child is a child in need. Local authority children's social care should ensure that the social work practitioners who are responding to referrals are supported by experienced first line managers competent in making sound evidence based decisions about what to do next. Further action by children's social care may also include referral to other agencies, the provision of information or advice – such as suggesting the completion of a common assessment by the referring agency or organisation – or no further action.

5.35 The parents' permission, or the child's where appropriate, should be sought before discussing a referral about them with other agencies unless permission-seeking may

---

87 ContactPoint provides an efficient way for people working with children to find out who else is working with the same child. Information is available at: www.dcsf.gov.uk/ecm/contactpoint

itself place the child at increased risk of suffering significant harm. When responding to referrals from a member of the public rather than another professional, local authority children's social care should bear in mind that personal information about referrers, including identifying details, should only be disclosed to third parties (including subject families and other agencies) with the consent of the referrer. In all cases where the police are involved, the decision about when to inform the parents (about referrals from third parties) will have a bearing on the conduct of police investigations.

5.36    Where local authority children's social care decides to take no further action at this stage, feedback should be provided to the referrer, who should be told of this decision and the reasons for making it. In the case of public referrals, this should be done in a manner consistent with respecting the confidentiality of the child. Sometimes it may be apparent at this stage that emergency action should be taken to safeguard and promote the welfare of a child (see paragraph 5.51). Such action should normally be preceded by an immediate strategy discussion between the police, local authority children's social care and other agencies as appropriate.

5.37    New information may be received about a child or family where the child or family member is already known to local authority children's social care. If the child's case is open and there are concerns that the child is, or is likely to be, suffering significant harm then a decision should be made about whether a strategy discussion should be held in order to consider whether to initiate section 47 enquiries (see paragraph 5.56). It may, also, be appropriate to consider undertaking a core assessment or to update a previous one in order to understand the child's current needs and circumstances and inform future decision making.

## Initial assessment

5.38    The initial assessment is a brief assessment of each child referred to local authority children's social care where it is necessary to determine whether:

- the child is in need;

- there is reasonable cause to suspect the child is suffering, or is likely to suffer, significant harm;

- any services are required and of what types; and

- a further, more detailed core assessment should be undertaken (paragraph 3.9 of the *Framework for the Assessment of Children in Need and their Families* (2000)).

5.39    The initial assessment should be completed by local authority children's social care, working with colleagues, within a maximum of 10 working days of the date of referral. An initial assessment is deemed to be completed once the assessment has been discussed with the child and family (or caregivers) and the team manager has viewed and authorised the assessment. The initial assessment period may be very brief if the criteria for initiating section 47 enquiries are met, i.e. it is suspected that the child is suffering, or is likely to suffer, significant harm. The initial assessment should be undertaken in accordance with statutory guidance, the *Framework for the Assessment of Children in Need and their Families* (Department of Health et al, 2000) (the 'Assessment Framework' – summarised in Appendix 2). Where a common assessment has been completed this information should be used to inform the initial assessment. Information should be gathered and analysed within the three domains of the Assessment Framework (see Figure1), namely:

- the child's developmental needs;

- the parents' or caregivers' capacity to respond appropriately to those needs; and

- the wider family and environmental factors.

*Figure 1.*

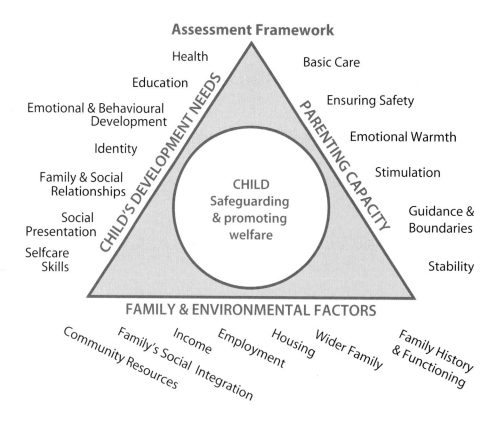

5.40    The initial assessment should address the following questions:

- what are the developmental needs of the child? What needs of the child are being met and how? What needs of the child are not being met and why not?

- are the parents able to respond appropriately to the child's identified needs? Is the child being adequately safeguarded from harm, and are the parents able to promote the child's health and development?

- what impact are family functioning (past and present) and history, and the wider family and environmental factors having on the parent's capacity to respond to their child's needs and the child's developmental progress?

- is action required to safeguard and promote the welfare of the child? Within what timescales should this action be taken?

5.41   The initial assessment should be led by a qualified and experienced social worker who is supervised by a highly experienced and qualified social work manager. It should be carefully planned, with clarity about who is doing what, as well as when and what information is to be shared with the parents. The planning process and decisions about the timing of the different assessment activities should be undertaken in collaboration with all those involved with the child and family. The process of initial assessment should involve:

- seeing and speaking to the child, including alone when appropriate;

- seeing and meeting with parents, the family and wider family members as appropriate;

- involving and obtaining relevant information from professionals and others in contact with the child and family; and

- drawing together and analysing available information (focusing on the strengths and positive factors as well as vulnerabilities and risk factors) from a range of sources (including existing agency records).

All relevant information (including information about the history and functioning of the family both currently and in the past, and adult problems such as domestic violence, substance misuse, mental illness and criminal behaviour/convictions) should be taken into account. This includes seeking information from relevant services if the child and family have spent time abroad. Professionals from agencies such as health, local authority children's social care or the police should request this information from their equivalent agencies in the country(ies) in which the child has lived. Information about who to contact can be obtained via the Foreign and Commonwealth Office or the appropriate Embassy or Consulate based in London[88].

5.42   The child should be seen by the lead social worker, without his or her caregivers present when appropriate, within a timescale which is appropriate to the nature of

---

88   See the London Diplomatic List (The Stationery Office), ISBN 0 11 591772 1, the FCO website www.fco.gov.uk or phone 020 7008 1500

concerns expressed at the time of the referral, according to the agreed plan. Seeing the child includes observing and communicating with the child in a manner appropriate to his or her age and understanding. Local authority children's social care is required by the Children Act 1989 (as amended by section 53 of the Children Act 2004) to ascertain the child's wishes and feelings and to give due consideration to the child's wishes and feelings, having regard to their age and understanding, when making decisions about what (if any) services to provide. Interviews with the child should be undertaken in the preferred language of the child. For some disabled children interviews may require the use of non-verbal communication methods.

5.43    **It will not necessarily be clear whether a criminal offence has been committed**, which means that even initial discussions with the child should be undertaken in a way that minimises distress to them and maximises the likelihood that she or he will provide accurate and complete information. It is important to avoid leading questions or suggesting answers.

5.44    Interviews with family members (which may include the child) should also be undertaken in their preferred language and where appropriate for some people by using non-verbal communication methods.

5.45    In the course of an initial assessment local authority children's social care should ascertain:

- is this a child in need? (section 17 of the Children Act 1989); and

- is there reasonable cause to suspect that this child is suffering, or is likely to suffer, significant harm? (section 47 of the Children Act 1989).

5.46    The focus of the initial assessment should be both on the safety and the welfare of the child. It is important to remember that even if the reason for a referral was a concern about abuse or neglect that is not subsequently substantiated, a child and family may still benefit from support and practical help to promote a child's health and development. When services are to be provided a child in need plan should be developed based on the findings from the initial assessment and on any previous plans, for example, those made following the completion of a common assessment. If the child's needs and circumstances are complex a more in-depth core assessment under section 17 of the Children Act 1989 will be required in order to decide what other types of services are necessary to assist the child and family (see the *Framework for the Assessment of Children in Need and their Families*). Appendix 1 sets out the statutory framework including relevant sections of the Children Act 1989. Appendix 3 *Using standardised assessment tools to evidence assessment and decision making* is intended for use by practitioners to support evidence-based assessment and decision making.

5.47   Once an initial assessment has been completed (see paragraph 5.39 for definition of completed) local authority children's social care should decide on the next course of action, following discussion with the child and family, unless such a discussion may place a child at increased risk of suffering significant harm. If there are concerns about a parent's ability to protect a child from harm, careful consideration should be given to what the parents should be told when and by whom, taking account of the child's welfare. Where it is clear that there should be a police investigation in parallel with a section 47 enquiry the considerations at paragraph 5.66 should apply. Whatever decisions are taken they should be endorsed at a managerial level agreed within local authority children's social care and recorded in writing. This information should be consistent with that contained in the Initial Assessment Record (Department of Health, 2002). The local authority record in relation to the child should include whether the child was seen and who else, if anyone, was present at the time of each visit and also the reasons for deciding (or not) to see the child alone. The local authority record should also set out the decisions made and future action to be taken. The family, the original referrer, and other professionals and services involved in the initial assessment should, as far as possible, be told what action has been and will be taken consistent with respecting the confidentiality of the child and family concerned, and not jeopardising further action in respect of concerns about harm (which may include police investigations). This information should be confirmed in writing to the agencies, the family and where appropriate the child.

## Next steps – child in need but no suspected actual or likely significant harm

5.48   An initial assessment may indicate that a child is a 'child in need' as defined by section 17 of the Children Act 1989 but that there are no substantiated concerns that the child may be suffering, or is likely to suffer, significant harm. There may be sufficient information available on which to decide what services (if any) should be provided by whom according to an agreed plan. On the other hand a more in-depth assessment may be necessary in order to understand the child's needs and circumstances. In these circumstances, the Assessment Framework provides guidance on undertaking a core assessment which builds on the findings from the initial assessment and addresses the central or most important aspects of the needs of a child and the capacity of his or her parents or caregivers to respond appropriately to these needs within the wider family and community context. This core assessment can provide a sound evidence base for professional judgements on what types of services are most likely to bring about good outcomes for the child. Family Group Conferences (see paragraphs 10.2–10.4) may be an effective vehicle for taking forward work in such cases.

5.49    The definition of a 'child in need' is wide and it will embrace children in a diverse range of circumstances. The types of services that may help such children and their families will vary greatly according to their needs and circumstances.

> The rest of the guidance in this chapter is concerned with the processes which should be followed where a child is suspected to be suffering, or is likely to suffer, significant harm.
>
> The Children Act 1989 introduced the concept of significant harm as the threshold that justifies compulsory intervention in family life, in the best interests of children. It gives local authorities a duty under section 47 to make enquiries when they have *reasonable cause to suspect that a child who lives, or is found, in their area is suffering, or likely to suffer, significant harm* to enable them to decide whether they should take action to safeguard or promote the child's welfare.
>
> This statutory guidance adopts specifically the legislative terminology of 'significant harm' in preference to the use of the word "risk", given the need both to reflect the legislative requirements and to avoid confusion with the wide variety of contexts and associated tools and methodologies associated with risk assessment/analysis. When assessing whether a child is suffering, or likely to suffer, significant harm local authority children's social care will of course draw on a wide variety of information including the outcomes of relevant risk assessments or judgments provided by other agencies and professionals to inform their own evidence based assessment.

## Next steps – suspicion that a child is suffering, or is likely to suffer, significant harm

5.50    Where it is suspected that a child is suffering, or is likely to suffer, significant harm the local authority is required by section 47 of the Children Act 1989 to make enquiries to enable it to decide whether it should take any action to safeguard and promote the welfare of the child. A section 47 enquiry should be carried out through a core assessment (see paragraph 5.62). The *Framework for the Assessment of Children in Need and their Families* provides a structured framework for collecting, drawing together and analysing available information about a child and family within and between the following three domains:

- the child's developmental needs;

- parenting capacity; and

- and family and environmental factors.

Using the framework will help to provide sound evidence on which to base often difficult professional judgements about whether to intervene to safeguard and promote the welfare of a child and if so, how best to do so and with what intended outcomes.

## Immediate protection

5.51   Where there is a risk to the life of a child or a likelihood of serious immediate harm, an agency with statutory child protection powers[89] **should act quickly to secure the immediate safety of the child**. Emergency action might be necessary as soon as a referral is received or at any point in involvement with a child/ren and their family (see Appendix 1, paragraph 18 for the range of emergency protection powers available). The need for emergency action may become apparent only over time as more is learned about the circumstances of a child or children. Neglect, as well as abuse, can result in a child suffering significant harm to the extent that urgent protective action is necessary. When considering whether emergency action is required, an agency should always consider whether action is also required to safeguard and promote the welfare of other children in the same household, the household of an alleged perpetrator or elsewhere.

5.52   Planned emergency action will normally take place following an immediate strategy discussion between the police, local authority children's social care and other agencies as appropriate (including NSPCC where involved). Where a single agency has to act immediately to protect a child, a strategy discussion should take place as soon as possible after such action to plan next steps. Legal advice should normally be obtained before initiating legal action, in particular, when an Emergency Protection Order (EPO) is to be sought. For further guidance on EPOs see pages 55–65 of Volume 1 of the Children Act 1989 Guidance and Regulations, Court Orders[90].

5.53   In some cases, it may be sufficient to secure a child's safety by a parent taking action to remove an alleged perpetrator or by the alleged perpetrator agreeing to leave the home. In other cases, it may be necessary to ensure either that the child remains in a safe place or that the child is removed to a safe place, either on a voluntary basis or by obtaining an EPO. The police also have powers to remove a child to suitable accommodation in cases of emergency. If it is necessary to remove a child a local authority should wherever possible – and unless a child's safety is otherwise at immediate risk – apply for an EPO. **Police powers should only be used in exceptional circumstances where there is insufficient time to seek an EPO or for reasons relating to the immediate safety of the child.**

---

89   Agencies with statutory child protection powers comprise the local authority, the police, and the NSPCC.

90   www.dcsf.gov.uk/everychildmatters/publications/documents/childrenactguidanceregulations/

5.54    The local authority in whose area a child is found in circumstances that require emergency action is responsible for taking that action. If the child is looked after by, or the subject of a child protection plan in another authority, the first authority should consult the authority responsible for the child. Only when the second local authority explicitly accepts responsibility is the first authority relieved of its responsibility to take emergency action. Such acceptance should be confirmed subsequently in writing.

5.55    Emergency action addresses only the immediate circumstances of the child(ren). The local authority should follow this action quickly by initiating section 47 enquiries as necessary. The agencies primarily involved with the child and family should be involved in the core assessment to understand the needs and circumstances of the child and family, and agree action to safeguard and promote the welfare of the child in the longer-term. Where an EPO applies, local authority children's social care will have to consider quickly whether to initiate care or other proceedings or to let the order lapse and the child return home.

## Strategy discussion

5.56    Whenever there is reasonable cause to suspect that a child is suffering, or is likely to suffer, significant harm there should be a strategy discussion involving local authority children's social care, the police, health and other bodies as appropriate (for example, children's centre/school or family intervention projects), in particular any referring agency. The strategy discussion should be convened and led by local authority children's social care and those participating should be sufficiently senior and able, therefore, to contribute to the discussion of available information and to make decisions on behalf of their agencies. If the child is a hospital patient (in- or out-patient) or receiving services from a child development team, the medical consultant responsible for the child's health care should be involved, as should the senior ward nurse if the child is an in-patient. Where a medical examination may be necessary or has taken place a senior doctor from those providing services should also be involved. Where the parents or adults in the household are experiencing problems such as domestic violence, substance misuse or mental illness it will also be important to consider involving the relevant adult services professional(s).

5.57    A strategy discussion may take place following a referral, or at any other time (for example, if concerns about significant harm emerge in respect of child receiving services under section 17). The discussion should be used to:

- share available information;

- agree the conduct and timing of any criminal investigation;

- decide whether section 47 enquiries should be initiated and therefore a core assessment be undertaken under section 47 of the Children Act 1989, or continued if it had already begun under section 17 of the Children Act 1989;

- plan how the section 47 enquiry should be undertaken (if one is to be initiated) including the need for medical treatment and who will carry out what actions, by when and for what purpose;

- agree what action is required immediately to safeguard and promote the welfare of the child, and/or provide interim services and support. If the child is in hospital decisions should also be made about how to secure the safe discharge of the child;

- determine what information from the strategy discussion will be shared with the family unless such information sharing may place a child at increased risk of suffering significant harm or jeopardise police investigations into any alleged offence(s); and

- determine if legal action is required.

5.58   Relevant matters will include:

- agreeing a plan for how the core assessment under section 47 of the Children Act 1989 will be carried out – what further information is required about the child(ren) and family and how it should be obtained and recorded;

- agreeing who should be interviewed, by whom, for what purpose and when. The way in which interviews are conducted can play a significant part in minimising any distress caused to children and increase the likelihood of maintaining constructive working relationships with families. When a criminal offence may have been committed against a child, the timing and handling of interviews with victims, their families and witnesses can have important implications for the collection and preservation of evidence;

- agreeing, in particular, when the child will be seen alone (unless to do so would be inappropriate for the child) by the lead social worker during the course of these enquiries and the methods by which the child's wishes and feelings will be ascertained so that they can be taken into account when making decisions under section 47 of the Children Act 1989;

- in the light of the race and ethnicity of the child and family, considering how these should be taken into account and establishing whether an interpreter will be required; and

- considering the needs of other children who may be affected – for example, siblings and other children, such as those living in the same establishment – in contact with alleged abusers.

5.59   A strategy discussion may take place at a meeting or by other means (for example, by telephone). In complex types of maltreatment a meeting is likely to be the most effective way of discussing the child's welfare and planning future action. More than one strategy discussion may be necessary. This is likely to be where the child's circumstances are very complex and a number of discussions are required to consider whether and if so, when to initiate section 47 enquiries as well as how best to undertake them. Such a meeting should be held at a convenient location for the key attendees, such as a hospital, school, police station or children's services office. Any information shared, all decisions reached and the basis for those decisions should be clearly recorded by the chair of the strategy discussion and circulated within one working day to all parties to the discussion. Local authority children's social care should record information in the child's file which is consistent with the information set out in the Record of Strategy Discussion (Department of Health, 2002). Any decisions about taking immediate action should be kept under constant review.

5.60   Significant harm to children gives rise to both child welfare and law enforcement concerns and section 47 enquiries may run concurrently with police investigations concerning possible associated crime(s). The police have a duty to carry out thorough and professional investigations into allegations of crime and the obtaining of clear strong evidence is in the best interests of a child, since it makes it less likely that a child victim will have to give evidence in criminal court. Enquiries may, therefore, give rise to information that is relevant to decisions that will be taken by both local authority children's social care and the police. The findings from the assessment and/or police investigation should be used to inform plans about future support and help to the child and family. They may also contribute to legal proceedings, whether criminal, civil or both.

5.61   Each LSCB should have in place a protocol for local authority children's social care and the police, to guide both agencies in deciding how section 47 enquiries and associated police investigations should be conducted jointly and in particular, in what circumstances section 47 enquiries and a linked criminal investigation are necessary and/or appropriate. When joint enquiries take place the police have the lead for the criminal investigation and local authority children's social care have the lead for the section 47 enquiries and the child's welfare.

## Section 47 enquiries and core assessment

5.62   The core assessment is the means by which a section 47 enquiry is carried out. It should be led by a qualified and experienced social worker. Local authority children's social care has lead responsibility for the core assessment under section 47 of the Children Act 1989. In these circumstances the objective of the local authority's involvement is to determine whether and what type of action is required to safeguard and promote the welfare of the child who is the subject of the section 47 enquiries. The *Framework for the Assessment of Children in Need and their Families* (2000) provides the structure for helping to collect and analyse information obtained in the course of section 47 enquiries. The core assessment should begin by focusing primarily on the information identified during the initial assessment as being of most importance or seriousness when considering whether the child is suffering, or is likely to suffer, significant harm. It should, however, cover all relevant dimensions in the Assessment Framework before its completion. Those making enquiries about a child should always be alert to the potential needs and safety of any siblings or other children in the household of the child in question. In addition, enquiries may also need to cover children in other households with whom the alleged offender may have had contact. At the same time, the police will have to (where relevant) establish the facts about any offence that may have been committed against a child and to collect evidence.

5.63   The Children Act 1989 places a statutory duty on health, education and other services to help the local authority in carrying out its social services functions under Part III of the Children Act 1989 and in undertaking section 47 enquiries. Assessing the needs of a child and the capacity of their parents or wider family network to ensure his or her safety, health and development, very often depends on building a picture of the child's situation on the basis of information from many sources. The local authority social worker, in leading the section 47 enquiry, should do his or her utmost to secure willing co-operation and participation from all professionals and services by being prepared to explain and justify the local authority's actions and to demonstrate that the process is being managed in a way that can help to bring about better outcomes for children. The LSCB has an important role to play in cultivating and promoting a climate of trust and understanding between different professionals and services.

5.64   The child's wishes and feelings should be ascertained and regard given to their age and understanding when making decisions about what (if any) services to provide. Section 47 enquiries should always involve interviews with the child who is the subject of concern. The child should be seen by the lead social worker and communicated with alone when appropriate. Some children may need to be seen, for example, with an interpreter or a person who can use their preferred method of communication (see paragraph 5.65). Others, such as babies, may need to be seen in the presence of their primary caregiver so as to minimise their distress. In addition, the enquiries should involve interviews with parents and/or caregivers (both with the child present and in the child's absence) and observations of the interactions between parents and child(ren) (where appropriate in a variety of settings).

Enquiries may also include:

- interviews with those who are personally (for example, wider family members) and professionally connected with the child;

- specific examinations or assessments of the child by other professionals (for example, medical or developmental checks, assessment of emotional or psychological state); and

- interviews with those who are personally and professionally connected with the child's parents and/or caregivers.

5.65 Individuals should always be enabled to participate fully in the enquiry process. Where a child or parent is disabled, it may be necessary to provide help with communication to enable the child or parent to express him/herself to the best of his or her ability. Where a child or parent speaks a language other than that spoken by the interviewer, an interpreter should be provided. If the child is unable to take part in an interview because of age or understanding, alternative means of understanding the child's wishes or feelings should be used, including observation where children are very young or where they have communication impairments.

5.66 Children are a key and sometimes the only source of information about what has happened to them especially in child sexual abuse cases but also in physical and other forms of abuse. Accurate and complete information is essential for taking action to safeguard and promote the welfare of the child, as well as for any criminal proceedings that may be instigated concerning an alleged perpetrator of abuse. When children are first approached, the nature and extent of any harm suffered by them may not be clear, nor whether a criminal offence has been committed. It is important that even initial discussions with children are conducted in a way that minimises any distress caused to them and maximises the likelihood that they will provide accurate and complete information. It is important, wherever possible, to have separate communication with a child. Leading or suggestive communication should always be avoided. Children may need time and more than one opportunity in order to develop sufficient trust to communicate any concerns they may have, especially if they have a communication impairment, learning disabilities, are very young or are experiencing mental health problems.

5.67 Exceptionally, a joint enquiry/investigation team may need to speak to a suspected child victim without the knowledge of the parent or caregiver. Relevant circumstances would include the possibility that a child would be threatened or otherwise coerced into silence, a strong likelihood that important evidence would be destroyed or that the child in question did not wish the parent to be involved at that stage and is competent to take that decision. As at paragraph 5.43 above, in all cases where the police are involved, the decision about when to inform the parent or caregiver will have a bearing on the conduct of police investigations and the strategy discussion should decide on the most appropriate timing of parental participation.

5.68   In accordance with the practice guidance *Achieving Best Evidence* (2007), all such joint interviews with children should be conducted by those with specialist training and experience in interviewing children. Additional specialist help may be required if:

- the child is very young;

- the child does not speak English at a level which enables him or her to participate in the interview;

- the child appears to have a degree of psychiatric disturbance but is deemed competent;

- the child has an impairment; or

- the interviewers do not have adequate knowledge and understanding of the child's racial, religious or cultural background.

Consideration should also be given to the gender of interviewers, particularly in cases of alleged sexual abuse.

5.69   Criminal justice legislation, in particular the Youth Justice and Criminal Evidence Act 1999, creates particular obligations for courts who are dealing with witnesses under 17 years of age. These include the presumption of evidence-giving through pre-recorded videos, as well as the use of live video links for further evidence-giving and cross examination.

## Child Assessment Orders

5.70   Local authority children's social care should make all reasonable efforts to persuade parents to co-operate with section 47 enquiries. If, despite these efforts, the parents continue to refuse access to a child for the purpose of establishing basic facts about the child's condition – but concerns about the child's safety are not so urgent as to require an EPO – a local authority may apply to the court for a child assessment order. In these circumstances, the court may direct the parents/caregivers to co-operate with an assessment of the child, the details of which should be specified. The order does not take away the child's own right to refuse to participate in an assessment, for example, a medical examination, so long as he or she is of sufficient age and understanding. For further guidance on child assessment orders see pages

52–55 of Volume 1 of the Children Act 1989 Guidance and Regulations, Court Orders[91].

## The impact of section 47 enquiries on the family and child

5.71   Section 47 enquiries should always be carried out in such a way as to minimise distress to the child and to ensure that families are treated sensitively and with respect. Local authority children's social care should explain the purpose and outcome of section 47 enquiries to the parents and to the child, (having regard to their age and understanding) and be prepared to answer questions openly, unless to do so would affect the safety and welfare of the child. It is particularly helpful for families if local authority children's social care provide written information about the purpose, process and potential outcomes of section 47 enquiries. The information should be both general and specific to the particular circumstances under enquiry. It should include information about how advice, advocacy and support may be obtained from independent sources.

5.72   In the great majority of cases, children remain with their families following section 47 enquiries even where concerns about abuse or neglect are substantiated. As far as possible, section 47 enquiries should be conducted in a way that allows for future constructive working relationships with families. The way in which a case is handled initially can affect the entire subsequent process. Where handled well and sensitively there can be a positive effect on the eventual outcome for the child.

5.73   Where a child is living in a residential establishment, consideration should be given to the possible impact on other children living in the same establishment. Paragraphs 6.10–6.13 set out a summary of the Government's practice guidance on dealing with complex abuse cases.

## The outcome of section 47 enquiries

5.74   Local authority children's social care should decide how to proceed following section 47 enquiries, after discussion between all those who have conducted, or been significantly involved in, those enquiries, including relevant professionals and agencies (as well as foster carers where involved) and the child and parents themselves. The information recorded on the outcome of the section 47 enquiries should be consistent with the information set out in the Outcome of the section 47 Enquiries Record (Department of Health, 2002). The local authority children's social care record for the child should set out clearly the dates on which the child was seen by the lead social worker during the course of the enquiries, if they were seen alone, and if not, who was present and for what reasons. Parents and children of sufficient age and appropriate level of understanding (together with professionals and agencies who have been significantly involved) should receive a copy of this record, in particular in advance of any initial child protection conference that is convened. This information should be conveyed in an appropriate format for younger children and those people whose preferred language is not English. Consideration should be given to whether the core assessment has been completed or what further work is required before it is completed. It may be valuable, following an evaluation of the outcome of enquiries, to make recommendations for action in an inter-disciplinary forum if the case is not going forward to a child protection conference. Enquiries may result in a number of outcomes. Where the child concerned is living in a residential establishment which is subject to inspection, the relevant inspectorate should be informed.

## Concerns are not substantiated

5.75   Section 47 enquiries may not substantiate the original concerns that the child was suffering, or was likely to suffer, significant harm but it is important that the core assessment is completed. In some circumstances it may be decided that completion of the section 47 enquiry means that the core assessment has been completed and no further action is necessary. However, local authority children's social care and other relevant agencies, as necessary, should always consider with the child and family what support and/or services may be helpful, how the child and family might be provided with these services (if they wish it) and by whom. The focus of section 47 enquiries is the welfare of the child and the assessment may well reveal a range of needs. The provision of services to these children and their family members should not be dependent on the presence of abuse and neglect. Help and support to children in need and their families may prevent problems escalating to a point where a child is abused or neglected.

5.76   In some cases, there may remain concerns about the child's safety and welfare despite there being no real evidence. It may be appropriate to put in place arrangements to monitor the child's welfare. Monitoring should never be used as a means of deferring or avoiding difficult decisions. The purpose of monitoring should always be clear, that is, what is being monitored and why, in what way and by whom. It will also be important to inform parents about the nature of any ongoing concerns. There should be a time set for reviewing the monitoring arrangements through the holding of a further discussion or meeting.

## Concerns are substantiated, but the child is not judged to be continuing to, or be likely to, suffer significant harm

5.77   There may be substantiated concerns that a child has suffered significant harm but it is agreed between the agencies most involved and the child and family, that a plan for ensuring the child's future safety and welfare can be developed and implemented without having a child protection conference or a child protection plan. Such an approach will be of particular relevance where it is clear to the agencies involved that there is the child is not continuing to suffer, or be likely to suffer, significant harm.

5.78    A child protection conference may not be required when there are sound reasons, based on an analysis of evidence obtained through section 47 enquiries, for judging that a child is not continuing to, or be likely to, suffer significant harm. This may be because, for example, the caregiver has taken responsibility for the harm they caused the child, the family's circumstances have changed or the person responsible for the harm is no longer in contact with the child. It may be because significant harm was incurred as the result of an isolated abusive incident (for example, abuse by a stranger).

5.79    The agencies most involved may judge that a parent, caregiver or members of the child's wider family are willing and able to co-operate with actions to ensure the child's future safety and welfare and that the child is therefore not continuing to, or be likely to, suffer significant harm. This judgement can only be made in the light of all relevant information obtained during a section 47 enquiry, and a soundly based assessment of the likelihood of successful intervention, based on clear evidence and mindful of the dangers of misplaced professional optimism. Local authority children's social care have a duty to ascertain the child's wishes and feelings and take these into account (having regard to the child's age and understanding) when deciding on the provision of services. A meeting of involved professionals and family members may be useful to agree what actions should be undertaken by whom and with what intended outcomes for the child's health and development, including the provision of therapeutic services. Whatever process is used to plan future action, the resulting plan should be informed by the core assessment findings. It should set out who will have responsibility for what actions including what course of action should be followed if the plan is not being successfully implemented. It should also include a timescale for review of progress against planned outcomes. Family Group Conferences (paragraphs 10.2–10.4) may have a role to play in fulfilling these tasks.

5.80    Local authority children's social care should take carefully any decision not to proceed to a child protection conference where it is known that a child has suffered significant harm. A suitably experienced and qualified social work manager within local authority children's social care should endorse the decision. Those professionals and agencies who are most involved with the child and family and those who have taken part in the section 47 enquiry, have the right to request that local authority children's social care convene a child protection conference if they have serious concerns that a child's welfare may not otherwise be adequately safeguarded. Any such request that is supported by a senior manager or a named or designated professional, should normally be agreed. Where there remain differences of view over the necessity for a conference in a specific case, every effort should be made to resolve them through discussion and explanation but as a last resort, LSCBs should have in place a quick and straightforward means of resolving differences of opinion.

## Concerns are substantiated and the child is judged to be continuing to, or be likely to, suffer significant harm

5.81   Where the agencies most involved judge that a child may continue to, or be likely to, suffer significant harm local authority children's social care should convene a child protection conference. The aim of the conference is to enable those professionals most involved with the child and family, and the family themselves, to assess all relevant information and plan how best to safeguard and promote the welfare of the child.

## The initial child protection conference

### Purpose

5.82   The initial child protection conference brings together family members, the child who is the subject of the conference (where appropriate) and those professionals most involved with the child and family, following section 47 enquiries. Its purpose is:

- to bring together and analyse, in an inter-agency setting, the information which has been obtained about the child's developmental needs and the parents' or carers' capacity to respond to these needs to ensure the child's safety and promote the child's health and development, within the context of their wider family and environment;

- to consider the evidence presented to the conference and taking into account the child's present situation and information about his or her family history and present and past family functioning, make judgements about the likelihood of the child suffering significant harm in future and decide whether the child is continuing to, or is likely to, suffer significant harm; and

- to decide what future action is required in order to safeguard and promote the welfare of the child, including the child becoming the subject of a child protection plan, what the planned developmental outcomes are for the child and how best to intervene to achieve these.

## Timing

5.83 The timing of an initial child protection conference will depend on the urgency of the case and on the time required to obtain relevant information about the child and family. If the conference is to reach well-informed decisions based on evidence, it should take place following adequate preparation and assessment of the child's needs and circumstances. At the same time, cases where children are continuing to, or are likely to, suffer significant harm should not be allowed to drift. Consequently, all initial child protection conferences should take place within 15 working days of the strategy discussion, or the strategy discussion at which the section 47 enquiries were initiated, if more than one has been held (see paragraph 5.57).

## Attendance

5.84 Those attending conferences should be there because they have a significant contribution to make, arising from professional expertise, knowledge of the child or family or both. The local authority social work manager should consider whether to seek advice from, or have present, a medical professional who can present the medical information in a manner which can be understood by conference attendees and enable such information to be evaluated from a sound evidence base. There should be sufficient information and expertise available – through personal representation and written reports – to enable the conference to make an informed decision about what action is necessary to safeguard and promote the welfare of the child, and to make realistic and workable proposals for taking that action forward. At the same time, a conference that is larger than it needs to be can inhibit discussion and intimidate the child and family members. Those who have a relevant contribution to make may include:

- the child, or his or her representative;

- family members (including the wider family);

- local authority children's social care staff who have led and been involved in an assessment of the child and family;

- foster carers (current or former);

- residential care staff;

- professionals involved with the child (for example, health visitors, midwife, school nurse, children's guardian, paediatrician, school staff, early years staff, the GP, NHS Direct, staff in the youth justice system including the secure estate);

- professionals involved with the parents or other family members (for example, family support services, adult services (in particular those from mental health, substance misuse, domestic violence and learning disability), probation, the GP, NHS Direct);

- professionals with expertise in the particular type of harm suffered by the child or in the child's particular condition, for example, a disability or long term illness;

- those involved in investigations (for example, the police);

- local authority legal services (child care);

- NSPCC or other involved voluntary organisations; and

- a representative of the armed services in cases where there is a service connection.

5.85    The relevant LSCB protocol should specify a required quorum for attendance and list those who should be invited to attend, provided that they have a relevant contribution to make. As a minimum, at every conference there should be attendance by local authority children's social care and at least two other professional groups or agencies who have had direct contact with the child, who is the subject of the conference. In addition, attendees may also include those whose contribution relates to their professional expertise or responsibility for relevant services. In exceptional cases, where a child has not had relevant contact with three agencies (that is, local authority children's social care and two others), this minimum quorum may be breached. Professionals and agencies who are invited to attend should make every effort to do so, but if unable to, they should submit a written report and, wherever possible, a well briefed agency representative should attend to speak to the report.

## Involving the child and family members

5.86    Before a conference is held, the purpose of a conference, who will attend and the way in which it will operate, should always be explained to a child of sufficient age and understanding, and to the parents, and involved family members. Where the child/family members do not speak English well enough to understand the discussions and express their views, an interpreter should be used. The parents (including absent parents) should normally be invited to attend the conference and helped to participate fully. Children's social care staff should give parents information about local advice and advocacy agencies and explain that they may bring an advocate, friend or supporter. The child, subject to consideration about age and understanding, should be invited to attend and to bring an advocate, friend or supporter if s/he wishes. Where the child's attendance is neither desired by him/her nor appropriate, the local authority children's social care professional who is working most closely with the child should ascertain what his/her wishes and feelings are and make these known to the conference.

5.87    The involvement of family members should be planned carefully. It may not always be possible to involve all family members at all times in the conference, for example, if one parent is the alleged abuser or if there is a high level of conflict between family members. Adults and any children who wish to make representations to the conference may not wish to speak in front of one another. Exceptionally, it may be necessary to exclude one or more family members from a conference, in whole or in part. The conference is primarily about the child and while the presence of the family is normally welcome, those professionals attending must be able to share information in a safe and non-threatening environment. Professionals may themselves have concerns about violence or intimidation, which should be communicated in advance to the conference chair.

5.88    LSCB procedures should set out criteria for excluding a parent or caregiver, including the evidence required. A strong risk of violence or intimidation by a family member at or subsequent to the conference, towards a child or anybody else, might be one reason for exclusion. The possibility that a parent/caregiver may be prosecuted for an offence against a child is not in itself a reason for exclusion although in these circumstances the chair should take advice from the police about any implications arising from an alleged perpetrator's attendance. If criminal proceedings have been instigated the view of the Crown Prosecution Service (CPS) should be taken into account. The decision to exclude a parent or caregiver from the child protection conference rests with the chair of the conference, acting within LSCB procedures. If the parents are excluded, or are unable or unwilling to attend a child protection conference, they should be enabled to communicate their views to the conference by another means.

## Chairing the conference

5.89    A professional who is independent of operational or line management responsibilities for the case should chair the conference[92]. The conference chair is accountable to the Director of Children's Services. The status of the chair should be sufficient to ensure inter-agency commitment to the conference and the child protection plan. Wherever possible, the same person should also chair subsequent child protection reviews in respect of a specific child. The responsibilities of the chair include:

- meeting the child and family members in advance, to ensure that they understand the purpose of the conference and what will happen;

---

92    In addition to this guidance *Putting Care into Practice,* the statutory guidance which accompanies the Care Planning, Placement and Case Review (England) Regulations 2010, sets out the expectations of the Independent Reviewing Officer (IRO) in relation to chairing the child protection review conference as part of the overarching review of the looked after child's case.

- setting out the purpose of the conference to all present, determining the agenda and emphasising the confidential nature of the occasion;

- enabling all those present, and absent contributors, to make their full contribution to discussion and decision-making;

- ensuring that the conference takes the decisions required of it in an informed, systematic and explicit way; and

- being accountable to the Director of Children's Services for the conduct of conferences.

5.90   A conference chair should be trained in the role and should have:

- a good understanding and professional knowledge of children's welfare and development, and best practice in working with children and families;

- the ability to look at objectively and assess the implications of the evidence on which judgements should be based;

- skills in chairing meetings in a way which encourages constructive participation, while maintaining a clear focus on the welfare of the child and the decisions which have to be taken;

- knowledge and understanding of anti-discriminatory practice; and

- knowledge of relevant legislation, including that relating to children's services and human rights.

## Information for the conference

5.91   Local authority children's social care should provide the conference with a written report that summarises and analyses the information obtained in the course of the initial assessment and the core assessment undertaken under section 47 of the Children Act 1989 (in as far as it has been completed within the available time period), and information in existing records relating to the child and family. Where decisions are being made about more than one child in a family there should be a report prepared on each child. The information in the report for a child protection conference, which is be likely to be in the current core assessment record, should be consistent with the information which is set out in the Initial Child Protection Conference Report (Department of Health, 2002). The conference report should include information on the dates the child was seen by the lead social worker during the course of the section 47 enquiries, if the child was seen alone and if not, who was present and for what reasons. The core assessment is the means by which a section 47 enquiry is carried out. Although a core assessment will have been commenced, it is unlikely it will have been completed in time for the conference given the 35 working day period that such assessments can take.

5.92    The child protection conference report should include:

- a chronology of significant events and agency and professional contact with the child and family;

- information on the child's current and past state of developmental needs;

- information on the capacity of the parents and other family members to ensure the child is safe from harm, and to respond to the child's developmental needs, within their wider family and environmental context;

- information on the family history and both the current and past family functioning;

- the expressed wishes and feelings of the child, and the views of parents and other family members;

- an analysis of the information gathered and recorded using the Assessment Framework dimensions to reach a judgement on whether the child is suffering, or likely to suffer, significant harm and consider how best to meet his or her developmental needs. This analysis should address:

  - how the child's strengths and difficulties are impacting on each other;

  - how the parenting strengths and difficulties are affecting each other;

  - how the family and environmental factors are affecting each other;

  - how the parenting that is provided for the child is affecting the child's health and development both in terms of resilience and protective factors, and vulnerability and risk factors; and

  - how the family and environmental factors are impacting on parenting and/or the child directly; and

- the local authority's recommendation to the conference.

5.93    Where appropriate, the parents and subject child should be provided with a copy of the report in advance of the conference. The contents of the report should be explained and discussed with the child and relevant family members in advance of the conference itself, in the preferred language(s) of the child and family members.

5.94    Other professionals attending the conference should bring with them details of their involvement with the child and family, and information concerning their knowledge of the child's developmental needs, capacity of the parents to meet the needs of their child within their family and environmental context. This information should include careful consideration of the impact that the current and past family functioning and family history are having on the parents' capacities to met the child's needs. Contributors should, wherever possible, provide a written report in advance to the conference and these should be made available to those attending.

5.95   The child and family members should be helped in advance to think about what they want to convey to the conference and how best to get their points across on the day. Some may find it helpful to provide their own written report, which they may be assisted to prepare by their adviser/advocate.

5.96   Those providing information should take care to distinguish between fact, observation, allegation and opinion. When information is provided from another source, i.e. it is second or third hand, this should be made clear.

## Action and decisions for the conference

5.97   The conference should consider the following questions when determining whether the child should be the subject of a child protection plan:

- has the child suffered significant harm? and

- is the child likely to suffer significant harm in the future?

5.98   The test for likelihood of suffering harm in the future should be that either:

- the child can be shown to have suffered ill-treatment or impairment of health or development as a result of physical, emotional, or sexual abuse or neglect, and professional judgement is that further ill-treatment or impairment are likely; or

- professional judgement, substantiated by the findings of enquiries in this individual case or by research evidence, is that the child is likely to suffer ill-treatment or the impairment of health or development as a result of physical, emotional, or sexual abuse or neglect.

5.99   If the child protection conference decides that the child is likely to suffer significant harm in the future, the child will therefore require inter-agency help and intervention to be delivered through a formal child protection plan. The primary purposes of this plan are to prevent the child suffering harm or a recurrence of harm in the future and to promote the child's welfare.

5.100  Child protection conference participants should base their judgements on all the available evidence obtained through existing records, the initial assessment and the in-depth core assessment undertaken following the initiation of section 47 enquiries, and any other relevant specialist assessments. The method of reaching a decision within the conference on whether the child should be the subject of a child protection plan should be set out in the relevant LSCB protocol. The decision making process should be based on the views of all agencies represented at the conference and also take into account any written contributions that have been made.

5.101 If the conference decided that the child is in need of a child protection plan, the chair should determine which category of abuse or neglect the child has suffered or is likely to suffer. The category used (that is physical, emotional, sexual abuse or neglect) will indicate to those consulting the child's social care record the primary presenting concerns at the time the child became the subject of a child protection plan.

5.102 It is the role of the initial child protection conference to formulate the outline child protection plan in as much detail as possible. The decision of the conference and, where appropriate, details of the category of abuse or neglect, the name of the lead social worker (i.e. the social worker who is the lead professional for the case) and the core group membership should be recorded in a manner that is consistent with the Initial Child Protection Conference Report (Department of Health, 2002) and circulated to all those invited to the conference within one working day.

5.103 Where a child has suffered, or is likely to suffer, significant harm in the future it is the local authority's duty to consider the evidence and decide what, if any, legal action to take. The information presented to the child protection conference should inform that decision making process but it is for the local authority to consider whether it should initiate, for example, care proceedings. In some situations the child may become accommodated and acquire looked after child status. Where a child who is the subject of a child protection plan becomes looked after by the local authority, the child protection plan should form part of the looked after child's overarching care plan (see paragraphs 5.144–5.148).

5.104 A decision may have been made that a child does not require a child protection plan but he or she may nonetheless require services to promote his or her health or development. In these circumstances, the conference together with the family should consider the child's needs and what further help would assist the family in responding to them. Subject to the family's views and consent, it may be appropriate to continue and to complete the core assessment to help determine what support might best help promote the child's welfare. Where the child's needs are complex, inter-agency working will continue to be important. Where appropriate, a child in need plan should be drawn up and reviewed at regular intervals – no less frequent than every six months (see paragraphs 4.33 and 4.36 of the *Framework for the Assessment of Children in Need and their Families*).

5.105  Where a child is to be the subject of a child protection plan it is the responsibility of the conference to consider and make recommendations on how agencies, professionals and the family should work together to ensure that the child will be safeguarded from harm in the future. This should enable both professionals and the family to understand exactly what is expected of them and what they can expect of others. Specific tasks include the following:

- appointing the lead statutory body (either local authority children's social care or the NSPCC) and a lead social worker (who is the lead professional), who should be a qualified, experienced social worker and an employee of the lead statutory body;

- identifying the membership of a core group of professionals and family members who will develop and implement the child protection plan as a detailed working tool;

- establishing how the child, their parents (including all those with parental responsibility) and wider family members should be involved in the ongoing assessment, planning and implementation process, and the support, advice and advocacy available to them;

- establishing timescales for meetings of the core group, production of a child protection plan, and for child protection review meetings;

- identifying in outline what further action is required to complete the core assessment and what other specialist assessments of the child and family are required to make sound judgements on how best to safeguard and promote the welfare of the child;

- outlining the child protection plan, especially, identifying what needs to change in order to achieve the planned outcomes to safeguard and promote the welfare of the child;

- ensuring a contingency plan is in place if agreed actions are not completed and/ or circumstances change, for example, if a caregiver fails to achieve what has been agreed, a court application is not successful or a parent removes the child from a place of safety;

- clarifying the different purposes and remit of the initial conference the core group, and the child protection review conference; and

- agreeing a date for the first child protection review conference and under what circumstances it might be necessary to convene the conference before that date.

5.106 The outline child protection plan should:

- identify factors associated with the likelihood of the child suffering significant harm and ways in which the child can be protected from harm through an inter-agency plan based on the current findings from the assessment, including information held by agencies on any previous involvement with the child and family;

- establish short-term and longer-term aims and objectives that are clearly linked to preventing the child suffering harm or a recurrence of the harm suffered, meeting the child's developmental needs and promoting the child's welfare, including contact with family members;

- be clear about who will have responsibility for what actions – including actions by family members – within what specified timescales;

- outline ways of monitoring and evaluating progress against the planned outcomes set out in the plan; and

- be clear about which professional is responsible for checking that the required changes have taken place and what action will be taken, by whom, and when they have not.

## Complaints about a child protection conference

5.107 Parents/caregivers and, on occasion children, may have concerns about which they may wish to make representations or complain, in respect of one or more of the following aspects of the functioning of child protection conferences:

- the process of the conference;

- the outcome, in terms of the fact of and/or the category of primary concern at the time the child became the subject of a child protection plan; and/or

- a decision for the child to become, or not to become, the subject of a child protection plan or not to cease the child being the subject of a child protection plan.

5.108 Complaints about individual agencies, their performance and provision (or non-provision) of services should be responded to in accordance with the relevant agency's complaints handling process. For example, local authority children's social care are required (by section 26 of the Children Act 1989) to establish complaints procedures to deal with complaints arising in respect of Part III of the Act.

5.109 Complaints about aspects of the functioning of conferences described above should be addressed to the conference chair. Such complaints should be passed on to local authority children's social care, which, since they relate to Part V of the

Children Act 1989, should be responded to in accordance with the Complaints Directions 1990[93]. (This section will be updated when regulations on the revision of Local Authority Complaints Procedures under the Children Act 1989 are revised). In considering and responding to complaints, the local authority should form an inter-agency panel made up of senior representatives from LSCB member agencies. The panel should consider whether the relevant inter-agency protocols and procedures have been observed correctly and whether the decision that is being complained about follows reasonably from the proper observation of the protocol(s).

5.110   In addition, representations and complaints may be received by individual agencies in respect of services provided (or not provided) as a consequence of assessments and conferences, including those set out in child protection plans. Such concerns should be responded to by the relevant agency in accordance with its own processes for responding to such matters.

## Administrative arrangements and record keeping

5.111   Those attending should be notified of conferences as far in advance as possible, and the conference should be held at a time and place likely to be convenient to as many people as possible. All child protection conferences, both initial and review, should have a dedicated administrative person to take notes and produce a record of the meeting. The record of the conference is a crucial working document for all relevant professionals and the family. It should include:

- the essential facts of the case;

- a summary of discussion at the conference, which accurately reflects contributions made;

- all decisions reached, with information outlining the reasons for decisions; and

- a translation of decisions into an outline or revised child protection plan enabling everyone to be clear about their tasks.

5.112   A copy should be sent as soon as possible after the conference to all those who attended or were invited to attend, including family members, except for any part of the conference from which they were excluded. This is in addition to sharing the main decisions within one working day of the conference (see paragraph 5.102). The record is confidential and should not be passed by professionals to third parties without the consent of either the conference chair or the lead social worker. However, in cases of criminal proceedings, the police may reveal the existence of the notes to the CPS in accordance with the Criminal Procedure and Investigation

---

93   The Directions are based on section 7B of the Local Authority Social Services Act 1970, inserted by section 50 of the National Health Service and Community Care Act 1990.

Act 1996. The record of the decisions of the child protection conference should be retained by the recipient agencies and professionals in accordance with their record retention policies.

## Action following the initial child protection conference

### The role of the lead social worker

5.113 When a conference decides that a child should be the subject of a child protection plan, one of the child care agencies with statutory powers (local authority children's social care or the NSPCC) should carry statutory responsibility for the child's welfare and designate a qualified and experienced member of its social work staff to be the lead social worker, i.e. the lead professional. Each child who is the subject of a child protection plan should have a named lead social worker.

5.114 The lead social worker is responsible for making sure that the outline child protection plan is developed into a more detailed inter-agency plan. S/he should complete the core assessment of the child and family, securing contributions from core group members and others as necessary. The lead social worker is also responsible for acting as the lead professional for the inter-agency work with the child and family. S/he should co-ordinate the contribution of family members and other agencies to planning the actions which need to be taken, putting the child protection plan into effect and reviewing progress against the planned outcomes set out in the plan. It is important that the role of the lead social worker is fully explained at the initial child protection conference and at the core group.

5.115 The lead social worker should see the child, alone when appropriate, in accordance with the plan. She or he should develop a therapeutic relationship with the child, regularly ascertain the child's wishes and feelings and keep the child up to date with the child protection plan and any developments or changes. The lead social worker should record in the child's local authority social care record when the child was seen and who else, if anyone, was present at the time of each visit and also the reasons for deciding (or not) to see the child alone.

### The core group

5.116 The core group is responsible for developing the child protection plan as a detailed working tool and implementing it within the outline plan agreed at the initial child protection conference. Membership should include the lead social worker, who chairs the core group, the child if appropriate, family members and professionals or foster carers who will have direct contact with the family. Although the lead social worker has lead responsibility for the formulation and implementation of the child protection plan, all members of the core group are jointly responsible for carrying out these tasks, refining the plan as needed and monitoring progress against the planned outcomes set out in the plan. Agencies should ensure that members of the core group undertake their roles and responsibilities effectively in accordance with the agreed child protection plan.

5.117   Core groups are an important forum for working with parents, wider family members and children of sufficient age and understanding. It can often be difficult for parents to accept the need for a child protection plan within the confines of a formal conference. Their co-operation may be gained later when details of the plan are worked out in the core group. Sometimes there may be conflicts of interest between family members who have a relevant interest in the work of the core group. The child's best interests should always take precedence over the interests of other family members.

5.118   The first meeting of the core group should take place within 10 working days of the initial child protection conference. The purpose of this first meeting is to flesh out the child protection plan. The meeting should also decide what steps need to be taken, by whom, to complete the core assessment on time so that future decisions and the provision of services can be fully informed when making decisions about the child's safety and welfare. Thereafter, core groups should meet sufficiently regularly to facilitate working together, monitor actions and outcomes against the child protection plan, and make any necessary alterations as circumstances change.

5.119   The lead social worker should ensure that there is a record of the decisions taken and actions agreed at core group meetings, as well as of the written views of those who were not able to attend. The child protection plan should be updated as necessary.

## Completion of the core assessment

5.120   Completion of the core assessment, within 35 working days, should include an analysis of the child's developmental needs and the parents' capacity to respond to those needs within the context of their family and environment. This analysis should include an understanding of the parents' capacity to ensure that the child is safe from harm. It should include consideration of the information gathered about the family's history and their present and past family functioning. It may be necessary to commission specialist assessments (for example, from child and adolescent mental health services, adult mental health or substance misuse services, or a specialist in domestic violence) which it may not be possible to complete within this time period. This should not delay the drawing together of the core assessment findings at this point. A core assessment is deemed complete once the assessment has been discussed with the child and family (or caregivers) and the team manager has viewed and authorised the assessment.

5.121 The analysis of the child's needs and the capacity of the child's parents or caregivers to meet these needs within their family and environment should provide evidence on which to base judgements and decisions on how best to safeguard and promote the welfare of a child and where possible to support parents in achieving this aim. Decisions based on this analysis should consider what the child's future will be like if his or her met needs continue to be met, and if his or her unmet needs continue to be unmet. The key questions are, what is likely to happen if nothing changes in the child's current situation? What are the likely consequences for the child? The answers to these questions should be used to decide what interventions are required when developing the child protection plan and, in particular, in considering what actions are necessary to prevent the child from suffering harm or to prevent a recurrence of the abuse or neglect suffered.

## The child protection plan

5.122 The initial child protection conference is responsible for agreeing an outline child protection plan. Professionals and parents/caregivers should develop the details of the plan in the core group. The overall aim of the plan is to:

- ensure the child is safe from harm and prevent him or her from suffering further harm by supporting the strengths, addressing the vulnerabilities and risk factors and helping meet the child's unmet needs;

- promote the child's health and development, i.e. his or her welfare; and

- provided it is in the best interests of the child, to support the family and wider family members to safeguard and promote the welfare of their child.

5.123 The child protection plan should be based on the findings from the assessment, following the dimensions relating to the child's developmental needs, parenting capacity and family and environmental factors, and drawing on knowledge about effective interventions. Where the child is also the subject of a care plan, the child protection plan should be part of the looked after child's care plan (see paragraph 5.103). The content of the child protection plans should be consistent with the information set out in the Child Protection Plan record (Department of Health, 2002). It should set out what work needs to be done, why, when and by whom. The plan should:

- describe the identified developmental needs of the child and what therapeutic services are required to meet these needs;

- include specific, achievable, child-focused outcomes intended to safeguard and promote the welfare of the child;

- include realistic strategies and specific actions to bring about the changes necessary to achieve the planned outcomes;

- set out when and in what situations the child will be seen by the lead social worker, both alone and with other family members or caregivers present;

- clearly identify and set out roles and responsibilities of family members and professionals including those with routine contact with the child (for example, health visitors, GPs and teachers) and the nature and frequency of contact by these professionals with the child and family members;

- include a contingency plan to be followed if circumstances change significantly and require prompt action (including initiating family court proceedings to safeguard and promote the child's welfare); and

- lay down points at which progress will be reviewed and the means by which progress will be judged.

5.124  The child protection plan should take into account the wishes and feelings of the child, and the views of the parents, insofar as they are consistent with the child's welfare. The lead social worker should make every effort to ensure that the child and parents have a clear understanding of the planned outcomes; that they accept the plan and are willing to work to it. If the parents are not willing to co-operate in the implementation of the plan the local authority should consider what action, including the initiation of family proceedings, it should take to safeguard the child's welfare.

5.125  The plan should be constructed with the family in their preferred language and they should receive a written copy in this language. If family members' preferences are not accepted about how best to safeguard and promote the welfare of the child, the reasons for this should be explained. Families should be told about their right to complain and make representations, and how to do so.

## Agreeing the plan with the child

5.126  The child protection plan should be explained to and agreed with the child in a manner which is in accordance with their age and understanding. An interpreter should be used if the child's level of English means that s/he is not able to participate fully in these discussions unless they are conducted in her/his own language. The child should be given a copy of the plan written at a level appropriate to his or her age and understanding, and in his or her preferred language.

### Negotiating the plan with parents

5.127 Parents should be clear about the evidence of significant harm which resulted in the child becoming the subject of a child protection plan, what needs to change and about what is expected of them as part of implementing the plan for safeguarding and promoting their child's welfare. All parties should be clear about the respective roles and responsibilities of family members and different agencies in implementing the plan. The parents should receive a written copy of the plan so that they are clear about who is doing what when and the planned outcomes for the child.

## Intervention

5.128 Decisions about how to intervene, including what services to offer, should be based on evidence about what is likely to work best to bring about good outcomes for the child[94]. A number of aspects of intervention should be considered in the context of the child protection plan, in the light of evidence from the assessment of the child's developmental needs, the parents' capacity to respond appropriately to the child's needs and the wider family and environmental circumstances. Particular attention should be given to family history (for example, of domestic and other forms of violence, childhood abuse, mental illness, substance misuse and/or learning disability) and present and past family functioning.

5.129 The following questions need to be considered:

- What are the options for interventions which might help support strengths and/ or help meet the child's identified unmet needs as well as addressing the known vulnerabilities and risk factors?

- What resources are available?

- With which agency or professional and with which approach is the family most likely to co-operate?

- Which intervention is most likely to produce the most immediate benefit and which might take time?

- What should be the sequence of interventions and why?

- Given the severity of any ill-treatment suffered or impairment to the child's health or development, the child's current needs and the capacity of the family to co-operate, what is the likelihood of achieving sufficient change within the child's time frame?

---

94    For further information from research findings on effective interventions see www.dcsf.gov.uk/nsdu/research.shtml

5.130   It is important that services are provided to give the child and family the best chance of achieving the required changes. If a child cannot be cared for safely by his or her caregiver(s) she or he will have to be placed elsewhere whilst work is being undertaken with the child and family. Irrespective of where the child is living, interventions should specifically address:

- the developmental needs of the child;

- the child's understanding of what has happened to him or her;

- the abusing caregiver/child relationship and parental capacity to respond to the child's needs;

- the relationship between the adult caregivers both as adults and parents;

- family relationships; and

- possible changes to the family's social and environmental circumstances.

5.131   Intervention may have a number of inter-related components:

- action to make a child safe from harm and prevent recurrence from harm;

- action to help promote a child's health and development, i.e. welfare;

- action to help a parent(s)/caregiver(s) in safeguarding a child and promoting his or her welfare;

- therapy for an abused or neglected child; and

- support or therapy for a perpetrator of abuse or neglect to prevent future harm to the child and where necessary to other children.

5.132   The development of secure parent–child attachments is critical to a child's healthy development. The quality and nature of the attachment will be a key issue to be considered in decision making, especially if decisions are being made about moving a child from one setting to another, re-uniting a child with his or her birth family or considering a permanent placement away from the child's family. If the plan is to assess whether the child can be reunited with the caregiver(s) responsible for the maltreatment, very detailed work will be required to help the caregiver(s) develop the necessary parenting skills.

5.133   A key issue in deciding on suitable interventions will be whether the child's developmental needs can be responded to within his or her family context and **within timescales that are appropriate for the child**. These timescales may not be compatible with those for the caregiver(s) who is/are in receipt of therapeutic help. The process of decision making and planning should be as open as possible, from an ethical as well as practical point of view. Where the family situation is not improving or changing fast enough to respond to the child's needs, decisions will be necessary about the long-term future of the child. In the longer term it may mean it will be in the best interests of the child to be placed in an alternative family context. Key to these considerations is what is in the child's best interests, informed by the child's wishes and feelings and by the parents' capacity to make the required changes.

5.134 Children who have suffered significant harm may continue to experience the consequences of this abuse irrespective of where they are living, whether remaining with or being reunited with their families or alternatively being placed in new families; this relates particularly to their behavioural and emotional development. Therapeutic work with the child should continue, irrespective of where the child is placed, as long as is required in order for their needs to be met.

5.135 More information to assist with making decisions about interventions is available in the Chapter 4 of the *Assessment Framework* and the accompanying practice guidance (Department of Health, 2000). Recent research evidence on effective interventions in safeguarding children has been published by DCSF and DH[95].

## The child protection review conference

### Timescale

5.136 The first child protection review conference should be held within three months of the initial child protection conference and further reviews should be held at intervals of not more than six months for as long as the child remains the subject of a child protection plan. Where the child is also looked after, the child protection review should be part of the looked after child review (see paragraphs 5.144–5.148). It is important to ensure that momentum is maintained in the process of safeguarding and promoting the welfare of the child. Where necessary, reviews should be brought forward to address changes in the child's circumstances. Attendees should include those most involved with the child and family in the same way as at an initial child protection conference, and the LSCB protocols for establishing a quorum should apply.

### Purpose

5.137 The purposes of the child protection review are to:

- review whether the child is continuing to suffer, or is likely to suffer, significant harm and their health and developmental progress against planned outcomes set out in the child protection plan;

---

- ensure that the child continues to be safeguarded from harm; and

- consider whether the child protection plan should continue or should be changed.

5.138 The reviewing of the child's progress and the effectiveness of interventions are critical to achieving the best possible outcomes for the child. The child's wishes and feelings should be sought and taken into account during the reviewing process. Every review should consider explicitly whether the child is suffering, or is likely to suffer, significant harm and hence continues to require safeguarding from harm through adherence to a formal child protection plan. If not, then the child should no longer be the subject of a child protection plan. If the child is considered to be suffering significant harm, the local authority should consider whether to initiate family court proceedings. For further guidance see Volume 1 of the Children Act 1989 Guidance and Regulations, Court Orders [96].

5.139 The same LSCB decision-making procedure should be used to reach a judgement on continuing to have a child protection plan as is used at the initial child protection conference. As with initial child protection conferences, the relevant LSCB protocol should specify a required quorum for attendance at review conferences. As a minimum, at every review conference there should be attendance by local authority children's social care and at least two other professional groups or agencies, which have had direct contact with the child who is the subject of the conference. In addition, attendees may also include those whose contribution relates to their professional expertise or responsibility for relevant services. In exceptional cases, where a child has not had relevant contact with three agencies (that is, local authority children's social care and two others), this minimum quorum may be breached.

5.140 The review requires as much preparation, commitment and management as the initial child protection conference. Each member of the core group has a responsibility to produce an individual agency report on the child and family for the child protection review. Together, these reports provide an overview of work undertaken by family members and professionals, and evaluate the impact of the interventions on the child's welfare against the planned outcomes set out in the child protection plan. Those unable to attend should send their report to the lead social worker prior to the core group meeting and where possible, delegate attendance to a well briefed colleague. The content of the report to the review child protection conference should be consistent with the information set out in the Child Protection Review (Department of Health, 2002).

---

## Discontinuing the child protection plan

5.141  A child should no longer be the subject of a child protection plan if:

- it is judged that the child is no longer continuing to, or be likely to, suffer significant harm and therefore require safeguarding by means of a child protection plan (for example, the likelihood of harm has been reduced by action taken through the child protection plan; the child and family's circumstances have changed; or re-assessment of the child and family indicates that a child protection plan is not necessary). Under these circumstances, only a child protection review conference can decide that a child protection plan is no longer necessary;

- the child and family have moved permanently to another local authority area. In such cases, the receiving local authority should convene a child protection conference within 15 working days of being notified of the move, only after which event may discontinuing the child protection plan take place in respect of the original local authority's child protection plan; or

- the child has reached 18 years of age (to end the child protection plan, the local authority should have a review around the child's birthday and this should be planned in advance), has died or has permanently left the UK.

5.142  When a child is no longer the subject of a child protection plan notification should be sent, at a minimum, to all those agency representatives who were invited to attend the initial child protection conference that led to the plan.

5.143  A child who is no longer the subject of a child protection plan may still require additional support and services. Discontinuing the child protection plan should never lead to the automatic withdrawal of help. The key worker should discuss with the parents and the child what services might be wanted and required, based upon the re-assessment of the needs of the child and family.

## Children looked after by the local authority

5.144  In most cases where a child who is the subject of a child protection plan becomes looked after it will no longer be necessary to maintain the child protection plan. There are however a relatively few cases where safeguarding issues will remain and a looked after child should also have a child protection plan. These cases are likely to be where a local authority obtains an interim care order in family proceedings but the child or young person who is the subject of a child protection plan remains at home, pending the outcome of the final hearing or where a young person's behaviour is likely to result in significant harm to themselves or others.

5.145   Where a looked after child remains the subject of a child protection plan it is expected that there will be a single planning and reviewing process, led by the Independent Reviewing Officer (IRO), which meets the requirements of both this guidance and the Care Planning, Placement and Case Review (England) Regulations 2010 and accompanying statutory guidance *Putting Care into Practice*.

5.146   The systems and processes for reviewing child protection plans and plans for looked after children should be carefully evaluated by the local authority and consideration given to how best to ensure the child protection aspects of the care plan are reviewed as part of the overall reviewing process leading to the development of a single plan. Given that a review is a process and not a single meeting, both reviewing systems should be aligned in an unbureaucratic way to enable the full range of the child's or young person's needs to be considered in the looked after child's care planning and reviewing processes.

5.147   It is recognised that there are different requirements for independence of the IRO function compared to the chair of the child protection conference. In addition, it is important to note that the child protection conference is required to be a multi-agency forum while children for the most part want as few external people as possible at a review meeting where they are present. However, it will not be possible for the IRO to carry out his or her statutory function without considering the child's safety in the context of the care planning process. In this context consideration should be given to the IRO chairing the child protection conference where a looked after child remains the subject of a child protection plan. Where this is not possible it will be expected that the IRO will attend the child protection review conference.

5.148   This means that the timing of the review of the child protection aspects of the care plan should be the same as the review under the Care Planning, Placement and Case Review (England) Regulations 2010, to ensure that up to date information in relation to the child's welfare and safety is considered within the review meeting and informs the overall care planning process. The looked after child's review when reviewing the child protection aspects of the plan should also consider whether the criteria continue to be met for the child to remain the subject of a child protection plan. Significant changes to the care plan should only be made following the looked after child's review.

## Pre-birth child protection conferences and reviews

5.149   Where a core assessment under section 47 of the Children Act 1989 gives rise to concerns that an unborn child may be likely to suffer significant harm local authority children's social care may decide to convene an initial child protection conference prior to the child's birth. Such a conference should have the same status, and proceed in the same way, as other initial child protection conferences, including decisions about a child protection plan. Similarly in respect of child protection review conferences. The involvement of midwifery services is vital in such cases.

## Recording that a child is the subject of a child protection plan

5.150    Local authority children's social care IT systems should be capable of recording in the child's case record when the child is the subject of a child protection plan, including where the child is also looked after by the local authority. A key purpose of having the IT capacity to record that a child is the subject of a child protection plan is to enable agencies and professionals, when appropriate, to be aware that these children are the subject of a child protection plan. It is equally important that agencies and professionals can obtain relevant information about any child in need who is known or has been known to the local authority. Consequently, agencies and professionals who have concerns about a child's safety and welfare should be able to obtain information about a child that is recorded on the local authority's ICS IT system[97]. It is essential that legitimate enquirers such as police and health professionals are able to obtain this information both in and outside office hours.

5.151    Children should be recorded as having been, or being likely to be abused or neglected under one or more of the categories of physical, emotional, or sexual abuse or neglect, according to a decision by the chair of the child protection conference. These categories help indicate the nature of the current concerns. Recording information in this way also allows for the collation and analysis of information locally and nationally and for its use in planning the provision of services. The categories selected should reflect all the information obtained in the course of the initial assessment and core assessment under section 47 or the Children Act 1989 and subsequent analysis, and should not just relate to one or more abusive incidents. The initial category may change as new information becomes available during the time that the child is the subject of a child protection plan.

## Managing and providing information about a child

5.152    Each local authority should designate a manager, normally an experienced social worker, who has responsibility for:

- ensuring that each local authority record on a child who has a child protection plan is kept up to date;

- ensuring enquiries about children about whom there are concerns or who have child protection plans are recorded and considered in accordance with paragraph 5.150;

- managing other notifications of movements of children into or out of the local authority area, such as children who have a child protection plan and looked after children;

- managing notifications of people who may pose a risk of significant harm to children who are either identified with the local authority area or have moved into the local authority area; and

- managing requests for checks to be made to ensure unsuitable people are prevented from working with children.

This manager should be accountable to the Director of Children's Services.

5.153   The child's individual case file should provide a record of information known to local authority children's social care about that child and therefore it should be kept up-to-date on the local authority's ICS IT system. The content of the child's record should be confidential, available only to legitimate enquirers. This information should be accessible at all times to such enquirers. The details of enquirers should always be checked and recorded on the system before information is provided.

5.154   If an enquiry is made about a child and the child's case is open to local authority children's social care, the enquirer should be given the name of the child's lead social worker and the lead social worker informed of this enquiry so that they can follow it up. If an enquiry is made about a child at the same address as a child who is the subject of a child protection plan, this information should be sent to the lead social worker of the child who is the subject of the child protection plan. If an enquiry is made but the child is not known to local authority children's social care, this enquiry should be recorded on a contact record together with the advice given to the enquirer. In the event of there being a second enquiry about a child who is not known to children's social care, not only should the fact of the earlier enquiry be notified to the later enquirer but the designated manager should ensure that local authority children's social care consider whether this is or may be a child in need.

5.155   The Department for Children, Schools and Families holds lists of the names of designated managers and should be notified of any changes in designated managers.

## Recording in individual case records

5.156 Keeping a good quality record about work with a child in need and his or her family is an important part of the accountability of all professionals to those who use their services. It helps to focus work and it is essential to working effectively across agency and professional boundaries. Clear and accurate records for each child ensure that there is a documented account of an agency's or professional's involvement with the child and/or his or her family or caregiver. They help with continuity when individual workers are unavailable or change and they provide an essential tool for managers to monitor work or for peer review. The child or adult's record is an essential source of evidence for investigations and inquiries, and may also be required to be disclosed in court proceedings. Where a child has been the subject of a section 47 enquiry which did not result in the substantiation of referral concerns, his or her record should be retained in accordance with agency retention policies. These policies should ensure that records are stored safely and can be retrieved promptly and efficiently.

5.157 To serve these purposes, records relating to work with the child and his or her family should use clear, straightforward language, be concise and be accurate not only in fact, but also in differentiating between opinion, judgement and hypothesis.

5.158 Well kept records about work with a child and his or her family provide an essential underpinning to good professional practice. Safeguarding and promoting the welfare of children requires information to be brought together from a number of sources and careful professional judgements to be made on the basis of this information. These records should be clear, accessible and comprehensive, with judgements made and decisions and interventions carefully recorded. Where decisions have been taken jointly across agencies, or endorsed by a manager, this should be made clear.

5.159 The records (Department of Health, 2002) produced to support the implementation of the Integrated Children's System contain the information requirements for local authority children's social care together with others when recording information about work with an individual child in need and his or her family. The appropriate type of record to use at different stages of the process of working with a child and his or her family has been referenced throughout this chapter.

5.160 The GP should retain child protection initial conference and review reports as part of the child's health record, where practicable. Ultimately, it is down to the individual GP, depending on their type of health recording system, to make the best judgement on how to incorporate this information into the child's health record.

## Request for a change of worker

5.161   Occasions may arise where relationships between parents, or other family members, are not productive in terms of working to safeguard and promote the welfare of their children. In such instances, agencies should respond sympathetically to a request for a change of worker, provided that such a change can be identified as being in the interests of the child who is the focus of concern.

# Flow chart 1: Referral

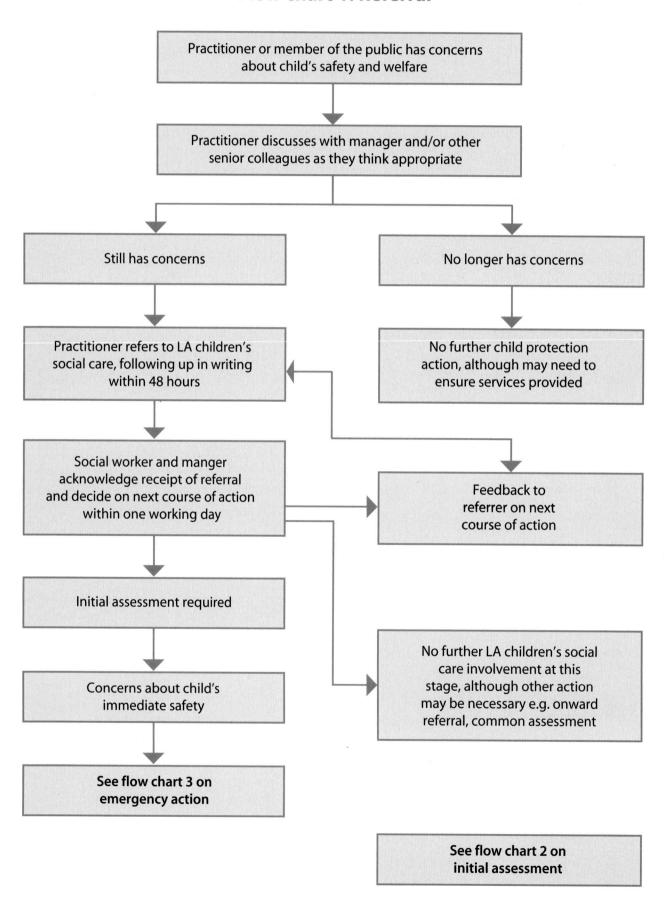

## Flow chart 2: What happens following initial assessment?

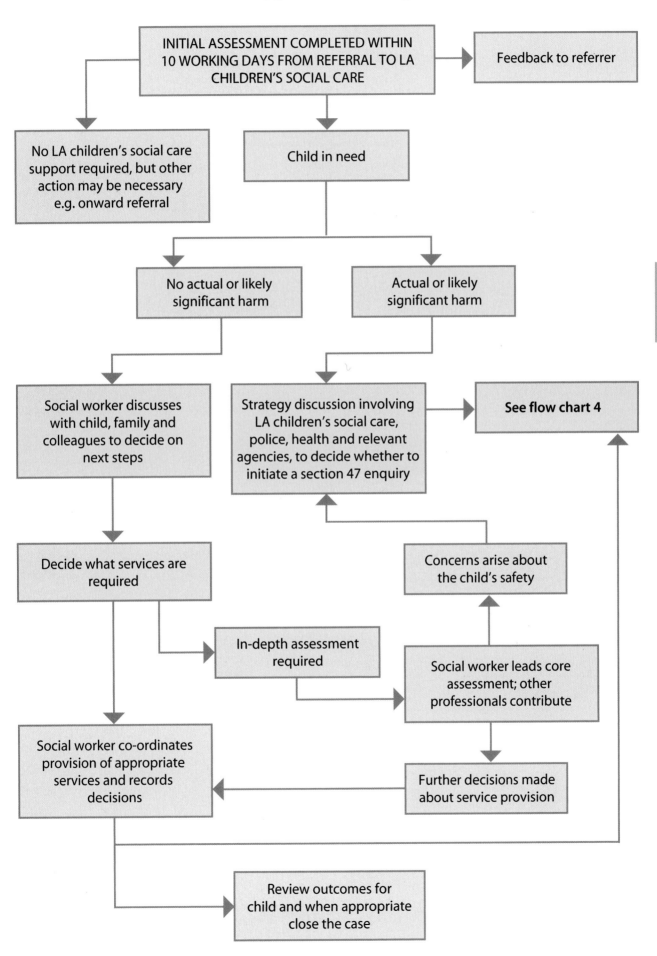

## Flow chart 3: Urgent action to safeguard children

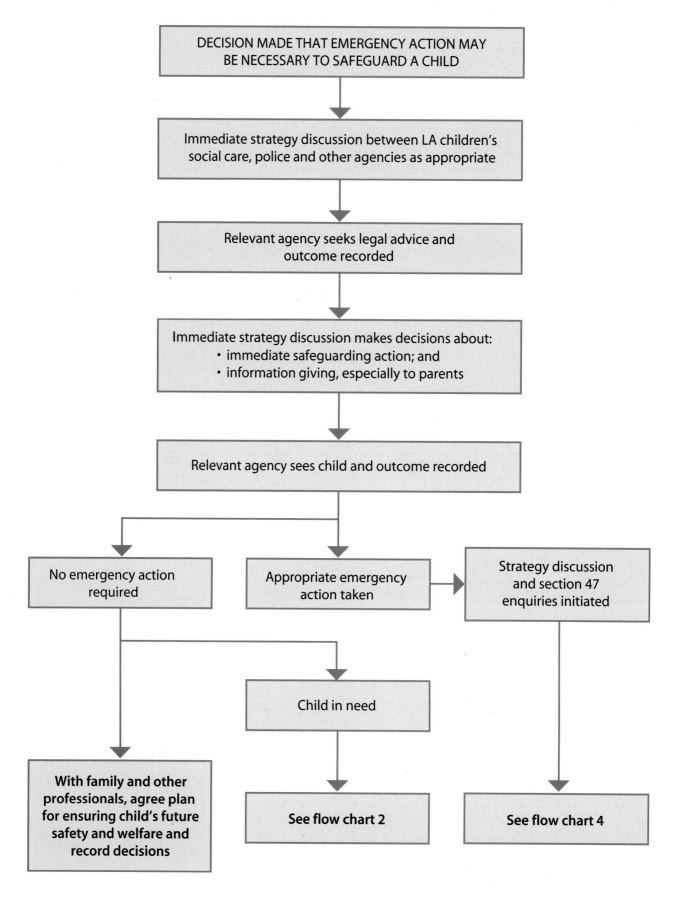

## Flow chart 4: What happens after the strategy discussion?

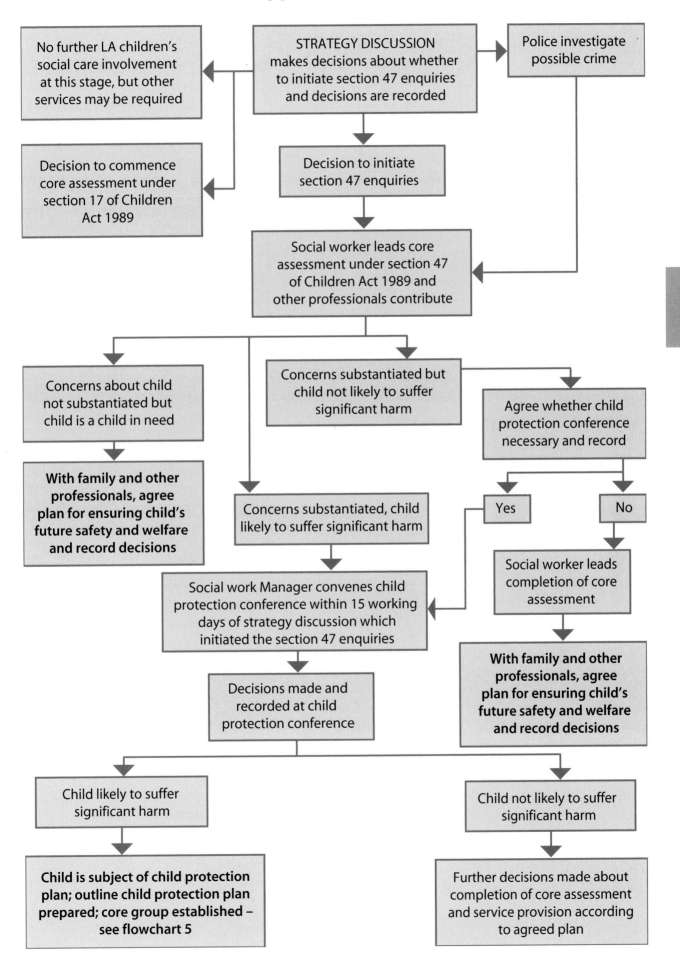

## Flow chart 5: What happens after the child protection conference, including the review process?

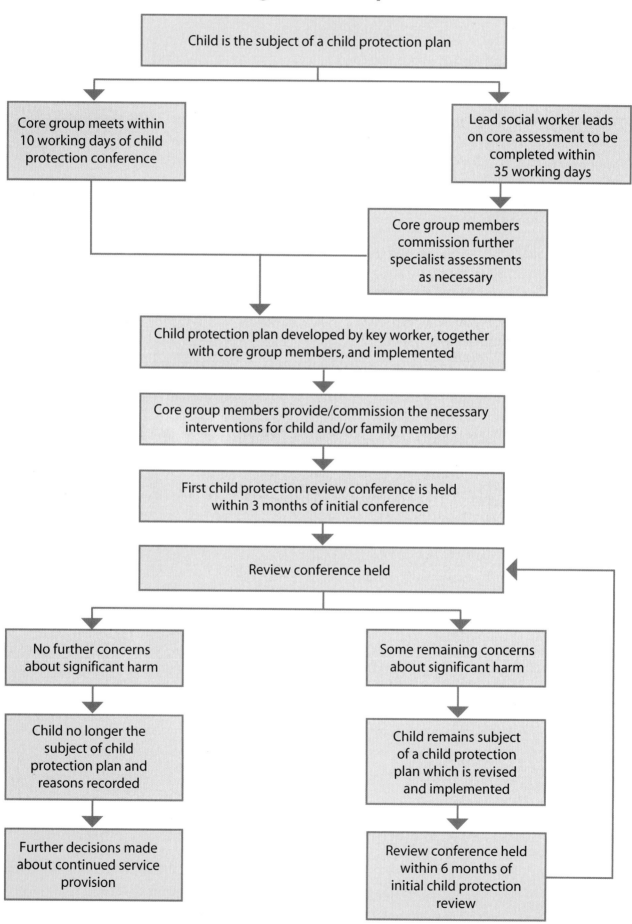

# Chapter 6 – Supplementary guidance on safeguarding and promoting the welfare of children

## Introduction

6.1    This chapter summarises supplementary guidance to *Working Together to Safeguard Children* and other guidance relevant to safeguarding and promoting children's welfare. The supplementary guidance follows the processes set out in Chapter 5 on how to respond to concerns about the welfare of a child or children, but is developed in more detail to reflect the specialist nature of the particular issues covered.

## Sexually exploited children

6.2    Children and young people who are sexually exploited are the victims of child sexual abuse, and their needs require careful assessment. They are likely to be in need of welfare services and – in many cases – protection under the Children Act 1989. This group may include children who have been sexually abused through the misuse of technology, coerced into sexual activity by criminal gangs or the victims of trafficking. Every Local Safeguarding Children Board (LSCB) should assume that sexual exploitation occurs within its area unless there is clear evidence to the contrary, and should put in place systems to monitor prevalence and responses. The DCSF published guidance in June 2009 on *Safeguarding Children and Young People from Sexual Exploitation*[98].

6.3    The guidance states that LSCBs should ensure that specific local procedures are in place covering the sexual exploitation of children and young people. The procedures should be a subset of the LSCB procedures for safeguarding and promoting the welfare of children, and be consistent with local youth offending protocols. The identification of a child who is being sexually exploited, or at risk of being sexually exploited, should always trigger the agreed local procedures to ensure the child's safety and welfare and to enable the police to gather evidence about abusers and coercers.

6.4    The strong links that have been identified between different forms of sexual exploitation, running away from home, gang activity, child trafficking and substance misuse should be borne in mind in the development of procedures. These should

---

include identifying signs of sexual exploitation, routes for referring concerns, advice on working with other professionals to disrupt sexual exploitation and support victims, gathering and preserving evidence about perpetrators, as well as how to deal with more complex issues such as those relating to the increasing use of the internet in sexual exploitation.

## Children affected by gang activity

6.5    Children and young people who become involved in gangs are at risk of violent crime and as a result of this involvement are deemed vulnerable. Agencies and professionals have a responsibility to safeguard these children and young people and to prevent further harm both to the young person and other potential victims. Risks associated with gang activity include access to weapons (including firearms), retaliatory violence and territorial violence with other gangs. Other risks include increased likelihood of involvement in knife crime, sexual violence and substance misuse. The recently published guidance on *Safeguarding Children and Young People who may be affected by Gang Activity*[99] is intended to assist agencies and professionals ensure the safeguarding process effectively responds to children and young people at risk of gang related violence. The guidance promotes an approach whereby agencies should work together to:

- clearly define the local problem;

- understand the risks posed by local gangs;

- effectively identify young people at risk;

- assess the needs of children, young people and their families;

- identify effective referral pathways;

- support professionals in delivering effective interventions; and

- define the role of the LSCB and other agencies.

## Fabricated or induced illness (FII)

6.6    Concerns may be raised when it is considered that the health or development of a child is likely to be significantly impaired or further impaired by a parent or caregiver who has fabricated or induced illness. These concerns may arise when:

- reported symptoms and signs found on examination are not explained by any medical condition from which the child may be suffering; or

---

99    http://publications.everychildmatters.gov.uk/default.aspx?PageFunction=productdetails&PageMode=publications&ProductId=DCSF-00064-2010

- physical examination and results of medical investigations do not explain reported symptoms and signs; or

- there is an inexplicably poor response to prescribed medication and other treatment; or

- new symptoms are reported on resolution of previous ones; or

- reported symptoms and found signs are not seen to begin in the absence of the carer; or

- over time the child is repeatedly presented with a range of signs and symptoms; or

- the child's normal, daily life activities are being curtailed, for example school attendance, beyond that which might be expected for any medical disorder from which the child is known to suffer.

There may be a number of explanations for these circumstances and each requires careful consideration and review. A full developmental history and an appropriate developmental assessment should be carried out. Consultation with peers, named or designated professionals or colleagues in other agencies will be an important part of the process of making sense of the underlying reason for these signs and symptoms. The characteristics of fabricated or induced illness are that there is a lack of the usual corroboration of findings with symptoms or signs, or, in circumstances of proven organic illness, lack of the usual response to proven effective treatments. It is this puzzling discrepancy which alerts the medical clinician to possible harm being suffered by the child.

6.7  There are three main ways of fabricating or inducing illness in a child. These are not mutually exclusive and include:

- fabrication of signs and symptoms. This may include fabrication of past medical history;

- fabrication of signs and symptoms and falsification of hospital charts and records, and specimens of bodily fluids. This may also include falsification of letters and documents; and

- induction of illness by a variety of means.

6.8  In 2008 the Government published statutory guidance *Safeguarding children in whom illness is fabricated or induced*[100]. This replaces the 2002 edition. This guidance provides a national framework within which agencies and professionals at a local level – individually and jointly – draw up and agree their own more detailed ways of

---

100    www.dcsf.gov.uk/everychildmatters/_download/?id=3161

working together where illness may be being fabricated or induced in a child by a caregiver who has parenting responsibilities for him or her. It is addressed to those who work in health, education, schools, probation, social care, the police and all others whose work brings them into contact with children and families. It is relevant to those working in the statutory, voluntary and independent sectors. It is intended that LSCBs' procedures should incorporate this guidance and its references to covert video surveillance, rather than having separate guidance on fabricated or induced illness in children. Within local procedures, the section on the use of covert video surveillance should make reference to the good practice advice for police officers which is available to them from the National Police Improvement Agency's Specialist Operations Centre.

6.9     To support the use of this statutory guidance the Government published *Incredibly Caring* in 2009. This training resource (in the form of a DVD) has been designed to assist both practitioners and managers promote the best outcomes for children where fabricated or induced illness is suspected; work sensitively with parents and carers in the child's best interests; and better exercise their professional judgement.

## Investigating complex (organised or multiple) abuse

6.10    This abuse may be defined as abuse involving one or more abusers and a number of children. The abusers concerned may be acting in concert to abuse children, sometimes acting in isolation, or may be using an institutional framework or position of authority to recruit children for abuse.

6.11    Complex abuse occurs both as part of a network of abuse across a family or community, and within institutions such as residential homes or schools. Such abuse is profoundly traumatic for the children who become involved. Its investigation is time-consuming and demanding work, requiring specialist skills from both police and social work staff. Some investigations become extremely complex because of the number of places and people involved, and the timescale over which abuse is alleged to have occurred. The complexity is heightened where, as in historical cases, the alleged victims are no longer living in the setting where the incidents occurred or where the alleged perpetrators are also no longer linked to the setting or employment role.

6.12    Each investigation of organised or multiple abuse will be different, according to the characteristics of each situation and the scale and complexity of the investigation. Although there has been much reporting in recent years about complex abuse in residential settings, complex abuse can occur in day care, in families and in other provisions such as youth services, sports clubs and voluntary groups. Cases of children being abused through the misuse of technology is also a new form of abuse which agencies are having to address.

6.13   Each complex abuse case requires thorough planning, good inter-agency working and attention to the welfare needs of the child victims or adult survivors involved. The guidance *Complex Child Abuse Investigations: Inter-agency issues* (Home Office and Department of Health, 2002)[101] seeks to help agencies confronted with difficult investigations by sharing the accumulated learning from Serious Case Reviews. It sets out the overarching policy and practice framework to inform and shape the detailed strategic plans that agencies will need to develop when confronted with a complex child abuse case. It does not, however, provide detailed operational guidance on all aspects of such investigations. This guidance is equally relevant to investigating organised or multiple abuse within an institution. In addition, Appendix A of this guidance identifies the issues which should be addressed in all major investigations, and which should be reflected in local procedures. The Association of Chief Police Officers (ACPO) have also recently issued revised guidance on *Investigating Child Abuse and Safeguarding Children*[102].

## Female genital mutilation

6.14   Female genital mutilation (FGM) is a collective term for procedures which include the removal of part or all of the external female genitalia for cultural or other non-therapeutic reasons. The practice is medically unnecessary, extremely painful and has serious health consequences, both at the time when the mutilation is carried out and in later life. The procedure is typically performed on girls aged between four and thirteen, but in some cases FGM is performed on new born infants or on young women before marriage or pregnancy. A number of girls die as a direct result of the procedure from blood loss or infection, either following the procedure or subsequently in childbirth.

6.15   FGM has been a criminal offence in the UK since the Prohibition of Female Circumcision Act 1985 was passed. The Female Genital Mutilation Act 2003 replaced the 1985 Act and made it an offence for UK nationals or permanent UK residents to carry out FGM abroad, or to aid, abet, counsel or procure the carrying out of FGM abroad, even in countries where the practice is legal. Further information about the Act can be found in *Home Office Circular 10/2004*[103].

6.16   FGM is much more common than most people realise, both worldwide and in the UK. It is reportedly practised in 28 African countries and in parts of the Middle and Far East but is increasingly found in Western Europe and other developed countries, primarily amongst immigrant and refugee communities. There are substantial populations from countries where FGM is endemic in London, Liverpool,

---

101   http://police.homeoffice.gov.uk/publications/operational-policing/child_abuse_guidancefb94. html?view=standard&pubID=184109

102   Available from www.ceop.police.uk.

103   Found at: www.homeoffice.gov.uk

Birmingham, Sheffield and Cardiff but it is likely that communities in which FGM is practised reside throughout the UK. It has been estimated that up to 24,000 girls under the age of 15 are at risk of FGM in the UK[104].

6.17 Suspicions may arise in a number of ways that a child is being prepared for FGM to take place abroad. These include knowing that the family belongs to a community in which FGM is practised and are making preparations for the child to take a holiday, arranging vaccinations or planning absence from school, and the child may talk about a 'special procedure' taking place. Indicators that FGM may have already occurred include prolonged absence from school with noticeable behaviour change on return and long periods away from classes or other normal activities, possibly with bladder or menstrual problems. Midwives and doctors may become aware that FGM has been practised on an older woman and this may prompt concern for female children in the same family.

6.18 A local authority may exercise its powers under section 47 of the Children Act 1989 if it has reason to believe that a child is likely to suffer or has suffered FGM. However, despite the very severe health consequences, parents and others who have this done to their daughters do not intend it as an act of abuse. They genuinely believe that it is in the girl's best interests to conform with their prevailing custom. So, where a child has been identified as at risk of significant harm, it may not be appropriate to consider removing the child from an otherwise loving family environment. Where a child appears to be in immediate danger of mutilation, consideration should be given to getting a prohibited steps order. If a child has already undergone FGM, particular attention should be paid to the potential risk of harm to other female children in the same family.

6.19 In local areas where there are communities who traditionally practice and positively promote FGM, consideration should be given to incorporating more detailed guidance on responding to concerns about FGM into existing procedures to safeguard and promote the welfare of children. LSCB policy should focus on a preventive strategy involving community education and be alert to the fact that the practice may also take place in this country. Further information in support of these guidelines can be found in *Local Authority Social Services Letter LASSL (2004)4*[105].

## Forced marriage and honour-based violence

6.20 The terms 'honour crime', 'izzat' or 'honour-based violence' embrace a variety of crimes of violence (mainly but not exclusively against women), including assault, imprisonment and murder where the person is being punished by their family or community. They are being punished for actually, or allegedly, undermining what

---

104    Dorkenoo et al, 2007. Available from FORWARD UK.
105    available at: www.dcsf.gov.uk

the family or community believes to be the correct code of behaviour. In transgressing against this correct code of behaviour, the person shows that they have not been properly controlled to conform by their family and this is to the 'shame' or 'dishonour' of the family.

6.21 Forced marriage and honour-based violence are human rights abuses and fall within the Government's definition of domestic violence. Forced marriage is defined as a marriage conducted without the full consent of both parties and where duress is a factor. There is a clear distinction between forced marriage and an arranged marriage. In arranged marriages, the families may take a leading role in arranging the marriage, but the choice whether or not to accept remains with the prospective spouses. In a forced marriage, one or both spouses do not consent to the marriage. The young person could be facing physical, psychological, sexual, financial or emotional abuse to pressure them into accepting the marriage.

6.22 Forced marriage affects victims from many communities. The majority of cases reported to date in the UK involve South Asian families, but there have been cases involving families from across Europe, East Asia, the Middle East and Africa. Some forced marriages take place in the UK with no overseas element, while others involve a partner coming from overseas or a British national being sent abroad.

6.23 If there are concerns that a child (male or female) is in danger of a forced marriage, in addition to safeguarding procedures set out in this publication, the Forced Marriage Unit should be contacted. The Forced Marriage Unit (a joint Home Office/ Foreign and Commonwealth Office Unit) was launched in January 2005. It is responsible for developing Government policy on forced marriage, for raising awareness and for casework. It runs a public helpline[106] that provides confidential advice and support to victims, and to practitioners handling cases of forced marriage. Caseworkers in the Unit have extensive experience of the cultural, social and emotional issues surrounding forced marriage. They can also directly assist to help British nationals facing forced marriage abroad by helping them to a place of safety and helping them to return to the UK.

6.24 Although there is no specific criminal offence in England and Wales of 'forcing someone to marry', criminal offences may nevertheless be committed. Perpetrators – usually parents or family members – could be prosecuted for offences including threatening behaviour, assault, kidnap, abduction, theft (of passport), threats to kill, imprisonment and murder. Sexual intercourse without consent is rape, regardless of whether this occurs within a marriage or not. A woman who is forced into marriage is likely to be raped and may be raped until she becomes pregnant.

---

106    The helpline number is 0207 008 0151 (www.fco.gov.uk/forcedmarriage).

6.25    Hundreds of people in the UK (particularly girls and young women), some as young as nine, are forced into marriage each year. Some are taken overseas to marry whilst others may be married in the UK. Suspicions that a young person may be forced into marriage may arise in a number of ways. These include a family history of older siblings leaving education early and marrying early; depressive behaviour including self-harming and attempted suicide; unreasonable restrictions such as being kept at home by their parents ('house arrest') or being unable to complete their education; and a person always being accompanied including to school and doctors' appointments. A young person may also talk about an upcoming family holiday that they are worried about, fears that they will be taken out of education and kept abroad, or directly disclose that they are worried they will be forced to marry.

6.26    There may be only one opportunity to speak to a potential victim of forced marriage, so an appropriate initial response is vital. Without the right information being taken down (for example, a traceable address overseas), a victim may never be seen again. It is important to gather as much information as possible about the victim immediately, but this should be done on their own, in a private place where the conversation cannot be overheard. Victims should be reminded of their rights – they have the right to choose who they marry, when and where, and the right to make decisions about their lives.

6.27    Many victims are terrified that their families will find out that they have asked for help. **Do not** inform the victim's family, friends or members of the community that the victim has sought help as this is likely to increase the risk to the victim significantly. Forced marriage is closely linked to honour-based violence and honour killings. All those involved will want to bear in mind that *mediation as a response to forced marriage can be extremely dangerous.* There have been cases of victims being murdered by their families during mediation. Mediation can also place someone at risk of further emotional and physical abuse.

6.28    All those with a duty to safeguard and promote the welfare of children should have regard to the statutory guidance *The Right to Choose: Multi-agency statutory guidance for dealing with forced marriage*[107]. This statutory guidance sets out the responsibilities of Chief Executives, directors and senior managers. It covers issues such as staff training, developing inter-agency policies and procedures, raising awareness and developing prevention programmes through outreach work.

6.29    In addition, all practitioners working with children should have access to *Multi-agency practice guidelines: Handling cases of Forced Marriage*[108], published in 2009. These guidelines provide advice and support to front line practitioners.

---

107    www.fco.gov.uk/resources/en/pdf/3849543/forced-marriage-right-to-choose
108    www.fco.gov.uk/resources/en/pdf/3849543/forced-marriage-guidelines09.pdf

6.30   Anyone threatened with forced marriage or forced to marry against their will can apply for a Forced Marriage Protection Order. Third parties, such as relatives, friends, voluntary workers and police officers, can also apply for a protection order with the leave of the court. Fifteen county courts deal with applications and make orders to prevent forced marriages. Local authorities can now seek a protection order for vulnerable adults and children without leave of the court. Guidance published by the Ministry of Justice explains how local authorities can apply for protection orders and provides information for other agencies[109].

6.31   Where a case of forced marriage has resulted in the serious harm of a child or young person, practitioners should also consider undertaking a Serious Case Review.

## Allegations of abuse made against a person who works with children

6.32   Children can be subjected to abuse by those who work with them in any setting. All allegations of abuse or maltreatment of children by a professional, staff member, foster carer, or volunteer must therefore be taken seriously and treated in accordance with consistent procedures. LSCBs have responsibility for ensuring there are effective inter-agency procedures in place for dealing with allegations against people who work with children, and monitoring and evaluating the effectiveness of those procedures – see Chapter 3.

6.33   In evaluating the effectiveness of local procedures LSCBs should have regard to the need to complete cases expeditiously. Data about allegations made against education staff show that it is reasonable to expect that 80% of cases should be resolved within one month, 90% within three months and that all but the most exceptional cases should be completed within 12 months, although it is unlikely that cases that require a criminal prosecution or a complex police investigation can be completed in less than three months.

6.34   All organisations which provide services for children, or provide staff or volunteers to work with or care for children, should operate a procedure for handling such allegations which is consistent with the guidance in Appendix 5.

---

109   This is available at www.justice.gov.uk/guidance/forced-marriage.htm

6.35   LSCB member organisations should have a named senior officer who has overall responsibility for:

- ensuring that the organisation operates procedures for dealing with allegations in accordance with the guidance in Appendix 5;

- resolving any inter-agency issues; and

- liaison with the LSCB on the subject.

County level and unitary local authorities should also designate officers (the Local Authority Designated Officer, or LADO) to be involved in the management and oversight of individual cases – providing advice and guidance to employers and voluntary organisations, liaising with the police and other agencies and monitoring the progress of cases to ensure that they are dealt with as quickly as possible consistent with a thorough and fair process.

6.36   Police forces should also identify officers to fill similar roles. There should be a senior officer to have strategic oversight of the arrangements, liaise with the LSCBs in the force area and ensure compliance, and others, perhaps unit managers, who will be responsible for liaising with the LADO(s), taking part in the strategy discussion (see Chapter 5), subsequently reviewing the progress of those cases in which there is a police investigation, and sharing information on completion of the investigation or any prosecution.

6.37   The scope of inter-agency procedures in this area is not limited to allegations involving significant harm or the risk of significant harm to a child. The guidance in Appendix 5 should be followed in respect of any allegation that a person who works with children has:

- behaved in a way that has harmed a child, or may have harmed a child;

- possibly committed a criminal offence against or related to a child; or

- behaved towards a child or children in a way that indicates s/he is unsuitable to work with children

in connection with the person's employment or voluntary activity. If concerns arise about the person's behaviour in regard to his/her own children, the police and/or children's social care need to consider informing the person's employer in order to assess whether there may be implications for children with whom the person has contact at work.

6.38   The child or children concerned should receive appropriate support. They, and their parents or carers, should be helped to understand the process, told the result of any enquiry or disciplinary process[110], and where necessary helped to understand the outcomes reached. The provision of information and advice must take place in a manner that does not impede the proper exercise of enquiry, disciplinary and investigative processes.

6.39    Staff, foster carers, volunteers and other individuals about whom there are concerns should be treated fairly and honestly, and should also be provided with support throughout the investigation process as should others who are also involved. They should be helped to understand the concerns expressed and the processes being operated, and be clearly informed of the outcome of any investigation and the implications for disciplinary or related processes. However, the police, and other relevant agencies, should always be consulted before informing a person who is the subject of allegations which may possibly require a criminal investigation.

6.40    There have been a number of widely reported cases of historical abuse, usually of an organised or multiple nature (see paragraph 6.12). Such cases have generally come to light after adults have reported abuse that they had experienced when children, while living away from home in settings provided by local authorities, the voluntary sector or independent providers. When such allegations are made, they should be responded to in the same way as contemporary concerns. In those cases it is also important to find out whether the person accused is still working with children and, if so, to inform the person's current employer or voluntary organisation.

6.41    Those undertaking investigations should be alert to any sign or pattern which suggests that the abuse is more widespread or organised than it appears at first sight, or that it involves other perpetrators or institutions. It is important not to assume that initial signs will necessarily be related directly to abuse, and to consider occasions where boundaries have been blurred, inappropriate behaviour has taken place, and matters such as fraud, deception or pornography have been involved.

6.42    If an allegation is substantiated, the managers or commissioners of the relevant service should think widely about the lessons of the case and how they should be acted upon. This should include whether there are features of the organisation which may have contributed to the abuse occurring, or failed to prevent the abuse occurring. In some circumstances, a Serious Case Review may be appropriate (see Chapter 8).

---

110     In deciding what information to disclose, careful consideration should be given to duties under the Data Protection Act 1998, the law of confidence and, where relevant, the Human Rights Act 1998.

202 Working Together to Safeguard Children

## Abuse of disabled children

6.43    In July 2009, the Government published *Safeguarding Disabled Children – Practice Guidance*[111]. This guidance provides a framework within which LSCBs, agencies and professionals at local level – individually and jointly – draw up and agree detailed ways of working together to safeguard disabled children.

6.44    The available UK evidence on the extent of abuse among disabled children suggests that disabled children are at increased risk of abuse, and that the presence of multiple disabilities appears to increase the risk of both abuse and neglect (see Standards 5, 7 and 8 of the *National Service Framework for Children, Young People and Maternity Services*). Disabled children may be especially vulnerable to abuse for a number of reasons:

- many disabled children are at an increased likelihood of being socially isolated with fewer outside contacts than non-disabled children;

- their dependency on parents and carers for practical assistance in daily living, including intimate personal care, increases their risk of exposure to abusive behaviour;

- they have an impaired capacity to resist or avoid abuse;

- they may have speech, language and communication needs which may make it difficult to tell others what is happening;

- they often do not have access to someone they can trust to disclose that they have been abused; and/or

- they are especially vulnerable to bullying and intimidation.

Looked after disabled children are not only vulnerable to the same factors that exist for all children living away from home, but are particularly susceptible to possible abuse because of their additional dependency on residential and hospital staff for day to day physical care needs.

6.45    Safeguards for disabled children are essentially the same as for non-disabled children. Particular attention should be paid to promoting a high level of awareness of the risks of harm and high standards of practice, and strengthening the capacity of children and families to help themselves. Measures should include:

- making it common practice to help disabled children make their wishes and feelings known in respect of their care and treatment;

---

111    www.dcsf.gov.uk/everychildmatters/_download/?id=6195

- ensuring that disabled children receive appropriate personal, health, and social education (including sex education);

- making sure that all disabled children know how to raise concerns, and giving them access to a range of adults with whom they can communicate. Those disabled children with communication impairments should have available to them at all times a means of being heard;

- an explicit commitment to, and understanding of disabled children's safety and welfare among providers of services used by disabled children;

- close contact with families, and a culture of openness on the part of services;

- guidelines and training for staff on good practice in intimate care; working with children of the opposite sex; handling difficult behaviour; consent to treatment; anti-bullying strategies; and sexuality and sexual behaviour among young people, especially those living away from home; and

- guidelines and training for staff working with disabled children aged 16 and over to ensure that decisions about disabled children who lack capacity will be governed by the Mental Health Capacity Act once they reach the age of 16.

6.46 Where there are concerns about the welfare of a disabled child, they should be acted upon in accordance with the guidance in Chapter 5, in the same way as with any other child. Expertise in both safeguarding and promoting the welfare of child and disability has to be brought together to ensure that disabled children receive the same levels of protection from harm as other children (see *Safeguarding Disabled Children – Practice Guidance (2009)*).

6.47 Where a disabled child has communication impairments or learning disabilities, special attention should be paid to communication needs, and to ascertain the child's perception of events, and his or her wishes and feelings. In every area, children's social care and the police should be aware of non-verbal communication systems, when they might be useful and how to access them, and should know how to contact suitable interpreters or facilitators. Agencies should not make assumptions about the inability of a disabled child to give credible evidence, or to withstand the rigours of the court process. Each child should be assessed carefully, and helped and supported to participate in the criminal justice process when this is in the child's best interest and the interests of justice.

6.48 In criminal proceedings under the Youth Justice and Criminal Evidence Act 1999[112] witnesses aged under 17 (to be raised to under 18 by the end of 2010) may be eligible for special measures assistance when giving evidence in court. There is a presumption that child witnesses should give their evidence by video recorded

112   www.opsi.gov.uk/acts/acts1999/ukpga_19990023_en_1

statement (if taken) and live link, which allows a witness to give evidence during a trial from outside the courtroom through a televised link to the courtroom. The other special measures available to vulnerable witnesses include clearing the public gallery in sexual offence cases and those involving intimidation, screens to shield the witness from seeing the defendant, and assistance with communication through an intermediary or communication aid. *Achieving Best Evidence in Criminal Proceedings: Guidance on vulnerable and intimidated witnesses including children*[113] gives detailed guidance on planning and conducting interviews with children and vulnerable adults and includes a section on interviewing disabled children and also those that are very young or psychologically disturbed.

## Child abuse linked to belief in 'spirit possession'

6.49    The belief in 'possession' and 'witchcraft' is relatively widespread. It is not confined to particular countries, cultures or religions, nor is it confined to new immigrant communities in this country.

6.50    The number of **identified** cases of child abuse linked to accusations of 'possession' are small, but the nature of the child abuse can be particularly disturbing and the children involved can suffer damage to their physical and mental health, capacity to learn, ability to form relationships and self-esteem.

6.51    There are a number of common factors which put a child at risk of harm, including rationalising misfortune by attributing it to spiritual forces and when a carer views a child as being 'different', attributes this difference to the child being 'possessed' or involved in 'witchcraft', and attempts to exorcise him or her. A child could be viewed as 'different' for a variety of reasons such as: disobedience; independence; bedwetting; nightmares; illness; or disability. The attempt to 'exorcise' may involve severe beating, burning, starvation, cutting or stabbing, and/or isolation, and usually occurs in the household where the child lives.

6.52    Agencies should look for these indicators, be able to identify children at risk of this type of abuse and intervene to prevent it. They should apply basic safeguarding children principles including: sharing information across agencies; being child-focused at all times; and keeping an open mind when talking to parents and carers. They should follow the guidance set out elsewhere in Working Together in their work with all children and families, ensure they liaise closely with colleagues and make connections with key people in the community, especially when working with new immigrant communities, so that they can ascertain the different dimensions of a family's cultural beliefs and how this might impact upon child abuse.

---

113    www.homeoffice.gov.uk/documents/ach-bect-evidence/

6.53   Good practice guidance for agencies, *Safeguarding Children from Abuse Linked to a Belief in Spirit Possession*[114], was published in April 2007.

## Child victims of trafficking

6.54   Trafficking in people involves a collection of crimes, spanning a variety of countries and involving an increasing number of victims – resulting in considerable suffering for those trafficked. It includes the exploitation of children through force, coercion, threat and the use of deception and human rights abuses such as debt bondage, deprivation of liberty and lack of control over one's labour. It includes the movement of people across borders and also the movement and exploitation within borders. The persons who are trafficked have very little choice in what happens to them and usually suffer abuse due to the threats and use of violence against them and/or their family.

6.55   The UK is a transit and destination country for trafficked children and young people. Children are trafficked for various reasons, including sexual exploitation, domestic servitude, labour, benefit fraud and involvement in criminal activity such as pickpocketing, theft and working in cannabis farms. There are a number of cases, too, of minors being exploited in the sex industry. Although there is no evidence of other forms of exploitation such as 'organ donation, or 'harvesting', all agencies should remain vigilant.

6.56   Such children enter the UK through various means. Some enter as unaccompanied asylum seekers, or students or as visitors. Children are also brought in by adults who state that they are their dependents, or are met at airports or other ports of entry by an adult who claims to be a relative. It has been suggested that children have been brought in via internet transactions, foster arrangements, and contracts as domestic staff. In some cases girls aged 16 or 17 will have been tricked into a bogus marriage for the purpose of sexual exploitation. If it is suspected that a child is the victim of trafficking, the police or children's social care should be informed. Agencies should work together to ensure a joined-up response.

6.57   The DCSF and the Home Office published joint guidance on *Safeguarding children who may have been trafficked*[115] in December 2007. It sets out a comprehensive strategy to improve the identification and safeguarding of child victims of trafficking. DCSF guidance on sexual exploitation and young runways includes details of how services must work to protect children from trafficking.

---

114   www.dcsf.gov.uk/everychildmatters/_download/?id=661

115   *Safeguarding Children who may have been trafficked* (HM Government, 2008) http://publications. everychildmatters.gov.uk/default.aspx?PageFunction=productdetails&PageMode=publications&Pro ductId=HMG-00994-2007&

6.58    Early identification is key to protecting these vulnerable children. The child trafficking assessment toolkit has been designed to help front line staff identify children who may have potentially been trafficked as part of a new National Referral Mechanism (NRM). The NRM is a multi-agency framework designed to enable frontline practitioners to work together to identify and support victims of trafficking. Designated expert 'Competent Authorities' within the UK Human Trafficking Centre (UKHTC) and the UK Border Agency (UKBA) are responsible for determining, from the evidence gathered, but in particular on the basis of advice from children's services, whether a child meets the Council of Europe Convention on Action Against Trafficking in Human Beings ('the Convention') definition of trafficking. It was launched on 1 April 2009 and will ensure consistency of approach across all relevant agencies.

6.59    Children do not have to be trafficked across international borders to be exploited in this way. There is evidence that some UK resident children, mainly young girls, are being groomed, coerced and moved around between towns and cities within the UK for the purposes of sexual exploitation. Relevant agencies should remain alert to the possibility that this can happen and work together to address it.

6.60    The NRM process is a key element of the Convention. The purpose of the Convention is to prevent and combat trafficking, to identify and protect the victims of trafficking and to safeguard their rights; and to promote international co-operation against trafficking. The UK signed the Convention on 23 March 2007. The convention was ratified on 17 December 2008 and it came into force on 1 April 2009.

6.61    Decisions about who is a victim of trafficking are made by trained specialists in designated 'Competent Authorities'. The UKHTC hosts one such Competent Authority. The UKHTC Competent Authority deals with cases referred by all external agencies such as the police, local authorities etc where the person is a UK or EEA national, or where there is an immigration issue but the person is not yet known to UKBA. A linked but separate Competent Authority sits in UKBA for situations where trafficking is raised as part of an asylum claim or in the context of another immigration process.

6.62    An integral part of the NRM is the provision of accommodation and support to victims, and local authorities will continue to take the lead in providing appropriate services for vulnerable children (including trafficked children). Further details of the NRM process, including the trafficking toolkit, can be found on the Home Office crime reduction website[116].

---

116    www.crimereduction.homeoffice.gov.uk/humantrafficking005.htm

6.63    The offence of trafficking for prostitution, introduced in the Nationality, Immigration and Asylum Act 2002, carries a tough maximum penalty of 14 years. The Sexual Offences Act 2003 introduced wide-ranging offences covering trafficking into, out of or within the UK for any form of sexual offence, which also carries a 14 year maximum penalty. It also introduced a range of offences covering the commercial sexual exploitation of a child, protecting children up to 18. These include buying the sexual services of a child (for which the penalty ranges from seven years to life imprisonment depending on the age of the child) and causing or inciting, arranging or facilitating and controlling the commercial sexual exploitation of a child in prostitution or pornography, for which the maximum penalty is 14 years imprisonment. An offence of trafficking for exploitation, which covers trafficking for forced labour and the removal of organs, was introduced in the Asylum and Immigration (Treatment of Claimants, etc.) Act 2004. These offences will also take into account the UK's international obligations under the UN Palermo Trafficking Protocol (supplementing the UN Convention Against Transnational Organised Crime 2000) and the EU Framework Decision on Trafficking for the Purposes of Sexual and Labour Exploitation.

6.64    At the local level, LSCBs should be aware of the child trafficking agenda within their local authority and ensure all suspected child victims of trafficking are referred through the NRM using the correct procedure.

6.65    LSCBs should also identify trafficking co-ordinators who can ensure a co-ordinated campaign of information-sharing to support the safeguarding agenda between local authorities, police and the NRM Competent Authorities to ensure a full picture is provided on child NRM referrals and secure the best safeguarding outcome for the child.

6.66    For those requiring more information on the nature and scale of child trafficking in the UK, please refer to the *Child Trafficking Strategic Threat Assessment 2008/09* produced by the Child Exploitation and Online Protection (CEOP) Centre[117].

---

117    This and other related documents is available from www.ceop.police.uk/publications.

# Chapter 7 – Child death review processes

## Introduction

7.1     This chapter sets out the processes to be followed when a child dies in the Local Safeguarding Children Board (LSCB) area(s) covered by a Child Death Overview Panel. There are two interrelated processes for reviewing child deaths (either of which can trigger a Serious Case Review (SCR) – see Chapter 8):

a.  rapid response by a group of key professionals who come together for the purpose of enquiring into and evaluating each unexpected death of a child (see paragraphs 7.48–7.93); and

b.  an overview of all child deaths up to the age of 18 years (excluding both those babies who are stillborn and planned terminations of pregnancy carried out within the law[118]) in the LSCB area(s), undertaken by a panel (see paragraphs 7.25–7.47).

7.2     A sub-committee of the LSCB(s) known as the Child Death Overview Panel (CDOP) should be responsible for reviewing the available information on all child deaths, and should be accountable to the LSCB Chair. The disclosure of information about a deceased child is to enable the LSCB to carry out its statutory functions relating to child deaths. The LSCB should use the aggregated findings from all child deaths, collected according to the nationally agreed minimum data set[119] to inform local strategic planning on how best to safeguard and promote the welfare of the children in their area.

7.3     Guidance in this chapter relates to the deaths of all children and young people from birth (excluding those deaths set out in paragraph 7.1b) **up to the age of 18 years**. Implementation of some parts of the guidance will therefore need to take into account the needs of different age groups.

---

118   Reviews of deaths which follow a planned termination under the law (Abortion Act 1967) should not be carried out by Child Death Overview Panels even in instances where a death certificate has been issued. If the LSCB has general concerns about local procedures relating to planned terminations, it should contact the Care Quality Commission (enquiries@cqc.org.uk). All other deaths (i.e. excluding those deaths which follow a planned termination of pregnancy under the law) which have been registered as live with the General Registrar's Office, should be reviewed by the Child Death Overview Panel.

119   The nationally agreed data set is available at: www.dcsf.gov.uk/everychildmatters/ safeguardingandsocialcare/safeguardingchildren/childdeathreviewprocedures/ nationaltemplatesforlscbs/lscbtemplates/

## Overall principles

7.4     Each death of a child is a tragedy for his or her family (including any siblings), and subsequent enquiries/investigations should keep an appropriate balance between forensic and medical requirements and the family's need for support. A minority of unexpected deaths are the consequence of abuse or neglect or are found to have abuse or neglect as an associated factor. In all cases, enquiries should seek to understand the reasons for the child's death, address the possible needs of other children in the household, the needs of all family members, and also consider any lessons to be learnt about how best to safeguard and promote children's welfare in the future.

7.5     Families should be treated with sensitivity, discretion and respect at all times, and professionals should approach their enquiries with an open mind.

7.6     Chronic illness, disability and life limiting conditions account for a large proportion of child deaths. Whilst it is to be expected that children with life limiting or life threatening conditions (LL/LT conditions) will die prematurely young, it is not always easy to predict when, or in what manner they will die. Professionals responding to the death of a child with a LL/LT condition should ensure that their response to these families is appropriate and supportive, does not cause any unnecessary distress at a time when they are dealing with the tragic but anticipated, natural death of their child, and that their child's expected death can be dignified and peaceful. End of life care plans may be in place and therefore families, where appropriate, should be supported, to choose where their child's body is cared for after death for example a children's hospice. The lives of children with LL/LT conditions are as valued and important as those of any other children, and hence the unexpected, death of a child with LL/LT conditions should be managed as for any other unexpected death so as to determine the cause of death and any contributory factors (see paragraphs 7.58–7.59). This is both out of respect for the child and family, and to fulfil any statutory requirements.

## Involvement of parents and family members (for all child deaths)

7.7     It is vitally important that LSCBs establish mechanisms for appropriately informing and involving parents and other family members[120] in both the child death overview and the rapid response processes (see paragraphs 7.4–7.12, 7.36, 7.50, 7.57–7.62, 7.73–7.75 and 7.91–7.92)[121].

---

120     Parents includes carers where appropriate, and family members includes siblings where appropriate.

121     A leaflet which can be given to parents, carers and family members to explain the child death review process is available to order from DCSF Publications, Tel: 0845 60 222 60, please quote reference: 00180-2010LEF-EN

7.8    Parents and family members should be informed that their child's death will be reviewed, and often have significant information and questions to contribute to the review process.

7.9    Parents and family members should be assured that the objective of the child death review process is to learn lessons in order to improve the health, safety and well being of children and ultimately, hopefully, to prevent further such child deaths. The process is not about culpability or blame.

7.10   The LSCB, acting through the CDOP should agree what information is to be shared with parents and family members and ensure that a professional known to the family conveys to them agreed information in a sensitive and timely manner. Decisions on information sharing (i.e. what information is shared, with whom, and why) must be recorded in each agency's records. It is not appropriate however, for parents to attend the CDOP meeting as this is a meeting for professionals to discuss not only the individual case but also wider public health issues. Parents should however be encouraged to contribute any comments or questions they might have to the review of their child's death.

7.11   Parents should be informed that all cases will be anonymised prior to discussion by the CDOP, information gathered will be stored securely and only anonymised data will be collated at a regional or national level. Parents should also be made aware that the CDOP will make recommendations and report on the lessons learned to the LSCB. The LSCB produces an annual report which is a public document, but it will not contain any personal information that could identify an individual child or their family.

7.12   CDOPs should ensure that whenever necessary, arrangements are made for the family to have the opportunity to meet with relevant professionals, for example a professional known to the family before their child died, a paediatrician or a police officer to help answer their questions.

## The Regulations relating to child deaths

7.13   One of the LSCB functions, set out in Regulation 6 of the Local Safeguarding Children Boards Regulations 2006, in relation to the deaths of any children normally resident in their area is as follows:

*(a) collecting and analysing information about each death with a view to identifying –*

> *(i)    any case giving rise to the need for a review mentioned in Regulation 5(1)(e);*

> *(ii)   any matters of concern affecting the safety and welfare of children in the area of the authority; and*

> (iii) *any wider public health or safety concerns arising from a particular death or from a pattern of deaths in that area; and*
>
> (b) *putting in place procedures for ensuring that there is a co-ordinated response by the authority, their Board partners and other relevant persons to an unexpected death.*

7.14   As explained in Chapter 3, the child death review functions became compulsory on 1 April 2008.

## Supply of information about child deaths by registrars

7.15   Registrars of Births and Deaths are required by the Children and Young Persons Act 2008 to supply LSCBs with information which they have about the deaths:

- of persons aged under 18 in respect of whom they have registered the death; or

- of persons in respect of whom the entry of death is corrected and it is believed that person was or may have been under the age of 18 at the time of death.

Registrars must also notify LSCBs if they issue *a Certificate of No Liability to Register* where it appears that the deceased was or may have been under the age of 18 at the time of death.

7.16   Registrars are required to send the information to the appropriate LSCB no later than seven days from the date of registration, the date of making the correction/ update or the date of issuing the certificate of no liability as appropriate. (The appropriate LSCB is the Board established by the children's services authority in England within whose area is situated the sub-district for which the register is kept). These requirements only apply in respect of deaths occurring on or after 1 April 2009.

7.17   In order to support these new responsibilities, it is a statutory requirement for each LSCB to make arrangements for the receipt of notifications from registrars and to publish these arrangements. In order to carry out this responsibility LSCBs are therefore required to notify the Department for Children, Schools and Families of the name and email address for the Child Death Overview designated person (hereafter referred to as the 'designated person') in each LSCB to whom child death notifications should be sent. This information is published by the Department on the *Every Child Matters* website[122].

---

122   A list of people designated by the Child Death Overview Panel to receive notifications of child death information is available at: www.dcsf.gov.uk/everychildmatters/resources-and-practice/IG00351/

## Duty and powers of coroners to share information

7.18   The Coroners Rules 1984 as amended by the Coroners (Amendment) Rules 2008 place a duty on coroners to inform the LSCB, for the area in which the child died, of the fact of an inquest or post mortem. It also gives coroners powers to share information with LSCBs for the purposes of carrying out their functions, which include reviewing child deaths and undertaking SCRs. Where there is more than one LSCB in a coroner's area, arrangements should be made between the coroner and the LSCBs as to which LSCB should be informed of the coroner's decisions.

7.19   On receipt of an initial report of a death of a child, the LSCB or LSCBs with an interest in this information should inform the coroner of the address(es) (including email address(es)) to which future information should be supplied. If any information comes to the attention of an LSCB which it believes should be drawn to the attention of the relevant coroner, then the LSCB should consider supplying it to the coroner as a matter of urgency[123].

## Duty and powers of Medical Examiners (MEs) to share information

7.20   In taking forward the proposed improvements to the process of death certification, the Department of Health will ensure that appropriate interfaces are established with these functions now being delivered by LSCBs. It is anticipated that under the Coroners and Justice Act 2009, MEs will be required to share information with LSCBs about child deaths that are not investigated by a coroner.

## Definition of an unexpected death of a child

7.21   In this guidance an unexpected death is defined as the death of an infant or child (less than 18 years old) which:

- was not anticipated as a significant possibility for example, 24 hours before the death; or

- where there was a similarly unexpected collapse or incident leading to or precipitating the events which led to the death[124,125].

---

123   For further guidance see: www.justice.gov.uk/guidance/coroners-guidance.htm

124   PJ. Fleming, P.S. Blair, C. Bacon, and P.J. Berry (2000) *Sudden Unexpected Death In Infancy. The CESDI SUDI Studies 1993-1996. The Stationary Office. London. ISBN 0 11 3222 9988.*

125   Royal College of Pathologists and the Royal College of Paediatrics and Child Health (2004) *Sudden unexpected death in infancy. A multi-agency protocol for care and investigation. The Report of a working group convened by the Royal College of Pathologists and the Royal College of Paediatrics and Child Health*. Royal College of Pathologists and the Royal College of Paediatrics and Child Health, London. www.rcpath.org

7.22   The designated paediatrician responsible for unexpected deaths in childhood (see paragraph 7.29) should be consulted where professionals are uncertain about whether the death is unexpected. If in doubt, the processes for unexpected child deaths should be followed until the available evidence enables a different decision to be made.

## Definition of preventable child deaths

7.23   For the purpose of producing aggregate national data, this guidance defines preventable child deaths as those in which modifiable factors may have contributed to the death. These factors are defined as those which, by means of nationally or locally achievable interventions, could be modified to reduce the risk of future child deaths.

7.24   In reviewing the death of each child, the CDOP should consider modifiable factors, for example in the family and environment, parenting capacity or service provision, and consider what action could be taken locally and what action could be taken at a regional or national level.

## LSCB responsibilities for the child death review processes

### Reviewing deaths of all children

7.25   The CDOP should undertake an overview of **all** child deaths (excluding those deaths set out in paragraph 7.1b) up to the age of 18 years in the LSCB area(s) covered by the CDOP. This is a paper based review, based on information available from those who were involved in the care of the child, both before and immediately after the death, and other sources including, perhaps, the coroner. The panel should:

- have a fixed core membership (see paragraph 7.27) to review these cases, with flexibility to co-opt other relevant professionals as and when appropriate;

- hold meetings at regular intervals to enable each child's case to be discussed in a timely manner (the length of the discussion may vary depending on the nature of the death in question and the quantity of information available);

- review the appropriateness of the professionals' responses to each death of a child, their involvement before and at the time of the death, and relevant environmental, social, health and cultural aspects of each death, to ensure a thorough consideration of how such deaths might be prevented in the future;

- determine whether or not the death was deemed preventable (as defined in paragraph 7.23). The decision must be agreed by the CDOP and approved by the Chair of the CDOP. This decision cannot be finalised however until the outcome of other investigations (for example SCRs, criminal proceedings, post mortem or inquests) is known;

- make recommendations to the LSCB or other relevant bodies as soon as these have been decided in order that prompt action can be taken to prevent future such deaths where possible; and

- identify any patterns or trends in the local data and report these to the LSCB.

7.26 Neighbouring LSCBs may decide to share a CDOP, depending on the local configuration of services and population served (experience shows that panels responsible for reviewing deaths from a total population greater than 500,000 gain experience more quickly, and review a sufficiently large number of deaths to be better able to identify significant recurrent contributory factors). In this situation LSCBs should agree lines of accountability with the CDOP in accordance with this guidance.

7.27 The CDOP has a permanent core membership drawn from the key organisations represented on the LSCB (see paragraph 3.70); although not all core members are necessarily involved in discussing all cases. The Panel should include a professional from public health as well as child health. Other members may be co-opted, either as permanent members to reflect the characteristics of the local population (for example, a representative of a large local ethnic or religious community), to provide a perspective from the independent or voluntary sector, or to contribute to the discussion of certain types of death when they occur (for example, fire fighters for house fires). The Panel will be chaired by the LSCB Chair or his or her representative, who will be a member of the LSCB. The Panel Chair should not be involved in providing direct services to children and families in the area.

7.28 Within each organisation represented on the LSCB, a senior person with relevant expertise should be identified as having responsibility for advising on the implementation of the local procedures on responding to child deaths. Each organisation should expect to be involved in a child death review at some time.

7.29 Each PCT should ensure that the LSCB, acting through the CDOP, has access to a consultant paediatrician whose designated role is to provide advice on:

- the commissioning of paediatric services from paediatricians with expertise in undertaking enquiries into unexpected deaths in childhood and the medical investigative services such as radiology, laboratory and histopathology services; and

- the organisation of such services.

The designated paediatrician for unexpected deaths in childhood may provide advice to more than one PCT, and is likely to be a member of the local CDOP. This is a separate role to the designated doctor for child protection, but does not necessarily need to be filled by a different person. These responsibilities should be recognised in the job plan agreed between the consultant and his or her employer.

7.30    The CDOP should have a clear relationship and agreed channels of communication with the local coronial service.

7.31    The LSCB should ensure that appropriate single and inter-agency training (see Chapter 4) is made available to ensure successful implementation of these processes. LSCB partner agencies should ensure that relevant staff have access to this training[126].

## Procedures to be followed by the local Child Death Overview Panel (for all child deaths)

7.32    In order for LSCBs to fulfil their child death reviewing responsibilities, the LSCB should be informed of all deaths of children normally resident in its geographical area. The LSCB Chair should decide who will be the designated person to whom the death notification and other data on each death should be sent[127]. The Chair of the CDOP is responsible for ensuring that this process operates effectively.

7.33    Deaths should be notified by the professional confirming the fact of the child's death. For unexpected deaths, this will be at the same time as they inform the coroner and the person designated by the LSCB to be notified of all children's deaths in the area in which the death occurred. If this is not the area in which the child is normally resident, the designated person should inform their opposite number in the area where the child normally resides[128].

7.34    In these situations, it should be decided on a case-by-case basis which Panel should take responsibility for gathering the necessary information for a Panel's consideration. In some cases this may be done jointly. Where partner agencies in more than one LSCB area have known about or have had contact with the child, the LSCB for the area in which the child was normally resident at the time of death should take lead responsibility for conducting the child death review. Any other LSCBs that have an interest or whose local agencies have had involvement in the case should co-operate as partners in jointly planning and undertaking the child death review. In the case of a looked after child, the LSCB for the area of the local authority looking after the child should exercise lead responsibility for conducting

---

126    *Responding when a child dies* – a multi-agency training resource to support LSCBs in implementing the child death review processes have been published to support the training of staff at all levels. The resources are available at: www.dcsf.gov.uk/everychildmatters/safeguardingandsocialcare/ safeguardingchildren/childdeathreviewprocedures/trainingmaterials/trainingmaterials/

127    See footnote 122.

128    See footnote 122.

the child death review, involving other LSCBs with an interest or whose local agencies have had involvement as appropriate. The Registrar has a duty to send a notification of each child's death to the LSCB (see paragraphs 7.15–7.17), and this provides a check to ensure that all child deaths have been notified to the designated person in each LSCB[129]. Any professional (or member of the public) hearing of a local child death in circumstances that mean it may not yet be known about (for example, a death occurring abroad) can inform the designated person in the LSCB.

7.35 Section 32 of the Children and Young Persons Act 2008 gives the Registrar General a power to share child death information with the Secretary of State. However information about children who die abroad may not reach the Registrar General for some time after the death has occurred. Therefore, LSCBs should continue to utilise other sources, such as professional contacts or the media, to inform the CDOP with information about the death of a child who is normally resident in England and who dies abroad.

7.36 The functions of the CDOP include:

- reviewing the available information on all child deaths of children aged up to 18 years (including deaths of infants aged less than 28 days but excluding those deaths set out in paragraph 7.1b) to determine whether the death was preventable. This decision should always be approved by the Chair of the CDOP;

- implementing, in consultation with the local coroner, local procedures and protocols that are in line with this guidance on enquiring into unexpected deaths, and evaluating these as part of the information set held on all deaths in childhood;

- collecting and collating an agreed minimum data set[130] on each child who has died and, seeking relevant information from professionals and family members;

- meeting frequently to review and evaluate the routinely collected data (see paragraph 7.25) on the deaths of all children, and thereby identifying lessons to be learnt or issues of concern, with a particular focus on effective inter-agency working to safeguard and promote the welfare of children;

- having a mechanism to evaluate specific cases in depth, where necessary, at subsequent meetings. This may involve revisiting child deaths after the outcome of other types of investigations is known (for example, outcomes from SCRs or criminal proceedings);

- monitoring the appropriateness of the response of professionals to an unexpected death of a child, reviewing the reports produced by the rapid response team on each unexpected death of a child, including the extent to

---

129 See footnote 122.
130 See footnote 119.

which the team has brought together any recorded wishes and feelings of the child, making a full record of this discussion and providing the professionals with feedback on their work. Where there is an ongoing criminal investigation, the Crown Prosecution Service must be consulted as to what it is appropriate for the Panel to consider and what actions it might take in order not to prejudice any criminal proceedings;

- referring to the Chair of the LSCB any deaths where, on evaluating the available information, the Panel considers there may be grounds to undertake further enquiries, investigations or a SCR and explore why this had not previously been recognised;

- informing the Chair of the LSCB where specific new information should be passed to the coroner or other appropriate authorities;

- providing relevant information to those professionals involved with the child's family so that they, in turn, can convey this information in a sensitive and timely manner to the family;

- monitoring the support and assessment services offered to families of children who have died;

- advising and monitoring the LSCB on the resources and training required locally to ensure an effective inter-agency response to child deaths[131];

- organising and monitoring the collection of data for the nationally agreed minimum data set[132], and making recommendations (to be approved by LSCBs) for any additional data to be collected locally;

- identifying any public health issues and considering, with the Director(s) of Public Health, how best to address these and their implications for both the provision of services and for training; and

- co-operating with regional and national initiatives – for example, by the Centre for Maternal and Child Enquiries (CMACE)[133] – to identify lessons on the prevention of child deaths.

### The process to be followed by Child Death Overview Panels (for all child deaths)

7.37    Any person notifying the designated person in the LSCB[134] of the death of a child should provide as much detail as is known to them in relation to the child and

---

131     See footnote 126.
132     See footnote 119.
133     found at: www.cmace.org.uk/
134     See footnote 122.

family and the circumstances of the death. They should inform the designated person of any professionals known to be involved with the child or family. Form A – The notification of the death of a child – is available at: www.dcsf.gov.uk/ everychildmatters/safeguardingandsocialcare/safeguardingchildren/ childdeathreviewprocedures/nationaltemplatesforlscbs/lscbtemplates/.

7.38 Following notification of the death of a child, the designated person should seek to establish which agencies and professionals have been involved with the child or family either prior to or at the time of death. A lead professional should be nominated in each agency to assist with this. Form B – Agency report form (and any relevant supplementary Form B's), is available at: www.dcsf.gov.uk/ everychildmatters/safeguardingandsocialcare/safeguardingchildren/ childdeathreviewprocedures/nationaltemplatesforlscbs/lscbtemplates/. Form B should be sent out to the lead professional in each agency and to any professionals known to be involved. If the death was either an early or a late neonatal death, the standard CMACE Perinatal Mortality Surveillance form should continue to be completed as normal and a copy should be sent to both the regional CMACE office and the relevant LSCB Child Death Overview designated person. This CMACE form is in addition to Form B2 having to be completed by the relevant professionals.

7.39 Professionals receiving an agency report form (Form B) should retrieve any relevant case records for the child or other family members to complete any information known to them or their organisation and return the form to the designated person within the requested time frame using a secure means of transfer. Normally this should be within three weeks of notification, although there will be circumstances where, because of ongoing medical or police investigations information may not be available for a longer period. It may be appropriate for the lead professional in each agency to collate information from all involved professionals within their agency.

7.40 Once all agency report forms are received by the designated person, the information should be collated onto a single Form B, anonymised and entered into a suitable database. The national agreed data set should be kept securely and separately from any identifiable data. The CDOP is likely to receive information that is personal data, including sensitive personal data, within the meaning of the Data Protection Act 1998 (DPA) for the purposes of child death reviews. CDOPs should be mindful of their obligations under the DPA when processing that information.

7.41 Prior to each panel meeting, anonymised, collated Form B's should be sent to all panel members in sufficient time to allow them to read all the material in preparation for the meeting. Panel members may wish for supplementary material (for example, individual case records, autopsy reports, scene photographs) to be made available at the panel meeting, but consideration should be given to its appropriateness for the meeting and issues of confidentiality. This information should be sent to the designated person before the meeting.

7.42    The CDOP should review each case brought before it to consider any factors contributing to the death, its classification of the death, and any lessons to be learnt from this death or from patterns of similar deaths in the area. Form C – the case review form (available at: www.dcsf.gov.uk/everychildmatters/ safeguardingandsocialcare/safeguardingchildren/childdeathreviewprocedures/ nationaltemplatesforlscbs/lscbtemplates/) may be used to facilitate this discussion and provides a template for local and national data collection. These forms should remain anonymous with a unique identifier but no identifiable information. For each death, the panel should classify the cause of death, make a decision as to the preventability of the death, identify any modifiable factors, and consider any recommendations that may be made about actions which could be taken to prevent such deaths in the future and to whom these recommendations should be addressed.

7.43    If the CDOP is unable to classify the death, or adequately review it from the information available, a decision should be made as to whether and what further information could be obtained to assist the panel. Where appropriate, the case should be rescheduled for discussion at a subsequent meeting. Where it is recognised that no further learning is likely, even with further information, the final review of the case should not be delayed.

7.44    Panels should consider whether groups of similar deaths (for example, all road traffic deaths, sudden unexpected death in infancy (SUDI), or deaths of children with life limiting conditions) should be discussed at designated panel meetings. In addition to standing panel members, specialists in relation to the type of death being discussed could be invited.

7.45    When reviewing neonatal deaths, these deaths should be discussed by the CDOP with appropriate representation of the professionals involved in this specialist area for example, midwifery, obstetrics, neonatal care. The process should focus on learning lessons from the deaths, and should use the minimum national data set when collecting information.

7.46    Any recommendations made by the CDOP should be directed at interventions that could help to prevent future child deaths, or improve the safety and welfare of children in the local area or further afield. The panel will not normally make direct recommendations in respect to individual case management. Recommendations should be few in number and should be carefully thought through to be Specific, Measurable, Achievable, Relevant and Timely.

7.47    Recommendations should be submitted to the LSCB or any other relevant body identified by the CDOP. The LSCB should make arrangements for following up on the recommendations to ensure that appropriate actions are taken.

## Roles and responsibilities when responding rapidly to an unexpected death of a child

7.48    The paragraphs below set out the roles of the various professionals for enquiring into and evaluating all unexpected child deaths (see paragraph 7.21 for a definition of unexpected child death). Information from this process should be considered by members of the CDOP which has responsibility for reviewing the deaths of all children normally resident in their area.

7.49    When a child dies unexpectedly, several investigative processes may be instigated, particularly when abuse or neglect is a factor. This guidance intends that the relevant professionals and organisations work together in a co-ordinated way, in order to minimize duplication and ensure that the lessons learnt contribute to safeguarding and promoting the welfare of children in the future.

7.50    It is intended that those professionals involved (before and/or after the death) with a child who dies unexpectedly should come together to respond to the child's death. This means that some roles may require an on-call rota for responding to unexpected child deaths in their area. The work of the team convened in response to each child's death should be co-ordinated, usually, by a local designated paediatrician responsible for unexpected deaths in childhood. LSCBs may choose to designate particular professionals to be standing members of a team because of their roles and particular expertise. The professionals who come together as a team will carry out their normal functions – for example, as a paediatrician, GP, nurse, health visitor, midwife, mental health professional, substance misuse worker, social worker, Youth Offending Team worker, probation or police officer in response to the unexpected death of a child in accordance with this guidance. They should also work according to a protocol agreed with the local coronial service. Other professionals known to the family from specialist agencies should be accessed on a case by case basis to support the core team; i.e. hospice support workers, children's community nurses. The joint responsibilities of these professionals include:

- responding quickly to the unexpected death of a child;

- making immediate enquiries into and evaluating the reasons for and circumstances of the death, in agreement with the coroner;

- undertaking the types of enquiries/investigations that relate to the current responsibilities of their respective organisations when a child dies unexpectedly.

This includes liaising with those who have ongoing responsibilities for other family members;

- collecting information in a standard, nationally agreed manner (see paragraph 7.2 and footnote 119);

- providing support to the bereaved family, and where appropriate referring on to specialist bereavement services; and

- following the death through and maintaining contact at regular intervals with family members and other professionals who have ongoing responsibilities for other family members, to ensure they are informed and kept up-to-date with information about the child's death.

## Other related processes

7.51   Where there is an ongoing criminal investigation, the Senior Investigating Officer and the Crown Prosecution Service must be consulted as to what it is appropriate for the professionals involved in reviewing a child's death to be doing, and what actions to take in order not to prejudice any criminal proceedings. Where a death of a young person occurs in custody, local agencies must co-operate with the Prisons and Probation Ombudsman.

7.52   Where a child dies unexpectedly, all registered providers of healthcare services are obliged to notify the Care Quality Commission, but may discharge this duty by notifying the National Patient Safety Agency (NHS providers) or the Care Quality Commission, as set out in Regulation 16 of the Care Quality Commission (Registration) Regulations 2009[135]. The results of these investigations should be made available to the CDOP in order to allow the information to be included in the Panel's discussions.

7.53   The Youth Justice Board for England and Wales (YJB) requires Youth Offending Teams (YOTs) to report and undertake local reviews of youth offending practice in cases where a child or young person has either died or attempted suicide whilst under supervision or within three months of the expiry of supervision. Where a child has died, the Local Management Review undertaken by the YOT in relation to the death should feed into the child death processes initiated by the CDOP.

7.54   If it is thought, at any time, that the criteria for a SCR might apply (see paragraphs 8.9–8.12), the Chair of the LSCB should be contacted and the SCR procedures set out in Chapter 8 should be followed. If a SCR is initiated, the CDOP will not be able to

---

135   See 'Outcome 18 – Notification of death' in Guidance about Compliance Essential Standards of Quality and Safety, CQC, 2009). NHS organisations should also follow locally agreed procedures for reporting and handling serious untoward and/or patient safety incidents.

conclude the child death reviewing process until after the SCR Executive Summary has been published. Similarly, the child death reviewing process will not be able to be completed if the CDOP is awaiting the outcomes of criminal proceedings and/or an inquest. This should **not**, however, prevent lessons from being learned and from being acted upon in a timely manner.

7.55   If, during the enquiries, concerns are expressed in relation to the needs of surviving children in the family, discussions should take place with local authority children's social care. It may be decided that it is appropriate to initiate an initial assessment using the *Framework for the Assessment of Children in Need and their Families (2000)*[136]. If concerns are raised at any stage about the possibility of surviving children in the household being abused or neglected, the inter-agency procedures set out in Chapter 5 in this guidance should be followed. Local authority children's social care has lead responsibility for safeguarding and promoting the welfare of children. The police will be the lead agency for any criminal investigation. The police must be informed immediately that there is a suspicion of a crime, to ensure that the evidence is properly secured and that any further interviews with family members and other relevant people accord with the requirements of the Police and Criminal Evidence Act 1984.

7.56   When a child dies unexpectedly and no doctor is able to issue a medical certificate of the cause of death, the child's death must be reported to the coroner. Agencies and professionals contributing to the processes described in this chapter should co-operate with their local coroner to ensure the inquest is able to proceed appropriately. The process of the rapid response can greatly assist the coroner in gathering information to inform the inquest, whilst providing ongoing support to the family. Any information pertaining to the death arising from the rapid response, including the outcome of a final local case discussion should be passed to the coroner. The CDOP members may attend an inquest at the discretion of HM Coroner and ask questions as a 'properly interested person'; there may be issues identified through the inquest that the CDOP would then be able to review to identify any wider public health concerns.

---

136   www.dh.gov.uk/en/Publicationsandstatistics/Publications/PublicationsPolicyandGuidance/ DH_4003256

## Processes for a rapid response from professionals to all unexpected deaths of children (0–18 years)[137]

### Care of parents/family members when a child dies unexpectedly

7.57   Where a child has died in, or been taken to, a hospital their parents/carers should be allocated a member of the hospital staff to remain with and support them throughout the process. The parents should normally be given the opportunity to hold and spend time with their baby or child. During this time the allocated member of staff should maintain a discreet presence.

7.58   Children dying at home or in a hospice or other setting who have been undergoing end of life care will not usually be considered to have died unexpectedly, and a rapid response to such deaths is rarely indicated.

7.59   When a child with a known life limiting and or life threatening condition dies in a manner or at a time that was not anticipated, the rapid response team should liaise closely and promptly with a member of the medical, palliative or end of life care team who knows the child and family, to jointly determine how best to respond to that child's death. This should include consideration of whether the child's body should be transferred to a hospital or hospice, and whether any investigations or inquiries are required. Where an end of life plan has been agreed by the end of life care team and is in place, this should be followed unless there are pressing reasons not to do so. For example, the coroner decides where the child's body may be taken and this decision may be different to what was set out in the family's prepared plan. The presence of a community children's nurse on call as part of the rapid response team could facilitate the process of communication and fact-finding.

7.60   Within the local rapid response procedures there should be provision for an identified professional to provide support to the family where their child has died and has not been taken to a hospital.

7.61   Where a child is living in England but their parents live abroad, careful consideration should be given to how best to contact and support the bereaved family members.

7.62   Parents/carers should be kept up-to-date with information about their child's death and the involvement of each professional, unless such sharing of information would jeopardise police investigations or other criminal justice processes.

---

137   Resources to assist in the conduct of a rapid response to an unexpected child death are available at: www.dcsf.gov.uk/everychildmatters/safeguardingandsocialcare/safeguardingchildren/childdeathreviewprocedures/advancedtrainingrapidresponse/rapidresponsetraining/

## Responding to the unexpected death of a child

7.63    The type of response to each child's unexpected death will depend to a certain extent on the age of the child, but there are some key elements that underpin all subsequent work. Supplementary information is required for making enquiries into, for example deaths of infants, those deaths in hospital that are the result of trauma, and suicides.

7.64    Once the death of a child has been referred to the coroner and s/he has accepted it, the coroner has jurisdiction over the body and all that pertains to it. Coroners must therefore be consulted over the local implementation of national guidance and protocols, and should be asked to give general approval for the measures agreed to reduce the need to obtain specific approval on each occasion.

7.65    A multi-professional approach is required to ensure collaboration among all involved, which may include ambulance staff, A&E department staff, coroners' officers, police, GPs, health visitors, school nurses, community children's nurses, midwives, paediatricians, palliative or end of life care staff, mental health professionals, substance misuse workers, hospital bereavement staff, voluntary agencies, coroners, pathologists, forensic medical examiners, local authority children's social care, YOTs, probation, schools, prison staff where a child has died in custody and any others who may find themselves with a contribution to make in individual cases (for example, fire fighters or faith leaders).

## Immediate response to the unexpected death of a child

7.66    Children who die suddenly and unexpectedly at home or in the community should normally be taken to an A&E department rather than a mortuary, and resuscitation should always be initiated unless clearly inappropriate. Resuscitation, once commenced, should be continued according to the *UK Resuscitation Guidelines* (2005)[138] until an experienced doctor (usually the consultant paediatrician on call) has made a decision that it is appropriate to stop further efforts. There may be some situations where it is inappropriate for a child to be transferred to a hospital (for example, if the circumstances of the death require the body to remain at the scene for forensic examination).

7.67    As noted above, children who die at home or in a hospice or other setting in which they have been in receipt of planned end of life care will not normally be considered to have died unexpectedly, and therefore should not usually be moved to a hospital A&E department. Parents whose children die at home in such circumstances may wish their child to remain at home, or be taken to a hospice cool room. This death

---

138    Found at: www.resus.org.uk/pages/guide.htm

will be subject to local coronial guidelines if the doctor is unable to issue a Medical Certificate of the Cause of Death.

7.68   As soon as practicable (i.e. as a response to an emergency) after arrival at a hospital, the baby or child should be examined by the consultant paediatrician on call (in some cases this might be together with a consultant in emergency medicine or, for some young people over 16 years of age, the consultant in emergency medicine may be more appropriate than a paediatrician). A detailed and careful history of events leading up to and following the discovery of the child's collapse should be taken from the parents/carers. This should begin the process of collecting a nationally agreed data set[139]. The purpose of obtaining high-quality information at this stage is to understand the cause of the death when appropriate and to identify anything suspicious about it. The paediatrician should carefully document the history and examination findings in the hospital notes. This should include a full account of any resuscitation and any interventions or investigations carried out. The use of a structured proforma may assist with documenting the history, but this should always include a narrative account by the carer of the events leading to the death. The examination findings, including any post mortem changes should be documented on a body chart. Templates for recording the history and examination are available on the *Every Child Matters* website at: www.dcsf.gov.uk/ everychildmatters/safeguardingandsocialcare/safeguardingchildren/ childdeathreviewprocedures/trainingmaterials/trainingmaterials/.

7.69   Where the cause of death or factors contributing to it is uncertain, investigative samples should be taken immediately on arrival and after the death is confirmed. In order to be compliant with the Human Tissue Act 2004 (HTA Act), the removal of these investigative samples must take place on Human Tissue Authority licensed premises with the authorisation of the coroner (or, where the coroner is not involved, the consent of a parent)[140]. These samples need to be agreed in advance with the coroner (see paragraph 7.64) and should include the standard set for SUDI (Royal College of Pathologists and Royal College of Paediatrics and Child Health, 2004) and standard sets for other types of death presentation as they are developed. The removal of tissue without such coronial authorisation or consent under the Human Tissue Act 2004 would be unlawful. Consideration should always be given to undertaking a full skeletal survey and, when appropriate, it should be made before the autopsy starts as this may significantly alter the required investigations.

7.70   When the baby or child is pronounced dead, the consultant clinician should inform the parents, having first reviewed all the available information. S/he should explain future police and coroner involvement, including the coroner's authority to order a post mortem examination. This may involve taking particular tissue blocks and

---

139   See footnote 119.
140   Further information can be found at: www.hta.gov.uk/

slides to ascertain the cause of death (see paragraph 7.69). Consent from those with parental responsibility for the child is required for tissue to be retained beyond the period required by the coroner (for example, for use in research or for possible future review).

7.71    The consultant clinician who has seen the child should inform the designated paediatrician with responsibility for unexpected deaths in childhood immediately after the coroner is informed.

7.72    The same processes apply to a child who is admitted to a hospital ward and subsequently dies unexpectedly in hospital.

7.73    In most circumstances following the unexpected death of a child, it will be appropriate to allow the parents to spend time with and hold their child. This should be facilitated by the hospital staff and rapid response team, with a quiet, designated area provided for the family to be with their child. In most circumstances it will be appropriate for a nurse or other professional to maintain a discreet presence at all times. In most situations the parents will have already handled their child after the death, and allowing them to hold their child will not in any way interfere with the investigation into the cause of death.

7.74    Support should be offered to the family, including where available, a bereavement counsellor, hospital chaplain or other faith leader. The hospital team should offer to contact any relatives or friends to support the parents at this time. The parents should be allowed to spend as much time as they wish with the child and any examination of the child or further investigations should where possible be carried out in a manner that causes least disruption to the family. Unless there are clear reasons not to (this matter should be discussed with the senior investigating police officer first), mementos such as a photograph, lock of hair, or hand and footprints should be offered to the family.

7.75    Before the parents leave the hospital, or in the case of a child who is not transferred to hospital, before the professionals leave the home, the parents should be provided with contact details for the lead professionals (consultant paediatrician, senior investigating police officer or coroners officer), and the details of who they should contact for information on the progress of any investigation or if they wish to visit the hospital to see their child. Following this immediate response, parents should be kept informed of the whereabouts of their child and any planned moves.

## Immediate response when a child is not transferred to a hospital

7.76   Where a child is not taken immediately to A&E, the professional confirming the fact of death should inform the designated paediatrician with responsibility for unexpected deaths in childhood at the same time as the coroner is informed.

7.77   The police will be involved and may decide that it is not appropriate to move the child's body. This may typically occur if there are clear signs that lead to suspicion. In most cases, however, it is expected that the child's body will already have been held or moved by the carer and, therefore, removal to A&E will not normally jeopardize an investigation.

7.78   The professional confirming the fact of death should consult the designated paediatrician with responsibility for unexpected deaths in childhood, who will ensure that relevant professionals (i.e. the coroner, the police and local authority children's social care) are informed of the death. This task may be undertaken by a person on behalf of the designated paediatrician. Contact may be required with more than one local authority if the child died away from home (see paragraphs 7.33–7.34 for more information about what should happen when a child who is normally resident within a LSCB area dies outside the area, including abroad). Any relevant information identified by local authority children's social care should be shared promptly with the police and on-call paediatrician. The health visitor or school nurse and GP should also be promptly informed as a matter of routine and relevant information should be shared.

7.79   When a child dies unexpectedly, a paediatrician (on-call or designated) should initiate an immediate information sharing and planning discussion between the lead agencies (i.e. health, police and local authority children's social care) to decide what should happen next and who will do what. This may also include the coroner's officer and consultant paediatrician on call, and any others who are involved (for example, the community children's nurse on call, other members of the primary health care team or other professionals who have been involved with the child and/ or family prior to, or around the time of death). The agreed plan should include a commitment to collaborate closely and communicate as often as necessary, often by telephone. Where the death occurred in a hospital, the plan should also address the actions required by the Trust's serious incidents protocol. Where the death occurred in a custodial setting, the plan should ensure appropriate liaison with the investigator from the Prisons and Probation Ombudsman.

7.80   For all unexpected deaths of children (including those not seen in A&E) urgent contact should be made with any other agencies who know or are involved with the child (including CAMHS, school or early years provider) to inform them of the child's death and to obtain information on the history of the child, the family and other members of the household. If a young person is under the supervision of a YOT, the YOT should also be approached.

7.81    The police will begin an investigation into the sudden or unexpected death of a child on behalf of the coroner. They will carry this out in accordance with relevant Association of Chief Police Officers guidelines.

7.82    When a baby or older child dies unexpectedly in a non-hospital setting, the senior investigating police officer and senior healthcare professional should make a decision about whether a visit to the place where the child died should be undertaken. This should almost always take place for infants who die unexpectedly (see paragraph 5.1 in the *Kennedy Report*)[141]. As well as deciding if the visit should take place, it should be decided how soon (within 24 hours) and who should attend. It is likely to be a senior investigating police officer and a healthcare professional (experienced in responding to unexpected child deaths (this will most commonly be a paediatrician or specialist nurse) who will visit, talk with the parents and evaluate the environment where the child died. They may make this visit together, or they may visit separately and then confer (details should be included in the local child death review protocol). After this visit the senior investigating police officer, visiting health care professional, GP, health visitor or school nurse and children's social care representative should review whether there is any additional information that could raise concerns about the possibility of abuse or neglect having contributed to the child's death. If there are concerns about surviving children in the household, the procedures set out in Chapter 5 should be followed. If there are grounds for considering initiating a SCR, the process set out in Chapter 8 should be followed.

## Involvement of coroner and pathologist

7.83    If s/he deems it necessary (and in almost all cases of an unexpected child death it will be), the coroner will order a post mortem examination to be carried out as soon as possible by the most appropriate pathologist available (this may be a paediatric pathologist, forensic pathologist or both) who will perform the examination according to the guidelines and protocols laid down by The Royal College of Pathologists. The designated paediatrician should collate information collected by those involved in responding to the child's death and share it with the pathologist conducting the post mortem examination in order to inform this process. Where the death may be unnatural, or the cause of death has not yet been determined, the coroner will in due course hold an inquest.

---

141    *Sudden Unexpected Death in Infancy: a multi-agency protocol for care and investigation. The report of a working party convened by the Royal Colleges of Pathologists and the Royal College of Paediatrics and Child Health (2004). London: RCPath.*

7.84   All information collected relating to the circumstances of the death – including a review of all relevant medical, social and educational records – must be included in a report for the coroner prepared jointly by the lead professionals in each agency. This report should be delivered to the coroner within 28 days of the death, unless some of the crucial information is not yet available.

## Case discussion following the preliminary results of the post mortem examination becoming available

7.85   The results of the post mortem examination belong to the coroner. In most cases it is possible for these to be discussed by the paediatrician and pathologist, together with the senior investigating police officer, as soon as possible, and the coroner should be informed immediately of the initial results. At this stage, the LSCB child death core data set[142] should be updated and, if necessary, previous information corrected to enable this change to be audited. If the initial post mortem findings or findings from the child's history suggest evidence of abuse or neglect as a possible cause of death, the police and local authority children's social care should be informed immediately, and the SCR processes in Chapter 8 of this guidance should be followed. If there are concerns about surviving children living in the household, the procedures set out in Chapter 5 should be followed with respect to these children.

7.86   In all cases, the designated paediatrician for unexpected child deaths or the paediatrician acting as his/her deputy should convene a further multi-agency discussion (usually on the telephone) very shortly after the initial post mortem results are available. This discussion usually takes place five to seven days after the death and should involve the pathologist, police, local authority children's social care and the paediatrician, plus any other relevant healthcare professionals, to review any further information that has come to light and that may raise additional concerns about safeguarding issues.

## Case discussion following the final results of the post mortem examination becoming available

7.87   A case discussion meeting should be held as soon as the final post mortem result is available. The timing of this discussion varies according to the circumstances of the death. This may range from immediately after the initial post mortem examination to three-four months after the death. The type of professionals involved in this meeting depends on the age of the child. The meeting should include those who knew the child and family and those involved in investigating the death, for

---

142   See footnote 119.

example, the GP, health visitor or school nurse, paediatrician(s), pathologist, senior investigating police officers and where appropriate, social workers.

7.88 The designated paediatrician with responsibility for unexpected deaths in childhood (or agreed deputy) should convene and chair this meeting. At this stage, the collection of the LSCB child death core data set[143] should be completed and if necessary, previous information corrected to enable this change to the information to be audited.

7.89 The main purpose of the case discussion is to share information to identify the cause of death and/or those factors that may have contributed to the death, and then to plan future care for the family. Potential lessons to be learnt may also be identified by this process. Another purpose is to inform the inquest.

7.90 There should be an explicit discussion of the possibility of abuse or neglect either causing or contributing to the death. If no evidence is identified to suggest maltreatment, this should be documented as part of the minutes of the meeting.

7.91 At the case discussion, it should be agreed how detailed information about the cause of the child's death will be shared, and by whom, with the parents, and who will offer the parents ongoing support.

7.92 The results of the post mortem examination, with the consent of HM Coroner, should be discussed with the parents at the earliest opportunity, except in those cases where abuse or neglect is suspected and/or the police are conducting a criminal investigation. In these situations, the paediatrician should discuss with local authority children's social care, the police and the pathologist what information should be shared with the parents and when. This discussion with the parents is usually part of the role of the lead paediatrician involved in the investigation of the child's death and she or he will, therefore, have responsibility for initiating and leading the meeting. A member of the primary healthcare team should attend this meeting whenever possible.

7.93 An agreed record of the case discussion meeting and all reports should be sent to the coroner, to take into consideration in the conduct of the inquest and, in the cause of death, notified to the Registrar of Births and Deaths. The record of the case discussions and the record of the core data set should also be made available to the relevant local CDOP. When a child dies away from their normal place of residence, a joint decision will need to be made by the rapid response team in the LSCB area in which the death occurred and the team in the child's normal area of residence as to which team will lead the investigation and in which LSCB area the case review meeting should be held. On occasion separate meetings may be appropriate in

---

143    See footnote 119.

both LSCB areas, but good communication between the teams is essential (see paragraphs 7.33–7.34). This information can then be analysed and decisions can be made about what actions should be taken by whom to prevent similar deaths in the future.

## Professionals meeting to discuss expected child deaths

7.94   When a child's death is not regarded as 'unexpected', the team looking after the child may choose to organise a discussion of the case, since it is likely that important lessons can be learnt that might improve the care of other children. Such a discussion may be conducted using the same format as a professionals' meeting, the output of which could be captured on the Analysis Proforma (Form C). Information from these discussions would provide the CDOP with evidence of good local practice and allow a wider engagement of professionals with the child death review process.

## Use of child death information to prevent future deaths

7.95   Each Child Death Overview Panel should prepare an annual report of relevant information for the LSCB. This information should in turn inform the LSCB annual report (see paragraph 3.35). This information should include the total numbers of deaths reviewed, recommendations made by the panel about required future actions to prevent child deaths, and any further description of the deaths that the panel deems appropriate. It should also include a review of actions taken to implement the recommendations from the previous year's report, and set out any such recommendations which have not yet been fully implemented which are to be carried forward. Appropriate care should be taken to ensure confidentiality of personal information and sensitivity to the bereaved families. Information which could lead to the identification of individual children or family members should not be included in the annual report. The LSCB annual report should serve as a powerful resource for driving public health measures to prevent child deaths and promote child health, safety and wellbeing.

7.96   The LSCB has responsibility for disseminating the lessons to be learned from the child death and other reviewing processes to all relevant organisations, ensures that relevant findings inform the Children and Young People's Plan and acts on any recommendations to improve policy, professional practice and inter-agency working to safeguard and promote the welfare of children. The LSCB is also required to supply anonymised data on child deaths to the Department for Children, Schools and Families, so that the Department can commission research and publish nationally comparable analyses of these deaths. The primary aims of this research are to support a reduction in the incidence of children whose deaths can be prevented, to improve inter-agency working and to safeguard and promote the welfare of children.

# Flow chart 6: Interface between the child death and serious case review processes

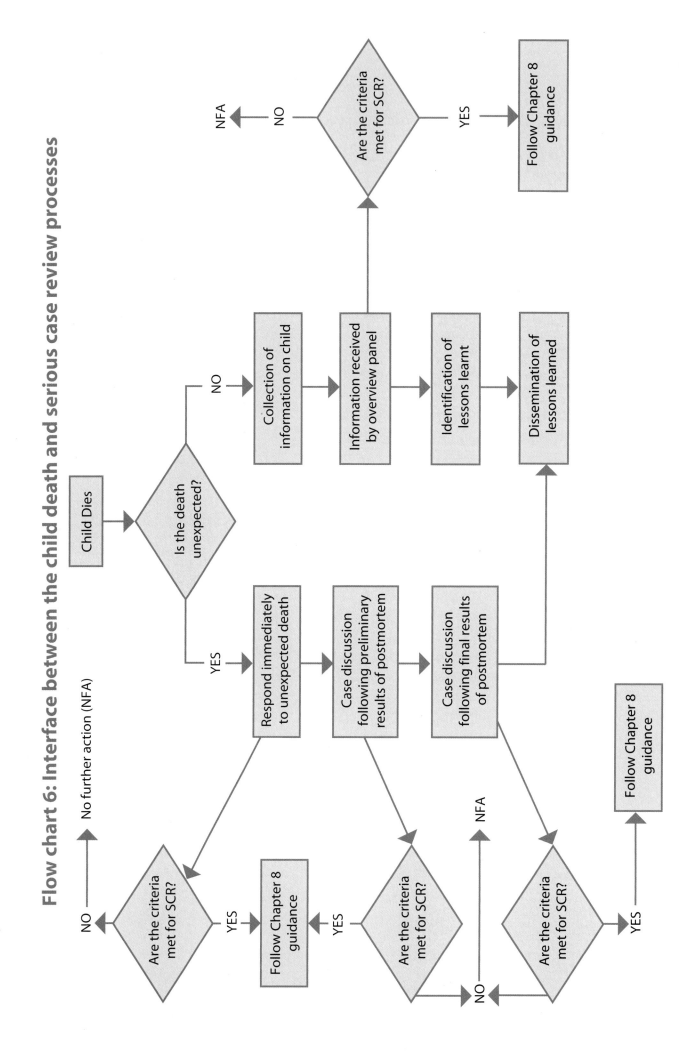

# Chapter 8 – Serious case reviews

## Reviewing and investigative functions of Local Safeguarding Children Boards

8.1 The prime purpose of a Serious Case Review (SCR) is for agencies and individuals to learn lessons to improve the way in which they work both individually and collectively to safeguard and promote the welfare of children. The lessons learned should be disseminated effectively, and the recommendations should be implemented in a timely manner so that the changes required result, wherever possible, in children being protected from suffering or being likely to suffer harm in the future. It is essential, to maximise the quality of learning, that the child's daily life experiences and an understanding of his or her welfare, wishes and feelings are at the centre of the SCR, irrespective of whether the child died or was seriously harmed. This perspective should inform the scope and terms of reference of the SCR as well as the ways in which the information is presented and addressed at all stages of the process, including the conclusions and recommendations. Reviews vary in their breadth and complexity but, in all cases, **where possible lessons should be acted upon quickly without necessarily waiting for the SCR to be completed**.

8.2 Any professional or agency may refer a case to the Local Safeguarding Children Board (LSCB) if they believe that there are important lessons for intra- and/or inter-agency working to be learned from the case.

8.3 Regulation 5 of the Local Safeguarding Children Boards Regulations 2006[144] requires LSCBs to undertake reviews of serious cases. They should be undertaken in accordance with the processes set out in this chapter. The same criteria apply to all children, including those with a disability[145].

8.4 Regulation 5 sets out that:

*(1) The functions of a LSCB in relation to its objective (as defined in section 14(1) of the Act) are as follows –*
*(e) undertaking reviews of serious cases and advising the authority and their Board partners on lessons to be learned.*
*(2) For the purposes of paragraph (1) (e) a Serious Case Review is one where –*
*(a) abuse or neglect of a child is known or suspected; and*
*(b) either –*
*(i) the child has died; or*

---

144 The Local Safeguarding Children Boards Regulations 2006, Statutory Instrument no. 2006/90.
145 *Safeguarding Disabled Children: Practice guidance* (2009). London: Department for Children, Schools and Families.

*(ii) the child has been seriously harmed and there is cause for concern as to the way in which the authority, their Board partners or other relevant persons have worked together to safeguard the child.*

## The purposes of Serious Case Reviews

8.5 The purposes of SCRs carried out under this guidance are to:

- establish what lessons are to be learned from the case about the way in which local professionals and organisations work individually and together to safeguard and promote the welfare of children;

- identify clearly what those lessons are both within and between agencies, how and within what timescales they will be acted on, and what is expected to change as a result; and

- improve intra- and inter-agency working and better safeguard and promote the welfare of children.

8.6 SCRs are not inquiries into how a child died or was seriously harmed, or into who is culpable. These are matters for coroners and criminal courts, respectively, to determine as appropriate.

8.7 Nor are SCRs part of any disciplinary inquiry or process relating to individual practitioners. Where information emerges in the course of a SCR indicating that disciplinary action would be appropriate, such action should be undertaken separately from the SCR process and in line with the relevant organisation's disciplinary procedures. SCRs may be conducted at the same time, but should be separate from disciplinary action. In some cases (for example, alleged institutional abuse) it may be necessary to initiate disciplinary action as a matter of urgency to safeguard and promote the welfare of other children.

## Safeguarding siblings or other children

8.8 When a child dies or is seriously harmed, and abuse or neglect is known or suspected to be a factor, the first priority of local organisations should be to consider immediately whether there are other children who are suffering, or likely to suffer, significant harm and who require safeguarding (for example, siblings or other children in an institution where abuse is alleged). Where there are concerns about the welfare of siblings or other children the guidance in Chapter 5 should be followed. Thereafter, organisations should consider whether there are any lessons to be learned about the ways in which they work individually and together to safeguard and promote the welfare of children.

## When should a LSCB undertake a Serious Case Review?

8.9    When a child dies (including death by suspected suicide) **and** abuse or neglect is known or suspected to be a factor in the death, the LSCB should **always** conduct a SCR into the involvement of organisations and professionals in the lives of the child and family. This is irrespective of whether local authority children's social care is, or has been, involved with the child or family. These SCRs should include situations where a child has been killed by a parent, carer or close relative with a mental illness, known to misuse substances or to perpetrate domestic abuse. In addition, a SCR should always be carried out when a child dies in custody, either in police custody, on remand or following sentencing, in a Young Offender Institution (YOI), a Secure Training Centre (STC) or secure children's home, or where the child was detained under the Mental Health Act 2005.

8.10   The death of every child is reviewed in accordance with the child death review processes outlined in Chapter 7 of this guidance. A SCR may be triggered at any point in the child death reviewing process if a rapid response team or Child Death Overview Panel (CDOP) considers a case may meet the criteria for a SCR (see paragraph 7.1). In the case of a looked after child, the LSCB for the area of the local authority looking after the child should exercise lead responsibility for conducting the child death review, involving other LSCBs with an interest or whose local agencies have had involvement as appropriate (see paragraph 7.34). This CDOP may refer a case to its LSCB Chair if it considers the criteria for a SCR may be met and a SCR has not been initiated. Chapter 7, flow chart 6, shows the interface between the child death review and SCR processes.

## When should a LSCB consider undertaking a Serious Case Review?

8.11   LSCBs should consider whether to conduct a SCR whenever a child has been seriously harmed in the following situations:

- a child sustains a potentially life-threatening injury or serious and permanent impairment of physical and/or mental health and development through abuse or neglect; or

- a child has been seriously harmed as a result of being subjected to sexual abuse; or

- a parent has been murdered and a domestic homicide review is being initiated under the Domestic Violence Act 2004[146]; or

---

146    The Home Office is working closely with other government departments to develop a process for undertaking domestic homicide reviews and will ensure that any relevant issues regarding SCRs, or any other statutory reviews, are fully considered and incorporated into that process.

- a child has been seriously harmed following a violent assault perpetrated by another child or an adult;

**and** the case gives rise to concerns about the way in which local professionals and services worked together to safeguard and promote the welfare of children. This includes inter-agency and/or inter-disciplinary working.

8.12 The following questions may also help in deciding whether a case should be the subject of a SCR. The answer 'yes' to one or more of these questions is likely to indicate that a SCR could yield useful lessons:

- Was there clear evidence of a child having suffered, or been likely to suffer, significant harm that was:

    - not recognised by organisations or professionals in contact with the child or perpetrator; **or**

    - not shared with others; **or**

    - not acted on appropriately?

- Was the child abused or neglected in an institutional setting (for example, school, nursery, children's or family centre, YOI, STC, immigration removal centre, mother and baby unit in a prison, children's home or Armed Services training establishment)?

- Was the child abused or neglected while being looked after by the local authority?

- Was the child a member of a family that has recently moved to the UK, for example as asylum seekers or temporary workers?

- Did the child suffer harm during an unauthorised absence from an institution, or having run away from home or other care setting?

- Does one or more agency or professional consider that its concerns about a child's welfare were not taken sufficiently seriously, or acted on appropriately, by another?

- Does the case indicate that there may be failings in one or more aspects of the local operation of formal safeguarding children procedures which go beyond the handling of this case?

- Was the child the subject of a child protection plan at the time of the incident, or had they previously been the subject of a plan or on the child protection register?

- Does the case appear to have implications for a range of agencies and/or professionals?

- Does the case suggest that the LSCB may need to change its local protocols or procedures, or that protocols and procedures are not being adequately promulgated, understood or acted on?

- Are there any indications that the circumstances of the case may have national implications for systems or processes, or that it is in the public interest to undertake a SCR?

## Which LSCB should take lead responsibility?

8.13   Where partner agencies of more than one LSCB have known about or have had contact with the child, the LSCB for the area in which the child is or was normally resident should take lead responsibility for conducting the SCR. Any other LSCBs that have an interest or involvement in the case should co-operate as partners in jointly planning and undertaking the SCR. In the case of a looked after child, the local authority looking after the child should exercise lead responsibility for conducting the SCR, again involving other LSCBs with an interest or involvement.

## Membership of SCR sub-committees and SCR Panels

8.14   Many LSCBs have a standing SCR sub-committee to oversee and quality assure all SCRs undertaken by the LSCB, and to provide advice to the LSCB Chair on whether the criteria for conducting a SCR have been met. A SCR sub-committee should involve representatives from local authority children's social care, health (commissioning Primary Care Trust (PCT) and other partners as relevant), education and the police at a minimum. Members of agencies which have responsibilities for completing Individual Management Reviews (IMRs) may be members of the SCR sub-committee but it should not consist solely of such people.

8.15   Following a decision by the LSCB Chair to undertake a SCR, the SCR sub-committee should commission a SCR Panel to manage the process. Where a LSCB does not have a standing SCR sub-committee, a SCR Panel should be convened by the LSCB to advise the LSCB Chair on whether the criteria for undertaking a SCR have been met and, where appropriate, to ensure the SCR is undertaken in accordance with this guidance. In such circumstances the same membership requirements apply to a SCR Panel as set out in paragraph 8.14 for a SCR sub-committee.

8.16   The Chair of the SCR sub-committee should be an experienced person and could be the independent Chair of the LSCB, or a member of the LSCB. The Chair of any SCR Panel should not be a member of the LSCB(s) involved in the SCR, an employee of any of the agencies involved in the SCR or the overview report author. The SCR

Panel Chair can be the independent LSCB Chair, someone from another LSCB which is not involved in the SCR or from an agency which is not involved in the case.

## Instigating a Serious Case Review

### Does the case meet the Serious Case Review criteria?

8.17    The LSCB Chair should consider whether a case might meet the criteria for a SCR, applying the criteria at paragraphs 8.9–8.12. Where the child has died, the LSCB Chair should also use information available from the professionals involved in reviewing the child's death (see Chapter 7) to assist in making this decision. In some cases, it may be valuable to conduct a single IMR rather than a full SCR, for example where there are lessons to be learned about the way in which staff worked within one agency rather than about how agencies worked together, or a smaller scale audit of an individual case that gives rise to concern but does not meet the criteria for a SCR. Methodologies such as those developed by Social Care Institute for Excellence (SCIE)[147] or root cause analysis used in the health service may be useful here. In such cases, arrangements should be made to share relevant findings with the SCR sub-committee or SCR Panel.

8.18    Where the LSCB Chair considers, in a particular case, that the criteria for a SCR may be met, he or she should request that the SCR sub-committee considers whether a SCR should take place. If the SCR sub-committee recommends that a SCR be undertaken, they should also recommend the scope and terms of reference for the review. These recommendations should be forwarded to the Chair of the LSCB, who has ultimate responsibility for deciding whether to conduct a SCR. The LSCB Chair should notify Ofsted of the outcome of this decision as soon as it has been made. Ofsted will then pass this information to the relevant Government Office (GO) and the Department for Children, Schools and Families (DCSF). PCT commissioners should ensure their Strategic Health Authority (SHA) and the Care Quality Commission (CQC) are notified. The police should also notify Her Majesty's Inspectorate of Constabulary (HMIC) and similarly the National Offender Management Service should notify Her Majesty's Inspectorate of Prisons (HMIP) and Her Majesty's Inspectorate of Probation (HMI Probation).

8.19    In all cases and at all stages in the SCR process from the first notification to Ofsted of a serious incident to the completion of the final SCR report, information relating to children, family members and professionals involved in the case (with the exception of the LSCB Chair, SCR Panel Chair and the overview report author) should be

---

147    Fish S., Munro E. and Bairstow S. (2008) *SCIE Report 19: Learning together to safeguard children: developing a multi-agency systems approach for case reviews.* London: Social Care Institute for Excellence.

anonymised by the LSCB before being submitted to any external organisation or body (including Ofsted, the relevant GO and DCSF).

## Determining the scope and terms of reference of the review

8.20   The SCR sub-committee should consider, in the light of current information known in each case, the scope of the SCR and draw up clear terms of reference. The LSCB Chair should ensure that the terms of reference address the key issues in the case and approve them. The GO Children and Learners Team will be able to assist LSCBs where policy advice on undertaking a SCR is required. Where necessary LSCBs should seek their own legal advice. Relevant issues to consider include the following:

- What appear to be the most important issues to address in identifying the learning from this specific case? How can the relevant information best be obtained and analysed, including, for instance, information on the mental health of relevant adults?

- When should the SCR start, and by what date should it be completed, bearing in mind the timescales for completion set out below? Are there any relevant court cases or investigations pending which could influence progress or the timing of the publication of the executive summary?

- Over what time period should events in the child's life be reviewed, i.e. how far back should enquiries extend and what is the cut-off point? What family history/ background information will help better to understand the recent past and the present?

- How should the child (where the review does not involve a death), surviving siblings, parents or other family members contribute to the SCR, and who should be responsible for facilitating their involvement? How will they be involved and contribute throughout the overall process?

- Are there any specific considerations around ethnicity, religion, diversity or equalities issues that may require special consideration?

- Did the family's immigration status have an impact on the child/children or on the parents' capacities to meet their needs?

- Which organisations and professionals should be asked to submit reports or otherwise contribute to the SCR including, where appropriate, for example the proprietor of an independent school or a playgroup leader?

- Who will make the link with relevant interests outside the main statutory organisations, for example independent professionals, independent schools, independent healthcare providers or voluntary organisations?

- Is there a need to involve organisations/professionals working in other LSCB areas (see paragraph 8.13), and what should be the respective roles and responsibilities of the different LSCBs with an interest?

- Will the LSCB need to obtain independent legal advice about any aspect of the proposed SCR?

- Who should be appointed as the independent author for the overview report (bearing in mind that this person should not be the Chair of the LSCB, the SCR sub-committee or the SCR Panel – see paragraph 8.33).

- Might it help the SCR Panel to bring in an outside expert at any stage, to help understand crucial aspects of the case?

- Will the case give rise to other parallel investigations of practice, for example, into the health or adult social care provided or multi-disciplinary suicide reviews, a domestic homicide review where a parent has been killed, a Prisons and Probation Ombudsman (PPO) Fatal Incidents Investigation[148] where the child has died in a custodial setting or a Serious Further Offence (SFO)[149] or MAPPA Serious Case Review (MSCR)[150] process where offenders are charged with serious further offences whilst subject to statutory supervision? And if so, how can a co-ordinated or jointly commissioned review process address all the relevant questions that need to be asked in the most effective way and with minimal delay? Arrangements should be agreed locally on how a NHS Serious Untoward Incident (SUI) investigation into the provision of healthcare should be co-ordinated with a SCR.

- How will the SCR terms of reference and processes fit in with those for other types of reviews – for example, for homicide, mental health or prisons?

- How should the review process take account of a coroner's inquiry, any criminal investigations (if relevant), family or other civil court proceedings related to the case? How will it be best to liaise with the coroner[151] and/or the Crown Prosecution Service (CPS) and to ensure that relevant information can be shared without incurring significant delay in the review process?

- How should the review process take account of relevant lessons learned from research (including the biennial overview reports of SCRs) and from SCRs which have been undertaken by the LSCB?

- How should any family, public and media interest be managed before, during and after the SCR? In particular, how should surviving children (where appropriate given their age and understanding) and family members be informed of the findings of the SCR?

---

148     See www.ppo.gov.uk/investigating-fatal-accidents.html

149     PC 22/2008 Revised Notification and Review Procedures for Serious Further Offences.

150     See www.probation.homeoffice.gov.uk/output/page30.asp

151     See www.justice.gov.uk/guidance/coroners-guidance.htm

8.21   Some of these issues may need to be revisited by the SCR Panel as the review progresses and new information emerges. This reconsideration of the issues may in turn mean that the terms of reference will need to be revised and agreed by the LSCB Chair.

## Timescales for initiating and undertaking a Serious Case Review

8.22   Reviews vary widely in their breadth and complexity but, in all cases, where lessons are able to be identified they should be acted upon as quickly as possible without necessarily waiting for the SCR to be completed. Within one month of a case coming to the attention of the LSCB Chair, he or she should decide, following a recommendation from the SCR sub-committee, whether a review should take place. An initial decision may need to be revisited if further information comes to light, for example through a criminal investigation or a child death review in accordance with Chapter 7. Ofsted and other inspectorates should be notified accordingly as set out in paragraph 8.18.

8.23   Serious case reviews should be completed within six months from the date of the decision to proceed. Sometimes the complexity of a case does not become apparent until the SCR is in progress. If it emerges that a SCR cannot be completed within six months of the LSCB Chair's decision to initiate it (perhaps because of judicial proceedings), the LSCB should revise its timetable and immediately consult the relevant GO in their capacity to provide advice, support and challenge.

8.24   Where an extension beyond the six month timeframe is necessary, an update on progress and a revised project plan should be produced quickly for the relevant GO to consider. This update should include recommendations for action where these are not dependent on the SCR being concluded until after other proceedings have ended. It should also include actions taken to date and an explanation for the extension to the timescale, including the revised completion date. Where a decision to extend the period for completion is made, this information will be passed to Ofsted by the relevant GO. LSCBs should be proactive in keeping GO Children and Learners Teams fully appraised of timing expectations, of risks of delay and of interdependencies with other parallel or related processes.

8.25   In some cases, criminal proceedings may follow the death or serious injury of a child. The Chair of the SCR Panel should discuss with the relevant criminal justice agencies such as the police and the CPS, at an early stage, how the review process should take account of such proceedings. For example, how does this affect timing and the way in which the SCR is conducted (including any interviews of relevant personnel), what is its potential impact on criminal investigations, and who should contribute at what stage? Much useful work to understand and learn from the case can often proceed without risk of contamination of witnesses in criminal proceedings. In some cases it may not be possible to finalise the IMRs and the overview report or to finalise and publish an executive summary until after coronial or criminal proceedings have been concluded, but this should not prevent early lessons learned from being acted upon.

8.26 SCRs should not be delayed as a matter of course because of outstanding family, civil or administrative court cases. The LSCB Chair should make these decisions on a case by case basis based on advice from the Chair of the SCR Panel and having consulted with the local authority where there are pending family cases. The LSCB Chair may also need to seek legal advice to assist in deciding how to proceed.

8.27 The final SCR report, including the executive summary, should take full account of salient, new information which becomes available during the course of these proceedings and the facts, conclusions and recommendations should be revised accordingly.

## Who should be involved in the Serious Case Review?

8.28 The initial scoping of the SCR should identify those who should contribute, although it may emerge, as further information becomes available, that the involvement of others, such as those providing specialist adult services, would be useful. As noted above in paragraph 8.21, information of relevance to the review may become available at a later stage through, for example, criminal proceedings or investigations such as those undertaken by the PPO.

8.29 Each relevant service should undertake an IMR of its involvement with the child and family. This should begin as soon as a decision is taken to proceed with a SCR, and even sooner if a case gives rise to concerns within the individual organisation. Relevant independent professionals should contribute reports of their involvement. Where Cafcass contributes to a review, the prior agreement of the courts should be sought so that the duty of confidentiality which the children's guardian has under the court rules can be waived to the degree necessary.

8.30 Designated safeguarding health professionals, on behalf of the PCT(s) as commissioners, should review and evaluate the practice of all involved health professionals, including GPs and providers commissioned by the PCT area. Where more than one PCT has commissioned services the PCTs will need to agree locally how they will work together. This may involve reviewing the involvement of individual practitioners and NHS trusts, and advising named professionals and managers who are compiling reports for the review. The designated professionals should produce an integrated health chronology and a health overview report focusing on how health organisations have interacted together. This may generate additional recommendations for health organisations. The health overview report will constitute the IMR for the PCTs as commissioners. Designated safeguarding health professionals also have an important role in providing guidance on how to balance confidentiality and disclosure issues to ensure an objective, just and thorough approach to identifying lessons in the IMR. If the designated health professional(s) have been clinically involved with the case the PCT should seek advice and help from another PCT designated professional as necessary.

8.31    The process of conducting an IMR requires access to records relevant to the child such as those from health bodies. The public interest served by this process warrants full disclosure of all relevant information within the child's own records. In some circumstances the person conducting the IMR may require access to information about third parties (for example, members of the child's immediate family or carers) that is either contained within the child's health records or in the health records of another person. While in most cases there will be a public interest in disclosing this information, the record holder(s) should ensure that any information they disclose about a third party is both necessary and proportionate. All disclosures of information about third parties need to be considered on a case by case basis, and the reasoning for either disclosure or non-disclosure should be fully documented. This applies to all records of NHS-commissioned care, whether provided under the NHS or in the independent or voluntary sector.

8.32    The SCR Panel, on behalf of the LSCB, should commission an overview report that brings together and analyses the findings of the various IMRs from organisations and others, and that makes recommendations for future action. It is crucial that the SCR Panel and the overview report author have access to all relevant documentation and where necessary individual professionals to enable both to undertake effectively their respective SCR functions.

8.33    The overview report should be commissioned from a person who is independent of all the local agencies and professionals involved and of the LSCB(s). The overview report author should not be the chair of the LSCB, the SCR sub-committee or the SCR Panel. Those conducting management reviews of individual services should not have been directly concerned with the child or family, or have been the immediate line manager of the practitioner(s) involved.

## Individual management reviews – general principles

8.34    Once it is known that a case is being considered for review, each organisation should secure its records relating to the case to guard against loss or interference. Once it is decided that a SCR will be undertaken, individual organisations, having secured their case records promptly, should begin quickly to draw up a chronology of their involvement with the child and family.

8.35    The aim of IMRs should be to look openly and critically at individual and organisational practice and at the context within which people were working to see whether the case indicates that improvements could and should be made and, if so, to identify how those changes can be brought about. The IMR reports should be quality assured by the senior officer in the organisation which has commissioned the report and when they are satisfied the findings accepted. This senior officer will be responsible also for ensuring that the recommendations of the IMR, and where appropriate the overview report, are acted on.

8.36    Where a child dies in or whilst under escort to or from a custodial setting such as a YOI or STC, the PPO will conduct a fatal incidents investigation and report on the circumstances surrounding the death of that child. The investigation will examine the child's period in custody and assess the clinical care they received as well as examining relevant factors which led to the child being placed in custody. In such cases a representative of the Youth Justice Board (YJB) should be a member of the SCR Panel to help ensure that relevant youth justice issues are covered. The PPO may be invited to attend SCR Panel meetings for specific, agreed purposes. The SCR terms of reference should set out how the PPO, the SCR Panel and the SCR sub-committee will work together to share relevant information during the process of undertaking the SCR[152].

8.37    The following outline format should guide the preparation of IMRs, to help ensure that the relevant questions are addressed and to ensure that information is provided to LSCBs in a consistent format to help prepare an overview report. The questions posed do not comprise a comprehensive checklist relevant to all situations. Each case may give rise to specific questions or issues that need to be explored, and each SCR should consider carefully the circumstances of individual cases and how best to structure the SCR in the light of the particular circumstances.

8.38    Where staff or others are interviewed by those preparing IMRs, a written record of such interviews should be made and this should be shared with the relevant interviewee. If the review finds that policies and procedures have not been followed, relevant staff or managers should be interviewed in order to understand the reasons for this.

8.39    On completion of each IMR report there should be a process of feedback and debriefing for the staff involved in the case, in advance of completion of the overview report. There should also be a follow-up feedback session with these staff once the SCR report has been completed and before the executive summary is published. It is important that the SCR process supports an open, just and learning

---

152    The DCSF and PPO are agreeing a memorandum which will set out in more detail how LSCBs and the PPO relate to each other when a fatal incidents investigation is being undertaken by the PPO and a SCR is being undertaken by a LSCB(s) with respect to the same child.

culture and is not perceived as a disciplinary-type hearing which may intimidate and undermine the confidence of staff.

## Scope and format of individual management reviews

*What was our involvement with this child and family?*

Construct a comprehensive chronology of involvement by the organisation and/or professional(s) in contact with the child and family over the period of time set out in the review's terms of reference. (This chronology should clearly set out when the child was seen and whether the wishes and feelings of the child were sought). Briefly summarise decisions reached, the services offered and/or provided to the child(ren) and family, and other action taken.

Where an agency has had relevant contact with the alleged perpetrator, the chronology should also cover these actions and should ask whether everything was done which might reasonably have been expected to manage effectively the risk of harm posed by the alleged perpetrator to the child.

*Analysis of involvement*

Consider the events that occurred, the decisions made, and the actions taken or not taken. Where judgements were made, or actions taken, which indicate that practice or management could be improved, try to get an understanding not only of what happened but **why** something either did or did not happen. Consider specifically the following:

- Were practitioners aware of and sensitive to the needs of the children in their work, and knowledgeable both about potential indicators of abuse or neglect and about what to do if they had concerns about a child's welfare?

- When, and in what way, were the child(ren)'s wishes and feelings ascertained and taken account of when making decisions about the provision of children's services? Was this information recorded?

- Did the organisation have in place policies and procedures for safeguarding and promoting the welfare of children and acting on concerns about their welfare?

- What were the key relevant points/opportunities for assessment and decision making in this case in relation to the child and family? Do assessments and decisions appear to have been reached in an informed and professional way?

- Did actions accord with assessments and decisions made? Were appropriate services offered/provided, or relevant enquiries made, in the light of assessments?

- Were there any issues, in communication, information sharing or service delivery, between those with responsibilities for work during normal office hours and others providing out of hours services?

- Where relevant, were appropriate child protection or care plans in place, and child protection and/or looked after reviewing processes complied with?

- Was practice sensitive to the racial, cultural, linguistic and religious identity and any issues of disability of the child and family, and were they explored and recorded?

- Were senior managers or other organisations and professionals involved at points in the case where they should have been?

- Was the work in this case consistent with each organisation's and the LSCB's policy and procedures for safeguarding and promoting the welfare of children, and with wider professional standards?

- Were there organisational difficulties being experienced within or between agencies? Were these due to a lack of capacity in one or more organisations? Was there an adequate number of staff in post? Did any resourcing issues such as vacant posts or staff on sick leave have an impact on the case?

- Was there sufficient management accountability for decision making?

*What do we learn from this case?*

Are there lessons from this case for the way in which this organisation works to safeguard and promote the welfare of children? Is there good practice to highlight, as well as ways in which practice can be improved? Are there implications for ways of working; training (single and inter-agency); management and supervision; working in partnership with other organisations; resources? Are there implications for current policy and practice?

*Recommendations for action*

What action should be taken by whom and when? What outcomes should these actions bring, and in what timescales, and how will the organisation evaluate whether they have been achieved? Are there any immediate statutory requirements for the notification of concerns and are there likely to be any media handling issues?

## The Serious Case Review overview report

8.40    The SCR overview report should bring together, and draw overall conclusions from, the information and analysis contained in the IMRs, information from the child death review processes, where relevant, and reports commissioned from any other relevant interests. Overview reports should be produced according to the following outline format although, as with IMRs, the precise format will depend on the features of the case. This outline is most applicable to abuse or neglect that has taken place in a family setting. In certain circumstances, for example abuse in institutional settings or complex situations, the reviews are likely to be more complex.

> ### Format of Serious Case Review overview report
>
> *Introduction*
>
> - Summarise the circumstances that led to a SCR being undertaken in this case.
>
> - State the terms of reference of the review.
>
> - Record the methodology used including the documents reviewed, and whether the information was provided in an interview or through written evidence.
>
> - List agencies or types of contributors to review and the nature of their contributions (for example, IMR by local authority, report through the PCT as commissioner from adult mental health service). List the names of the LSCB Chair, SCR Panel Chair, the author of the overview report and the job titles and employing organisations of all the SCR Panel members.
>
> - List parallel processes, if any, that are being conducted (for example, criminal proceedings, PPO investigation following the death of a child in custody or independent investigation of adverse events in mental health services).
>
> *The facts*
>
> - Prepare an anonymised genogram showing membership of family, extended family and household.
>
> - Compile an integrated chronology of involvement with the child and family on the part of all relevant organisations, professionals and others who have contributed to the review process. Note specifically in the chronology each occasion on which the child was seen, if the child was seen alone and whether the child's wishes and feelings were sought or expressed.

- Consider explicitly any relevant ethnic, cultural or other equalities issues and whether these are relevant to the behaviours and approach taken by the organisations and professionals involved.

- Summarise the relevant information that was known to the agencies and professionals involved about the parents/carers, any perpetrator and the home circumstances of the children.

*Analysis*

This part of the overview report should look at how and why events occurred, decisions were made and actions taken or not taken. This is the part of the report where reviewers can consider, with the benefit of hindsight, whether different decisions or actions may have led to an alternative course of events. It is important that this is objective and open, being clear where systems could improve. The analysis section is also where any examples of good practice should be highlighted. The findings from this SCR should be considered alongside learning from previous SCRs undertaken by the LSCB and findings from relevant research.

*Conclusions and recommendations*

This part of the report should summarise what lessons are to be drawn from the case, and how those lessons should be translated into recommendations for action, and to what timescales. Recommendations should include, but should not simply be limited to, the recommendations made in individual reports from each organisation. Recommendations should usually be few in number, focused and specific, and capable of being implemented. If there are lessons for national as well as local policy and practice, these should also be highlighted and the information sent to the relevant government department.

## SCR Panel responsibilities for the overview report

8.41    The SCR Panel should:

- ensure that it actively manages the SCR process, seeking legal advice as necessary, so that the findings from other relevant processes such as care or criminal proceedings, an inquest or inquiry/investigation are incorporated into the SCR report;

- ensure that contributing organisations and individuals are satisfied that their information is fully and fairly represented in the overview report;

- ensure that the overview report is of a high standard and is written in accordance with this guidance;

- commission and agree the content of the executive summary for publication, ensuring that it accurately represents the full SCR, includes the action plan in full and is fully anonymised apart from including the names of the LSCB Chair, SCR Panel Chair and the overview author and the job titles and the employing organisations of all the SCR Panel members;

- translate recommendations into an action plan that should be signed up to by the senior manager in each of the organisations which will be involved in implementing the action plan. The plan should set out who will do what, by when, with what intended outcome and how success will be measured. The plan should set out the means by which improvements in practice/systems will be monitored and reviewed;

- clarify to whom in which agencies or organisations the executive summary and the action plan of the SCR should be made available to support implementation of the recommendations and the learning of the lessons; and

- make arrangements to provide feedback and debriefing to the child (if surviving) and family members/carers of the subject child as appropriate, following completion of the executive summary.

## The executive summary

8.42    In all cases, the SCR overview report and the IMRs should be used to produce an executive summary that should be made public and which accurately reflects the full overview report. The executive summary should include information about the review process, key issues arising from the case, the recommendations and the action plan (including any actions that have been completed). The content of the executive summary needs to be suitably anonymised in order to protect the identity of children, relevant family members and others and to comply with the Data Protection Act 1998. The executive summary should, however, include the names of the LSCB Chair, SCR Panel Chair, the overview report author, and the job titles and employing organisations of all the SCR Panel members. Executive summaries should be produced according to the following outline format although, as with IMRs and overview reports, the precise format will depend on the features of the case.

## Format of Serious Case Review executive summary

*Introduction*

- Summarise the circumstances that led to a SCR being undertaken in this case and the process followed by the review.

- List the names of the LSCB Chair, SCR Panel Chair and the author of the overview report, and the job titles and employing organisations of all SCR Panel members.

- Note the parallel processes, where relevant, that are being or have been conducted and how they have interrelated with the processes followed by the review (for example, criminal proceedings, PPO investigation following the death of a child in custody, or independent investigation of adverse events in mental health services).

- Note the extent to which the family (and the child, where he or she has been seriously harmed) have been involved in the review.

*The facts/summary of events*

- Summarise the key facts of the case and the sequence of events. This should be an accurate précis of circumstances of the child and their family and of the chronology of the involvement of the relevant agencies. The narrative should be consistent with the detailed chronology in the full overview report.

- Care should however be taken to ensure that the summary is appropriately anonymised and sensitive to the child and family in respect of information that will be available in the public domain.

*Key issues or themes arising from the case*

- Summarise the key issues or themes arising from the analysis in the overview report, and highlight the key decisions taken in respect of the child and their family and the opportunities for early intervention where they existed. With hindsight could or should different decisions or actions have been taken at the time?

*Priorities for learning and change*

- Describe clearly the conclusions and lessons learned from the review, both for individual agencies and for inter-agency working through the LSCB and the Children's Trust Board, ensuring these are in the context of the issues or themes that arose from the case.

- Identify examples of good practice as well as being clear where systems should improve.

*Recommendations and action plan*

- Reproduce the recommendations and action plan from the full SCR.

- The action plan should highlight which recommendations are relevant to which agencies, the agency/ies responsible for taking forward specific recommendations, how action will be monitored and by whom. It should also set out the progress that has already been made in implementing or completing recommendations and plans to evaluate the impact of these changes.

## LSCB action on receiving the Serious Case Review report

8.43    The SCR sub-committee, on behalf of the LSCB, should quality assure the final SCR – that is, the IMR reports, the overview report, the executive summary and the action plan.

8.44    The LSCB should approve the final SCR and:

- provide an anonymised copy of the IMRs, overview report, executive summary and the individual and multi-agency action plans and chronologies to Ofsted, the relevant GO Children and Learners Team, the SHA and DCSF. All personal information relating to children, family members and professionals involved in the case (with the exception of the names of the LSCB and SCR Panel chairs and the overview report author) should be anonymised in all the SCR documentation submitted to Ofsted and the relevant GO. If the child died in a custodial setting, copies of the anonymised SCR should be made available to the YJB and copies of the executive summary should be provided to the PPO;

- make arrangements to provide feedback and debriefing to staff and the media as appropriate;

- disseminate the executive summary and key findings to relevant interested parties;

- publish only the SCR executive summary once the SCR has been completed;

- implement those actions for which the LSCB has lead responsibility and monitor the timely implementation of the SCR action plan;

- on receipt of the evaluation letter from Ofsted, take action as necessary to amend the action plan and/or the SCR report if the SCR executive summary has been published before receiving Ofsted's feedback; and

- formally conclude the review process when the action plan has been implemented and inform the relevant GO of this decision.

8.45 The LSCB should decide on a case by case basis when to publish the executive summary. This decision should take account of the timing of the conclusion of relevant court cases and statutory processes such as inquests or a PPO investigation. The LSCB, on advice from the SCR Panel and where relevant the CPS, the police or its lawyers, should decide whether new information may become available from these other processes which is likely to have an impact on the lessons to be learned from the SCR. If the findings are not likely to have an impact, then there should be no delay in publishing the SCR executive summary. On the other hand, in some cases it may be best to undertake the IMRs and finalise them and the SCR overview report in the light of this new information or findings before publication of the SCR executive summary. In addition, LSCBs may decide to take account of any points raised in Ofsted's evaluation of the SCR before publishing the SCR executive summary but, depending on local circumstances, it may be necessary for the LSCB to publish it prior to the completion of an evaluation by Ofsted.

8.46 All SCRs are evaluated by Ofsted and, in line with the arrangements agreed between inspectorates, the evaluation may involve other inspectorates notably the CQC and HMIC. The evaluation will be shared with the LCSB and, together with the SCR reports as appropriate, with partner inspectorates and Government. Where a SCR has been evaluated as 'inadequate' the LSCB should convene a SCR Panel, to be chaired by an independent person, to reconsider the review. The LSCB is then required to submit to Ofsted, within three months, an action plan that addresses the inadequacies of the SCR.

## Reviewing institutional abuse

8.47 When serious abuse takes place in an institution, or multiple abusers are involved, the same principles of review apply. SCRs in these circumstances are likely to be more complex, on a larger scale, and may require more time (see paragraphs 6.10–6.13) on investigating complex (organisational or multiple) abuse. Terms of reference need to be carefully constructed to explore the issues relevant to the specific case. For example, if children are abused in a residential school, it is important to explore whether and how the school has taken steps to create a safe environment for children, and to respond to specific concerns raised.

8.48   There needs to be clarity over the interface between: the different processes of investigation (including criminal investigations); case management, including help for abused children and immediate measures to ensure that other children are safe; learning lessons from the SCR to reduce the chance of such events happening again. These three different processes should inform each other. Any proposals for review should be agreed with those leading criminal investigations, to make sure that they do not prejudice possible criminal proceedings.

## Accountability and disclosure

8.49   LSCBs should consider carefully who might have an interest in SCRs – for example, elected and appointed members of authorities, staff, the child who was seriously harmed and the subject of the SCR, members of the child's family, the public, the media – and what information should be made available to each of these interests. There are difficult interests to balance, including:

- the need to maintain confidentiality in respect of personal information contained within reports on the child, family members and others;

- the accountability of public services and the importance of maintaining public confidence in the process of internal review;

- the need to secure full and open participation from the different agencies and professionals involved;

- the responsibility to provide relevant information to those with a legitimate interest; and

- constraints on public information sharing when criminal proceedings are ongoing, in that providing access to information may not be within the control of the LSCB.

8.50   It is important to anticipate requests for information and plan in advance how they should be met. For example, a lead agency may take responsibility for debriefing the child (where the SCR was undertaken in respect of a child who was seriously harmed) and family members, or for responding to media interest about a case, in liaison with contributing agencies and professionals. The publication of the executive summary needs to be timed in accordance with the conclusion of any related criminal court proceedings. Neither the SCR overview report nor the IMRs should be made publicly available.

8.51   The LSCB should ensure that the relevant GO Children and Learners Team, Ofsted and all other relevant bodies including the SHA, the CQC, HMIC, HMIP and HMI Probation are appropriately briefed in advance about the publication of the executive summary. Where a child has died in a custodial setting, this briefing should include the YJB and the PPO. The SHA should brief the Department of Health.

## Learning lessons locally

8.52    As the purpose of SCRs is to learn lessons for improving both individual agency and inter-agency working, it is essential that the lessons are learned and acted upon. This means that at least as much effort should be spent on implementing the recommendations as on conducting the review. The following may help in getting maximum benefit from the review process:

- as far as possible, conduct the review in such a way that the process is a learning exercise in itself for all those who have been involved in the case;

- consider what type and level of information needs to be disseminated, how and to whom, in the light of a SCR. Be prepared to communicate both examples of good practice and areas where change is required, as well as to integrate this information with that from other serious case or local reviews;

- incorporate the learning into local training programmes; and

- focus recommendations on a small number of key areas, with Specific, Measurable, Achievable, Relevant and Timely proposals for change and intended outcomes.

In addition:

- the LSCB should put in place a means of monitoring and auditing the actions of all agencies against recommendations and intended outcomes; and

- PCTs should seek feedback from SHAs who should use it to inform their performance management role, and the CQC may use the findings of SCRs to inform its processes for regulating NHS and independent sector provider organisations. PCTs will monitor the implementation of the recommendations by provider organisations.

8.53    The role of GOs in relation to safeguarding includes giving support and challenge to LSCBs and to Children's Trust Boards in relation to SCR and CDOP activity and implementation. This includes seeking assurance that LSCB and Children's Trust plans are in place and action is being taken to effectively address recommendations.

8.54    Day-to-day good practice can help ensure that reviews are conducted successfully and in a way most likely to maximise learning:

- establish a culture of audit and review. Make sure that tragedies are not the only reason inter-agency work is reviewed;

- have in place clear, systematic case recording and record-keeping systems;

- develop good communication and mutual understanding between different disciplines and different LSCB members;

- communicate with the local community and media to raise awareness of the positive and 'helping' work of statutory services with children, so that attention is not focused disproportionately on tragedies; and

- make sure staff and their representatives understand what can be expected in the event of a child death/SCR.

8.55   The SCR sub-committee should provide information to relevant LSCB(s) on the actions taken in response to SCRs which have been completed by the LSCB(s) in the previous year. LSCBs will draw on this information when publishing their annual reports (paragraph 3.36 sets out LSCB's annual reporting requirements in relation to SCRs). Appropriate care should be taken to ensure confidentiality of personal information and sensitivity to the families whose child is the subject of a SCR. The LSCB annual report should support the driving forward of measures to prevent child deaths and serious harm where abuse and neglect have been factors and to safeguard and promote the welfare of children.

## Learning lessons nationally

8.56   Taken together, child death reviews and SCRs are an important source of information to inform national policy and practice. The DCSF is responsible for identifying and disseminating common themes and trends across review reports, and acting on lessons for policy and practice. The DCSF commissions regular reports, drawing out key findings of SCRs and their implications for policy and practice to assist the process of learning lessons. In the future relevant findings from the work of the local child death overview teams will be integrated into these reports.

## Flow chart 7: Overview of Serious Case Review process

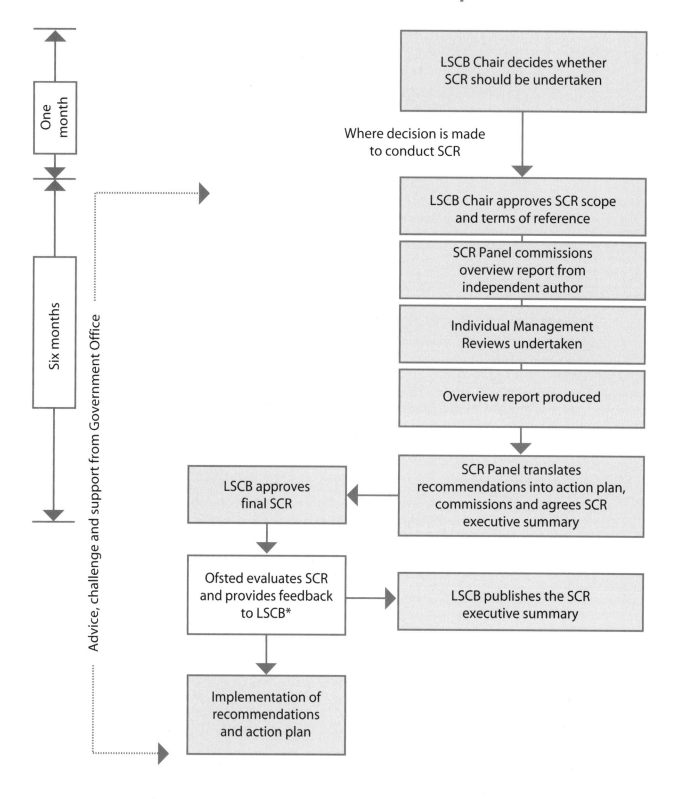

\*        Where a SCR has been evaluated as 'inadequate' the LSCB should convene a SCR Panel, to be chaired by an
         independent person, to reconsider the review. The LSCB is then required to submit to Ofsted within three months,
         an action plan that addresses the inadequacies of the SCR.

# Part 2: Non-statutory practice guidance

# Chapter 9 – Lessons from research

## Introduction

9.1 Our knowledge and understanding of children's welfare – and how to respond in the best interests of a child to concerns about maltreatment (abuse and neglect) – develops over time, informed by research, experience and the critical scrutiny of practice. Sound professional practice involves making judgements supported by evidence: evidence derived from research and experience about the nature and impact of maltreatment, and when and how to intervene to improve outcomes for children; and evidence derived from a thorough assessment of a specific child's health, development and welfare, and his or her family circumstances.

9.2 This chapter summarises what is known about the impact of maltreatment on children's health and development, and sources of stress in families that may also have an impact on children's developmental progress (see also *The Developing World of the Child*, 2006). Further information on findings from the joint Department for Children, Schools and Families and Department of Health Safeguarding Children Research Initiative and other related research can be found on the NSDU research website[153].

## The impact of maltreatment on children

9.3 The maltreatment of children – physically, emotionally, sexually or through neglect – can have major long-term effects on all aspects of a child's health, development and wellbeing. **The immediate and longer-term impact can include anxiety, depression, substance misuse, eating disorders and self-destructive behaviours, offending and anti-social behaviour.** Maltreatment is likely to have a deep impact on the child's self-image and self-esteem, and on his or her future life. Difficulties may extend into adulthood: the experience of long-term abuse may lead to difficulties in forming or sustaining close relationships, establishing oneself in work, and to extra difficulties in developing the attitudes and skills necessary to be an effective parent.

9.4 It is not only the stressful events of maltreatment that have an impact, but also the context in which they take place. Any potentially abusive incident has to be seen in context to assess the extent of harm to a child and decide on the most appropriate intervention. Often, it is the interaction between a number of factors that increases the likelihood or level of significant harm.

9.5    For every child and family, there may be factors that aggravate the harm caused to the child, and those that protect against harm. Relevant factors include the individual child's means of coping and adapting, support from a family and social network, and the impact of any interventions. The effects on a child are also influenced by the quality of the family environment at the time of maltreatment, and by subsequent life events. The way in which professionals respond also has a significant bearing on subsequent outcomes.

9.6    Serious Case Reviews[154], together with other research findings, show that children under one year of age and in particular very young babies are extremely vulnerable to being seriously injured or to dying as a result of abuse or neglect. Young people aged 11 and over also have a heightened level of vulnerability and likelihood of suffering harm, yet their needs and distress are often missed or deemed too challenging for services.

9.7    Some children may be living in families that are considered resistant to change. A knowledge review on effective practice to protect children living in such families, undertaken by C4EO, has identified practices which can enable practitioners to engage with these types of families and improve outcomes for children (see www. c4eo.org.uk/themes/safeguarding/default.aspx?themeid=11&accesstypeid=1).

## Physical abuse

9.8    Physical abuse can lead directly to neurological damage, physical injuries, disability or, at the extreme, death. Harm may be caused to children both by the abuse itself and by the abuse taking place in a wider family or institutional context of conflict and aggression, including inappropriate or inexpert use of physical restraint. Physical abuse has been linked to aggressive behaviour in children, emotional and behavioural problems and educational difficulties. Violence is pervasive and the physical abuse of children frequently coexists with domestic violence[155].

---

154    Brandon, M., Bailey, S., Belderson, P., Gardner, R., Sidebottom, P., Dodsworth, J., Warren, C. and Black, J. (2009) *Understanding Serious Case Reviews and their Impact: A Biennial Analysis of Serious Case Reviews 2005-7*. London: Department for Children Schools and Families.

155    Montgomery, P.Ramchandani, P. Gardner, F. and Bjornstad,G. (2009) *Systematic reviews of interventions following physical abuse: helping practitioners and expert witnesses improve the outcomes of child abuse.* London: Department for Children, Schools and Families.

## Emotional abuse

9.9 There is increasing evidence of the adverse long-term consequences for children's development where they have been subject to sustained emotional abuse, including the impact of serious bullying[156]. Emotional abuse has an important impact on a developing child's mental health, behaviour and self-esteem. It can be especially damaging in infancy. Underlying emotional abuse may be as important, if not more so, as other more visible forms of abuse in terms of its impact on the child. Domestic violence is abusive in itself. Adult mental health problems and parental substance misuse may be features in families where children are exposed to such abuse.

## Sexual abuse

9.10 Disturbed behaviour – including self-harm, inappropriate sexualised behaviour, sexually abusive behaviour, depression and a loss of self-esteem – has been linked to sexual abuse. Its adverse effects may endure into adulthood. The severity of impact on a child is believed to increase the longer the abuse continues, the more extensive the abuse, and the older the child. A number of features of sexual abuse have also been linked with severity of impact, including the relationship of the abuser to the child, the extent of premeditation, the degree of threat and coercion, sadism, and bizarre or unusual elements. A child's ability to cope with the experience of sexual abuse, once recognised or disclosed, is strengthened by the support of a non-abusive adult carer who believes the child, helps the child understand the abuse, and is able to offer help and protection. The reactions of practitioners also have an impact on the child's ability to cope with what has happened, and on his or her feelings of self worth. (For further information see *Child Sexual Abuse: Informing Practice from Research*)[157].

9.11 A proportion of adults and children and young people who sexually abuse children have themselves been sexually abused as children. They may also have been exposed as children to domestic violence and discontinuity of care. However, it would be quite wrong to suggest that most children who are sexually abused inevitably go on to become abusers themselves.

## Neglect

9.12 Severe neglect of young children has adverse effects on children's ability to form attachments and is associated with major impairment of growth and intellectual

156 Barlow, J and Schrader-MacMillan, A. (2009) *Safeguarding Children From Emotional Abuse – What Works?*. London: Department for Education and Skills. DCSF-RBX-09-09.

157 Jones, D.P.H. and Ramchandani, P. (1999) *Child Sexual Abuse. Informing Practice from Research*. Abingdon: Radcliffe Medical Press Ltd.

development. Persistent neglect can lead to serious impairment of health and development, and long-term difficulties with social functioning, relationships and educational progress. Neglected children may also experience low self-esteem, and feelings of being unloved and isolated. Neglect can also result, in extreme cases, in death. The impact of neglect varies depending on how long children have been neglected, the children's age, and the multiplicity of neglectful behaviours children have been experiencing[158,159].

## Sources of stress for children and families

9.13   Many families under great stress succeed in bringing up their children in a warm, loving and supportive environment in which each child's needs are met. Sources of stress within families may, however, have a negative impact on a child's health, development and wellbeing, either directly, or because when experienced during pregnancy they may result in delays in the physical and mental development of infants, or because they affect the capacity of parents to respond to their child's needs[160]. This is particularly so when there is no other significant adult who is able to respond to the child's needs, for example where children experience a parent in prison as a result of offending behaviour.

9.14   Undertaking assessments of children and families requires a thorough understanding of the factors that influence children's development: the developmental needs of children; the capacities of parents or caregivers to respond appropriately to those needs; and the impact of wider family and environmental factors on both children's development and parenting capacity. An analysis of how these three domains of children's lives interact enables practitioners to understand the child's developmental needs within the context of the family and to provide appropriate services to respond to those needs. (See the *Framework for the Assessment of Children in Need and their Families 2000*.)

9.15   The following sections summarise some of the key research findings on parental mental illness, learning disability, substance misuse and domestic violence[161]. The information should be drawn on when assessing children and families, providing services to meet their identified needs and reviewing whether the planned

---

158   Daniel, B. Taylor, J. and Scott, J. (2009) *Noticing and helping the neglected child.* London: Department for Children, Schools and Families. DCSF-RBX-09-03.

159   Stein, M. Rees, G. Hicks, L. and Gorin, S. (2009) *Neglected adolescents: a review of the research and the preparation of guidance for multi-disciplinary teams and a guide for young people.* London: Department for Children, Schools and Families. DCSF-RBX-09-04.

160   Chapter 6 of the Government's strategy document *Carers at the heart of 21st Century families and communities* (2008) addresses the needs of young carers.

161   Cleaver, H. Unell, I. and Aldgate, A. (2010) Children's Needs – Parenting Capacity: The impact of parental mental illness, learning disability, problem alcohol and drug use, and domestic violence on children's safety and development. 2nd Edition. London: The Stationery Office.

outcomes for each child have been achieved. In each section the issue is defined, information on its prevalence given, and the likely impact on the child identified. The research findings are explored in relation to four stages of childhood: the unborn child, babies and infants (under 5 years), middle childhood (5 to 10 years) and adolescence (11 to 16 plus years).

## Social exclusion

9.16    Many of the families who seek help for their children, or about whom others raise concerns in respect of a child's welfare, are multiply disadvantaged. These families may face chronic poverty, social isolation, racism, and the problems associated with living in disadvantaged areas, such as high crime rates, poor housing, childcare, transport and education services, and limited employment opportunities. Many lack a wage earner. Poverty may mean that children live in crowded or unsuitable accommodation, have poor diets, health problems or disability, are vulnerable to accidents, and lack ready access to good educational and leisure opportunities. When children themselves become parents this exacerbates disadvantage and the potential for social exclusion. Racism and racial harassment are an additional source of stress for some families and children, as is violence in the communities in which they live. Social exclusion can also have an indirect effect on children, through its association with parental substance misuse, depression, learning disability, and long-term physical health problems.

## Domestic violence

9.17    The Home Office[162] defines domestic violence as 'Any incident of threatening behaviour, violence or abuse (psychological, physical, sexual, financial or emotional) between adults who are or have been intimate partners or family members, regardless of gender or sexuality'. Nearly a quarter of adults in England are victims of domestic violence. Although both men and women can be victimised in this way, a greater proportion of women experience all forms of domestic violence, and are more likely to be seriously injured or killed by their partner, ex-partner or lover.

9.18    Domestic violence affects both adults and children within the family. Some 200,000 children (1.8%) in England live in households where there is a known risk of domestic violence or violence[163]. Prolonged and/or regular exposure to domestic violence can have a serious impact on children's safety and welfare, despite the best

---

162    Home Office (2009) *What is Domestic Violence?* London: Home Office.
163    Lord Laming (2009) *The Protection of Children in England: Progress Report.* London: The Stationery Office.

efforts of parents to protect them. An analysis of Serious Case Reviews found evidence of past or present domestic violence present in over half (53%) of cases[164].

9.19   Domestic violence rarely exists in isolation. Many parents also misuse drugs or alcohol, experience poor physical and mental ill health and have a history of poor childhood experiences themselves. The co-morbidity of issues compounds the difficulties parents experience in meeting the needs of their children, and increases the likelihood that the child will experience abuse and/or neglect.

9.20   Domestic violence has an impact on children in a number of ways. Children are at increased risk of physical injury during an incident, either by accident or because they attempt to intervene. Even when not directly injured, children are greatly distressed by witnessing the physical and emotional suffering of a parent. Children's exposure to parental conflict, even where violence is not present, can lead to serious anxiety and distress which may express itself in anti-social or criminal behaviour. Although separating from a violent partner should result in women and children being safe from harm, the danger does not automatically end. Moreover, the point of leaving an abusive relationship is the time of highest risk for a victim. Contact arrangements can be used by violent men not only to continue their controlling, manipulative and violent behaviour but also as a way of establishing the whereabouts of the victim(s).

9.21   Domestic violence also affects children because it impacts on parenting capacity. A parent (in most families, the mother) may have difficulty in looking after the children when domestic violence results in injuries, or in extreme cases, death. The impact on parenting, however, is often more subtle. Exposure to psychological and emotional abuse has profound negative effects on women's mental health resulting in a loss of confidence, depression, feelings of degradation, problems with sleep, isolation, and increased use of medication and alcohol. These are all factors that can restrict the mother's capacity to meet the developmental needs of her child. Moreover, belittling and insulting a mother in front of her children undermines not only her respect for herself, but also the authority she needs to parent confidently. A mother's relationship with her children may also be affected because, in attempts to avoid further outbursts of violence, she prioritises her partner's needs over those of her children.

9.22   The impact of domestic violence on children increases when directly abused, witnessing the abuse of a parent, or colluding (willingly or otherwise) in the concealment of assaults. Other relevant factors include the chronicity and degree of violence, and its co-existence with other issues such as substance misuse. No age

164   Brandon, M., Bailey, S., Belderson, P., Gardner, R., Sidebottom, P., Dodsworth, J., Warren, C. and Black, J. (2009) *Understanding Serious Case Reviews and their Impact: A Biennial Analysis of Serious Case Reviews 2005-7*. London: Department for Children Schools and Families.

group is particularly protected from or damaged by the impact of domestic violence. Children's ability to cope with parental adversity is related to their age, gender and individual personality. However, regardless of age, support from siblings, wider family, friends, school and community can act as protective factors. Key to the safety of women and children subjected to violence and the threat of violence is an alternative, safe and supportive residence[165].

9.23    An exploration of the possible impact on the unborn child shows the foetus is at risk of injury because violence towards women increases both in severity and frequency during pregnancy, and often involves punches or kicks directed at the women's abdomen. Such assaults can result in a greater rate of miscarriage, still or premature birth, foetal brain injury and fractures. Domestic violence is also associated with women's irregular or late attendance for ante-natal care. Poor attendance may be the result of low self esteem and depression or due to an abusive partner controlling and restricting women's use of medical services. Once born, the baby continues to be at risk of injury. For example, the infant may be in his or her mother's arms when an assault occurs. A young child's health and development may also be compromised when violence results in the mother having difficulty in concentrating, becoming depressed, or self medicating. When domestic violence undermines the mother's capacity to provide her infant with a sense of safety and security it can impact on the attachment process. Finally, domestic violence may influence a young child's social relationships, increasing their outbursts of anger, peer aggression and other behaviour problems.

9.24    Children in middle childhood, who live with domestic violence, continue to be at risk of being physically injured. Injuries may occur when the child is caught in the cross-fire or when trying to intervene to protect his or her mother. There is also evidence to link domestic violence with elevated levels of child sexual abuse[166],[167]. Witnessing domestic violence affects children's emotions and behaviour and can lead to temper tantrums and aggression which are directed at family and peers, and cruelty towards animals. Exposure to domestic violence is also associated with children being more anxious, sad, worried, fearful and withdrawn, than children who are not exposed[168]. Some children cope with the stress and fear of violence by seeking to escape. During middle childhood this may be through fantasy and make-believe, or by withdrawing into themselves, or seeking a place of safety.

165    Cleaver, H., Unell, I. and Aldgate, A. (2010) *Children's Needs – Parenting Capacity: The impact of parental mental illness, learning disability, problem alcohol and drug use, and domestic violence on children's safety and development. 2nd Edition*. London: The Stationery Office.

166    Humphreys, C. and Stanley, N. (eds) (2006) *Domestic Violence and Child Protection*. London: Jessica Kingsley Publishers.

167    Hester, M., Pearson, C. and Harwin, N. with Abrahams, H. (2007). *Making an impact: children and domestic violence. A reader. 2nd Edition*. London: Jessica Kingsley Publishers.

168    Onyskiw, J. E. (2003) 'Domestic Violence and Children's Adjustment: A Review of Research.' *Journal of Emotional Abuse 3*, 1/2, 11-45.

Experiencing domestic violence and seeing parents unable to control themselves or their circumstances may result in feelings of helplessness and confusion. Children may blame themselves for their parent's violence and feel inadequate and guilty when unable to stop the violent episode or prevent its reoccurrence.

9.25    Adolescents exposed to domestic violence may live in constant fear of violent arguments, being threatened, or actual physical violence being directed at a parent (usually the mother) or themselves. The likelihood of being physically injured continues. Furthermore, in a recent survey of 13 to 17-year-old girls in intimate relationships, one in six girls said they had been hit by their boyfriends (4% regularly)[169] and one in sixteen said they had been raped[170]. Experiencing domestic violence has a serious emotional impact: feelings can include fear, sadness, loneliness, helplessness and despair, and anger. In the home teenagers may focus their anger on both parents, towards the abuser for inflicting the violence and towards the victim for accepting the behaviour. Witnessing the abuse of a parent or experiencing intimate partner violence may result in adolescents exhibiting behavioural problems, both at home and in school, which have an impact on friendships and educational progress. Education can suffer when adolescents stay home to protect their parent or themselves from an abusive partner. Friends are highly valued by teenagers as confidants and sources of support, but behavioural difficulties may jeopardise friendships. Many adolescents cope with the stress of domestic violence by distancing themselves from their family or friends. They may withdraw emotionally through music, reading or participating in on-line virtual worlds, or physically by spending long periods out of the home, or running away.

9.26    Assessments, judgements and plans for children living with domestic or intimate partner violence benefit from the expertise of practitioners working in services for domestic violence. Services for children and families and young people need to take a proactive, collaborative approach to identifying and responding appropriately to domestic and intimate partner violence. Children and families and adolescents experiencing domestic and intimate partner violence are likely to need well targeted support from a range of different agencies. Mothers and children need safe places to stay and children and adolescents need mentors to ensure their needs are identified and met and their welfare is safeguarded and promoted.

## Mental illness of a parent or carer

9.27    A wide range of mental ill health can affect parents and their families. This includes depression and anxiety, and psychotic illnesses such as schizophrenia or bipolar disorder. Depression and anxiety are common. At any one time one in six adults in

---

169    Body Shop YouGov survey (2004).
170    NSPCC and University of Bristol (2009) *Partner exploitation and violence in teenage intimate relationships.* London: NPSCC.

Great Britain may be affected. Psychotic disorders are much less common with about one in two hundred individuals being affected. Mental illness may also be associated with alcohol or drug use, personality disorder and significant physical illness. Approximately 30% of adults with mental ill health have dependent children[171], mothers being more at risk than fathers.

9.28    Appropriate treatment and support usually means that mental illness can be managed effectively and as a result parents are able to care successfully for their children[172]. Mental ill health in a parent or carer does not necessarily have an adverse impact on a child's development. Just as there is a range in severity of illness, so there is a range of potential impact on families. The consequent likelihood of harm being suffered by a child will range from a minimal effect to significant one. It is essential to assess the implications of parental ill health for each child in the family. This would include assessment of the impact on the family members of the social, physical ill heath or substance use difficulties that a parent with mental illness may also be experiencing. After assessment appropriate additional support should be provided where needed[173].

9.29    Given the wide range of mental ill health, the effect on parents and the potential impact on their capacity to meet the needs of their children is varied. Depression can result in the individual experiencing feelings of worthlessness and hopelessness which may lead to everyday activities being left undone. Parents may neglect their own and their children's physical and emotional needs. In psychotic disorders such as schizophrenia, when the person is actively psychotic, they can lose contact with reality, experiencing hallucinations and delusions with consequent inability to understand and respond to their children's needs. In some people with chronic psychotic illness self-neglect in a range of areas of life may be an issue and this may have an impact on their capacity to care for their children. Overall children with mothers who have mental ill health are five times more likely to have mental health problems themselves. Parental mental illness, particularly in the mother, is also associated with poor birth outcomes[174], increased risk of sudden infant death[175] and

171    Meltzer, D. (2003) 'Inequalities in mental health: A systematic review.' *The research findings register, Summary No. 1063*. London: Department of Health.

172    Reupert, A. and Maybery, D. (2007) 'Families Affected by Parental Mental Illness; A Multiperspective Account of Issues and Interventions.' *American Journal of Orthopsychiatry 77*, 3, 362-369.

173    New Horizons: A Shared Vision for Mental Health (2009). London: Department of Health. http://www.newhorizons.dh.gov.uk

174    King-Hele S, Webb R, Mortensen PB, Appleby L, Pickles A, Abel KM. Risk of stillbirth and neonatal death linked with maternal mental illness: a national cohort study. *Archives of Disease in Childhood Fetal & Neonatal Edition* 2009; 94: F105-F110.

175    Webb RT, Wicks S, Dalman C, Pickles AR, Appleby L, Mortensen PB, Haglund B, Abel KM. Influence of environmental factors in higher risk of sudden infant death syndrome linked with parental mental illness. *Archives of General Psychiatry* 2010; 67: 69-77.

increased mortality in offspring[176] – probably through complex interaction of sociological, biological and risk behaviours such as smoking. This research indicates that these vulnerable families need additional support and help.

9.30   The majority of parents with a history of mental ill health present no risk to their children. However, in rare cases a child may sustain severe injury, profound neglect, or even die. Very serious risks may arise if the parent's illness incorporates delusional beliefs about the child, and/or incorporates the child in a suicide plan. Information from the National Confidential Inquiry into Suicides and Homicides suggests that there are about 30 convictions a year where a parent or step parent kills a child (this excludes those cases where the parent then goes on to commit suicide). In 37% of these cases the parent was found to have a mental disorder including depressive illness or bipolar affective disorder, personality disorder, schizophrenia, and/or substance or alcohol dependence[177]. In a review of Serious Case Review reports where children had either died or been seriously harmed, current or past mental illness was found in two thirds of cases[178].

9.31   The potential impact of a parental mental illness and the child's ability to cope with it is related to age, gender and individual personality.

9.32   For babies and infants post natal depression may hamper the mother's capacity to empathise with, and respond appropriately to, her baby's needs. A consistent lack of warmth and negative responses increases the likelihood that the infant will become insecurely attached. Depression may also reduce the level of interaction and engagement between mother and child. Parents in these circumstances may have greater difficulty in listening to their children and offering praise and encouragement. Mothers who experience psychotic symptoms after giving birth, and those who continue to be depressed at six months after the birth, are more likely than other mothers to regard their babies negatively and ignore cries for warmth and comfort[179]. Women with a history of severe mental illness are at particular risk of relapse post partum and should be under the care of a psychiatrist, as should any mother who develops psychotic symptoms post birth[180]. Mood swings, a common feature in mental disorders, can result in inconsistent parenting, emotional unavailability and unexpected and unplanned for separations, which

---

176   Webb RT, Abel KM, Pickles AR, Appleby L, King-Hele SA, Mortensen PB. Mortality risk among offspring of psychiatric inpatients: a population-based follow-up to early adulthood. *American Journal of Psychiatry* 2006; 163: 2170-7.

177   NPSA Alert. Preventing harm to children from parents with mental health needs. NPSA, 2009.

178   Brandon, M., Bailey, S., Belderson, P., Gardner, R., Sidebottom, P., Dodsworth, J., Warren, C. and Black, J. (2009) *Understanding Serious Case Reviews and their Impact: A Biennial Analysis of Serious Case Reviews 2005-7.* London: Department for Children Schools and Families.

179   Egeland, B. (2009) 'Taking stock: Childhood emotional maltreatment and developmental psychopathology.' *Child Abuse & Neglect 33*, 1, 22-27.

180   NICE (2007) *Guidelines on antenatal and postnatal care.* London: NICE.

infants find bewildering and frightening. Young children can be supported by the vigilance of primary health care workers, the presence of an alternative caring adult, the support of wider family, and good community facilities.

9.33 Parental mental disorders affect children in middle childhood rather differently. Children react to parenting difficulties which result from mental disorders with an increased level of behavioural problems. Some children experience depression and anxiety disorders[181] while others show high rates of conduct disorder[182]. It is widely accepted that boys are more likely to act out their distress with anti social and aggressive behaviours while girls tend to respond by internalising their worries. Children of this age can escape into fantasy to cope with disturbing parental behaviour, or use more down to earth methods such as withdrawing into themselves, or escaping to a safe place. Relatives, particularly grandparents, can provide children with the emotional and practical support they need. However, children of this age are acutely aware of the social stigma of mental illness and consequently maybe reluctant to talk about family problems. Relatives and other adults who would be able to offer help and support may be unaware of what the child is experiencing. Same age friendships can also be supportive, although a fear of ridicule could keep children from discussing their circumstances with friends. Nonetheless, play and the companionship of friends can offer children respite from family concerns.

9.34 The prevalence of mental ill health in children increases with the advent of adolescence. A survey of children's mental health suggests 11% of children aged 11-16 years have a mental disorder[183]. Parental mental ill health exacerbates the likelihood of young people experiencing psychological and behavioural symptoms[184]. The volatility of this age group means that the impact of parental mental illness, while similar to that at a young age, maybe more intense. Teenagers whose mothers suffer from depression show more behaviour problems than those whose mothers are well[185]. Conduct disorders, depression and a preoccupation with family problems affect young people's ability to concentrate and education and learning may be impaired. Education may also be interrupted when parental mental health problems become severe and young people stay at home in order to look

---

181 Tunnard, J. (2004) Parental Mental Health Problems: Key Messages from Research, Policy and Practice. Dartington: Research in Practice.

182 Klein, D., Clark, D., Dansky, L. and Margolis, E.T. (1988) 'Dysthymia in the offspring of parents with primary unipolar affective disorder.' *Journal of Abnormal Psychology 94*, 1155-1127.

183 Green, H., McGinnity, A., Meltzer, H., Ford, T. and Goodman, R. (2005) *Mental health of children and young people in Great Britain, 2004*. London: Office for National Statistics.

184 Weissman, M.M., John, K., Merikangas, K.R., Prusoff, B.A., Wickramaratne, P., Gammon, G.D., Angold, A. and Warner, V. (1986) 'Depressed parents and their children: General health, social and psychiatric problems.' *American Journal of Diseases of Children 140*, 801-805.

185 Somers, V. (2007) 'Schizophrenia: The Impact of Parental Illness on Children.' *British Journal of Social Work 37*, 8, 1319-1334.

after their parent or younger siblings. Although relationships between parent and child may suffer as a result of parental mental illness, the opposite may also be true. As children reach adolescence, and their understanding and empathy develops, parental mental health problems may strengthen the bond between them. However, this can also result in accelerating the normal pace of emotional maturity, resulting in a loss of childhood. Young people may not only become responsible for shouldering the burden of practical tasks, but also assume the emotional responsibility for a parent or younger siblings. To do this young people may curtail their leisure time and restrict their friendships. Friendships can be a great source of support, but an acute awareness of the stigma of mental illness may result in young people coping alone. It is essential that the needs of young carers are assessed to ensure they receive the support they need. Many families in these circumstances would benefit from practical and domestic help. Young people value the support of sympathetic and trusted adults with whom they can discuss sensitive issues, a mutual friend and knowing who to contact in the event of a crisis regarding their parent.

9.35   It is important not to assume that all young people will have problems just because they grow up living with a parent who has mental ill health. Research has shown that the adverse effects on children and young people are less likely when parental disorders are mild, last only a short time, are not associated with family disharmony and do not result in the family breaking up. Children may also be protected from harm when the other parent or a family member can respond to the child's needs, and the child or young person has the support of friends and other caring adults[186].

9.36   Advice to services in responding to the needs of families where there is parental mental ill health is found in the NPSA Alert[187] and in practice guidance produced by SCIE[188].

---

186    Cleaver, H., Unell, I. and Aldgate, A. (2010) *Children's Needs – Parenting Capacity: The impact of parental mental illness, learning disability, problem alcohol and drug use, and domestic violence on children's safety and development.* 2nd Edition. London: The Stationery Office.

187    National Patient Safety Agency (2009) *Rapid Response Report NPSA/2009/RRR003: Preventing harm to children from parents with mental health needs.* London: National Patient Safety Agency. See www.npsa.nhs.uk/patientsafety/alerts-and-directives.

188    Social Care Institute for Excellence (2009) *Think child, think parent, think family.* London: SCIE.

## Parental problem drug use

9.37    The Government's 2008 Drug Strategy refers to that group of illegal drug misusers who present the greatest problems overall – i.e. those using opiates such as heroin and/or crack cocaine – as 'Problem Drug Users' (PDUs). Whilst the 'PDUs' are a priority group for policy and for access to services, these services are at the same time available for all those with problems with their drug use.

9.38    Although as many as one in three adults have used illicit drugs at least once, problem drug users are less than one percent of the population in England[189]. It is hard to know with any degree of certainty how many children are living with parents who are problem drug users as such behaviour is against the law and characterised by denial and secrecy. In England and Wales it is estimated that one per cent of babies are born each year to women with problem drug use, and that two to three per cent of children under the age of 16 years have parents with problem drug use. Not all these children will be living with their parents and only about a third of fathers and two-thirds of mothers with problem drug use are still living with their own children[190]. It is not only their parents whose drug misuse may place the child at risk of suffering significant harm, but problem drug use of other family members such a parent's new partner, siblings, or other individuals within the household.

9.39    To understand how problem drug use can affect parents' capacity to meet the developmental needs of their children is far from simple and it is important not to generalise or make assumptions about the impact on children of parental drug misuse. Consideration needs to be given to both the type of drug used and its effects on the individual; the same drug may affect different people in different ways. The situation is further complicated because the same drug may have very different consequences for the individual depending on their current mental state, experience and/or tolerance of the drug, expectations, personality, the environment in which it is taken, the amount used and the way it is consumed. When parents, or others in the home, stop taking drugs children can be particularly vulnerable. For example, the withdrawal symptoms both physical and psychological may interfere, at least for a while, with parent's capacity to meet the needs of their children. Problematic drug use is likely to continue over time, and although treatment may prolong periods of abstinence or controlled use, for some individuals relapse should be expected. Assumptions about the use or abstinence of drugs should not be based on whether or not parents, or others in the home, are engaged with services for their problem drug use.

---

189    Hoare, J. and Flatley, J. (2008) *Drug Misuse Declared: Finding from the 2007/08 British Crime Survey, England and Wales*. London: Home Office Statistical Bulletin.

190    Advisory Council on the Misuse of Drugs (2003) *Hidden harm: Responding to the needs of children of problem drug users*. London: Home Office.

9.40    Parental problem drug misuse is generally associated with some degree of child neglect and emotional abuse. It can result in parents or carers experiencing difficulty in organising their own and their children's lives, being unable to meet children's needs for safety and basic care, being emotionally unavailable and having difficulty in controlling and disciplining their children[191,192]. Difficulty in organising day to day living means that important events such as birthdays or holidays are disrupted and family rituals and routines such as meal or bed times, which cement family relationships, are difficult to sustain. Problem drug misuse may cause parents to become detached from reality or lose consciousness. When there is no other responsible adult in the home, children are left to fend for themselves. Some problem drug using parents may find it difficult to give priority to the needs of their children. Finding money for drugs may reduce what is available to meet basic needs, or may draw families into criminal activities. Poverty and a need to have easy access to drugs may lead families to live in unsafe communities where children are exposed to harmful anti-social behaviour and environmental dangers such as dirty needles in parks and other public places. At its extreme, parental problem drug misuse can be implicated in the serious injury or death of a child. The study of Serious Case Reviews[193] found that in a third of cases there was a current or past history of parental drug misuse.

9.41    Such negative scenarios are not inevitable. A significant proportion of children who live with parents who are problem drug users will show no long term behavioural or emotional disturbance. Some problem drug users ensure their children are looked after, clean and fed, have all their needs met and that drugs are stored safely. A caring partner, spouse or relative who does not use drugs can provide essential support and continuity of care for the child. Other protective factors include drug treatment, wider family and primary health care services providing support, the child's attendance at nursery or day care, sufficient income and good physical standards in the home. Many parents, however, who are problem drug users often base their social activities around the procurement and use of the drug and are isolated and rejected by their communities. Drug related debts and angry neighbours may result in unplanned moves which disrupt children's schooling, community links and friendships. The safety, health and development of a considerable number of children are adversely affected by parental problem drug

---

191    Hogan, D. and Higgins L. (2001) When Parents Use Drugs: Key Findings from a Study of Children in the Care of Drug-using Parents. Dublin: The Children's Research Centre.

192    Cleaver, H., Nicholson, D., Tarr, S. and Cleaver, D. (2007) *Child Protection, Domestic Violence and Parental Substance Misuse: Family Experiences and Effective Practice*. London: Jessica Kingsley Publishers.

193    Brandon, M., Bailey, S., Belderson, P., Gardner, R., Sidebottom, P., Dodsworth, J., Warren, C. and Black, J. (2009) *Understanding Serious Case Reviews and their Impact: A Biennial Analysis of Serious Case Reviews 2005-7*. London: Department for Children Schools and Families.

misuse and would benefit from services to meet the needs of both children and parents.

9.42 The impact of parental problem drug misuse will depend on the child's age and stage of development as well as this or her personality and ability to cope. Drug use while pregnant may endanger the unborn child depending on the pharmacological make-up of the drug, the gestation of pregnancy and the route/amount/duration of drug use. Structural damage to the foetus is most likely during 4-12 weeks of gestation; drugs taken later can affect growth or cause intoxication or abstinence syndromes[194]. However, gauging the impact of maternal drug use on the unborn child is complicated when mothers take a combination of substances. Some of the problems associated with maternal problem drug misuse can be ameliorated by good ante-natal care. Unfortunately, some pregnant problem drug users do not seek ante-natal care, either because the drugs affect menstruation and leave women uncertain of dates, or because they fear that revealing their drug use to health professionals will result in judgemental attitudes, the involvement of children's social care services and the possible loss of the baby once it is born. For pregnant drug users in general, irrespective of the substance used, especially where poor social conditions prevail, there is an increased risk of low birth weight, premature delivery, perinatal mortality and cot death[195]. While there is general agreement that problem drug use while pregnant can increase the risk of impairment to the unborn child's development, it is also probable that most women who misuse drugs will give birth to healthy children who suffer from no long term effects[196].

9.43 Maternal problem drug misuse can impact on the attachment relationship between mother and child in a number of ways. Babies who need treatment for withdrawal symptoms may become sleepy and unresponsive. Mothers who undergo rapid drug reduction or abstinence may find it difficult to respond appropriately to their new-born baby. Problem drug misuse may also affect the parents' ability to empathise with the baby. Research has shown that many parents who misuse drugs, particularly heroin, are often emotionally unavailable to their children[197]. A consistent lack of warmth and negative responses may result in the infant becoming insecurely attached. Babies and young children who are exposed to dramatic and sometimes frightening parental mood swings may become

194 Julien, R.M. (1995) *A Primer of Drug Action: A Concise, Non-Technical Guide to the Actions, Uses, and Side Effects of Psychoactive Drugs. 7th Edition*. New York: W.H. Freeman and Co.

195 Standing Conference on Drug Misuse (SCODA) (1997) *Working with Children and Families Affected by Parental Substance Misuse*. London: Local Government Association Publications.

196 Powell, J. and Hart, D. (2001) 'Working with Parents who Use Drugs.' In R. Gordon and E. Harran (eds) *Fragile handle with care: protecting babies from harm: Reader*. Leicester: NSPCC.

197 Hogan, D. and Higgins L. (2001) *When Parents Use Drugs: Key Findings from a Study of Children in the Care of Drug-using Parents*. Dublin: The Children's Research Centre.

unnaturally vigilant as they try to alter their behaviour according to their parent's state of mind. Serious drug dependency may result in parents placing their own needs before the safety and welfare of their children. For example, young children may be left alone at home, or in the care of unsuitable and unsafe people, while the parent prioritises the acquisition of drugs.

9.44    Parental problem drug misuse also affects children during middle childhood. Research suggests that children's education and performance in school may suffer because parental problems dominate the child's thoughts and can affect concentration[198]. Some children feel responsible for their parent's actions, believing they are to blame for their parent's drug taking. This can lead to feelings of inadequacy and guilt when their actions fail to make any impact on their parent's use of drugs. Parental problem drug misuse may have very negative effects on the parent/child relationship. The need for drugs is paramount and children may believe that they take second place in their parent's lives, leaving them with feelings of anger, betrayal and worthlessness. Children may also have to grow up too quickly, as parental problem drug use may result in some children having to assume adult responsibilities. Children may be left to take care of themselves for much of the time, which can lead to school work being neglected, erratic school attendance, curtailment of friendships, and a general loss of childhood. Parental problem drug use is associated with higher levels of aggressive, noncompliant, disruptive, destructive and antisocial behaviours in children[199]. For some children school and friendships offer respite and a safe haven from a troubled home situation. Other protective factors for this age group include: the presence in the home of an alternative, caring adult who does not misuse drugs, a supportive older sibling and/ or members of the wider family, regular school attendance, vigilant and sympathetic teachers, learning different ways of coping and developing the confidence to know what to do when parents are incapacitated.

9.45    As children grow up parental problem drug use affects them in different ways. Adolescence ushers in great physical changes. Parental problem drug misuse may mean parents are unaware of children's worries over their changing body and fail to provide support and advice. Children's health may be affected because parental problem drug use is associated with an increased risk during adolescence, of children experimenting with drugs. Some young people learn to mirror their parents coping strategies and come to depend on drugs to deal with difficult situations and negative feelings[200]. The relationship, however is complex and most

---

198    Cleaver, H., Unell, I. and Aldgate, A. (2010) *Children's Needs – Parenting Capacity: The impact of parental mental illness, learning disability, problem alcohol and drug use, and domestic violence on children's safety and development. 2ⁿᵈ Edition*. London: The Stationery Office.

199    Barnard, M. (2007) *Drug Addiction and Families*. London: Jessica Kingsley Publishers.

200    Covell, K. and Howe, R.B. (2009) *Children, families and violence: Challenges for children's rights*. London: Jessica Kingsley Publishers.

children of parents with drug problems do not themselves become problem drug users. The likelihood that children's education is affected continues into adolescence as young people take on greater responsibility for looking after the home and assuming the care of a parent and younger siblings. Nonetheless, the majority of adolescent children whose parents are problem drug users attend school regularly. When parents are unable to look after adolescent children adequately, the normal pace of emotional maturity can be accelerated and for some the relationship between parent and child is reversed. Problem drug use can result in parents continuing to put their own needs above those of their adolescent children, leading to feelings of worthlessness and anger. To deal with these emotions young people may resort to self harm, illicit drug use, spending long periods outside the home, or leaving home altogether.

9.46 Parental problem drug use is a feature in the backgrounds of many young homeless people. Loneliness and isolation are not the experience of all adolescents whose parents misuse drugs. Friendships are valued highly and many teenagers of parents with drug problems gain solace and support from friends, regardless of whether they are able to discuss family problems. Sadly for some, unplanned moves, often as a result of drug related issues, mean adolescents experience school changes, lose ties with their community and perhaps most mourned, lose the support and love of close friends. The key factors that support young people living with parental problem drug use include practical and domestic help, a trusted mentor with whom the adolescent can discuss sensitive issues, a mutual friend, and the ability to separate safely, either psychologically or physically, from stressful situations.

## Parental problem alcohol use

9.47 The Government's strategy on alcohol reduction defines harmful drinking as:

*'Drinking at levels that lead to significant harm to physical and mental health and at levels that may be causing substantial harm to others... Women who regularly drink over 6 units a day (or over 35 units a week) and men who regularly drink over 8 units a day (or 50 units a week) are at highest risk of such alcohol-related harm'*[201].

9.48 Findings from the *General Lifestyle Survey 2008* suggest that 7% of men and 4% of women regularly drink at higher-risk levels: rates which have fallen slightly over the past few years. In addition to regular higher-risk drinking, problems can also result from binge drinking or, for example, drinking before driving. Nearly a fifth of men and 14% of women are drinking more than twice the lower-risk limit at least one day per week, a figure that is used as a proxy for 'binge drinking' at a population

---

201 Department of Health, Home Office, Department for Education and Skills and Department for Culture, Media and Sport (2007) *Safe. Sensible. Social. The next steps in the National Alcohol Strategy.* London: Department of Health and Home Office. Page 3.

level[202]. It is estimated that up to 1.3 million children are affected by parental alcohol problems in England (Strategy Unit 2004). An analysis of calls received by ChildLine[203] shows that the majority (57%) of callers identified their father or father figure as the problem drinker, a third their mother or mother figure and 7% indicated both parents had a drink problem.

9.49   The impact of excessive alcohol consumption on parents' capacity to look after their children will depend on their current mental state and personality, their experience and tolerance of alcohol and the amount of alcohol consumed. For example, parenting may be affected because excessive drinking can affect concentration, induce sleep or coma, or reduce psychomotor co-ordination. In addition inhibitions may be lost, which can result in diminished self control and violence.

9.50   Parental problem drinking can be associated with violence within the family and the physical abuse of children, but who has the alcohol problem is relevant. Alcohol misuse by a father or father figure can be related to violence and the physical abuse of children, while mothers with an alcohol problem are more likely to neglect their children[204]. Children are most at risk of suffering significant harm when alcohol misuse is associated with violence. If parents with a chronic drink problem stop drinking, the physical reactions they experience may also affect their capacity to meet the children's needs. As noted in relation to chronic drug misuse, severe and chronic alcohol problems are likely to continue over time and, although treatment may result in abstinence, relapse is possible. The adverse effects of parental alcohol misuse on children are less likely when not associated with violence, family discord, or the disorganisation of the family's day to day living. Particularly important is the presence of a parent or family member who does not have an alcohol problem and is able to respond to the child's developmental needs.

9.51   Many of the problems associated with problem alcohol use during pregnancy could be ameliorated to some extent by good ante-natal care. However, pregnant women with alcohol problems may not attend ante-natal care until late in pregnancy because they fear professionals will judge them. The effect of drinking on the developing foetus is related to the amount and pattern of alcohol consumed by the mother, and the stage of gestation. The foetus is most vulnerable to damage during the first three months but is at risk throughout pregnancy. Drinking during pregnancy, particularly in the first three months, is associated with an increased rate of miscarriage. Heavy drinking can cause Fetal Alcohol Syndrome (FAS), whose features include growth deficiency for height and weight, a distinct pattern of facial

---

202   General Lifestyle Survey 2008, *Smoking and Drinking among adults 2008*. ONS: 2010.

203   ChildLine (1997) *Beyond the limit: children who live with parental alcohol misuse*. London: ChildLine.

204   Cleaver, H., Unell, I. and Aldgate, A. (2010) *Children's Needs – Parenting Capacity: The impact of parental mental illness, learning disability, problem alcohol and drug use, and domestic violence on children's safety and development. 2nd Edition*. London: The Stationery Office.

features and physical characteristics and central nervous system dysfunction. A syndrome that does not show the full characteristic features of FAS, Fetal Alcohol Spectrum Disorder, has been reported, and may develop at lower levels of drinking than is reported for FAS. The Chief Medical Officer and NICE both advise pregnant women or women trying to conceive to avoid drinking alcohol. If they choose to drink, to minimise the risk to the baby, they should not drink more than one to two units of alcohol once or twice a week and should not get drunk. The NICE guidelines emphasise the importance of avoiding alcohol especially during the first three months of pregnancy as this is the key time for organ and nervous system development[205]. It is generally accepted that heavy alcohol consumption during pregnancy increases the risk of damage to the foetus. Most mothers with alcohol problems, however do give birth to healthy babies. Only approximately 4% of pregnant women who drink heavily give birth to a baby with Fetal Alcohol Spectrum Disorder[206].

9.52    Once born, babies may be likely to suffer significant harm. When alcohol problems result in parents being pre-occupied with their own feelings and emotions they may fail to notice or respond appropriately to their baby. Chronic alcohol problems may limit the mother's capacity to engage with and stimulate her baby. A consistent lack of warmth can result in the infant becoming insecurely attached. Supervision is essential to keep the more mobile infant safe from harm, but harmful drinking can affect parents' concentration and lead to a lack of oversight. Chronic drinking may also mean parents fail to recognise when their baby or infant is unwell, or delay seeking medical help for minor injuries if these have resulted from a lack of supervision. The infant's health may also be affected because high levels of alcohol consumption can depress appetite, and parents may fail to respond to their child's need for food. Research suggests parental problem drinking may also impact on the young child's cognitive development. Babies and infants are more likely to be protected from significant harm when one parent does not have an alcohol problem and is able to respond to the emotional and cognitive needs of the child, there is sufficient income and good physical standards in the home and the parent who is drinking at harmful levels acknowledges their problem and receives treatment[207].

9.53    Parental alcohol problems continue to affect the health and development of children during middle childhood. For example, children's health may be

205    National Institute for Health and Clinical Excellence (2008) *Updated NICE guideline published on care and support that women should receive during pregnancy.* www.nice.org.uk/media/E5D/8B/2008022AntenatalCare.pdf

206    Abel, E.L. (1998) 'Fetal Alcohol Syndrome: The American Paradox.' *Alcohol and Alcoholism 33*, 3, 195-201.

207    Cleaver, H., Unell, I. and Aldgate, A. (2010) *Children's Needs – Parenting Capacity: The impact of parental mental illness, learning disability, problem alcohol and drug use, and domestic violence on children's safety and development. 2nd Edition.* London: The Stationery Office.

endangered because, although alcohol consumption is not common during this period of childhood, maternal drinking increases the likelihood that children aged 10 years will start drinking[208]. Learning may also be affected. Children of parents with chronic alcohol problems are more likely to experience reading problems, poor concentration and low academic performance[209]. When parents are intoxicated they may not be capable of encouraging the child to learn, or of providing sufficient support with schooling. Alcohol can make parents behave in inconsistent and unexpected ways, loving and caring at one moment and rejecting and cold at another. This can leave children feeling betrayed, let down, angry, and uncertain that they are loved. Middle year children tend to feel guilty and blame themselves for their parents' drinking; emotions which are compounded when parents deny the problem. A further possible consequence of parental problem drinking is that children may grow up too quickly, having to look after themselves, younger siblings and their alcoholic parent. It should not be assumed that all children in middle childhood who live with a parent with alcohol problems experience emotional and behavioural difficulties. Older siblings and close relatives can provide children with much needed emotional and practical support. Unfortunately, wider family and friends are often unaware of the family difficulties as a fear of stigma and ridicule may keep all family members silent. There is considerable evidence to suggest that the combination of parental chronic drinking with domestic violence causes a more detrimental impact on children than parental alcohol misuse in isolation[210].

9.54   To ensure children understand the physical changes that result from puberty and how to cope safely with new relationships, they need the support of their parents or carers. When alcohol problems dominate parents' lives children may be left to deal with these issues alone. Chronic alcohol problems may also result in parents failing to provide adolescents with adequate supervision. Research suggests youngsters aged 11-12 years are more likely to use alcohol, cannabis and tobacco if their parents have an alcohol problem[211]. Young people who start drinking at an early age are at greater risk of poor health and being involved in accidents and accidental injury. The relationship between parental problem drinking and young people's drinking patterns is complex, because observing the devastating effect alcohol has

208   Macleod, J., Hickman, M., Bowen, E., Alati, R., Tilling, K. and Davey Smith, G. (2008) 'Parental drug use, early adversities, later childhood problems and children's use of tobacco and alcohol at age 10: birth cohort study.' *Addiction 103*, 1731-43.

209   Cleaver, H., Nicholson, D., Tarr, S. and Cleaver, D. (2007) *Child Protection, Domestic Violence and Parental Substance Misuse: Family Experiences and Effective Practice*. London: Jessica Kingsley Publishers.

210   Cleaver, H., Unell, I. and Aldgate, A. (2010) *Children's Needs – Parenting Capacity: The impact of parental mental illness, learning disability, problem alcohol and drug use, and domestic violence on children's safety and development. 2nd Edition*. London: The Stationery Office.

211   Li, C., Pentz, A. and Chou, C-P. (2002) 'Parental substance use as a modifier of adolescent substance use risk.' *Addiction 97*, 1537-50.

on their parents' lives may act as a strong deterrent[212]. Young people's education may continue to be affected by their parents' alcohol problems and they may find themselves facing the stress of examinations with little or no support. Education may also be interrupted because teenagers feel compelled to stay at home to look after their parent or younger siblings. A lack of educational attainment has long term effects on young people's life chances. However, generalisations should not be made. For some young people school offers an escape from the problems at home and an opportunity to build a different life from that of their parents. Relationships between teenagers and their parents can also be affected. Chronic alcohol problems may result in parents putting their own needs above those of their children, leaving teenagers feeling let down, angry and worthless. Teenagers may experience physical neglect when drinking takes precedence and there is not sufficient money for household essentials and clothes. Such neglect may jeopardise friendships or lead to bullying. To keep up appearances some young people may resort to stealing or other illegitimate ways of obtaining money to keep up appearances. Others may seek to escape the difficulties within the home by withdrawing into themselves, using alcohol or drugs, or leaving home altogether[213]. Many young people who leave home will experience homelessness which is associated with poorer mental and physical health and an increased likelihood of substance misuse[214].

9.55    It is important not to assume that all young people will have problems just because they grow up living with a parent who has alcohol problems. The majority outgrow their childhood problems[215]. Research suggests that the following factors can support young people: sufficient income and good physical standard in the home, regular medical and dental checks, a trusted adult, a mutual friend, supportive and harmonious family environment, and regular attendance at school, work-based training or a job[216].

## Parents with a learning disability

9.56    The cause of learning disabilities can have its roots in genetic factors, infection before birth, brain injury at birth, brain infections or brain damage after birth. A learning disability may be mild, moderate, severe or profound, but it is a life-long

212    Velleman, R. and Orford, J. (2001) *Risk and Resilience: Adults who were the children of problem drinkers.* Amsterdam: Harwood Academic Publishers.

213    Velleman, R. and Orford, J. (2001) *Risk and Resilience: Adults who were the children of problem drinkers.* Amsterdam: Harwood Academic Publishers.

214    Quilgars, D., Johnsen, S. and Pleace, N. (2008) *Youth homelessness in the UK. A decade of progress?* York: Joseph Rowntree Foundation.

215    Velleman, R. and Orford, J. (2001) *Risk and Resilience: Adults who were the children of problem drinkers.* Amsterdam: Harwood Academic Publishers.

216    Cleaver, H., Unell, I. and Aldgate, A. (2010) *Children's Needs – Parenting Capacity: The impact of parental mental illness, learning disability, problem alcohol and drug use, and domestic violence on children's safety and development. 2nd Edition.* London: The Stationery Office.

condition. Traditionally, scores on standardised intelligence tests have been used to define learning disability. However, difficulties arise over how to classify those with borderline IQs (70 to 85), and individuals who exhibit different ability levels across the components of IQ tests. The Department of Health's definition of learning disability encompasses people with a broad range of disabilities. *'Learning disability includes the presence of:*

- *a significantly reduced ability to understand new or complex information, to learn new skills (impaired intelligence); with*

- *a reduced ability to cope independently (impaired social functioning);*

- *which started before adulthood, with a lasting effect on development'*[217].

9.57 The most recent research estimates that there are 985,000 people in England with a learning disability, equivalent to an overall prevalence rate of 2% of the adult population[218]. Estimates of the number of adults with learning disabilities who are parents vary widely from 23,000 to 250,000[219].

9.58 It is important not to generalise or make assumptions about the parenting capacity of parents with learning disabilities. Parental learning disability is not correlated with child abuse or wilful neglect, although there is evidence that children may suffer neglect from omission where parents are not adequately supported or where there was no early intervention. In most cases where physical or sexual abuse occurs it is the mother's male partner who is responsible[220]. A study of Serious Case Reviews found that in 15% of cases parents had a learning disability[221].

9.59 Parents with learning disabilities will need support to develop the understanding, resources, skills and experience to meet the needs of their children. Such support is particularly important when parents experience additional stressors such as having a disabled child, domestic violence, poor physical and mental health, substance misuse, social isolation, poor housing, poverty and a history of growing up in care. It is these additional stressors when combined with a learning disability that are most likely to lead to concerns about the care and safety of a child. A study of children

---

217  Cm 5086 (2001) *Valuing People: A New Strategy for Learning Disability for the 21st Century*. London: The Stationery Office. Cm 5086 2001, p.14, paragraph 1.5.

218  Emerson E. and Hatton, C. (2008) *People with Learning Disabilities in England*. Lancaster: Centre for Disability Research.

219  Department of Health and Department for Education and Skills (2007) *Good practice guidance on working with parents with a learning disability*. London: Department of Health.

220  Booth, T. and Booth, W. (2002) 'Men in the Lives of Mothers with Intellectual Disabilities'. *Journal of Applied Research in Intellectual Disabilities 15*, 187-199.

221  Brandon, M., Bailey, S., Belderson, P., Gardner, R., Sidebottom, P., Dodsworth, J., Warren, C. and Black, J. (2009) *Understanding Serious Case Reviews and their Impact: A Biennial Analysis of Serious Case Reviews 2005-7*. London: Department for Children Schools and Families.

living with learning disabled parents who had been referred to local authority child's social care services highlighted the need for collaborative working between children's and adults' services and support for the family that lasts until the children reach adulthood[222]. There are many examples of positive practice in supporting parents with learning disabilities[223].

9.60    Parental learning disability may impact on the unborn child because if affects parents in their decision-making and preparation for the birth. Many women with learning disabilities are poorly informed about contraception and the significance of changes in their menstrual pattern and, as a result, may fail initially to recognize their pregnancy. The quality of the woman's ante-natal care is often jeopardized by late presentation and poor attendance. When women with learning disabilities do attend antenatal care they may experience difficulty in understanding and putting into practice the information and advice they receive.

9.61    For new born babies to thrive they need love, adequate nutrition, sleep, warmth, and to be kept clean. Mothers with learning disabilities may not know what is appropriate food for the baby and developing infant and experience difficulty in establishing a beneficial routine. Health checks may be missed and when the baby is unwell a mother with learning disabilities may not recognise the seriousness of the illness. As the infant develops and becomes more mobile, parents with learning disabilities may not realise the importance of supervising bath times and ensuring the infant is protected from potential dangers within the home. The ongoing support and advice from their wider family and health workers will be essential to ensure parents adapt to their babies changing needs. The infant's cognitive development may be delayed due to an inherited learning disability. However, the environment can still make a difference; children brought up in a warm and stimulating environment will have better outcomes than those with inherited learning disabilities that are not[224]. Mothers with learning disabilities may experience difficulty in engaging with and providing sufficient stimulation for the infant's development and learning. For example, a learning disability may curtail parents' ability to read simple stories to their children and result in a restricted repertoire of nursery rhymes and other songs. Finally, babies and infants may be left with unsafe

---

222    Cleaver, H. and Nicholson, D. (2007) *Parental Learning Disability and Children's Needs: Family Experiences and Effective Practice*. London: Jessica Kingsley Publishers.

223    Working Together with Parents Network (2009), *Supporting parents with learning disabilities and difficulties: stories of positive practice* Norah Fry Research Centre.; DH/DCSF *Joint Good Practice Guidance on Supporting Parents with a Learning Disability*. www.dh.gov.uk/en/Publicationsandstatistics/Publications/PublicationsPolicyAndGuidance/ DH_075119; *SCIE Knowledge Review on disabled parents and parents with additional support needs*. www.scie.org.uk/publications/knowledgereviews/kr11.pdf.

224    Cleaver, H., Unell, I. and Aldgate, A. (2010) *Children's Needs – Parenting Capacity: The impact of parental mental illness, learning disability, problem alcohol and drug use, and domestic violence on children's safety and development. 2nd Edition*. London: The Stationery Office.

adults because parents fail to recognise the threat they pose, or lack the self confidence to prevent them having access to the child. Babies and young children can be supported by the presence of a non-abusive, caring adult, other responsible adults such as grandparents involved in the care of the child, on-going support for the parent, stable home, adequate finances, and harmonious family relationships[225].

9.62   The impact of parental learning disability on children becomes more evident during middle childhood[226]. Children's health may suffer because of a lack of hygiene and a poor diet. Health problems may not be recognised or adequately dealt with, for example dental and doctor's appointments may be missed. Learning may also be affected. Parents with literacy and numeracy problems will have difficulty in helping with school work and encouraging learning. Children's school attendance may be erratic or frequently late. Parents' own poor school experiences may mean they are reluctant to attend school events, and they may experience difficulty in understanding and putting into practice the advice teachers give them. A learning disability may affect parents' capacity to set boundaries and exert authority as their children reach middle childhood; a situation that can be exacerbated if the child is more able than their parent. Children's self image and self esteem may be affected if parents do not understand the importance of recognising the individuality of their children. Parental learning disabilities may also affect children's relationships within the family and with their peers. Inconsistent parenting can cause children to become anxious and uncertain of their parents' affection; emotions which will be exacerbated if parents fail to protect their children from childhood abuse. The consequences of abuse and neglect, particularly in relation to hygiene, low self esteem, and poor control over emotions and behaviour, may result in children being rejected and bullied by their peers. Finally, growing up with parents with learning disability may mean that an able child assumes a major caring role within the family, and as a consequence loses out on his or her own childhood. Positive outcomes for middle year children are associated with the provision of emotional and practical support by relatives, particularly grandparents, regular attendance at school, empathic and vigilant teachers, sufficient income, good physical standards in the home, and belonging to organised out of school activities[227].

9.63   Teenagers of parents with learning disabilities may be left to cope alone with the physical and emotional changes that result from puberty. Parents themselves do not fully understand the significance of puberty and they may fail to educate,

225   Cleaver, H., Unell, I. and Aldgate, A. (2010) *Children's Needs – Parenting Capacity: The impact of parental mental illness, learning disability, problem alcohol and drug use, and domestic violence on children's safety and development. 2nd Edition.* London: The Stationery Office.

226   Cleaver, H. and Nicholson, D. (2007) *Parental Learning Disability and Children's Needs: Family Experiences and Effective Practice.* London: Jessica Kingsley Publishers.

227   Cleaver, H. and Nicholson, D. (2007) *Parental Learning Disability and Children's Needs: Family Experiences and Effective Practice.* London: Jessica Kingsley Publishers.

support or protect their children. The problems are compounded when parents need to care for an adolescent child with profound learning and physical disabilities. Physical and emotional neglect, low self esteem and inadequate supervision increases the likelihood that young people will engage in risky behaviour, such as drinking and drug taking, self harming, and early sexual relationships. When children are more intellectually able than their parents, acting effectively and setting boundaries as they reach adolescence becomes more difficult[228]. The likelihood that education will suffer continues into adolescence. Learning disabilities can result in parents not attending meetings and other school events and not having the capacity to support teenagers through the stress of examinations. Research suggests that many children of parents with learning disabilities experience school related problems such as being suspended for aggressive behaviour, truancy, frequent punishment, being bullied and having few friends[229]. Teenagers who are more able than their parents are increasingly likely to take on the parenting role, becoming responsible for housework, cooking, correspondence, dealing with authority figures, and the general care of their parents and younger siblings. When parents become increasingly dependent on their teenage children it may lead both parties to feel resentful and angry. For many teenagers peer friendships are a source of great support, but low self esteem and behavioural and emotional problems can make it more difficult for teenagers to make friends. Young people whose parents have a learning disability will benefit from factual information about sex and contraception, a trusted adult or peer with whom they can discuss sensitive issues, a good friend, regular attendance at school, training or work, practical help in the home, and access to a young carers projects.

9.64     To support families where a parent has a learning disability a specialist assessment will often be needed and is recommended[230]. Where specialist assessments have not been carried out and/or learning disability support services have not been involved, evidence from inspections has shown that crucial decisions could be made on inadequate information[231].

9.65     Adult learning disability services, and community nurses, can provide valuable input to core assessments and there are also validated assessment tools available[232].

---

228     James, H. (2004) 'Promoting Effective Working with Parents with Learning Disabilities.' *Child Abuse Review 13*, 1, 31-41.

229     Cleaver, H., Unell, I. and Aldgate, A. (2010) *Children's Needs – Parenting Capacity: The impact of parental mental illness, learning disability, problem alcohol and drug use, and domestic violence on children's safety and development. 2nd Edition.* London: The Stationery Office.

230     Department of Health, Department for Education and Employment, Home Office (2000) *Framework for the Assessment of children in Need and their Families.* London: The Stationery Office. Paragraph 6.18-6.21.

231     Social Services Inspectorate (2000) *A Jigsaw of Services: Supporting disabled adults in their parenting role.* London: Department of Health. Paragraph 1.29.

232     McGaw, S. and Newman, T. (2005) *What works for parents with learning disabilities.* Essex: Barnardo's.

However, most parents with learning disabilities do not meet eligibility criteria for adult services and a lack of co-operation between children's and adults' services can create great difficulties.

9.66   A comparative study of methods of supporting parents with learning disabilities found that group education combined with home based support, increases parenting capacity[233]. In some areas, services provide accessible information, advocacy, peer support, multi-agency and multi-disciplinary assessments and on-going home based and other support. This 'parenting with support' appears to yield good results for both parents and children[234].

---

233   McGaw, S., Ball, K. and Clark, A. (2002) 'The effect of group intervention on the relationships of parents with intellectual disabilities'. *Journal of Applied Research in Intellectual Disabilities 15*, 4, 354-366.

234   Tarleton, B., Ward, L. and Howarth, J. (2006) *Finding the right support? A review of issues and positive practice to support parents with learning difficulties and their children.* London: The Baring Foundation.

# Chapter 10 – Implementing the principles on working with children and their families

## Introduction

10.1    The general principles set out in Chapter 5 draw on findings from research. They underpin work with children and their families to safeguard and promote the welfare of children[235]. This chapter sets out in more detail specific aspects of working with children and their families.

## Family group conferences

10.2    A family group conference (FGC) is a decision making and planning process whereby the wider family group makes plans and decisions for children and young people who have been identified either by the family or by service providers as being in need of a plan that will safeguard and promote their welfare. FGCs do not replace or remove the need for child protection conferences, which should always be held when the relevant criteria are met. FGCs may be valuable, for example:

- for children in need, in a range of circumstances where a plan is required for the child's future welfare;

- where section 47 enquiries do not substantiate concerns about significant harm, but where support and services are required; and

- where section 47 enquiries progress to a child protection conference, the conference may agree that an FGC is an appropriate vehicle for the core group to use to develop the outline child protection plan into a fully worked-up plan.

10.3    It is essential that all parties are provided with clear and accurate information, which will make effective planning possible. The family is the primary planning group in the process. Family members need to be able to understand what the issues are from the perspective of the professionals. The family and involved professionals should be clear about:

- what the professional findings are from any core assessment of the child and family;

---

235    See also paragraph 2.18 in *Statutory guidance on making arrangements to safeguard and promote the welfare of children under section 11 of the Children Act 2004* (2007) London: HM Government.

- what the family understands about their current situation;

- what decisions are required;

- what decisions have already been taken;

- the family's scope for decision-making, and whether there are any issues/decisions that are not negotiable; and

- what resources are, or might be, available to implement any plan. Within this framework, agencies and professionals should agree to support the plan if it does not place the child at risk of suffering significant harm, and if the resources requested can be provided.

10.4   Where there are plans to use FGCs in situations where there are concerns about possible harm to a child, they should be developed and implemented under the auspices of the Local Safeguarding Children Board (LSCB). This work should involve all relevant organisations and individuals, and ensure that their use is applicable to other relevant LSCB policies and procedures. Inter-agency training is necessary to build the relevant skills required to work with children and families in this way, and to promote confidence in, and develop a shared understanding of, the process.

## Support, advice and advocacy to children and families

10.5   Children and families may be supported through their involvement in safeguarding processes by advice and advocacy services, and they should always be informed of services that exist locally and nationally. Independent advocates provide independent and confidential information, advice, representation and support, and can play a vital role in ensuring children have appropriate information and support to communicate their views in formal settings, such as child protection conferences and court proceedings.

10.6   Where children and families are involved as witnesses in criminal proceedings, the police, witness support services and other services, such as those provided by Victim Support and Youth Offending Team work with young victims of crime, can do a great deal to explain the process, make it feel less daunting, and ensure that children are prepared for and supported in the court process. The practice guidance *Provision of Therapy for Child Witnesses prior to a Criminal Trial* (2001)[236] makes it clear that the best interests of a child are paramount when deciding whether, and in what form, therapeutic help is given to child witnesses. Information about the Criminal Injuries Compensation Scheme should also be provided in relevant cases.

---

236   www.cps.gov.uk/publications/prosecution/therapychild.html

## Communication and information

10.7  The local authority has a responsibility to make sure children and adults have all the information they require to help them understand the processes that are followed when there are concerns about a child's welfare. Information should be clear and accessible and available in the family's preferred language.

10.8  Family members or friends should not be used as interpreters, since the majority of domestic and child abuse is perpetrated by family members or adults known to the child. Children should not be used as interpreters.

## Race, ethnicity and culture

10.9  Children from all cultures are subject to abuse and neglect. All children have a right to grow up safe from harm. In order to make sensitive and informed professional judgements about a child's needs, and parents' capacity to respond to their child's needs, it is important that professionals are sensitive to differing family patterns and lifestyles and to child-rearing patterns that vary across different racial, ethnic and cultural groups. **At the same time they must be clear that child abuse cannot be condoned for religious or cultural reasons**.

10.10  Professionals should also be aware of the broader social factors that serve to discriminate against black and minority ethnic people. Working in a multi-racial and multicultural society requires professionals and organisations to be committed to equality in meeting the needs of all children and families and to understand the effects of racial harassment, racial discrimination and institutional racism, as well as cultural misunderstanding or misinterpretation.

10.11  The assessment process should maintain a focus on the needs of the individual child. It should always include consideration of the way religious beliefs and cultural traditions in different racial, ethnic and cultural groups influence their values, attitudes and behaviour and the way in which family and community life is structured and organised. Cultural and religious factors should not be regarded as acceptable explanations for child abuse or neglect and are not acceptable grounds for inaction when there are concerns that a child is or may be suffering or likely to suffer harm. Professionals should be aware of, and work with, the strengths and support systems available within families, ethnic groups and communities, which can be built on to help safeguard children and promote their welfare.

10.12  Professionals should guard against myths and stereotypes – both positive and negative – of black and minority ethnic families. Anxiety about being accused of racist practice should not prevent the necessary action being taken to safeguard and promote a child's welfare. Careful assessment – based on evidence – of a child's needs, and a family's strengths and difficulties, understood in the context of the wider social environment, will help to avoid any distorting effect of these influences on professional judgements.

10.13   All children, whatever their religious or cultural background, must receive the same care and safeguards with regard to abuse and neglect.

## Children in 'Families at risk' having very poor outcomes

10.14   'Families at risk' is a shorthand term for families whose members experience, or are at risk of, multiple and complex problems – such as worklessness, poor mental health or substance misuse, offending behaviour by adults or children – which frequently lead to very poor outcomes for children, young people and adults within the families. The safety and welfare of children living within these families are more likely to be a cause for concern than those from the population as a whole.

10.15   The term 'families at risk' was first was adopted following the Families at Risk Review undertaken by the Cabinet Office's Social Exclusion Taskforce with the Department for Children's Schools and Families[237].

10.16   The review found that families at risk, because of the multiple difficulties they face, have a significant likelihood of facing a crisis situation without preventative support. Problems experienced by family members, could include combinations of the following factors:

- poverty, debt, inactivity or worklessness and low aspirations;

- low parental education and skills;

- domestic violence;

- relationship conflict;

- child neglect and poor parenting and family functioning;

- poor mental health;

- poor physical health and disabilities;

- teenage pregnancy;

- learning disability;

- poor school attendance and attainment;

- involvement in crime, anti-social behaviour, substance misuse; and

---

237   See www.cabinetoffice.gov.uk/social_exclusion_task_force/families_at_risk.aspx.

- poor housing and homelessness.

10.17 Early action to prevent and address problems for children and young people is critical to stop children living in these circumstances having poor outcomes in life. This means a co-ordinated approach across services to identify and intervene early with families with children who are at the greatest risk of having poor outcomes. An agreed list of warning signs which could prompt concerns being raised about a child's welfare (such as a permanent exclusion from school, repeated truancy or involvement in anti-social behaviour, knife crime, violence, and/or gangs) should identify that whole family intervention may be necessary to safeguard and promote a child's welfare. Targeted parenting and family support is provided through services such as Family Intervention Projects (FIPs) and parenting programmes and services as set out in the local authority's Parenting Strategy.

## Think Family practice

10.18 'Think Family' is an approach promoted by Government based on co-ordinating the support provided by adult and children's services to a single family in order to secure better outcomes for the children through the use of targeted, specialised and whole-family approaches to addressing family needs. It is about making sure the different parts of the systems around families work together in a way which intervenes early in family dysfunction. In addition, that they tailor the support provided to individual family members, taking into account the needs of the family as a whole and how addressing family needs can contribute to safeguarding and promoting each child's welfare.

10.19 Services of all types come into contact with families at risk of poor outcomes: universal, targeted and specialist; statutory, voluntary and independent; and children, adult and family. The Social Exclusion Taskforce research showed that whilst families at risk of very poor outcomes are often in contact with a wide range of services, evidence suggests that the support provided is only effectively co-ordinated and persistent when a crisis occurs. This was despite the fact that universal services such as schools, GPs and health visitors had often identified them as highly vulnerable to poor outcomes very early in their involvement.

10.20 Effective interventions for children in families at risk of very poor outcomes depends upon the ability of services and the practitioners already working with family members, to 'assess' and then 'decide' on the most appropriate types of interventions to support and achieve better outcomes for each child whilst at the same time, whenever possible, helping the child's parents and other adult family members if they are experiencing problems which are having an impact on the families ability to function effectively. However, focusing on the full range of needs within a family should not detract from the over-riding duty to safeguard and promote the welfare of the children within the family.

10.21   'Think Family' practice depends on children's services developing arrangements with local adult services so that the impact of any problems that mothers, fathers and other key carers are experiencing are seen in the context of the welfare of the children for whom they are responsible. Adult services also have a crucial role to play in minimising the risk of parental problems such as domestic violence, learning disability, substance misuse or worklessness affecting children's outcomes.

## Effectiveness of parenting and family interventions

10.22   Supporting mothers and fathers and key carers can be a sustainable way of securing better outcomes for children. Research suggests that using evidence-based parenting and family support programmes, for example, through the Parenting Early Intervention Programme, can have lasting effects in improving behaviour even in cases where they are initially reluctant to accept help. Providing help with parenting impacts upon a range of outcomes for children and young people. A meta-analysis of over 40 studies conducted in 2003 showed Family Based Interventions had substantial desirable effects[238]. A review by the National Institute for Clinical Excellence (NICE) highlighted the value of parenting programmes in improving the behaviour of children with conduct disorder[239]. Eleven out of fifteen studies showed statistical long terms effects (between one and ten years). Conduct disorder is one of the main reasons for referrals to Children and Adolescent Mental Health Services (CAMHS) and the estimated cost of a one-year cohort of children with conduct disorders in the UK is £5.2 billion[240].

10.23   Parenting interventions tend to work best when both parents are included in the intervention (or separate partner-support is provided). The ability of workers to engage parents effectively and consistently and to achieve 'buy in' to what is often a demanding and rigorous change management programme, is crucial to the success of any intervention. There is considerable skill, tenacity, determination and tolerance required by parenting practitioners and key workers who will need to identify the appropriate drivers for change in their clients. They need to understand the underlying reasons for the behaviours displayed by families and agencies, be solution focused in their approach and be able to draw on the necessary support themselves to enable them to set and sustain realistic goals.

---

238   Farrington and Welsch (2007). *Saving children from a life of crime*; Farrington and Welsh (2003). Meta analysis in ANZJC.

239   NICE (2006). Parent – Training/education programmes in the management of children with conduct disorders. In NICE Technology appraisal guidance 102.

240   Friedli and Parsonage (2007). *Mental Health Promotion: Building an Economic Case*. Northern Ireland Association for Mental Health.

## Working with fathers

10.24 When working with families it is important to 'Think Fathers' as well, including where the father is himself a young person. A child's father can have a significant, positive impact on the child's outcomes but only where he is causing no harm to the child – for example, research shows that children with highly involved fathers do better at school and are more empathic in the way that they behave. More and more fathers want to be involved within their family and in their children's upbringing even if they are no longer living with the children and their mother. However, many fathers find this difficult and feel they are not recognised or encouraged to get involved, by schools or health services. For example, children's services as a whole can still be very mother-focused and fathers can, often inadvertently, be made to feel unwelcome or uncomfortable when they try to use them. Managers and commissioners should therefore make sure that their services take account of the needs of fathers and actively look for ways to engage them. *The Dad Test* (2009)[241] sets out practical steps organisations can take to remove these barriers to fathers' participation.

## Family Intervention Projects

10.25 Joint work with FIPs funded through the local authority 'Think Family' Grant may also be appropriate where the needs of a family are complex and require a high level of face to face contact and family-focused interventions. All local authorities receive funding to set up at least one FIP. The health contribution is key to this and is currently funded centrally to pay for a part-time health professional to work with the FIP team in every local authority. With their systematic contact with families FIPs can help identify earlier, children about whom there are concerns that they are, or may be, suffering or be likely to suffer harm. In these situations, a member of the FIP team should make a referral to children's social care. Family involvement with FIPs does not replace or remove the need for the processes set out in Chapter 5 to be followed. Where a FIP team is involved with a family they should continue to be involved, as appropriate, in any assessments, section 47 enquiries and subsequent work led by children's social care.

10.26 Chief Executives will need to nominate an officer responsible for reporting to the Director of Children's Services (DCS) on the adequacy of safeguarding arrangements between FIPs and children's social care. In addition, the FIP also should have a designated person for safeguarding with clear lines of accountability through their manager to the Head of Quality and Safeguarding in their relevant service and through them to the DCS/Chief Executive for ensuring the implementation of effective practice with regard to safeguarding and promoting the welfare of children.

---

241    See www.think-fathers.org.

## Family Nurse Partnership

10.27 The Family Nurse Partnership is an evidence based, intensive preventive programme for vulnerable, young first time mothers that is being tested across England. The programme is voluntary and family nurses visit from early pregnancy until the child is two years old. The family nurses build close relationships with clients and use the programme methods and materials to improve antenatal health, child health and development and parents' economic self-sufficiency.

10.28 The family nurse works with vulnerable young people and their babies. They play a key role in the prevention and early identification of babies and young people who may have been, or are likely to be, abused or neglected. They will refer a child to children's social care as a 'child in need', when appropriate, and will act on concerns that a child may suffering or likely to suffer significant harm. Family nurses receive weekly supervision and together with the supervisor work closely with named professionals with safeguarding responsibilities.

10.29 Family nurses have close contact with and in depth knowledge of children and families which means they have an important role at all stages of the safeguarding and child protection process. This includes completing common assessments, taking on the lead professional role where appropriate, information sharing, contributing to assessments, and involvement in implementing a child protection plan. Family nurses will make available relevant information to child protection conferences about a child and family, whether or not they are able to attend.

# Chapter 11 – Safeguarding and promoting the welfare of children who may be particularly vulnerable

## Introduction

11.1 This chapter outlines some groups of children who may be particularly vulnerable. The purpose of this chapter is simply to help inform the procedures in Chapter 5, which sets out the basic framework of action to be taken in **all** circumstances when a parent, professional, or any other person has concerns about the welfare of any child. This chapter cannot provide a comprehensive list of every group of vulnerable children, but highlights some specific groups of particular concern in relation to safeguarding, and some specific issues in relation to promoting their welfare.

## Children living away from home

### General

11.2 Previous high profile inquiries and reports into abuse of children living away from home have raised awareness of the particular vulnerability of these children. We should not be complacent that such abuse could not occur again. We need to be continually vigilant so that children today do not suffer as others have.

11.3 All settings where children live away from home should provide the same basic safeguards against abuse, founded on an approach which promotes their general welfare, protects them from harm of all kinds and treats them with dignity and respect. The current regulatory system, including the regulations and National Minimum Standards which apply to such settings, has a clear focus on safeguarding children and promoting their welfare and development. All those who work with children should be able to recognise evidence that a child's welfare or development may be being impaired and know how to act on such evidence.

11.4 Local Safeguarding Children Board (LSCB) procedures for safeguarding and promoting the welfare of children should apply in every situation and to all settings, including those where children are living away from home. Individual agencies that provide care for children living away from home should implement clear and unambiguous procedures to respond to potential matters of concern about children's welfare in line with the relevant legal requirements and LSCB's arrangements. Where children are living away from their home area it is essential that there is clarity about the respective and complementary roles and responsibilities of the local authority and agencies involved. Specifically it is important that the local authority covering the area where the child comes from but is currently not resident understands its continuing responsibilities in relation to safeguarding the child.

## Essential safeguards

11.5    There are a number of essential safeguards that should be observed in all settings in which children live away from home, including children in care, private fostering, healthcare, boarding schools (including residential special schools), prisons, young offenders' institutions, secure training centres and secure units, and when children are detained whilst within the immigration system. Detailed guidance and standards are in place for service providers in each of these sectors. Where services are not directly provided essential safeguards should be explicitly addressed in contracts with external providers. These safeguards should ensure that:

- children feel valued and respected and their self-esteem is promoted;

- there is an openness on the part of the institution to the external world and to external scrutiny, including contact with families and the wider community;

- staff and foster carers are trained in all aspects of safeguarding children, alert to children's vulnerabilities and risks of harm and knowledgeable about how to implement safeguarding children procedures;

- children who live away from home are listened to, and their views and concerns responded to;

- children have ready access to a trusted adult outside the institution – for example, a family member, the child's social worker, independent visitor or children's advocate. Children should be made aware of the help they could receive from independent advocacy services, external mentors and ChildLine;

- staff recognise the importance of ascertaining the wishes and feelings of children and understand how individual children communicate by verbal or non-verbal means;

- there are clear procedures for referring safeguarding concerns about a child to the relevant local authority;

- complaints procedures are clear, effective, user-friendly and are readily accessible to children and young people including those with disabilities and those for whom English is not their preferred language. Procedures should address informal as well as formal complaints. Systems that do not promote open communication about 'minor' complaints will not be responsive to major ones and a pattern of 'minor' complaints may indicate more deeply seated problems in management and culture that needs to be addressed. Records of complaints should be kept by providers of children's services or secure settings – for example, there should be a complaints register in every children's home and secure establishment that records all representations or complaints, the action taken to address them and the outcomes. Children should genuinely be able to raise concerns and make suggestions for changes and improvements which should be taken seriously;

- bullying is effectively countered;

- recruitment and selection procedures are rigorous and create a high threshold of entry to deter abusers;

- there is effective supervision and support that extends to temporary staff and volunteers;

- contractor staff are effectively checked and supervised when on site or in contact with children;

- clear procedures and support systems are in place for dealing with expressions of concern by staff and carers about other staff or carers. Organisations should have a code of conduct instructing staff on their duty to their employer and their professional obligation to raise legitimate concerns about the conduct of colleagues or managers. There should be a guarantee that procedures can be invoked in ways that do not prejudice the 'whistle-blower's' own position and prospects;

- there is respect for diversity and sensitivity to race, culture, religion, gender, sexuality and disability; and

- staff and carers are alert to the risks of harm to children in the external environment from people prepared to exploit the additional vulnerability of children living away from home.

## Looked after children

11.6    The full range of safeguards which apply to all looked after children are set out in the relevant regulations, statutory guidance and National Minimum Standards. This section highlights certain issues of particular relevance to safeguarding.

11.7    Local authorities placing children in another local authority area are required to notify the host authority prior to placement.

11.8    As part of their statutory responsibilities for planning children's care, social workers are required to maintain a regular up to date assessment of child's needs, see looked after children in foster care on their own and take appropriate account of the child's wishes and feelings. Evidence of their engagement with the child must be recorded so that the plan for the child's care is kept up to date, with the child being offered the right services to respond to the full range of their needs.

11.9    Independent Reviewing Officers (IROs) are responsible for chairing meetings that must be scheduled at prescribed intervals to review the child's care plan. IROs have specific responsibilities to ensure that the plan has taken the child's wishes and feelings into account and that their care plan remains appropriate in view of the child's needs, including their need to be effectively safeguarded.

11.10   Foster carers should be provided with full information about the foster child and his/her family, including details of the child's previous experiences of harm and/or neglect so that they can provide an appropriate pattern of care for the child, which takes into account the child's needs and those of the carers own children.

11.11   Carers must be properly aware of the whereabouts of the children they look after, their patterns of absence and contacts. Carers should follow the recognised procedure of their agency whenever a child is missing from their home[242]. This involves notifying the placing authority and, where necessary, the police of any unauthorised absence by a child.

11.12   The local authority's duty to undertake section 47 enquiries, when there are concerns about significant harm to a child, applies on the same basis to looked after children as it does to children who live with their own families. Enquiries should consider the safety of any other child living in the household/placement, including foster carers' own children. The local authority in which the child is living has the responsibility to convene a strategy discussion, which should include representatives from the responsible local authority that placed the child. At the strategy discussion it should be decided which local authority should take responsibility for the next steps, which may include a section 47 enquiry. For further details on this see Chapter 5.

## Private fostering

11.13   A private fostering arrangement is essentially one that is made privately (i.e. without the involvement of a local authority) for the care of a child under the age of 16, under 18 if disabled, by someone other than a parent or close relative for 28 days or more, in the carer's own home.

11.14 Privately fostered children are a diverse and potentially vulnerable group. They include:

- children where arrangements are made due to parental illness or distress or when parents' work or study involves long or anti-social hours;

- young people who stay with friends because they have fallen out with their parents and who may not be in touch with agencies such as education services;

- children staying with families while attending a school away from their home area; and

- children from overseas whose parents do not reside in this country.

11.15 Under the Children Act 1989, private foster carers and those with parental responsibility are required to notify the local authority of their intention to privately foster; or to have a child privately fostered, or where a child is privately fostered in an emergency. Teachers, health and other professionals, such as Youth Offending Team (YOT) workers, should notify the local authority of a private fostering arrangement that comes to their attention where they are not satisfied that the local authority has been, or will be, notified of the arrangement.

11.16 It is the duty of every local authority to satisfy itself that the welfare of children who are privately fostered within its area is being satisfactorily safeguarded and promoted, and to ensure that such advice as appears to be required is given to private foster carers. In order to do so, local authority officers must visit privately fostered children at regular intervals and the minimum visiting requirements are set out in the Children (Private Arrangements for Fostering) Regulations 2005. The local authority officer should visit a child alone unless the officer considers it inappropriate. Local authorities must also arrange for visits to be made to the privately fostered child, the private foster carer, or parent of the child when reasonably requested to do so. Children should be given contact details of the social worker who will be visiting them while they are being privately fostered.

11.17 Local authorities must satisfy themselves as to such matters as the suitability of the private foster carer and the private foster carer's household and accommodation. They have the power to impose requirements on the private foster carer or, if there are serious concerns about an arrangement, to prohibit it.

11.18 The Children Act 1989 creates a number of offences in connection with private fostering, including for failure to notify an arrangement or to comply with any requirement or prohibition imposed by the authority. Certain people are disqualified from being private foster carers.

11.19   Local authorities are required to promote awareness in their area of notification requirements, and to ensure that such advice as appears to be required is given to those concerned with children who are, or are proposed to be, privately fostered. This includes private foster carers (proposed and actual) and parents.

11.20   The Children (Private Arrangements for Fostering) Regulations 2005 require local authorities to satisfy themselves of the suitability of a proposed arrangement before it commences (where advance notice is given).

11.21   The private fostering regulations require local authorities to monitor their compliance with all their duties and functions in relation to private fostering, and place a duty on them to appoint an officer for this purpose.

11.22   In addition, local authorities are inspected against the National Minimum Standards for private fostering.

11.23   The Children Act 2004 and regulations strengthen and enhance the private fostering notification scheme, and provide additional safeguards for privately fostered children. These measures, along with the National Minimum Standards and the role of LSCBs in relation to private fostering, focus local authorities' attention on private fostering and require them to take a more proactive approach to identifying arrangements in their area.

11.24   Private fostering is a key area of child protection. Privately fostered children may be very vulnerable if private fostering arrangements have not been notified to the local authority. Local authorities are expected to improve notification rates and compliance with the existing legislative framework for private fostering to safeguard privately fostered children.

11.25   All professionals working with children have an important role in relation to safeguarding privately fostered children. If they become aware of a private fostering arrangement, and they are not confident that it has been notified to the local authority, they should contact the local authority themselves. LSCBs can play a vital role in helping protect children who are privately fostered, exercising leadership and raising awareness in the community of the requirements and issues around private fostering.

11.26   Children Act 1989 guidance on private fostering, issued in July 2005[243], reflects the new measures on private fostering in the Children Act 2004 and in the regulations.

---

243   This guidance, along with the National Minimum Standards and guidance for local authorities on promoting awareness within their areas, is available at: www.dcsf.gov.uk/everychildmatters/_download/?id=2596

## Children and young people in hospital

11.27   *The National Service Framework for Children, Young People and Maternity Services (NSF), (2004)* sets out standards for children and young people's healthcare. Standard 6, 'Children who are Ill' should be used in conjunction with Standard 7 'Children in Hospital', which was published in 2003 to meet the commitment made in the Government's response to *The Report of the Public Enquiry into Children's Heart Surgery at the Bristol Royal Infirmary 1984-1995: Learning from Bristol to develop hospital services for children and young people.* The Healthcare Commission undertook an improvement review of the NHS implementation of the hospital standard in 2006[244].

11.28   Children and young people should be cared for at home wherever possible providing it is safe and sustainable to do so. When admission to hospital is unavoidable the highest standards of privacy and dignity must be maintained and care should be provided in a location and environment that is safe, healthy, child friendly and suitable to the age and stage of development of the child or young person *(NSF Standard 7, 2003).* Care should be provided by staff who have been trained and educated in the care of children and young people. Nursing care should be delivered by a ratio of staff supervised by registered children's nurses to ensure safe standards of care. Children should not be cared for in an adult ward; where treatment and care will continue into adulthood arrangements should be in place to plan and facilitate a smooth transition to adult services at a time when the young person is ready to make this change. Where there is no adolescent unit available hospitals should take the additional needs of adolescents into account and provide appropriate facilities. Wherever possible, children and young people should be consulted about where they would prefer to stay in hospital and their views should be taken into account and respected. Hospital admission data should include the age of children so that hospitals can monitor whether they are being given appropriate care in appropriate wards.

11.29   When children are in hospital, this should not in itself jeopardise the health of the child or young person further. The NSF requires hospitals to ensure that their facilities are secure and regularly reviewed. There should be policies relating to breaches of security involving the police and local safeguarding procedures should be followed should there be suspicion of child abuse. The local authority where the hospital is located is responsible for the welfare of children in its hospitals. Primary Care Trusts (PCTs) are responsible for ensuring hospitals commissioned to provide services for their children and young people population have processes in place to protect them including out of area services.

---

244   www.cqc.org.uk/_db/_documents/children_improving_services_Tagged.pdf

11.30    Additionally, section 85 of the Children Act 1989 requires PCTs to notify the 'Responsible Authority' – i.e. the local authority for the area where the child is ordinarily resident, or where the child is accommodated if this is unclear – when a child has been, or will be, accommodated by the PCT for three months or more for example, in hospital. This is so that the local authority can assess the child's needs and decide whether services are required under the Children Act 1989. Arrangements for this notification process should be included by PCTs in local contracts.

## Children in contact with the youth justice system

11.31    In fulfilling their statutory function of reducing offending and reoffending by children and young people, YOTs have dual responsibilities in the area of safeguarding as well as public protection, including protection of other children and young people. It is important that public protection in a youth justice context is seen as integral to wider approaches to working effectively with children and young people.

11.32    These complex responsibilities are discharged both by YOTs' involvement in prevention work, including initiatives such as Safer Schools Partnerships, as well as work with victims of crime. YOTs co-operate with various partner agencies, including the police, Multi-agency Public Protection Agencies (MAPPA) and Crime and Disorder Reduction Partnerships (CDRPs), in initiatives aimed at making communities safer, including projects to reduce gang violence and violent extremism, thus directly contributing to the safeguarding of children and young people from violence in their communities. All partners working in the youth justice system should see *When to share information: best practice guidance for everyone working in the youth justice system*[245]; joint Department of Health, Department for Children, Schools and Families, Youth Justice Board and Prison Service, which includes best practice case studies used to identify when, what, where and how information needs to be shared to ensure improved outcomes for children and young people.

11.33    In order to effectively manage the risk posed by young people in the youth justice system, it is important that managers and practitioners distinguish clearly between risk (likelihood) of reoffending, risk of serious harm to others and risk to the young person either from themselves or others.

11.34    All young people involved with the formal youth justice system are referred to a YOT at the earliest stage and will have a named responsible caseworker. In many cases, this work requires the active engagement of broader children's health and

---

245    www.dh.gov.uk/en/Publicationsandstatistics/Publications/PublicationsPolicyAndGuidance/ DH_084703

family services – specifically, when assessing and addressing the needs of individual children and young people in order to safeguard the child or young person and address the causes of vulnerability as well as improve outcomes.

11.35　Key partner agencies are required to support YOTs in fulfilling these duties as set out under the Crime and Disorder Act 1998. As outlined in the NSF, this includes Children and Adolescent Mental Health Services (CAMHS) services, as well as other generic and specialist health and social care services delivered locally.

*Children and young people in custody*

11.36　Children and young people sentenced or remanded in custody are among the most vulnerable. Specific consideration to the safeguarding of this particular group is therefore called for and requires ongoing support from children's services and LSCBs in addition to the establishment's day to day duty of care.

11.37　The functions, powers, duties, responsibilities and obligations imposed on local authorities by the Children Act 1989 – in particular, by sections 17 and 47 – do not cease to arise merely because a child is in the secure estate. Such functions, powers, duties and responsibilities operate subject to the necessary requirements of imprisonment. Prisons have a legal obligation to safeguard the wellbeing of children in their care.

11.38　It is important that agreed procedures between the secure establishment and the local authority (in particular the LSCB) with that establishment in its geographical area are in place outlining how to deal with and undertake child in need assessments as well as how to deal with child protection allegations. In discharging these duties, local authority children's social care services should consider seconding social workers to work in secure establishments and establish effective links with a child or young person's home local authority. The home local authority and YOT have continuing responsibilities to children and young people in custody.

11.39　Continuity of services when children and young people transfer into and out of the secure estate is a vital element of good safeguarding practice and good resettlement planning. This includes ensuring that young people have suitable supported accommodation, help with mental health and substance misuse issues and with identifying appropriate education, training or employment.

11.40　Issues of transition to adult services can cause particular problems for children and young people in the youth justice system. The different thresholds for children's and adult services and the complexity of need posed by many young people in the youth justice system, as well as emotional immaturity, can result in a breakdown of services, including accommodation, substance misuse and health services. Standard

4 of the Core Standards in the Children's NSF describes that 'Young people with additional and sometimes complex needs, such as mental health problems or disabilities may find it more difficult to make these transitions successfully and they and their families may require additional support'. High quality transition services should be delivered in a multi-agency context.

11.41 *Healthy Children, Safer Communities: a strategy and action plan to promote the health and well being of those in contact with the youth justice system*[246] incorporates coverage of transition issues as a key element. Children's services transitions and leaving care teams are also key agencies in ensuring successful transition.

11.42 *Healthy Children, Safer Communities* is designed to try to ensure that the health and wellbeing needs of children and young people in contact with the youth justice system are addressed and responded to with appropriate and timely mainstream services wherever possible. In addition it aims to encourage co-ordinated, multi-faceted care tailored to individual needs, continuity of care between the community and the secure estate, and a safe and effective transition to appropriate adult provision. The strategy also responds to the three recommendations for children in Lord Bradley's review of people with mental health problems or learning disabilities in the criminal justice system (April 2009)[247].

*Looked after children and custody*

11.43 Where a looked after child who is the subject of a care order, meaning that their responsible authority shares parental responsibility for them, enters a young offender institution (YOI), either on sentence or on remand, the responsible authority has continuing responsibilities as a corporate parent to visit and continue to assess their needs. The responsible authority must make arrangements for regular contact with the looked after child, continue to ensure that reviews of their care plan take place at the prescribed intervals and facilitate ongoing contact with parents and siblings where that is part of the care plan. These responsibilities will mean that the responsible authority must be closely involved in making plans for resettling the child in their community once they are able to be released from custody. For some children this will involve them returning to foster care or other kind of supported placement.

11.44 Where a child under 16 who has previously been accommodated as a result of a voluntary agreement under section 20 of the Children Act enters custody they do not remain a looked after child. However, regulations to be enacted as a result of

---

246 www.dh.gov.uk/en/Publicationsandstatistics/Publications/PublicationsPolicyAndGuidance/ DH_109771

247 www.dh.gov.uk/en/Publicationsandstatistics/Publications/PublicationsPolicyAndGuidance/ DH_098694

section 15 of the Children and Young Persons Act 2008 will require a responsible local authority to ensure that they appoint a representative to visit all children and young people who have ceased to be accommodated. The representative will be responsible for assessing the child's needs in order to make recommendations about the support they will need whilst detained, and, in particular, the support necessary on release which could include planning for the child to become looked after again.

11.45    Children aged 16+ who were looked after prior to being sentenced may well be 'relevant children' as defined by section 23A of the Children Act 1989[248]. Their responsible authority must appoint a personal adviser and prepare a pathway plan setting out the support that they will provide to prepare the child for the responsibilities of adulthood. The pathway plan must include information about where the child will live on release and the support they will receive to re-establish themselves in their communities with positive plan for their futures, to minimise the possibility of their re-offending.

## Abuse by children and young people

### Peer abuse

11.46    Children, particularly but not exclusively those living away from home, are also vulnerable to physical, sexual and emotional bullying and abuse by their peers. Such abuse should always be taken as seriously as abuse perpetrated by an adult. Whenever a child may have harmed another, all agencies must be aware of their responsibilities to both children and multi-agency management of both cases must reflect this. Agencies should also be alert to the possibility that a child or young person who has harmed another may well also be a victim. However, the interests of the identified victim must always be the paramount consideration and professionals should also be alert to the fact that there is likely to be a risk to children other than the current victim. A significant proportion of sex offences are committed by teenagers although, on occasion, such offences are committed by younger children. Staff working with children, including carers of children living away from home need clear guidance and training to identify the difference between consenting and abusive, and between appropriate and exploitative peer relationships. Staff should not dismiss some abusive sexual behaviour as 'normal' between young people, and should not develop high thresholds before taking action.

11.47    Work with children and young people who abuse others, including those who sexually abuse/offend, should recognise that such children are likely to have considerable needs themselves, and that they may pose a significant risk of harm to other children. Evidence suggests that children who abuse others may have suffered considerable disruption in their lives, been exposed to violence within the family, may have witnessed or been subject to physical or sexual abuse, have problems in their educational development and may have committed other offences. Such children and young people are likely to be children in need, and some will, in addition, be suffering, or at risk of suffering, significant harm, and may themselves be in need of protection. Children and young people who abuse others should be held responsible for their abusive behaviour, while being identified and responded to in a way that meets their needs as well as protecting others.

11.48 A cross-government service delivery framework for young people who display sexually harmful behaviour is due for publication in early 2010. The purpose of the framework is to deliver a document that sets service development across the pathway from early intervention, through the community, and within custody, ensuring that there are clear plans for this group of children and young people. The framework aims to ensure that services that address health, wellbeing and education needs are delivered equitably to all children and young people, including those who display sexually harmful behaviour, and that services are delivered, based on evidence for what is effective for meeting specific needs.

11.49 The Ofsted survey *Exclusion from school of children from four to seven* (May 2009) highlighted the issue of sexually inappropriate behaviour in very young children as one faced by a small number of schools and early years settings. The survey acknowledged that exclusions from school generally and sexually inappropriate behaviours specifically were extremely rare in children from this age group, but where they did occur they highlighted important underlying issues which schools and early years settings need to be equipped to address.

11.50 Three key principles should guide work with children and young people who abuse others:

- there should be a co-ordinated multi-agency approach including youth justice (where appropriate), children's social care, education (including educational psychology) and health (including child and adolescent mental health) agencies and police;

- the needs of children and young people who abuse others should be considered separately from the needs of their victims; and

- a multi-agency assessment should be carried out in each case, appreciating that these children may have considerable unmet developmental needs, as well as specific needs arising from their behaviour.

11.51 LSCBs and YOTs should ensure that there is a clear operational framework in place within which assessment, decision-making and case-management take place. Neither child welfare nor criminal justice agencies should embark on a course of action that has implications for the others without appropriate consultation.

11.52 In assessing a child or young person who abuses another, relevant considerations include:

- the nature and extent of the abusive behaviours. In respect of sexual abuse, there are sometimes perceived to be difficulties in distinguishing between normal childhood sexual development and experimentation, and sexually inappropriate or aggressive behaviour. Expert professional judgement may be required, within the context of knowledge about normal child sexuality;

- the context of the abusive behaviours;

- the child's development, and family and social circumstances;

- needs for services, specifically focusing on the child's harmful behaviour as well as other significant needs; and

- the risks to self and others, including other children in the household, extended family, school, peer group or wider social network. This risk is likely to be present unless the opportunity for further abuse is ended, the young person has acknowledged the abusive behaviour and accepted responsibility and there is agreement by the young abuser and his/her family to work with relevant agencies to address the problem.

11.53 Decisions for local agencies (including the Crown Prosecution Service where relevant) according to the responsibilities of each include:

- the most appropriate course of action within the youth justice system if the child is above the age of criminal responsibility;

- whether the young person who perpetrated the abuse should be the subject of a child protection conference; and

- what plan of action should be put in place to address the needs of the young abuser, detailing the involvement of all relevant agencies.

11.54 A young abuser should be the subject of a child protection conference if he or she is considered personally to be at risk of continuing significant harm. Where there is no reason to hold a child protection conference there is likely to be a need for a multi-agency approach if the young abuser's needs are complex. Issues regarding suitable educational and accommodation arrangements often require skilled and careful consideration.

11.55   Children with inappropriate sexual or very violent behaviour who are re-entering the community following a custodial sentence or time in secure accommodation, or who move into an area from another local authority, require the multi-agency response (assessment/intervention) initiated at the earliest opportunity. Where a child who has been convicted of sexual offences involving the abuse of other children is released into the community, the MAPPA must be invoked.

## Bullying

11.56   Bullying may be defined as deliberately hurtful behaviour, usually repeated over a period of time, where it is difficult for those bullied to defend themselves. It can take many forms, but the three main types are:

- physical (for example, hitting, kicking, theft);

- verbal (for example, racist or homophobic remarks, threats, name-calling); and

- emotional (for example, isolating an individual from the activities and social acceptance of their peer group).

11.57   The damage inflicted by bullying (including bullying via the internet) can frequently be underestimated. It can cause considerable distress to children, to the extent that it affects their health and development or, at the extreme, causes them significant harm (including self-harm). All settings in which children are provided with services or are living away from home should have in place rigorously enforced anti-bullying strategies.

11.58   Since 1999 schools have been under a legal duty to put measures in place to promote good behaviour, respect for others and to prevent all forms of bullying among pupils. In practice schools need to draw up an anti-bullying policy linked to the behaviour policy.

11.59   In cases of sexist, sexual and transphobic bullying schools must always consider whether safeguarding processes need to be followed. This is because of the potential seriousness of violence (including sexual violence) that these forms of bullying characterise through inappropriate sexual behaviour. It is important for schools to consider whether to apply safeguarding procedures both to young people being bullied and to perpetrators. Young people being bullied may need to be protected from the child or young person engaging in bullying behaviour using safeguarding processes. If a young person is engaging in these behaviours this may be an indication that they are acting out the prejudices they see, to fit in. It could also be an indication that the young person could be experiencing abuse at home and therefore require some form of safeguarding intervention[249].

11.60   The Department for Children, Schools and Families (DCSF) has produced a comprehensive suite of guidance for schools under the title *Safe to Learn: Embedding Anti-bullying Work in Schools*. This includes overarching guidance and specialist materials on cyberbullying, homophobic bullying (launched in 2007) which links to existing guidance on bullying around race, religion and culture (2006)[250]. Materials on bullying, preventing and tackling the cyberbullying of teachers, and bullying related to special educational needs and disabilities were launched in April and May 2008 respectively.

11.61   In addition the *Safe from Bullying* suite of guidance documents on tackling bullying outside of schools was published in April 2009. This includes guidance for practitioners in several target settings, such as children's homes and journeys to and from schools; it also includes a guide for local authorities and a set of training resources for staff.

11.62   New *Guidance for schools on preventing and tackling sexist, sexual and transphobic bullying*[251] was published in December 2009, following the DVD resource pack on bullying related to SEN and disabilities[252] launched in September 2009.

11.63   The DCSF provides support and challenge to local authorities and schools on bullying issues through a universal programme of support provided by the National Strategies and a more targeted programme provided by the Anti-Bullying Alliance. The Anti-Bullying Alliance provides support also to local areas to tackle bullying in their communities. Ofsted has a challenge role with schools in looking at how children and young people are being kept safe from bullying as part of their inspections and canvass views direct from parents and children and young people as part of this process. If weaknesses are identified these will be flagged up in the Ofsted report.

11.64   The LSCB, Children's Trust partners and all organisations involved with providing services to children are required to share information and work together to safeguard and promote the welfare of children and young people who should also be consulted on issues that affect them as individuals and collectively. Children's Trust partners should consider tackling bullying as part of their wider role in

---

249   For more detailed guidance please see Chapter 2 of the document, 'The law, policy and guidance for schools' and the tackling school bullying guidance at: http://publications.teachernet.gov.uk/default. aspx?PageFunction=productdetails&PageMode=publications&ProductId=DCSF-00668-2007

250   www.teachernet.gov.uk/wholeschool/behaviour/tacklingbullying/racistbullying/

251   www.teachernet.gov.uk/wholeschool/behaviour/tacklingbullying/ sexistsexualandtransphobicbullying/

252   www.teachernet.gov.uk/wholeschool/behaviour/tacklingbullying/sendisab/

safeguarding children and young people. The role of Government Offices is to support and challenge on how local authorities and their partners are delivering improved outcomes in respect of keeping children and young people safe from bullying.

## Children whose behaviour indicates a lack of parental control

11.65 When children are brought to the attention of the police or the wider community because of their behaviour, this may be an indication of vulnerability, poor supervision or neglect in the wider sense. It is important to consider whether these are children in need and to offer them assistance and services that reflect their needs. This should be done on a multi-agency basis. A range of powers should be used to engage families to improve the child's behaviour where engagement cannot be secured on a voluntary basis.

11.66 A child safety order (CSO) is a compulsory intervention available below the threshold of the child being at risk of significant harm. A local authority can apply for a CSO where a child has committed an act that would have been an offence if s/he were aged 10 or above, where it is necessary to prevent such an act, or where the child has caused harassment, distress or harm to others (i.e. behaved anti-socially). It is designed to help the child improve his or her behaviour, and is likely to be used alongside work with the family and others to address any underlying problems.

11.67 A parenting order can be made alongside a CSO or when a CSO is breached. This provides an effective means of engaging with and supporting parents, while helping them develop their ability to undertake their parental responsibilities. A parenting order consists of two elements:

- a requirement on the parent to attend counselling or guidance sessions (for example, parenting education or parenting support classes). This is the core of the parenting order and lasts for three months; and

- a requirement on the parent to comply with such requirements as are determined necessary by the court. This element can last up to 12 months.

11.68 Harassment and anti social behaviour by children can have a major impact on adults and other children living in a neighbourhood. Arrangements should ideally exist whereby local community safety teams can seek help or advice about when antisocial behaviour by children should be regarded as evidence of need.

11.69 Children may also be members of households in which a vulnerable adult is being neglected or mistreated and may participate in such neglect or mistreatment themselves. Arrangements should ideally exist in which local safeguarding adults' teams can seek help or advise about appropriate interventions for children in such cases. Staff working with children in need in households in which there are vulnerable adults should be alert to the possibilities of mistreatment of the vulnerable adult.

11.70    In case of behaviour problems at school, schools will need to make use of a full range of strategies when working to engage with parents, families and communities, including:

- offering specific support for parents and carers who need help either because their child is being bullied or in managing their child's behaviour. There is a range of support mechanisms available in schools and through partner agencies but parents and carers need to feel this support is accessible to them;

- employing some of the formal strategies for parental engagement including the use of parenting contracts and home-school agreements. Many parents will react positively to such offers of help and particularly value group support;

- some schools find that the use of an education related parenting contract for behaviour is helpful in protecting the interests of the child. This is a voluntary arrangement between the parent and school/local authority; and

- parenting orders can also be applied for by a school or local authority where a parent has refused or failed to comply with a parenting contract and where the court considers that parenting is a factor in the child's behaviour.

11.71    An education related parenting order is a civil court order which consists of the same two elements as standard parenting orders, except that they focus specifically on improving the behaviour and attendance of the child[253].

11.72    Parent Support Advisers (PSAs) can enable the school-home relationship to grow and flourish. There is a comprehensive package of materials available from the Training and Development Agency for Schools on PSAs, which local authorities can draw upon when considering what information to include in their training materials. Guidance on securing parental involvement in managing pupil behaviour is due to be updated in 2010.

## Race and racism

11.73    Racism can be a significant factor in cases of abuse. The experience of racism is also likely to affect the responses of the child and family to assessment and enquiry processes. Failure to consider the effects of racism undermines efforts to protect

---

253    More information can be found at:
www.teachernet.gov.uk/wholeschool/behaviour/pcspospns/

children from other forms of significant harm. The effects of racism differ for different communities and individuals and should not be assumed to be uniform. Attention should be given to the specific needs of all children. Evidence from research and previous abuse enquiries suggests particular issues for children of mixed parentage and refugee children. The need for neutral, high-quality translation or interpretation services should be taken into account when working with children and families whose preferred language is not English. All organisations working with children, including those operating in areas where black and minority ethnic communities are numerically small, should address institutional racism defined in the *Macpherson Inquiry Report* (2000) as 'the collective failure by an organisation to provide an appropriate and professional service to people on account of their race, culture and/or religion'.

## Violent extremism

11.74 Exposure to, or involvement with, groups or individuals who condone violence as a means to a political end is a particular risk for some children. Children and young people can be drawn into violence themselves or they can be exposed to messages if a family member is involved in an extremist group.

11.75 Experience suggests that young people from their teenage years onwards can be particularly vulnerable to getting involved with radical groups through direct contact with members or, increasingly, through the internet. This can put a young person at risk of being drawn in to criminal activity and has the potential to cause significant harm.

11.76 The cross-Government strategy to stop people becoming terrorists or supporting violent extremism is known as 'Prevent'[254]. One of Prevent's primary objectives is to support individuals who are vulnerable to recruitment or have already been recruited by violent extremists. There are a number of local projects across the country that contribute to this aim. All local authority areas should have an agreed process in place for safeguarding vulnerable children and young people susceptible to violent extremism. All staff should understand the nature of the risk and how to respond.

11.77 Levels of risk vary across different areas so LSCBs, safeguarding adults boards and children's services practitioners should ensure they are informed of the particular risks in their area. Most local authority areas have a Prevent partnership group that is responsible for co-ordinating work on this agenda across all agencies. Children's services departments should be involved in this partnership group to ensure services that support children and young people are contributing to Prevent.

---

254    For more information on the Prevent Strategy, visit www.dcsf.gov.uk/violentextremism

11.78   All children and young people's partnerships should have an agreed process in place for safeguarding vulnerable individuals, including children's, transition and vulnerable adult services. In some areas there is a bespoke multi-agency process known as 'Channel', which is an agreed mechanism for referring those at risk and providing support. Channel guidance states that if a referred individual is under the age of 18[255] the Channel co-ordinator must liaise with the common assessment framework (CAF) co-ordinator/manager or social care office in children and young people's services (who should be represented on the Prevent partnership and multi-agency Channel panel) to agree how best to handle the case. Following initial discussion a decision needs to be made on how to progress the case (for example, as a safeguarding issue, under Channel, CAF, or another support process) and establish how this will be reviewed. This decision can be taken on a case by case basis or a decision can be made by all local partners to use one particular system for the referral of all under 18s. If an area does not have Channel, local areas should incorporate referrals of under 18s within safeguarding procedures.

## Domestic violence

11.79   As outlined in Chapter 9, children may suffer both directly and indirectly if they live in households where there is domestic violence. Domestic violence includes any incident of threatening behaviour, violence or abuse (psychological, physical, sexual, financial or emotional) between adults, or young people, who are or have been intimate partners, family members or extended family members, regardless of gender and sexuality. Domestic violence is likely to have a damaging effect on the health and development of children, who are likely to suffer emotional and psychological maltreatment, and it will often be appropriate for them to be regarded as children in need. Women are more likely to experience the most serious forms of domestic violence but it is important to acknowledge that there are female perpetrators and male victims and that domestic violence also occurs within same-sex relationships. Professionals should be aware to these possibilities.

11.80   Everyone working with women and children should be alert to the frequent inter-relationship between domestic violence and the abuse and neglect of children (*National Service Framework for Children, Young People and Maternity Services*, 2004). There may be serious effects on children who witness domestic violence, which often result in behavioural issues, low self esteem, depression, absenteeism, ill health, bullying, antisocial or criminal behaviour, drug and alcohol misuse, self-harm and psychosocial impacts. Where there is evidence of domestic violence the implications for any children in the household should be considered, including the possibility that the children may themselves be subject to violence or may be

---

255   The Channel guidance also makes clear that children and young people's services may have responsibility for care beyond the age of 25 if additional vulnerabilities are present such as for children in care, care leavers or disability.

harmed by witnessing or overhearing the violence. Children affected by domestic violence often find disclosure difficult or go to great lengths to hide it.

11.81   The three central imperatives of any intervention for children living with domestic violence are:

- to protect the child/ren, including unborn child/ren;

- to empower the mother to protect herself and her child/ren; and

- to identify the abusive partner, hold him accountable for his violence and provide him with opportunities to change.

11.82   Professionals in all agencies are in a position to identify or receive a disclosure about domestic violence. Professionals should ask direct questions about domestic violence and be alert to the signs that a child or mother may be experiencing domestic violence or that a father/partner may be perpetrating domestic violence. Similarly, professionals should ask young people direct questions about whether they are experiencing intimate partner violence. Everyone working with women and children should be alert to the frequent inter-relationship between domestic violence and other issues which should be considered, such as drugs and alcohol misuse, deprivation and social exclusion, homelessness and housing needs, mental health difficulties, or child abuse and/or animal abuse.

11.83   Conversely, where it is believed that a child is being abused those involved with the child and family should check whether there is domestic violence within the family or in a young person's partner relationship. Professionals should offer all children, young people and women, accompanied or not, the opportunity of being seen alone (including in all assessments) with a female practitioner, wherever practicable, and asked whether they are experiencing or have previously experienced domestic violence. Professionals in all agencies should take all disclosures seriously and the impact of the domestic violence on the mother and her child/ren should be clearly explained to her. She should be provided with full information about her legal rights and the extent and limits of statutory duties and powers. Maintaining and strengthening the mother/child relationship is in most cases key to helping the child/ren to survive and recover from the impact of the violence and abuse. Children who are experiencing domestic violence are likely to benefit from a range of support and services.

11.84   As soon as a professional becomes aware of domestic violence within a family or a young person's relationship they should help the young person or mother and each child, according to their age and understanding, develop a safety plan. Children's safety plans should emphasise that the best thing a child can do for themselves and their mother is not to try to intervene but to keep safe and, where appropriate, to get away and seek help.

11.85 Separation itself does not ensure safety, it often at least temporarily increases the risk to the child/ren or mother. Where a mother's safety plan is to separate from the abusive partner the possibility of removing the abusive partner rather than the mother and child/ren should be considered first. Professionals should ensure that there is sufficient support in place to enact this plan. Where a mother proposes to remain with the abusive partner a multi-agency assessment should be undertaken of whether the safety plan is sufficient to safeguard the children.

11.86 The police are often (but not always) the first point of contact with families in which domestic violence takes place. When responding to incidents of violence the police should find out whether there are any children living in the household. They should see any children present in the house to assess their immediate safety. There should be arrangements in place between the police and children's social care to enable the police to find out whether any such children are the subject of a child protection plan. The police are already required to determine whether any court orders or injunctions are in force in respect of members of the household. The police should make an assessment of risk of harm to the children and their mother using a dedicated assessment tool for example, the Domestic Abuse, Stalking and Harassment and Honour Based Violence (DASH) 2009 Risk Assessment Model. If they have specific concerns about the safety or welfare of a child they should make a referral to children's social care and to a Multi-Agency Risk Assessment Conference (MARAC) – a multi-agency meeting that focuses on the safety of high-risk domestic violence victims. MARACs and LSCBs should agree joint working arrangements for identifying, protecting and supporting children affected by domestic violence.

11.87 It is also important that there is clarity about whether the family is aware that a referral is to be made. Any response by children's social care to such referrals should be discreet in terms of making contact with victims in ways that will not further endanger them or their child/ren. In some cases, a child may be in need of immediate protection. The amendment to the Children Act 1989 made in section 120 of the Adoption and Children Act 2002 clarifies the meaning of 'harm' in the Children Act to make explicit that 'harm' includes, for example, impairment suffered from seeing or hearing the ill-treatment of another.

11.88 Normally one serious or several lesser incidents of domestic violence where there is a child in the household indicate that children's social care should carry out an initial assessment of the child and family, including consulting existing records. Babies under 12 months old are particularly vulnerable to violence. Where there is domestic violence in families with a child under 12 months old (including an unborn child), even if the child was not present, professionals should make a referral to children's social care if there is any single incident of domestic violence.

11.89   Children's social care should assess the child/ren and their family using the *Framework for the Assessment of Children in Need and their Families* (DH, 2000), taking into account such factors as the:

- nature of the abuse;

- risks to the child posed by the abuser;

- risks of serious injury or death;

- abuser's pattern of assault and coercive behaviours;

- impact of the abuse on the mother;

- impact of the abuse on the child;

- impact of the abuse on parenting roles;

- protective factors; and

- outcome of the mother's past help-seeking.

Contact can be a mechanism for the abusive partner to locate the mother and children. Professionals should complete an assessment of the risks from contact to the mother and child/ren.

11.90   Education, early years and health service professionals are well placed to identify domestic violence. Safe information sharing arrangements are necessary to ensure that staff are confident about when and how to share information between education, children's social care, health and the police is key. Guidance on best practice for health service staff is available in the toolkit *Improving safety, Reducing harm: Children, young people and domestic violence – A practical toolkit for front line practitioners*[256]. The toolkit provides information on children and domestic violence, including the ways children experience domestic violence and the impact of abuse.

11.91   Domestic Violence Forums have been set up in many areas to raise awareness of domestic violence, to promote co-ordination between agencies in preventing and responding to violence, and to encourage the development of services for those who are subjected to violence or suffer its effects. LSCBs should have clearly defined links with their local Domestic Violence Forums, including cross-membership and jointly-undertaken workstreams. The LSCB and the Domestic Violence Forum should jointly contribute – in the context of the Children and Young People's Plan – to an assessment of the incidence of children and young people experiencing domestic

---

256      www.dh.gov.uk/prod_consum_dh/groups/dh_digitalassets/documents/digitalasset/dh_108704.pdf

violence, their needs, the adequacy of local arrangements to meet those needs and the implications for local services. Other work might include developing joint protocols, safe information sharing arrangements and training. Local authorities and health, together with the police and other partner agencies, need to assure themselves that they have in place the services and responses which will satisfy the *Every Child Matters* Outcomes Framework target: Children affected by domestic violence are identified, protected and supported. To have in place appropriate local integrated services, planners and commissioners are encouraged to take guidance from *A Vision for Services for Children and Young People affected by Domestic Violence* (LGA, ADSS, Women's Aid and Cafcass, 2005)[257]. This guidance focuses on meeting the needs of children affected by domestic violence within the planning of integrated children's services and provides a framework to ensure that the range of different needs that children/young people experience in relation to domestic violence are identified and addressed.

11.92   There is an extensive range of services for women and children, delivered mainly through the voluntary sector, which includes Independent Domestic Violence Advisors for high risk victims of abuse, refuges, outreach services and a 24 hour domestic violence helpline. There is also probation service provision of Women's Safety Workers for partners of male perpetrators of domestic abuse where they are on a domestic abuse treatment programme (in custody or in the community). These services have a vital role in contributing to an inter-agency approach in child protection cases where domestic violence is an issue. In responding to situations where domestic violence may be present, considerations include:

- asking direct questions about domestic violence;

- checking whether domestic violence has occurred whenever child abuse is suspected and considering the impact of this at all stages of assessment, enquiries and intervention;

- identifying those who are responsible for domestic violence in order that relevant family law or criminal justice responses may be made;

- taking into account that there may be continued or increased risk of domestic violence towards the abused parent and/or child after separation especially in connection with post-separation child contact arrangements;

- providing women with full information about their legal rights and about the extent and limits of statutory duties and powers;

- helping victims and children to get protection from violence by providing relevant practical and other assistance;

- supporting non-abusing parents in making safe choices for themselves and their children; and

- working separately with each parent where domestic violence prevents non-abusing parents from speaking freely and participating without fear of retribution.

## Child abuse and information communication technology (ICT)

11.93   The range of child abuse definitions and concepts (described in Part 1 of this guidance) are now being seen in an ICT environment. As technology develops the internet and its range of content services can be accessed through various devices.

11.94   The internet has, in particular, become a significant tool in the distribution of indecent photographs/pseudo photographs of children. Internet chat rooms, discussion forums and bulletin boards are used as a means of contacting children with a view to grooming them for inappropriate or abusive relationships, which may include requests to make and transmit pornographic images of themselves, or to perform sexual acts live in front of a webcam. Contacts made initially in a chat room are likely to be carried on via email, instant messaging services, mobile phone or text messaging. There is also growing cause for concern about the exposure of children to inappropriate material via interactive communication technology – for example, adult pornography and/or extreme forms of obscene material. Allowing or encouraging a child to view such material may warrant further enquiry. Children themselves can engage in text bullying and use mobile phone cameras to capture violent assaults of other children for circulation.

11.95   Where there is evidence of a child using ICT excessively, this may be a cause for concern more generally about the child's welfare or development in the sense that it may inhibit the development of real-world social relationships or become a factor contributing to obesity.

11.96   There is some evidence that people found in possession of indecent photographs/ pseudo photographs of children are likely to be involved directly in child abuse. Thus, when somebody is discovered to have placed or accessed such material on the internet the police should normally consider the likelihood that the individual is involved in the active abuse of children. In particular, the individual's access to children should be established, within the family, employment contexts and in other settings (for example, work with children as a volunteer or in other positions of trust). If there are particular concerns about one or more specific children it may be necessary to undertake, in accordance with the guidance set out in Chapter 5, section 47 enquiries (see the Memorandum of Understanding with the police for the appropriate notification to the Internet Watch Foundation of concerns about possible child pornography and other illegal materials on the internet).

11.97 As part of their role in preventing abuse and neglect LSCBs should consider activities to raise awareness about the safe use of the internet. LSCBs are a key partner in the development and delivery of training and education programmes with the Child Exploitation and Online Protection Centre[258] (CEOP). This includes building on the work of the British Educational Communications and Technology Agency (BECTA), the Home Office and the ICT industry in raising awareness about the safe use of interactive communication technologies by children.

## Children with families whose whereabouts are unknown

11.98 Local agencies and professionals should bear in mind, when working with children and families where there are outstanding concerns about the children's safety and welfare (including where the concerns are about an unborn child who may be at future risk of significant harm), that a series of missed appointments may indicate that the family has moved out of the area or overseas. Children's social care and the police should be informed as soon as such concerns arise. In the case of children taken overseas it may be appropriate to contact the Consular Directorate at the Foreign and Commonwealth Office[259], which offers assistance to British nationals in distress overseas. They may be able to follow up a case through their consular post(s) in the country concerned.

11.99 Particular consideration needs to be given to appropriate legal interventions where it appears that a child for whom there are outstanding concerns about their safety and welfare may be removed from the UK by his/her family in order to evade the involvement of agencies with safeguarding responsibilities. Particular consideration should also be given to appropriate legal interventions when a child who is subject to a care order has been removed from the UK. Children's social care, the police Child Abuse Investigation Unit and the Child Abduction Section at the Foreign and Commonwealth Office should be informed immediately.

## Children who go missing

11.100 Children who decide to run away are unhappy, vulnerable and in danger. As well as short term risks to their immediate safety there are longer term implications as well

---

258 The Child Exploitation and Online Protection Centre, which came into being in April 2006, is a partnership between Government, law enforcement, NGOs (including children's charities) and industry, with the common aim of protecting children. It works to protect children, families and society from paedophiles and sex offenders – in particular, those who seek to exploit children sexually online.

259 www.fco.gov.uk, 020 7008 1500

with children and young people who run away being less likely to fulfil their potential and live happy, health and economically productive lives as adults. In July 2009 the Government published new statutory guidance setting how local authorities and agencies should respond when a child or young person goes missing[260].

11.101  Local and regional Runaway and Missing from Home and Care protocols should be agreed between children's services, the police and other agencies and relevant voluntary sector agencies. Protocols should define roles and responsibilities when a child goes missing and when they return and should include:

- an agreed definition of a missing or runaway child or young person;

- an agreed inter-agency framework for classifying the degree of risk when a child goes missing from home or when a missing young person comes to agency notice;

- guidance on the threshold for referrals to social care;

- where CAF would be beneficial and the parents/carers agree, details of who should carry out a CAF and how this information should be shared, where appropriate;

- the basis on which agencies offer 'Return interviews' for children who have run away from home; and

- details of preventative approaches.

11.102  Return interviews for children and young people missing from both home and care are a crucial element in exploring the reasons they ran away and instances where the young person has run away from care, referring on, or linking into, care planning as appropriate. Where there is the possibility that the young person has runaway or gone missing as a result of child protection concerns the local authority where the child is placed, in liaison with the authority responsible for the child's placement and in partnership with the police, must follow its procedures to safeguard and promote the welfare of children in the area where the child is living (see also the National Minimum Standards for fostering services and residential care).

## Children who go missing from education

11.103  If a child or young person is receiving an education not only do they have the opportunity to fulfil their potential but they are also in an environment that enables local agencies to safeguard and promote their welfare. If a child goes missing from education they could be at risk of significant harm.

11.104 There are a number of reasons why children go missing from education. These can include:

- failing to start appropriate provision and hence never entering the system;

- ceasing to attend due to exclusion (for example, illegal unofficial exclusions) or withdrawal; and

- failing to complete a transition between providers (for example, being unable to find a suitable school place after moving to a new local authority area).

11.105 Children's personal circumstances, or those of their families, may contribute to the withdrawal process and the failure to make a transition.

11.106 Certain groups of vulnerable children are more likely than others to go missing from education:

- young people who have committed offences;

- children living in women's refuges;

- children of homeless families, perhaps living in temporary accommodation;

- young runaways;

- children with long-term medical or emotional problems;

- looked after children;

- children with a gypsy/traveller background;

- young carers;

- children from transient families;

- teenage mothers;

- children who are permanently excluded from school;

- migrant children, whether in families seeking asylum or economic migrants; and

- children/teenagers being forced into marriage.

11.107 There is a Child Missing Education (CME) named point of contact in every local authority. Every practitioner working with a child has a responsibility to inform their CME contact if they know or suspect that a child is not receiving education. To help local agencies and professionals find children who are missing from education and identify those at risk of going missing from education, guidance was issued in July

2004, *Identifying and maintaining contact with children missing, or at risk of going missing, from education*[261].

## Children of families living in temporary accommodation

11.108 Placement in temporary accommodation, often at a distance from previous support networks or involving frequent moves, can lead to individuals and families falling through the net and becoming disengaged from health, education, social care and welfare support systems. Some families who have experienced homelessness and are placed in temporary accommodation by local authorities under the main homeless duty, can have very transient lifestyles.

11.109 It is important that effective systems are in place to ensure that children from homeless families receive services from health and education, as well as any other specific types of services, because these families move regularly and may be at risk of becoming disengaged from services. Where there are concerns about a child or children the procedures set out in Chapter 5 should be followed.

11.110 Statutory guidance on making arrangements under section 11 of the Children Act 2004 to safeguard and promote the welfare of children sets out local authorities' responsibilities for homeless families.

## Migrant children

11.111 In recent years the number of migrant children in the UK has increased for a variety of reasons including the expansion of the global economy and incidence of war and conflict. Local agencies should have due regard to the need to safeguard and promote the welfare of these children offering the same level of support and protection as for children who are UK nationals. Given that migrant children may have serious health needs, in addition to their complex other social needs, particular attention should be given to ensuring that they receive appropriate health care services.

## Unaccompanied asylum-seeking children (UASC)

11.112 A UASC is an asylum-seeking child under the age of 18 who is not living with their parent, relative or guardian in the UK. In most cases UASC will be referred to local authorities by the UK Border Agency (UKBA) shortly after they arrive in the United Kingdom.

---

261    http://publications.everychildmatters.gov.uk/default.aspx?PageFunction=productdetails&PageMode =publications&ProductId=LEA%2F0225%2F2004&

11.113 Local authorities should adopt the same approach to assessing the needs of a UASC as they use to assess other children in need in their area. The child will not have a parent, relative or other suitable adult carer in the United Kingdom, and will likely to have to be accommodated under section 20 of the Children Act.

11.114 The child's immigration status should not affect the quality of care, support and services that are provided as a result of the assessment. Immigration status will, however, have a bearing on the child's future and very careful thought should therefore be given to the range of services provided to the proportion of the children that are not granted asylum or long term leave to remain in the UK – with a view to making sure that the children are equipped for life in their countries of origin as well as the United Kingdom. These considerations should be reflected in the child's care (or their pathway plan for those aged 16+), which will be subject to the same statutory review process, chaired by an Independent Reviewing Officer, appropriate for other looked after children.

11.115 In assessing the needs of UASC and providing effective care local authorities will normally need to build close links with the UKBA 'case owner' responsible for resolving the child's immigration status. This should extend to sharing key information necessary to safeguard the child's welfare, including:

- information relevant to the assessment of the child's identity and age (given that most UASCs may not have reliable documentary evidence of their age and identity);

- information that might be relevant to the immigration decision made in respect of the child (where, for example, the child has complex medical needs or is suffering from trauma); and

- information about any efforts to trace the location of family members in the country of origin (many UASCs will have lost contact with family members because of the circumstances of their journey to the United Kingdom).

11.116 In order to plan appropriately for the future of unaccompanied asylum seeking children it will be necessary for their social worker or personal adviser to seek up to date information on the progress of their asylum case from the UK Border Agency. It should not be assumed that a UASC will remain permanently in the UK, unless and until they have been granted British Nationality, refugee status or indefinite leave to remain. Opportunities available in the country of origin should be addressed in the care or pathway plan review to prepare for the eventuality that the child may decide to or be required to return to their country of origin.

11.117 Where there are safeguarding concerns relating to the care and welfare of any UASC[262] then these must be investigated in line with the LCSB procedures in the area where they are living, in the same way as any other looked after child.

---

262 See for example para. 2.23 of the Statutory Guidance to the UK Border Agency on Making Arrangements to Safeguard and Promote the Welfare of Children.

# Chapter 12 – Managing individuals who pose a risk of harm to children

## Introduction

12.1    This section provides practice guidance and information about a range of mechanisms that are available when managing adults, or children and young people, who have been identified as presenting a risk, or potential risk, of harm to children. Areas covered include:

- collaborative working between organisations and agencies to identify and manage individuals who present a risk of harm to children;

- the Multi-Agency Public Protection Arrangements (MAPPA), which enable agencies to work together within a statutory framework for managing risk of harm to the public; and

- other processes and mechanisms for working with individuals who present a risk of harm to children.

## Collaborative working

12.2    The Children Act 1989 recognised that the identification and investigation of child abuse, together with the protection and support of victims and their families, requires multi-agency collaboration. This is rightly focused on the child and the supporting parent/carer. As part of that protection, action has been taken, usually by the police and children's social care services, to prosecute known offenders and/ or control their access to vulnerable children.

12.3    This work, while successful in addressing the safety of particular victims, has not always acknowledged the ongoing risk of harm that an individual perpetrator may present to other children in the future. Nor does it acknowledge that a young person may also be a perpetrator and that the same young person may simultaneously be both suffering, or likely to suffer harm, and present a risk of harm to other children and young people.

## Use of the term 'Schedule One offender'

12.4    The terms 'Schedule One offender' and 'Schedule One offence' have been commonly used for anyone convicted of an offence against a child listed in

Schedule One of the Children and Young Person's Act 1933. However, a conviction for an offence in Schedule One does not trigger any statutory requirement in relation to child protection issues, and inclusion on the schedule was determined solely by the age of the victim and offence for which the offender was sentenced, and not by an assessment of whether the offender may pose a future risk of harm to children.

12.5    **Therefore the term 'Schedule One offender' is no longer used. It has been replaced with 'Risk to children'.** This clearly indicates that the person has been identified as presenting a risk, or potential risk, of harm to children.

12.6    *Guidance on offences against children (Home Office Circular 16/2005)*[263], explains how those people who present a risk, or potential risk, of harm to children should be identified. The circular explains that the present method of automatically identifying as a risk of harm to children an offender who has been convicted of an offence listed in Schedule One of the Children and Young Person's Act 1933 fails to focus on those who **continue** to present a risk of harm.

12.7    Practitioners working in this area should use the new list of offences as a 'trigger' to a further assessment, including consideration of previous offences and behaviours, to determine if an offender should be regarded as presenting a continuing risk of harm to children. This allows agencies to focus resources on the correct group of individuals, and not include those who have been identified solely because a child was harmed during the offence, for example, as in the case of a road traffic accident. An offender who has harmed a child might not continue to present a risk or harm towards that child or other children. Where a child or young person (aged under 18 years) offends against another child, a thorough and specialist assessment should be undertaken to establish the extent to which the young person who has offended continues to pose a risk of harm to other children and young people. They should be alert to the possibility that there may be little or no continuing risk of harm to other children and young people, but never losing sight of taking all possible actions to ensure that children are adequately protected from any future harm. Practitioners should also assess and put in place services to respond to the, often complex, needs of the young person who has offended.

12.8    Once an individual has been sentenced and identified as presenting a risk of harm to children, agencies have a responsibility to work collaboratively to monitor and manage the risk of harm to others. Where an offender is given a community sentence, Offender Managers or Youth Offending Team (YOT) workers will monitor the individual's risk of harm to others and their behaviour, and liaise with partner agencies as appropriate.

---

263    See www.homeoffice.gov.uk/about-us/publications/home-office-circulars/circulars-2005/016-2005/index.html

12.9　In cases where an offender has been sentenced to a period of custody, prison establishments undertake a similar responsibility and, in addition, notify other agencies prior to any period of release. Similarly for offenders released on licence into the community who are assessed as potentially presenting a risk of harm to children, consideration will be given to including licence conditions which seek to prevent the offender's contact with children.

## New offences targeted at those who sexually exploit children and young people

12.10　The Sexual Offences Act 2003 introduced a number of new offences to deal with those who sexually exploit children and young people. The offences protect children up to the age of 18 and can attract tough penalties. They include:

- paying for the sexual services of a child;

- causing or inciting child prostitution;

- arranging or facilitating child prostitution; and

- controlling a child prostitute.

12.11　These are not the only charges that may be brought against those who sexually exploit children or young people. Abusers and coercers often physically, sexually and emotionally abuse these children, and may effectively imprison them. If a child is a victim of serious offences, the most serious charge that the evidence will support should always be used.

## Multi-Agency Public Protection Arrangements (MAPPA)

12.12　MAPPA provide a national framework in England and Wales for the assessment and management of the risk of serious harm posed by specified sexual and violent offenders, including offenders (including young people) who are considered to pose a risk, or potential risk, of serious harm to children. The arrangements are statutory. Sections 325–327 of the Criminal Justice Act 2003 require the police, prisons and probation services (the 'Responsible Authority') in each area to establish and monitor the arrangements. A number of other agencies – including children's and adult's social care services, health, housing, YOTs, Jobcentre Plus and electronic monitoring providers – are under a statutory duty to co-operate with the Responsible Authority in this work.

12.13　National MAPPA Guidance (2009)[264] further develops processes particularly with regard to young people who pose a risk and the role of YOTs.

---

264　See www.probation.homeoffice.gov.uk/output/page30.asp.

12.14   MAPPA's focus is on specified sexual and violent offenders in, and returning to, the community, and its aims are to:

- ensure more comprehensive risk assessments are completed, taking advantage of co-ordinated information sharing across the agencies; and

- share information, assess and manage risk and direct the available resources to best protect the public from serious harm.

12.15   Offenders eligible for MAPPA are identified and information is gathered/shared about them across relevant agencies. The extent to which they pose a risk of serious harm is assessed and a risk management plan is implemented to protect the public.

12.16   Each area has a MAPPA Strategic Management Board (SMB) attended by senior representatives of each of the responsible authority and duty to co-operate agencies, plus two lay advisers. It is the SMB's role to ensure that the MAPPA are working effectively and to establish and maintain working relationships with the Local Safeguarding Children Boards (LSCBs).

## Identifying MAPPA eligible offenders

12.17   There are three categories of offender eligible for MAPPA:

- **registered sexual offenders** (Category 1) – sexual offenders who are required to notify the police of their name, address and other personal details and notify any changes subsequently;

- **violent offenders** (Category 2) – offenders sentenced to imprisonment/ detention for 12 months or more, or detained under hospital orders (in relation to murder or offences specified in schedule 15 of the Criminal Justice Act 2003). This category also includes a small number of sexual offenders who do not qualify for registration, and offenders disqualified from working with children; and

- **other dangerous offenders** (Category 3) – offenders who do not qualify under categories 1 or 2 but who currently pose a risk of serious harm, there is a link between the offending and the risk posed, and they require active multi-agency management.

## Sharing of relevant information

12.18   Exchange of information is essential for effective public protection. The MAPPA guidance[265] details how MAPPA agencies may/should exchange information among themselves to better manage offenders. It also explains why and how information

---

265     See www.probation.homeoffice.gov.uk/output/page30.asp.

may be disclosed to those not involved in the MAPPA management of the offender. The expectation is that information on offenders will be disclosed to others – for example, partners, employers, schools – where this is required to manage the risks posed by the offender.

## ViSOR

12.19    ViSOR is a national database which currently carries details of MAPPA eligible offenders and other potentially dangerous individuals. The police have been using ViSOR since 2005 and probation and prisons have had access since 2008–09. The benefit is that, for the first time, all three responsible authority agencies can access the same IT system, thus improving the quality and timeliness of risk assessments and of interventions to prevent offending.

## Assessment of the risk of serious harm

12.20    The National Offender Management Service (NOMS) assesses risk of serious harm using the Offender Assessment System (OASys) supplemented by additional assessment procedures, depending on the nature of the offending and the specific risks identified. The Youth Justice Board uses ASSET for under-18-year-olds. The levels of risk are as follows:

- **low**: current evidence does not indicate likelihood of causing serious harm;

- **medium**: identifiable indicators of risk of serious harm. The offender has the potential to cause serious harm, but is unlikely to do so unless there is a change in circumstances, for example, failure to take medication, loss of accommodation, relationship breakdown, drug or alcohol misuse;

- **high**: identifiable indicators of risk of serious harm. The potential event could happen at any time, and the impact would be serious; and

- **very high**: an imminent risk of serious harm. The potential event is more likely than not to happen imminently, and the impact to be serious.

12.21    Risk is categorised by reference to the potential subject of the harm. This includes children who may be vulnerable to harm of various kinds, including violent or sexual behaviour, emotional harm or neglect. In this context, MAPPA works closely with LSCBs to ensure the best local joint arrangements can be made for any individual child being considered by either setting.

## Managing risk of serious harm

12.22    In most cases, a MAPPA eligible offender will be managed without recourse to MAPPA meetings under the ordinary arrangements applied by the agency or agencies with supervisory responsibility. This will generally be the police for registered sexual offenders who are not on a licence to probation, and probation for violent offenders and those on a licence, but YOTs will lead with young offenders and Mental Health Services with those on hospital orders. A number of offenders, though, require active multi-agency management and their risk management plans will be formulated and monitored via multi-agency public protection (MAPP) meetings attended by various agencies.

12.23   There are 3 levels of management within the MAPPA framework, which are based upon the level of multi-agency co-operation required to implement the risk management plan effectively:

- **Level 1 – Ordinary Management**. These offenders are subject to the usual management arrangements applied by whichever agency is supervising them. But this does not rule out information sharing between agencies, via ViSOR and other routes;

- **Level 2 – Active Multi-Agency Management**. The risk management plans for these offenders require the active involvement of several agencies via regular MAPP meetings; and

- **Level 3 – Active Multi-Agency Management**. As with level 2 but these cases additionally require the involvement of senior officers to authorise the use of special resources, such as police surveillance or specialised accommodation, and/or to provide ongoing senior management oversight.

Offenders will be moved up and down levels as appropriate.

12.24   YOTs have a duty to identify cases that meet MAPPA criteria and make appropriate referrals. However, the guidance emphasises that young people should be assessed and managed differently from adults, using age-appropriate assessment tools and always bearing in mind the need to safeguard the welfare of the young offender as well as to protect others from harm. Children's social care services should **always** be represented at MAPPA meetings when a young person is being discussed.

12.25   The national MAPPA guidance sets out the framework in full. The guidance and the area annual reports, which describe how the arrangements are working locally, are available on the National Probation Service website[266].

---

266   www.probation.homeoffice.gov.uk/output/page30.asp

## Other processes and mechanisms

### Multi-Agency Risk Assessment Conference (MARAC)

12.26 A MARAC is a multi-agency meeting which has the safety of high risk victims of domestic abuse as its focus. The identification of high risk victims has been made possible by the use of a risk identification tool[267], for use across a wide range of agencies. This has permitted practitioners, both within and outside of the criminal justice system, to identify high risk victims of domestic abuse. As a result many more high risk victims are being identified and, in response, the MARAC is being rolled out across England and Wales with a view to meeting this need.

12.27 The MARAC is a process involving the participation of all the key statutory and voluntary agencies who might be involved in supporting a victim of domestic abuse. This includes those from the criminal justice system, those supporting children, those from the health service, the local authority, housing, substance misuse and, critically, specialist domestic violence services most frequently in the form of an Independent Domestic Violence Advisor (IDVA). The IDVA is a specialist caseworker who receives accredited training to work with high risk victims of domestic abuse from the point of crisis and whose focus is very much on the MARAC.

12.28 At a typical MARAC meeting 15 to 20 high risk cases are discussed in half a day with a very brief and focused information sharing process followed by a simple multi-agency action plan being put into place to support the victim and to make links with other public protection procedures, particularly safeguarding children, vulnerable adults and, of course, the management of perpetrators.

12.29 It is important to understand the MARAC meeting as part of a wider process which hinges on the early involvement and support from an IDVA and continued specialist case management, both before and after the meeting. The MARAC should combine the best of specialist support together with the co-ordination of the generic agencies whose resources and involvement will be needed to keep victims and their children safe.

12.30 Where an offender is being managed at MAPPA Level 2 or Level 3, to avoid duplication of effort and resources, the MAPP meeting should take the lead over the MARAC. The reason for this is that the MAPPA is a statutory set of arrangements and therefore it takes precedence over the MARAC.

---

267  See www.caada.org.uk/Practitioner_resources/Quick%20Start%20Guidance%20&%20RIC%20 09062009.doc

## Offending behaviour programmes

12.31   Rehabilitation of offenders is the best guarantee of long-term public protection. A range of independently accredited treatment programmes, which have been developed or commissioned by NOMS, have been 'tried and tested' at a national level. Examples include sex offender treatment programmes, programmes for offenders convicted of internet-related sexual offences, and programmes for perpetrators of domestic abuse.

## The Vetting and Barring Scheme

12.32   The Vetting and Barring Scheme (VBS) aims to ensure that unsuitable people do not work with children, whether in paid employment or on a voluntary basis. The scheme comprises:

- two barred lists, maintained by the Independent Safeguarding Authority (ISA). One list comprises persons barred from working with children, and the other is for persons barred from working with vulnerable adults. From 12 October 2009 these lists replaced the list held under section 142 of the Education Act 2002 known as 'List 99', the list held under the Protection of Children Act 1999 and the list held under the Protection of Vulnerable Adults Scheme. It is a criminal offence for a barred person to engage in 'regulated activity' (see below) or for an employer knowingly to engage a barred person to carry out such work; and

- a register of those wishing to work with vulnerable groups. Except where there is a specific exception, from November 2010 all new entrants to the children's workforce will be required to register with the Scheme before being allowed to engage in any relevant duties. From this date, it will be a criminal offence for anyone entering the sector to work in regulated activity or for an organisation to allow a non-registered individual to do so. Registration for existing workers will be phased in over the period 2011-2015, and employers will be expected to facilitate the registration, at the appropriate time, of staff that carry out regulated activity. Guidance on the coverage of the scheme, on the exceptions from registration and on phasing will be made available on the ISA website[268].

12.33   Since October 2009, the duties to refer concerns regarding individuals under List 99 and the Protection of Children Act 1999 were replaced with a duty to refer information to the ISA. The circumstances where a referral must be made are where:

   a.   an individual has been removed from 'regulated activity' (or would or might have been removed if they had not already left); and

b.   the employer/volunteer manager thinks that 'relevant conduct' has occurred, or the individual poses a risk of harm.

12.34   The duties to refer and to provide information to the ISA on request are placed on regulated activity providers and certain other bodies, including local authorities in their children's services and adult social care capacities. Failure by regulated activity providers to carry out the duty is a criminal offence. Compliance by local authorities is subject to local government performance management systems. 'Regulated activity' is defined in guidance on the ISA's website[269].

12.35   'Relevant conduct' is defined as:

a.   conduct which endangers a child or is likely to endanger a child;

b.   conduct which, if repeated against or in relation to a child, would endanger that child or would be likely to endanger him;

c.   conduct involving sexual material relating to children (including possession of such material);

d.   conduct involving sexually explicit images depicting violence against human beings (including possession of such images), if it appears to the Independent Safeguarding Authority that the conduct is inappropriate; or

e.   conduct of a sexual nature involving a child, if it appears to the ISA that the conduct is inappropriate.

12.36   Full guidance on referrals and the VBS can be found on the ISA's website. The Secretary of State has issued guidance on what constitutes 'inappropriate' in 12.35(d) and 12.35(e) above. This guidance is available on the ISA's website.

12.37   The new barred lists will in time replace the regime of disqualification orders imposed by the courts under the Criminal Justice and Court Services Act 2000 (CJCSA), as amended by the Criminal Justice Act 2003. Until the VBS is fully phased in, individuals working with children could be either barred or subject to disqualification orders. Either way, they must be removed from such work and commit an offence if they carry out such work.

## Criminal Records Bureau (CRB)

12.38   The Criminal Records Bureau (CRB) is an executive agency of the Home Office. The CRB's Disclosure Service aims to help employers make safer recruitment decisions by identifying candidates who may be unsuitable for certain types of work. In some

---

269   At the time of writing, the guidance on the ISA's website should be read alongside information about Sir Roger Singleton's recommendations relating to regulated activity, also available on the ISA website. These recommendations will be incorporated into the ISA guidance in due course.

cases, employers must ask successful candidates to apply to the CRB for a Standard or Enhanced Disclosure, depending on the duties of the particular position or job involved. In other cases, employers are eligible to ask for disclosures. Relevant sectoral guidance sets out the requirements and eligibility in detail.

12.39   In addition to information about a person's criminal record, enhanced disclosures supplied in connection with work with children contain details of whether a person is registered with the ISA, or barred. It should be noted that barred status is no longer shown on a standard disclosure. Enhanced disclosures may contain details of acquittals or other non-conviction information held on local police records, relevant to the position or post for which the person has been selected, and the police may also provide additional information to employers in a separate letter. Further information, including details of how to apply for disclosures, is available on the CRB website[270]. The Government is shortly to consult on proposals to amend its requirements for CRB disclosures once individuals have been ISA registered.

## The Sex Offenders Register

12.40   The notification requirements of Part 2 of the Sexual Offences Act 2003 (known as the Sex Offenders Register) are an automatic requirement on offenders, including young people who have offended, who receive a conviction or caution for certain sexual offences. The notification requirements are intended to ensure that the police are informed of the whereabouts of offenders in the community. The notification requirements do not bar offenders from certain types of employment or from being alone with children.

12.41   Offenders must notify the police of certain personal details within three days of their conviction or caution for a relevant sexual offence (or, if they are in prison on this date, within three days of their release).

12.42   Such an offender must then notify the police, within three days, of any change to the notified details and whenever they spend seven days or more at another address.

12.43   All offenders must reconfirm their details at least once every twelve months, and notify the police seven days in advance of any travel overseas for a period of three days or more.

12.44   The period of time for which an offender must comply with these requirements depends on whether they received a conviction or caution for their offence and, where appropriate, the sentence they received.

---

270   www.crb.gov.uk

12.45    Failure to comply with these requirements is a criminal offence, with a maximum penalty of five years' imprisonment. The police should be contacted if such an offence is committed.

## Child Sex Offender Review Disclosure Process

12.46    In June 2007, the Government published the *Review of the Protection of Children from Sex Offenders*. Action 4 of the Review created a process which allows members of the public to register a child protection interest in an identified individual who has access to, or a connection with, a particular child or children.

12.47    If an individual is found to have convictions for sexual offences against children and poses a risk of causing serious harm, there is a presumption that this information will be disclosed to the person who is best placed to protect the child or children, where it is necessary to do so for this purpose.

12.48    It should be noted that, under the scope of the Disclosure Process, the presumption for disclosure will only exist in cases where the individual has convictions for child sexual offences. However, it is felt that to restrict access to information regarding convicted child sexual offenders would severely limit the effectiveness of the process and ignore significant issues regarding offences committed against children.

12.49    The Disclosure Process will therefore include routes for managed access to information regarding individuals who are not convicted child sexual offenders but who pose a risk of harm to children. This may include:

●   persons who are convicted of other offences for example, serious domestic violence; and

●   persons who are unconvicted but about whom the police, or any other agency, holds intelligence indicating that they pose a risk of harm to children.

There would not however be a presumption to disclose such information.

12.50    It is important that the disclosure of information about previous convictions, for offences which are not child sex offences, is able to continue as it is not the intention of the Disclosure Process to make access to information concerning safeguarding children more restricted.

12.51    It should be stressed that the Disclosure Process will build on existing procedures such as MAPPA and will provide a clear access route for the public to raise child protection concerns and be confident that action will follow.

12.52   It is of paramount importance to all involved in delivering this process that we ensure that children are being protected from harm. By making a request for disclosure, a parent, guardian or carer will often also be registering their concerns about possible risks to the safety of their child or children. For that reason, it is essential to this process that police forces, local authority children's social care and LSCBs work closely together to ensure that any possible risks of harm to the child or children are fully assessed and managed.

12.53   This process is due to be rolled-out nationally from August 2010. The roll-out will be regionally staggered and full details of progress and national and local contact details can be found on the Home Office website[271].

12.54   For full guidance on this process please see ACPO *Guidance on Protecting the Public: Managing Sexual Offenders and Violent Offenders*. Prior to this visit the Home Office Circular website[272].

## Notification Orders

12.55   Notification Orders are intended to ensure that British citizens or residents, as well as foreign nationals, can be made subject to the notification requirements (the Sex Offenders Register) in the UK if they receive convictions or cautions for sexual offences overseas. The provisions also apply to young people who have offended.

12.56   Notification Orders are made on application from the police to a magistrates' court. Therefore, if an offender is identified who has received a conviction or caution for a sexual offence overseas, the case should be referred to the local police for action.

12.57   If a Notification Order is in force, the offender becomes subject to the requirements of the Sex Offenders Registration.

12.58   For example, a Notification Order could ensure that the notification requirements apply to a British man who, while on holiday in Southeast Asia, received a caution for a sexual offence on a child.

12.59   Any information that an individual has received a conviction or caution for a sexual offence overseas should, where appropriate, be shared with the police.

## Sexual Offences Prevention Orders (SOPOs)

12.60   Introduced by the Sexual Offences Act 2003, SOPOs are civil preventative orders designed to protect the public from serious sexual harm. A court may make a SOPO

---

271     www.homeoffice.gov.uk
272     www.homeoffice.gov.uk/about-us/publications/home-office-circulars/

when it deals with an offender, including a young person who has offended, who has received a conviction for an offence listed at Schedule 3 (sexual offences) or Schedule 5 (violent and other offences) to the Act and is assessed as posing a risk of serious sexual harm. The police can also apply for a SOPO to a magistrates' court in respect of an offender who has a previous conviction or caution for a Schedule 3 or 5 offence and who poses a risk of serious sexual harm.

12.61   SOPOs include such prohibitions as the court considers appropriate. For example, a sex offender who poses a risk of serious sexual harm to children could be prohibited from loitering near schools or playgrounds. The offender will also, if s/he is not already, become subject to the notification requirements for the duration of the order.

12.62   SOPOs can be made on application from the police, so any violent or sex offender who poses a risk of serious sexual harm should be referred to MAPPA agencies, and the police in particular. In an application for an order, the police can set out the prohibitions they would like the court to consider.

12.63   Breach of any of the prohibitions in a SOPO is a criminal offence, with a maximum punishment of five years imprisonment. Therefore the police should be contacted whenever a SOPO is breached.

12.64   SOPOs can be particularly helpful in the management of sex offenders who are assessed as continuing to pose a high risk of harm, but are no longer subject to statutory supervision.

## Risk of Sexual Harm Orders (RSHOs)

12.65   Introduced by the Sexual Offences Act 2003, RSHOs are civil preventative orders. They cannot be applied to young people under the age of 18. They are used to protect children from the risks of harm posed by individuals who do not necessarily have a previous conviction for a sexual or violent offence but who have, on at least two occasions, engaged in sexually explicit conduct or communication with a child or children, and who pose a risk of further such harm. For a RSHO to be made, it is not necessary for there to be a risk that the defendant will commit a sexual offence against a child – the risk may be that s/he intends to communicate with children in a sexually explicit way. The RSHO can contain such prohibitions as the court considers necessary. For example, in the case of an adult found regularly communicating with young children in a sexual way in internet chat rooms, a RSHO could be used to prohibit the person from using the internet in order to stop him/her from such harmful activity.

12.66   RSHOs are made on application from the police, so any person who is thought to pose a risk of sexual harm to children should be referred to the police. In an application for an order, the police can set out the prohibitions they would like the court to consider.

12.67   Breach of any of the prohibitions in a RSHO is a criminal offence, with a maximum punishment of five years imprisonment. It is also an offence that makes the offender subject to the notification requirements. The police should be contacted whenever a RSHO is breached.

## Violent Offender Orders (VOOs)

12.68   Violent Offender Orders (VOOs) are civil preventative orders that came into effect on 3 August 2009 (contained in Part 7 of the Criminal Justice and Immigration Act 2008). VOOs were developed as a tool to help the Police Service to manage those offenders who continue to pose a risk of serious violent harm to the public even after their release from prison or when their licence has ceased. Although not specifically designed as a tool to protect children, there may be circumstances where VOOs would be an appropriate mechanism to manage an individual who poses a serious risk of harm to children.

12.69   VOOs are available on application by a chief officer of police to a Magistrates' Court and, if granted, will contain such restrictions, prohibitions or conditions authorised by section 102 of the Act as the court considers necessary to protect the public from the risk of serious violent harm caused by the offender. This may include prohibiting their access to certain places, premises, events or people to whom they pose the highest risk.

12.70   Breach of any of the prohibitions, restrictions or conditions contained in a VOO without reasonable excuse is a criminal offence, with a maximum punishment of five years' imprisonment.

12.71   Full guidance on VOOs is available on the Home Office's Crime Reduction website[273].

---

273     www.crimereduction.homeoffice.gov.uk/violence/violence027.htm

# Appendix 1 – Statutory framework

1.     All organisations that work with children and families share a commitment to safeguard and promote their welfare, and for many agencies that is underpinned by a statutory duty or duties.

2.     This appendix briefly explains the legislation most relevant to work to safeguard and promote the welfare of children.

## Children Act 2004

3.     **Section 10** requires each local authority to make arrangements to promote co-operation between the authority, each of the authority's relevant partners (see Table A below) and such other persons or bodies working with children in the local authority's area as the authority considers appropriate. The arrangements are to be made with a view to improving the wellbeing of children in the authority's area – which includes protection from harm or neglect alongside other outcomes. This section of the Children Act 2004 is the legislative basis for children's trust arrangements.

4.     **Section 11** requires a range of organisations (see Table A) to make arrangements for ensuring that their functions, and services provided on their behalf, are discharged with regard to the need to safeguard and promote the welfare of children.

5.     **Section 12** enables the Secretary of State to require local authorities to establish and operate databases relating to the section 10 or section 11 duties (above) or the section 175 duty (below), or to establish and operate databases nationally. This section limits the information that may be included in those databases, and sets out which organisations can be required to, and which can be enabled to, disclose information to be included in the databases. This section is the statutory basis for ContactPoint.

6.     **Section 12A** was inserted by section 194 of the Apprenticeships, Skills Children and Learning Act 2009 and requires the co-operation arrangements made under section 10 to include the establishment of a Children's Trust Board.

7.     **Section 13** requires each children's services authority to establish a Local Safeguarding Children Board (LSCB). It also requires a range of organisations (see the list in column 5 of Table A) to take part in LSCBs. Sections 13–16 set out the framework for LSCBs, and the LSCB Regulations set out the requirements in more detail, in particular on LSCB functions.

*Table A: Bodies covered by key duties (in addition to local authorities)*

| Body | CA 2004 Section 10 – duty to co-operate | CA 2004 Section 11 – duty to s'guard & promote welfare | Ed Act 2002 Section 175 – duty to s'guard & promote welfare + and regs | CA 2004 Section 12A – statutory partners on CTBs | CA 2004 Section 13 – statutory partners in LSCBs | CA 1989 Section 27 – help with children in need | CA 1989 Section 47 – help with enquiries about sig harm |
|---|---|---|---|---|---|---|---|
| District councils | X | X | | X | X | X | X |
| Police authority | X | X | | X | | | |
| Chief officer of police | X | X | | X | X | | |
| Local probation board | X | X | | X | X | | |
| SoS re functions in s2-3 of the Offender Management Act 2007 | X | X | | X | X | | |
| Provider of probation services required under s3(2) OMA 2007 | X | X | | X | X | | |
| British Transport Police | | X | | | | | |
| Prison or secure training centre | | X | | | X (which detains children) | | |
| Youth offending team | X | X | | X | X | | |
| Strategic Health Authority | X | X | | X | X | X | X |
| Primary Care Trust | X | X | | X | X | X | X |

| Body | CA 2004 Section 10 – duty to co-operate | CA 2004 Section 11 – duty to s'guard & promote welfare | Ed Act 2002 Section 175 – duty to s'guard & promote welfare + and regs | CA 2004 Section 12A – statutory partners on CTBs | CA 2004 Section 13 – statutory partners in LSCBs | CA 1989 Section 27 – help with children in need | CA 1989 Section 47 – help with enquiries about sig harm |
|---|---|---|---|---|---|---|---|
| Special Health Authority | | X (as designated by the Secretary of State) | | | | X | X |
| NHS trust | | X | | | X | X | X |
| NHS foundation trust | | X | | | X | X | X |
| Connexions Service | X | X | | X | X | | |
| Learning and Skills Council | X | X | | X | | | |
| Cafcass | | | | | X | | |
| Maintained schools | X | | X | X | | | |
| FE colleges | X | | X | X | | | |
| Independent schools | X | | X | X | | | |
| Contracted services | | X | X | | | | |
| SoS re functions in section 2 Employment and Training Act 1973 | X | | | X | | | |
| Such other persons as the authority considers appropriate | X | | | X (after consulting partners) | | | |

## Education Act 2002

8.      **Section 175** puts a duty on local education authorities, maintained (state) schools and further education institutions, including sixth-form colleges, to exercise their functions with a view to safeguarding and promoting the welfare of children – children who are pupils, and students under 18 years of age in the case of schools and colleges.

9.      The same duty is put on independent schools, including academies, by Regulations made under section 157 of that Act.

## Children Act 1989

10.     The Children Act 1989 places a duty on local authorities to promote and safeguard the welfare of children in need in their area.

> Section 17(1) of the Children Act 1989 states that:
>
> It shall be the general duty of every local authority:
>
> - to safeguard and promote the welfare of children within their area who are in need; and
>
> - so far as is consistent with that duty, to promote the upbringing of such children by their families, by providing a range and level of services appropriate to those children's needs.
>
> Section 17(10) states that a child shall be taken to be in need if:
>
> a)  he is unlikely to achieve or maintain, or to have the opportunity of achieving or maintaining, a reasonable standard of health or development without the provision for him of services by a local authority under this Part;
>
> b)  his heath or development is likely to be significantly impaired, or further impaired, without the provision for him of such services; or
>
> c)  he is disabled.
>
> (Children Act 1989, section 17)

11.     The primary focus of legislation about children in need is on how well they are progressing and whether their development will be impaired without the provision of services.

12.     It also places a specific duty on other local authority services and health bodies to co-operate in the interests of children in need in section 27. Section 322 of the

Education Act 1996 places a duty on social services to assist the local education authority where any child has special educational needs.

> Where it appears to a local authority that any authority mentioned in sub-section (3) could, by taking any specified action, help in the exercise of any of their functions under this Part, they may request the help of that other authority, specifying the action in question. An authority whose help is so requested shall comply with the request if it is compatible with their own statutory or other duties and obligations and does not unduly prejudice the discharge of any of their functions.
>
> The authorities are:
>
> a. *any local authority;*
>
> b. *any local education authority;*
>
> c. *any local housing authority;*
>
> d. *any health authority, special health authority, Primary Care Trust, National Health Service Trust or NHS Foundation Trust; and*
>
> e. *any person authorised by the Secretary of State for the purpose of this section.*
>
> (Children Act 1989, section 27)

13. Under section 47 of the Children Act 1989, the same agencies are placed under a similar duty to assist local authorities in carrying out enquiries into whether or not a child is at risk of significant harm.

14. Section 47 also sets out duties for the local authority itself, around making enquiries in certain circumstances to decide whether they should take any action to safeguard or promote the welfare of a child.

> **Section 47(1) of the Children Act 1989 states that:**
>
> Where a local authority:
>
> a. are informed that a child who lives, or is found, in their area (i) is the subject of an emergency protection order, or (ii) is in police protection, or (iii) has contravened a ban imposed by a curfew notice imposed within the meaning of Chapter I of Part I of the Crime and Disorder Act 1998; or
>
> b. have reasonable cause to suspect that a child who lives, or is found, in their area is suffering, or is likely to suffer, significant harm:
>
> The authority shall make, or cause to be made, such enquiries as they consider necessary to enable them to decide whether they should take any action to safeguard or promote the child's welfare.
>
> In the case of a child falling within paragraph (a) (iii) above, the enquiries shall be commenced as soon as practicable and, in any event, within 48 hours of the authority receiving the information.
>
> (Children Act 1989, section 47)

15. Under section 17 of the Children Act 1989, local authorities carry lead responsibility for establishing whether a child is in need and for ensuring that services are provided to that child as appropriate. This does not necessarily require local authorities themselves to be the provider of such services.

16. Section 17(5) of the Children Act 1989 enables the local authority to make arrangements with others to provide services on their behalf.

> Every local authority:
>
> a. shall facilitate the provision by others (including in particular voluntary organisations) of services which the authority have power to provide by virtue of this section, or section 18, 20, 23, 23B to 23D, 24A or 24B; and
>
> b. may make such arrangements as they see fit for any person to act on their behalf in the provision of any such service.
>
> (Children Act 1989, section 17(5))

17. Section 53 of the Children Act 2004 amends both section 17 and section 47 of the Children Act 1989, to require in each case that before determining what services to provide or what action to take, the local authority shall, so far as is reasonably practicable and consistent with the child's welfare:

- ascertain the child's wishes and feelings regarding the provision of those services or the action to be taken; and

- give due consideration (with regard to the child's age and understanding) to such wishes and feelings of the child as they have been able to ascertain.

## Emergency protection powers

18.	There is a range of powers available to local authorities and others such as the NSPCC and the police to take emergency action to safeguard children.

*Emergency protection orders*

The court may make an emergency protection order under section 44 of the Children Act 1989, if it is satisfied that there is reasonable cause to believe that a child is likely to suffer significant harm if:

- s/he is not removed to different accommodation; or

- s/he does not remain in the place in which s/he is then being accommodated.

An emergency protection order may also be made if enquiries (for example, made under section 47) are being frustrated by access to the child being unreasonably refused to a person authorised to seek access, and the applicant has reasonable cause to believe that access is needed as a matter of urgency.

An emergency protection order gives authority to remove a child, and places the child under the protection of the applicant.

*Exclusion requirement*

The court may include an exclusion requirement in an interim care order or emergency protection order (sections 38A and 44A of the Children Act 1989). This allows a perpetrator to be removed from the home instead of having to remove the child. The court must be satisfied that:

- there is reasonable cause to believe that if the person is excluded from the home in which the child lives, the child will cease to suffer, or cease to be likely to suffer, significant harm, or that enquires will cease to be frustrated; and

- another person living in the home is able and willing to give the child the care that it would be reasonable to expect a parent to give, and consents to the exclusion requirement.

*Police protection powers*

Under section 46 of the Children Act 1989, where a police officer has reasonable cause to believe that a child would otherwise be likely to suffer significant harm, s/he may:

- remove the child to suitable accommodation and keep him or her there; or

- take reasonable steps to ensure that the child's removal from any hospital, or other place in which the child is then being accommodated is prevented.

No child may be kept in police protection for more than 72 hours.

## Homelessness Act 2002

19.    Under section 12 (which inserts section 213A of the Housing Act 1996), housing authorities are required to refer to adult social care services homeless persons with dependent children who are ineligible for homelessness assistance, or are intentionally homeless, as long as the person consents. If homelessness persists, any child in the family could be in need. In such cases, if social services decide the child's needs would be best met by helping the family to obtain accommodation, they can ask the housing authority for reasonable advice and assistance in this, and the housing authority must give reasonable advice and assistance.

# Appendix 2 – Framework for the Assessment of Children in Need

1.  The *Framework for the Assessment of Children in Need and their Families* (outlined at Figure 1) provides a systematic basis for collecting and analysing information to support professional judgements about how to help children and families in the best interests of the child. Practitioners should use the framework to gain an understanding of:

    -   a child's developmental needs;

    -   the capacity of parents or caregivers to respond appropriately to those needs, including their capacity to keep the child safe from harm; and

    -   the impact of wider family and environmental factors on the parents and child.

    Each of the three main aspects of the framework is outlined in more detail in Boxes 1, 2 and 3 respectively.

2.  The framework is to be used for the assessment of all children in need, including those where there are concerns that a child may be suffering significant harm. The process of engaging in an assessment should be viewed as being part of the range of services offered to children and families. Use of the framework should provide evidence to help, guide and inform judgements about children's welfare and safety from the first point of contact, through the processes of initial and more detailed core assessments, according to the nature and extent of the child's needs. The provision of appropriate services need not and should not wait until the end of the assessment process, but should be determined according to what is required, and when, to promote the welfare and safety of the child.

3.  Evidence about children's developmental progress – and their parents' capacity to respond appropriately to the child's needs within the wider family and environmental context – should underpin judgements about:

    -   the child's welfare and safety;

    -   whether, and if so how, to provide help to children and family members;

    -   what form of intervention will bring about the best possible outcomes for the child; and

    -   the intended outcomes of intervention.

# Box 1: Dimensions of children's developmental needs

## Health

Includes growth and development as well as physical and mental wellbeing. The impact of genetic factors and of any impairment need to be considered. Involves receiving appropriate health care when ill, an adequate and nutritious diet, exercise, immunisations where appropriate and developmental checks, dental and optical care and, for older children, appropriate advice and information on issues that have an impact on health, including sex education and substance misuse.

## Education

Covers all areas of a child's cognitive development which begins from birth. Includes opportunities:

- for play and interaction with other children;

- to access books;

- to acquire a range of skills and interests; and

- to experience success and achievement.

Involves an adult interested in educational activities, progress and achievements, who takes account of the child's starting point and any special educational needs.

## Emotional and behavioural development

Concerns the appropriateness of response demonstrated in feelings and actions by a child, initially to parents and caregivers and, as the child grows older, to others beyond the family. Includes nature and quality of early attachments, characteristics of temperament, adaptation to change, response to stress and degree of appropriate self control.

## Identity

Concerns the child's growing sense of self as a separate and valued person. Includes the child's view of self and abilities, self image and self esteem, and having a positive sense of individuality. Race religion, age, gender, sexuality and disability may all contribute to this. Feelings of belonging and acceptance by family, peer group and wider society, including other cultural groups.

## Family and social relationships

Development of empathy and the capacity to place self in someone else's shoes. Includes a stable and affectionate relationship with parents or caregivers, good relationships with siblings, increasing importance of age appropriate friendships with peers and other significant persons in the child's life and response of family to these relationships.

## Social presentation

Concerns the child's growing understanding of the way in which appearance, behaviour, and any impairment are perceived by the outside world and the impression being created. Includes appropriateness of dress for age, gender, culture and religion; cleanliness and personal hygiene; and availability of advice from parents or caregivers about presentation in different settings.

## Self care skills

Concerns the acquisition by a child of practical, emotional and communication competencies required for increasing independence. Includes early practical skills of dressing and feeding, opportunities to gain confidence and practical skills to undertake activities away from the family and independent living skills as older children. Includes encouragement to acquire social problem solving approaches. Special attention should be given to the impact of a child's impairment and other vulnerabilities, and on social circumstances affecting these in the development of self care skills.

## Box 2: Dimensions of parenting capacity

### Basic care

Providing for the child's physical needs, and appropriate medical and dental care. Includes provision of food, drink, warmth, shelter, clean and appropriate clothing and adequate personal hygiene.

### Ensuring safety

Ensuring the child is adequately protected from harm or danger. Includes protection from significant harm or danger, and from contact with unsafe adults/other children and from self-harm. Recognition of hazards and danger both in the home and elsewhere.

## Emotional warmth

Ensuring the child's emotional needs are met giving the child a sense of being specially valued and a positive sense of own racial and cultural identity. Includes ensuring the child's requirements for secure, stable and affectionate relationships with significant adults, with appropriate sensitivity and responsiveness to the child's needs. Appropriate physical contact, comfort and cuddling sufficient to demonstrate warm regard, praise and encouragement.

## Stimulation

Promoting the child's learning and intellectual development through encouragement and cognitive stimulation and promoting social opportunities. Includes facilitating the child's cognitive development and potential through interaction, communication, talking and responding to the child's language and questions, encouraging and joining the child's play, and promoting educational opportunities. Enabling the child to experience success and ensuring school attendance or equivalent opportunity. Facilitating child to meet challenges of life.

## Guidance and boundaries

Enabling the child to regulate their own emotions and behaviour. The key parental tasks are demonstrating and modelling appropriate behaviour and control of emotions and interactions with others, and guidance which involves setting boundaries, so that the child is able to develop an internal model of moral values and conscience, and social behaviour appropriate for the society within which they will grow up. The aim is to enable the child to grow into an autonomous adult, holding their own values, and able to demonstrate appropriate behaviour with others rather than having to be dependent on rules outside themselves. This includes not over protecting children from exploratory and learning experiences. Includes social problem solving, anger management, consideration for others, and effective discipline and shaping of behaviour.

## Stability

Providing a sufficiently stable family environment to enable a child to develop and maintain a secure attachment to the primary caregiver(s) in order to ensure optimal development. Includes: ensuring secure attachments are not disrupted, providing consistency of emotional warmth over time and responding in a similar manner to the same behaviour. Parental responses change and develop according to child's developmental progress. In addition, ensuring children keep in contact with important family members and significant others.

## Box 3: Family and environmental factors

### Family history and functioning

Family history includes both genetic and psycho-social factors. Family functioning is influenced by:

- who is living in the household and how they are related to the child;
- significant changes in family/household composition;
- history of childhood experiences of parents;
- chronology of significant life events and their meaning to family members;
- nature of family functioning, including sibling relationships and its impact on the child;
- parental strengths and difficulties, including those of an absent parent; and
- the relationship between separated parents.

### Wider family

Who are considered to be members of the wider family by the child and the parents? This includes related and non-related persons and absent wider family. What is their role and importance to the child and parents and in precisely what way?

### Housing

Does the accommodation have basic amenities and facilities appropriate to the age and development of the child and other resident members? Is the housing accessible and suitable to the needs of disabled family members? Includes the interior and exterior of the accommodation and immediate surroundings. Basic amenities include water, heating, sanitation, cooking facilities, sleeping arrangements and cleanliness, hygiene and safety and their impact on the child's upbringing.

### Employment

Who is working in the household, their pattern of work and any changes? What impact does this have on the child? How is work or absence of work viewed by family members? How does it affect their relationship with the child? Includes children's experience of work and its impact on them.

## Income

Income available over a sustained period of time. Is the family in receipt of all its benefit entitlements? Sufficiency of income to meet the family's needs. The way resources available to the family are used. Are there financial difficulties which affect the child?

## Family's social integration

Exploration of the wider context of the local neighbourhood and community and its impact on the child and parents. Includes the degree of the family's integration or isolation, its peer groups, friendship and social networks and the importance attached to them.

## Community resources

Describes all facilities and services in a neighbourhood, including universal services of primary health care, day care and schools, places of worship, transport, shops and leisure activities. Includes availability and standard of resources and impact on the family, including disabled members.

# Appendix 3 – Using standardised assessment tools to evidence assessment and decision making

1.   **The Strengths and Difficulties Questionnaires** (Goodman et al, 1997; Goodman et al, 1998). These scales are a modification of the very widely used instruments to screen for emotional and behavioural problems in children and adolescents – the Rutter A + B scales for parents and teachers. Although similar to Rutter's, the Strengths and Difficulties Questionnaire's wording was re-framed to focus on a child's emotional and behavioural strengths as well as difficulties. The actual questionnaire incorporates five scales: pro-social, hyperactivity, emotional problems, conduct (behavioural) problems, and peer problems. In the pack, there are versions of the scale to be completed by adult caregivers, or teachers for children from age three to sixteen, and children between the ages of 11 to 16. These questionnaires have been used with disabled children and their teachers and carers. They are available in 40 languages on the following website: www.sdqinfo.com/

2.   **The Parenting Daily Hassles Scale** (Crinic and Greenberg, 1990; Crinic and Booth, 1991) aims to assess the frequency and intensity/impact of 20 potential parenting 'daily' hassles experienced by adults caring for children. It has been used in a wide variety of research studies concerned with children and families – particularly families with young children. It has been found that parents (or caregivers) generally like filling it out, because it touches on many aspects of being a parent that are important to them.

3.   **The Recent Life Events Questionnaire** (Taken from Brugha et al, 1985) helps to define negative life events over the last 12 months, but could be used over a longer time-scale, and significantly whether the respondent thought they have a continuing influence. Respondents are asked to identify which of the events still affects them. It was hoped that use of the scale will:

   ●  result in a fuller picture of a family's history and contribute to greater contextual understanding of the family's current situation;

   ●  help practitioners explore how particular recent life events have affected the carer and the family; and

   ●  in some situations, identify life events which family members have not reported earlier.

4.   **The Home Conditions Assessment** (Davie et al, 1984) helps make judgements about the context in which the child was living, dealing with questions of safety, order and cleanliness which have an important bearing where issues of neglect are the focus of concern. The total score has been found to correlate highly with indices of the development of children.

5.   **The Family Activity Scale** (derived from The Child-Centredness Scale – Smith, 1985) gives practitioners an opportunity to explore with carers the environment provided for their children, through joint activities and support for independent activities. This includes information about the cultural and ideological environment in which children live, as well as how their carers respond to their children's actions (for example, concerning play and independence). They aim to be independent of socio-economic resources. There are two separate scales; one for children aged two to six, and one for children aged seven to twelve.

6.   **The Alcohol Scale** was developed by Piccinelli et al (1997). Alcohol abuse is estimated to be present in about 6% of primary carers, ranking it third in frequency behind major depression and generalised anxiety. Higher rates are found in certain localities, and particularly amongst those parents known to social services. Drinking alcohol affects different individuals in different ways. For example, some people may be relatively unaffected by the same amount of alcohol that incapacitates others. The primary concern therefore is not the amount of alcohol consumed, but how it impacts on the individual and, more particularly, on their role as a parent. This questionnaire has been found to be effective in detecting individuals with alcohol disorders and those with hazardous drinking habits.

7.   **Adult Wellbeing Scale** (Irritability, Depression, Anxiety – IDA Scale. Snaith et al, 1978). This scale, which was based on the Irritability, Depression and Anxiety Scale, was devised by a social worker involved in the pilot. The questions are framed in a 'personal' fashion (that is, I feel, my appetite is…). This scale looks at how an adult is feeling in terms of their depression, anxiety and irritability. The scale allows the adult to respond from four possible answers, which enables the adult some choice, and therefore less restriction. This could enable the adult to feel more empowered.

8.   **The Adolescent Wellbeing Scale** (Self-rating Scale for Depression in Young People. Birleson, 1980) was originally validated for children aged between seven and sixteen. It involves 18 questions each relating to different aspects of a child or adolescent's life, and how they feel about these. As a result of the pilot the wording of some questions was altered in order to be more appropriate to adolescents. Although children as young as seven and eight have used it, older children's thoughts and beliefs about themselves are more stable. The scale is intended to enable practitioners to gain more insight and understanding into how an adolescent feels about their life.

9.     **The Home Inventory** (Cox and Walker, 2002) assessment through interview and observation provides an extensive profile of the context of care provided for the child and is a reliable approach to assessment of parenting. It gives a reliable account of the parents' capacities to provide learning materials, language stimulation, and appropriate physical environment, to be responsive, stimulating, providing adequate modelling variety and acceptance. A profile of needs can be constructed in these areas, and an analysis of how considerable the changes would need to be to meet the specific needs of the significantly harmed child; and the contribution of the environment provided by the parents to the harm suffered. The HOME Inventory has been used extensively to demonstrate change in the family context as a result of intervention, and can be used to assess whether intervention has been successful.

10.     **The Family Assessment** (Bentovim and Bingley Miller, 2001) provides a systematic and systemic assessment in complex child care cases of family functioning, family relationships, the quality of parenting and the parents' capacity to adapt to the children's needs as well as the impact of family history. It provides a standardised evidence-based approach to assessing current family strengths and difficulties which have played a role in the significant harm of the child, and also in assessing the capacity for change, resources in the family to achieve a safe context for the child, and the reversal of family factors which may have played a role in significant harm, and aiding the recovery and future health of the child. The Family Assessment Profile draws together the assessment and provides qualitative and quantitative information on the parents' understanding of the child's state, and the level of responsibility they take for any significant harm or likelihood of harm, the capacity of the parents to adapt to the children's changing needs in the past and future, their abilities to promote development, provide care-giving which enables their children to have secure attachments with them as care-givers, provide adequate guidance, care and to manage conflict, make decisions and relate to the wider family and community.

# Appendix 4 – MOD child protection contacts

1.   Appendix 4 offers points of contact for the relevant Service agencies in child protection matters.

## Royal Navy

2.   All child protection matters within the Royal Navy are managed by the Naval Personal and Family Service (NPFS), the Royal Navy's social work department. This provides a confidential and professional social work service to all Naval personnel and their families, liaising as appropriate with local authority children's social care services. Child protection issues involving the family of a member of the Royal Navy should be referred to the relevant Area Officer, NPFS.

| | | |
|---|---|---|
| NPFS Eastern Area Portsmouth | (02392) 722712 | Fax: 725803 |
| NPFS Northern Area Helensburgh | (01436) 672798 | Fax: 674965 |
| NPFS Western Area Plymouth | (01752) 555041 | Fax: 555647 |

## Royal Marines

3.   The Royal Marines Welfare Service is staffed by trained but unqualified Royal Marine senior non-commissioned officers (NCOs). They are accountable to a qualified social work manager at Headquarters Royal Marines, Portsmouth. For child protection matters involving Royal Marines families, social services departments should notify SO3 (WFS) at Portsmouth. Tel: (02392) 547542.

## Army

4.   Staffed by qualified civilian Social Workers and trained and supervised Army Welfare Workers, the Army Welfare Service (AWS) provides professional welfare support to Army personnel and their families. AWS also liaises with local authorities where appropriate, particularly where a child is subject to child protection concerns. Local Authorities who have any enquiries or concerns regarding safeguarding or promoting the welfare of a child from an Army Family should contact the Senior Army Welfare Worker in the nearest AWS team location or:

Chief Personal Support Officer
HQ AWS
HQ Land Command
Erskine Barracks
Wilton
Salisbury
SP2 0AG

Tel: 01722 436564
Fax: 01722 436307
e-mail: LF-AWS-CPSO@mod.uk

## Royal Air Force

5.    Welfare Support for families in the RAF is managed as a normal function of Command and co-ordinated by each Station's Personnel Officer, the Officer Commanding Personnel Management Squadron (OCPMS) or the Officer Commanding Administrative Squadron (OCA), depending on the size of the Station.

6.    A number of qualified SSAFA Forces Help Social Workers and trained professionally supervised Personal and Family Support Workers are located throughout the UK to assist the chain of Command in providing welfare support.

7.    Any Local Authority who have any enquiries or concerns regarding safeguarding or promoting the welfare of a child from an RAF family should contact the parent's unit, or if this is not known, contact the OC PMS/OCA of the nearest RAF Unit. Additionally, the SSAFA Forces Help Head of Service RAF can be contacted at:

Head of Service
SSAFA-Forces Help
HQ Air Command
RAF High Wycombe
Buckinghamshire
HP14 4UE

Tel: 01494 496477
Fax: 01494 497971

e-mail: AirPersPol-SSAFAForcesHelpHd@mod.uk

Or

Director of Social Work SSAFA-Forces Help
19 Queen Elizabeth Street
London SE1 2LP

Tel: 020 7403 8783
Fax: 020 7403 8815

Email: directorofsocialwork@ssafa.org.uk

## Overseas

The following should be consulted:

### Royal Navy

Area Officer (NPFS) Eastern
HMS Nelson
Queen Street
Portsmouth
PO1 3HH

Tel: (02392) 722712
Fax: (02392) 725083

### Army and Royal Air Force

Director of Social Work SSAFA-Forces Help
Contact details shown above.

*For **any** child being taken abroad and subject to child protection procedures or the subject of a child protection plan, the Director of Social Work SSAFA-Forces Help **must** be consulted, using the same contact details shown above.*

# Appendix 5 – Procedures for managing allegations against people who work with children

## Scope

1.  The framework for managing cases set out in this guidance applies to a wider range of allegations than those in which there is reasonable cause to believe a child is suffering, or is likely to suffer, significant harm. It also caters for cases of allegations that might indicate that s/he is unsuitable to continue to work with children in their present position, or in any capacity. It should be used in respect of all cases in which it is alleged that a person who works with children has:

    ● behaved in a way that has harmed a child, or may have harmed a child;

    ● possibly committed a criminal offence against or related to a child; or

    ● behaved towards a child or children in a way that indicates s/he is unsuitable to work with children.

2.  There may be up to three strands in the consideration of an allegation:

    ● a police investigation of a possible criminal offence;

    ● enquiries and assessment by children's social care about whether a child is in need of protection or in need of services; and

    ● consideration by an employer[274] of disciplinary action in respect of the individual.

---

274  For convenience the term employer is used throughout this guidance to refer to organisations that have a working relationship with the individual against whom the allegation is made. That includes organisations that use the services of volunteers, or people who are self employed, as well as service providers, voluntary organisations, employment agencies or businesses, contractors, fostering services, regulatory bodies such as Ofsted in the case of childminders, and others that may not have a direct employment relationship with the individual, but will need to consider whether to continue to use the person's services, or to provide the person for work with children in future, or to deregister the individual. N.B. In some circumstances the term 'employer' for these purposes will encompass more than one organisation. For example, where staff providing services for children in an organisation are employed by a contractor, or where temporary staff are provided by an agency. In those circumstances both the contractor or agency, and the organisation in which the accused individual worked will need to be involved in dealing with the allegation.

3.      Some cases will also need to be referred to the ISA for consideration of including the person on the ISA barred lists, or for consideration by professional bodies or regulators.

## Supporting those involved

4.      Parents or carers of a child or children involved should be told about the allegation as soon as possible if they do not already know of it (subject to paragraph 15 below). They should also be kept informed about the progress of the case, and told the outcome where there is not a criminal prosecution. That includes the outcome of any disciplinary process. NB. The deliberations of a disciplinary hearing, and the information taken into account in reaching a decision, cannot normally be disclosed, but those concerned should be told the outcome.

5.      In cases where a child may have suffered significant harm, or there may be a criminal prosecution, children's social care, or the police as appropriate, should consider what support the child or children involved may need.

6.      The employer should also keep the person who is the subject of the allegations informed of the progress of the case, and arrange to provide appropriate support to the individual while the case is ongoing (that may be provided via occupational health or employee welfare arrangements where those exist). If the person is suspended the employer should also make arrangements to keep the individual informed about developments in the workplace. As noted in paragraph 16, if the person is a member of a union or professional association s/he should be advised to contact that body at the outset.

## Confidentiality

7.      Every effort should be made to maintain confidentiality and guard against publicity while an allegation is being investigated/considered. In accordance with ACPO guidance, the police will not normally provide any information to the Press or media that might identify an individual who is under investigation, unless and until the person is charged with a criminal offence (In exceptional cases where the police might depart from that rule, for example, an appeal to trace a suspect, the reasons should be documented and partner agencies consulted beforehand). The system of self-regulation, overseen by the Press Complaints Commission, also provides safeguards against the publication of inaccurate or misleading information.

## Resignations and 'compromise agreements'

8.      The fact that a person tenders his or her resignation, or ceases to provide their services, must not prevent an allegation being followed up in accordance with these

procedures. It is important that every effort is made to reach a conclusion in all cases of allegations bearing on the safety or welfare of children including any in which the person concerned refuses to co-operate with the process. Wherever possible the person should be given a full opportunity to answer the allegation and make representations about it, but the process of recording the allegation and any supporting evidence, and reaching a judgement about whether it can be regarded as substantiated on the basis of all the information available should continue even if that cannot be done or the person does not co-operate. It may be difficult to reach a conclusion in those circumstances, and it may not be possible to apply any disciplinary sanctions if a person's period of notice expires before the process is complete, but it is important to reach and record a conclusion wherever possible.

9.      By the same token so called 'compromise agreements' by which a person agrees to resign, the employer agrees not to pursue disciplinary action, and both parties agree a form of words to be used in any future reference, must not be used in these cases. In any event, such an agreement will not prevent a thorough police investigation where appropriate. Nor can it override an employer's statutory duty to make a referral to the Independent Safeguarding Authority where circumstances require that.

## Record keeping

10.     It is important that employers keep a clear and comprehensive summary of any allegations made, details of how the allegation was followed up and resolved, and details of any action taken and decisions reached, on a person's confidential personnel file and give a copy to the individual. Such information should be retained on file, including for people who leave the organisation, at least until the person reaches normal retirement age or for 10 years if that will be longer. The purpose of the record is to enable accurate information to be given in response to any future request for a reference. It will provide clarification in cases where a future CRB Disclosure reveals information from the police that an allegation was made but did not result in a prosecution or a conviction. And it will prevent unnecessary re-investigation if, as sometimes happens, allegations re-surface after a period of time.

## Timescales

11.     It is in everyone's interest to resolve cases as quickly as possible consistent with a fair and thorough investigation. Every effort should be made to manage cases to avoid any unnecessary delay. Indicative target timescales are shown for different actions in the summary description of the process. Those are not performance indicators: the time taken to investigate and resolve individual cases depends on a

variety of factors including the nature, seriousness, and complexity of the allegation, but they provide useful targets to aim for that are achievable in many cases.

## Oversight and monitoring

12. LSCB member organisations, county level and unitary local authorities, and police forces should each have officers who fill the roles described in paragraphs 6.35 and 6.36.

13. Other employers' procedures should identify a senior manager within the organisation to whom allegations or concerns that a member of staff or volunteer may have abused a child should be reported, and should make sure that all staff and volunteers know who that is. The procedures should also identify an alternative person to whom reports should be made in the absence of the named senior manager, or in cases where that person is the subject of the allegation or concern, and include contact details for the local authority designated officer responsible for providing advice, liaison, and monitoring the progress of cases to ensure that they are dealt with as quickly as possibly consistent with a fair and thorough process.

## Initial considerations

14. Procedures need to be applied with common sense and judgement. Some allegations will be so serious as to require immediate referral to children's social care and the police for investigation. Others may be much less serious and at first sight might not seem to warrant consideration of a police investigation, or enquiries by children's social care. However, it is important to ensure that even apparently less serious allegations are seen to be followed up, and that they are examined objectively by someone independent of the organisation concerned. Consequently, the local authority designated officer should be informed of all allegations that come to the employer's attention and appear to meet the criteria in paragraph 1, so that s/he can consult police and social care colleagues as appropriate. The local authority designated officer should also be informed of any allegations that are made directly to the police (which should be communicated via the police force designated officer) or to children's social care.

15. The local authority designated officer should first establish, in discussion with the employer, that the allegation is within the scope of these procedures, see paragraph 1, and may have some foundation. If the parents/carers of the child concerned are not already aware of the allegation, the designated officer will also discuss how and by whom they should be informed. In circumstances in which the police or children's social care may need to be involved, the local authority officer should consult those colleagues about how best to inform parents. However, in some circumstances an employer may need to advise parents of an incident involving

their child straight away, for example if the child has been injured while in the organisation's care and requires medical treatment.

16. The employer should inform the accused person about the allegation as soon as possible after consulting the local authority designated officer. However, where a strategy discussion is needed, or it is clear that police or children's social care may need to be involved, that should not be done until those agencies have been consulted and have agreed what information can be disclosed to the person. If the person is a member of a union or professional association s/he should be advised to seek support from that organisation.

17. If there is cause to suspect a child is suffering or is likely to suffer significant harm, a strategy discussion should be convened in accordance with paragraph 5.56. NB. In these cases the strategy discussion should include a representative of the employer (unless there are good reasons not to do that), and take account of any information the employer can provide about the circumstances or context of the allegation.

18. In cases where a formal strategy discussion is not considered appropriate because the threshold of 'significant harm' is not reached, but a police investigation might be needed, the local authority designated officer should nevertheless conduct a similar discussion with the police, the employer, and any other agencies involved with the child to evaluate the allegation and decide how it should be dealt with (NB. The police must be consulted about any case in which a criminal offence may have been committed). Like a strategy discussion that initial evaluation may not need to be a face to face meeting. It should share available information about the allegation, the child, and the person against whom the allegation has been made, consider whether a police investigation is needed and, if so, agree the timing and conduct of that. In cases where a police investigation is necessary the joint evaluation should also consider whether there are matters which can be taken forward in a disciplinary process in parallel with the criminal process, or whether any disciplinary action will need to wait completion of the police enquiries and/or prosecution.

19. If the complaint or allegation is such that it is clear that investigations by police and/ or enquiries by children's social care are not necessary, or the strategy discussion or initial evaluation decides that is the case, the local authority designated officer should discuss next steps with the employer. In those circumstances options open to the employer will range from taking no further action to summary dismissal or a decision not to use the person's services in future. The nature and circumstances of the allegation and the evidence and information available will determine which of the range of possible options is most appropriate.

20.    In some cases further investigation will be needed to enable a decision about how to proceed. If so, the local authority designated officer should discuss with the person's employer how and by whom the investigation will be undertaken. That should normally be undertaken by the employer. However in some circumstances appropriate resources may not be available in the employer's organisation or the nature and complexity of the allegation might point to the employer commissioning an independent investigation.

## Suspension

21.    The possible risk of harm to children posed by an accused person needs to be effectively evaluated and managed – in respect of the child(ren) involved in the allegations, and any other children in the individual's home, work or community life. In some cases that will require the employer to consider suspending the person. Suspension should be considered in any case where there is cause to suspect a child is at risk of significant harm, or the allegation warrants investigation by the police, or is so serious that it might be grounds for dismissal. People must not be suspended automatically, or without careful thought. Employers must consider carefully whether the circumstances of a case warrant a person being suspended from contact with children until the allegation is resolved. NB. Neither the local authority, the police, nor children's social care can require an employer to suspend a member of staff or a volunteer. The power to suspend is vested in the employer alone. However, where a strategy discussion or initial evaluation discussion concludes that there should be enquiries by children's social care and/or an investigation by the police, the local authority designated officer should also canvass police/children's social care views about whether the accused member of staff needs to be suspended from contact with children, to inform the employer's consideration of suspension.

## Monitoring progress

22.    The local authority designated officer should regularly monitor the progress of cases either via review strategy discussions or by liaising with the police and/or children's social care colleagues, or the employer as appropriate. Reviews should be conducted at fortnightly or monthly intervals depending on the complexity of the case.

23.    If the strategy discussion or initial evaluation decides that a police investigation is required, the police should also set a target date for reviewing the progress of the investigation and consulting the Crown Prosecution Service (CPS) to consider whether to charge the individual, continue to investigate or close the investigation. Wherever possible that review should take place **no later than four weeks** after the initial action meeting. Dates for subsequent reviews, at fortnightly or monthly intervals, should be set at the meeting if the investigation continues.

## Information sharing

24. In the initial consideration at a strategy discussion or joint evaluation the agencies concerned, including the employer, should share all relevant information they have about the person who is the subject of the allegation, and about the alleged victim.

25. Wherever possible the police should obtain consent from the individuals concerned to share the statements and evidence they obtain with the employer, and/or regulatory body, for disciplinary purposes. That should be done as the investigation proceeds rather than after it is concluded. That will enable the police and CPS to share relevant information without delay at the conclusion of their investigation or any court case.

26. Children's social care should adopt a similar procedure when making enquiries to determine whether the child or children named in the allegation is in need of protection or services so that any information obtained in the course of those enquiries which is relevant to a disciplinary case can be passed to the employer or regulatory body without delay.

## Action following a criminal investigation or a prosecution

27. The police or the CPS should inform the employer and local authority designated officer straightaway when a criminal investigation and any subsequent trial is complete, or if it is decided to close an investigation without charge, or not to prosecute after the person has been charged. In those circumstances the local authority designated officer should discuss with the employer whether any further action is appropriate and, if so, how to proceed. The information provided by the police and/or children's social care should inform that decision. Action by the employer, including dismissal, is not ruled out in any of those circumstances. The range of options open will depend on the circumstances of the case and the consideration will need to take account the result of the police investigation or trial, as well as the different standard of proof required in disciplinary and criminal proceedings.

## Action on conclusion of a case

28. If the allegation is substantiated and the person is dismissed or the employer ceases to use the person's services, or the person resigns or otherwise ceases to provide his/her services, the local authority designated officer should discuss with the employer whether a referral to the Independent Safeguarding Authority is required, or advisable, and the form and content of a referral. A referral must always be made if the employer thinks that the individual has harmed a child or poses a risk of harm to children. Also, if the person is subject to registration or regulation by a

professional body or regulator, for example by the General Social Care Council, General Medical Council, Ofsted etc. the designated officer should advise on whether a referral to that body is appropriate.

29.   If it is decided on the conclusion of the case that a person who has been suspended can return to work the employer should consider how best to facilitate that. Most people will benefit from some help and support to return to work after a very stressful experience. Depending on the individual's circumstances, a phased return and/or the provision of a mentor to provide assistance and support in the short term may be appropriate. The employer should also consider how the person's contact with the child or children who made the allegation can best be managed if they are still in the workplace.

## Learning lessons

30.   At the conclusion of a case in which an allegation is substantiated the employer should review the circumstances of the case to determine whether there are any improvements to be made to the organisation's procedures or practice to help prevent similar events in the future. This should include issues arising from any decision to suspend a member of staff, the duration of the suspension and whether or not suspension was justified.

## Action in respect of unfounded or malicious allegations

31.   If an allegation is determined to be unfounded or malicious, the employer should refer the matter to children's social care to determine whether the child concerned is in need of services, or may have been abused by someone else. In the rare event that an allegation is shown to have been deliberately invented or malicious, the police should be asked to consider whether any action might be appropriate against the person responsible.

## Summary of Process

### Allegation made to employer

32.   The allegation should be reported to the senior manager identified in the employer's procedure immediately unless that person is the subject of the allegation in which case it should be reported to the designated alternative.

33.   If the allegation meets any of the criteria set out in paragraph 1 the employer should report it to the local authority designated office within 1 working day.

## Allegation made to the police or children's social care

34.     If an allegation is made to the police, the officer who receives it should report it to the force designated liaison officer without delay and the designated liaison officer should in turn inform the local authority designated officer straight away. Similarly if the allegation is made to children's social care the person who receives it should report it to the local authority designated officer without delay.

## Initial consideration

35.     The local authority designated officer will discuss the matter with the employer and where necessary obtain further details of the allegation and the circumstances in which it was made. The discussion should also consider whether there is evidence/information that establishes that the allegation is false or unfounded.

36.     If the allegation is not patently false and there is cause to suspect that a child is suffering or is likely to suffer significant harm, the local authority designated officer will immediately refer to children's social care and ask for a strategy discussion to be convened straight away. In those circumstances the strategy discussion should include the local authority designated officer and a representative of the employer.

37.     If there is not cause to suspect that 'significant harm' is an issue, but a criminal offence might have been committed, the local authority designated officer should immediately inform the police and convene a similar discussion to decide whether a police investigation is needed. That discussion should also involve the employer.

## Action following initial consideration

38.     Where the initial evaluation decides that the allegation does not involve a possible criminal offence it will be dealt with by the employer. In such cases, if the nature of the allegation does not require formal disciplinary action, appropriate action should be instituted **within three working days**. If a disciplinary hearing is required and can be held without further investigation, the hearing should be held **within 15 working days**.

39.     Where further investigation is required to inform consideration of disciplinary action the employer should discuss who will undertake that with the local authority designated officer. In some settings and circumstances it may be appropriate for the disciplinary investigation to be conducted by a person who is independent of the employer or the person's line management to ensure objectivity. In any case the investigating officer should aim to provide a report to the employer **within 10 working days**.

40. On receipt of the report of the disciplinary investigation, the employer should decide whether a disciplinary hearing is needed **within two working days,** and if a hearing is needed it should be held **within 15 working days**.

41. In any case in which children's social care has undertaken enquiries to determine whether the child or children are in need of protection, the employer should take account of any relevant information obtained in the course of those enquiries when considering disciplinary action.

42. The local authority designated officer should continue to liaise with the employer to monitor progress of the case and provide advice/support when required/requested.

## Case subject to police investigation

43. If a criminal investigation is required, the police will aim to complete their enquiries as quickly as possible consistent with a fair and thorough investigation and will keep the progress of the case under review. They should at the outset set a target date for reviewing progress of the investigation and consulting the CPS about whether to proceed with the investigation, charge the individual with an offence, or close the case. Wherever possible that review should take place **no later than four weeks** after the initial evaluation, and if the decision is to continue to investigate the allegation dates for subsequent reviews should be set at that point (it is open to the police to consult the CPS about the evidence that will need to be obtained in order to charge a person with an offence at any stage).

44. If the police and/or CPS decide not to charge the individual with an offence, or decide to administer a caution, or the person is acquitted by a Court, the police should pass all information they have which may be relevant to a disciplinary case to the employer without delay. In those circumstances the employer and the local authority designated officer should proceed as described in paragraphs 37–41 above.

45. If the person is convicted of an offence the police should also inform the employer straight away so that appropriate action can be taken.

## Referral to the Independent Safeguarding Authority

46. If the allegation is substantiated and on conclusion of the case the employer dismisses the person or ceases to use the person's services, or the person ceases to provide his/her services, the employer should consult the local authority designated officer about whether a referral to the Independent Safeguarding Authority and/or to a professional or regulatory body is required. If a referral is appropriate the report should be made within one month. A referral must always be made if the employer thinks that the individual has harmed a child or poses a risk of harm to children.

# Appendix 6 – Faith community contacts and resources

Appendix 6 offers points of contact for faith communities in child protection matters and outlines some key resources that may be useful.

## Faith community contacts

| Organisation | Telephone number | Website |
|---|---|---|
| Baptist Church | 01235 517 700 | www.baptist.org.uk |
| Catholic Church – CSAS | 0121 237 6076 | www.csas.uk.net |
| Church of Jesus Christ and the Latter-day Saints | 0121 712 1251 | www.lds.org.uk |
| Church in Wales | 0292 034 8234 | www.churchinwales.org.uk |
| Methodist and Church of England | 020 7467 5189 | www.methodistchurch.org.uk |
| Mosques and Imams National Advisory Board (MINAB) | 020 8993 7141 | www.minab.org.uk |
| Movement for Reform Judaism | 020 8349 5656 | www.reformjudaism.org.uk |
| Muslim Council of Britain | 0845 2626 786 | www.mcb.org.uk |
| Religious Society of Friends | 020 7663 1023 | www.quaker.org.uk |
| Salvation Army | 020 7367 4772 | www.salvationarmy.org.uk |
| United Reform Church | 020 7916 2020 | www.urc.org.uk |
| United Synagogue | 020 8343 8989 | www.theus.org.uk |

For those from Hindu or Sikh faith, please contact the local temple.

For other faiths including independent Christian churches, please contact the Churches' Child Protection Advisory Service (CCPAS) who are an independent christian child care charity working across the faith sector. Please ring 0845 120 4550, visit www.ccpas.co.uk or email info@ccpas.co.uk.

## Faith community resources

CCPAS, together with the Lucy Faithful Foundation, have produced materials to assist faith communities in working with offenders, including a DVD, *SOS Supporting Offenders Safely*, and a booklet, *Help... a sex offender has joined my church*.

CCPAS has also produced *Safe and Secure*, ten safeguarding standards for faith communities, which contains both policies and procedures, as well as an hour long safeguarding DVD drama documentary set around the 10 standards

Faith communities should also refer to Section 6.49 to 6.53 Child abuse linked to belief in 'spirit possession' and the DCSF good practice guidance *Safeguarding Children from Abuse Linked to a belief in Spirit Possession* (DCSF, 2007). Further information is available on '*Good Practice for Working with Faith Communities – Spirit Possession & Abuse*' from CCPAS.

# Appendix 7 – A guide to acronyms in the document

| | |
|---|---|
| A&E | Accident and Emergency |
| ACPO | Association of Chief Police Officers |
| AWS | Army Welfare Service |
| BECTA | British Educational Communications and Technology Agency |
| CAF | Common Assessment Framework |
| Cafcass | Children and Family Court Advisory and Support Service |
| CAIUs | Child abuse investigation units |
| CAMHS | Child and Adolescent Mental Health Services |
| CCPAS | Churches' Child Protection Advisory Service |
| CDOP | Child Death Overview Panel |
| CDRPs | Crime and Disorder Reduction Partnerships |
| CEOP | Child Exploitation and On-Line Protection Centre |
| CJCSA | Criminal Justice and Court Services Act |
| CMACE | Centre for Maternal and Child Enquiries |
| CME | Child Missing Education |
| CPS | Crown Prosecution Service |
| CPSU | Child Protection in Sport Unit |
| CQC | Care Quality Commission |
| CRB | Criminal Record Bureau |
| CSAS | Catholic Safeguarding Advisory Service |
| CSO | Child Safety Order |
| CT | Children's Trust |
| CTB | Children's Trust Board |
| CWDC | Children's Workforce Development Council |
| CYPP | Children and Young People's Plan |
| DASH | Domestic Abuse, Stalking and Harassment and Honour Based Violence |
| DCPs | Dental practitioners and dental care professionals |
| DCS | Director of Children's Services |
| DCSF | The Department for Children, Schools and Families |
| DH | The Department of Health |
| DPA | Data Protection Acts |
| EEA | European Economic Area |
| EPO | Emergency Protection Order |
| EYFS | Early Years Foundation Stage |
| FAS | Fetal Alcohol Syndrome |
| FCO | Foreign and Commonwealth Office |
| FE | Further Education |
| FGCs | Family Group Conferences |

| | |
|---|---|
| FGM | Female Genital Mutilation |
| FII | Fabricated or induced illness |
| FIPs | Family Intervention Projects |
| GMC | General Medical Council |
| GO | Government Office |
| GP | General Practitioner |
| HMI Probation | Her Majesty's Inspectorate of Probation |
| HMIC | Her Majesty's Inspectorate of Constabulary |
| HMIP | Her Majesty's Inspectorate of Prisons |
| ICS | Integrated Children's System |
| ICT | Information Communication Technology |
| IDVA | Individual Domestic Violence Advisor |
| IMR | Individual Management Review |
| INI | IMPACT Nominal Index |
| IRO | Independent Reviewing Officer |
| ISA | Independent Safeguarding Authority |
| JSP | Joint Service Publication |
| LADO | Local authority Designated Officer |
| LASSL | Local Authority Social Services Letter |
| LAYS | Local authority youth services |
| LL/LT | Life Limiting or Life Threatening |
| LSCB | Local Safeguarding Children Board |
| MAPPA | Multi Agency Public Protection Arrangements |
| MARAC | Multi Agency Risk Assessment Conference |
| MEs | Medical Examiners |
| MSCR | MAPPA Serious Case Review |
| NICE | The National Institute for Health and Clinical Excellence |
| NOMS | National Offenders Management Service |
| NPFS | Naval Personal and Family Service |
| NPIA | The National Police Improvement Agency |
| NRM | National Referral Mechanism |
| NSF | National Service Framework |
| OSSys | Offender Assessment System |
| PACE | Police and Criminal Evidence Act |
| PCTs | Primary Care Trusts |
| PDUs | Problem Drug Users |
| PND | Police National Database |
| PPO | Probation and Prisons Ombudsman |
| PSAs | Parenting Support Advisers |
| PSHE | Personal, Social and Health Education |
| RN | Royal Navy |
| RSHOs | Risk of Sexual Harm Orders |
| RSLs | Registered Social Landlords |

| | |
|---|---|
| SARCs | Sexual Assault Referral Centres |
| SARS | Sexual Assault Referral Services |
| SCHs | Secure Children's Homes |
| SCRs | Serious Case Reviews |
| SEN | Special Education Needs |
| SFO | Serious Further Offence |
| SHAs | Strategic Health Authorities |
| SMB | Strategic Management Board |
| SOPOs | Sexual Offences Prevention Orders |
| SSAFA-FH | Sailors Airmen and Families Association-Forces Help |
| STCs | Secure Training Centres |
| SUDI | Sudden Unexpected Deaths in Infancy |
| TAC | Team around the Child |
| TSA | Tenant Services Authority |
| UASC | Unaccompanied Asylum Seeking Child |
| UK | United Kingdom |
| UKBA | United Kingdom Border Agency |
| UKHTC | UK Human Trafficking Centre |
| US | United States |
| VBS | Vetting and Barring Scheme |
| VISOR | The Violent and Sexual Offenders Register |
| VOOs | Violent Offender Orders |
| YCWs | Youth and community workers |
| YJB | Youth Justice Board |
| YJS | Youth Justice System |
| YOIs | Young Offender Institutions |
| YOTs | Youth Offending Teams |

# References and internet links

## Chapter 1

*Every Child Matters* Green Paper.
Internet link:
http://publications.everychildmatters.gov.uk/eOrderingDownload/CM5860.pdf

*The Protection of Children in England: A Progress Report*.
Internet link:
http://publications.everychildmatters.gov.uk/eOrderingDownload/HC-330.pdf

*The Protection of Children in England: Action Plan*.
Internet link:
http://publications.dcsf.gov.uk/eOrderingDownload/DCSF-Laming.pdf

*Guidance on the roles and responsibilities of the Director of Children's Services and Lead Member for children's services*.
Internet link:
http://publications.everychildmatters.gov.uk/default.aspx?PageFunction=productdetails&
PageMode=publications&ProductId=DCSF-00686-2009

Adcock, M. and White, R. (1998). *Significant Harm: its management and outcome*. Surrey: Significant Publications.

Jones, D. P. H. (2003). *Communicating with Vulnerable Children: a Guide for Practitioners*. London: Gaskell.

## Chapter 2

Children Act 2004
Internet link:
www.opsi.gov.uk/acts/acts2004/ukpga_20040031_en_1

*Making Arrangements to Safeguard and Promote the Welfare of Children*.
Internet link:
www.everychildmatters.gov.uk/resources-and-practice/IG00042/

Education Act 2002
Internet link:
www.opsi.gov.uk/acts/acts2002/ukpga_20020032_en_1

*Safeguarding Children and Safer Recruitment in Education.*
Internet link:
www.dcsf.gov.uk/everychildmatters/resources-and-practice/IG00175/

Children Act 1989.
Internet link:
www.opsi.gov.uk/acts/acts1989/ukpga_19890041_en_1

National Minimum Standards.
Internet link:
www.dh.gov.uk/en/PublicationsAndStatistics/Legislation/ActsAndBills/DH_4001911

Childcare Act 2006.
Internet link:
www.opsi.gov.uk/acts/acts2006/ukpga_20060021_en_1

Criminal Justice and Court Services Act 2000.
Internet link:
www.opsi.gov.uk/Acts/acts2000/ukpga_20000043_en_1

Borders, Citizenship and Immigration Act 2009.
Internet link:
www.opsi.gov.uk/acts/acts2009/ukpga_20090011_en_1

*Arrangements to Safeguard and Promote Children's Welfare in the United Kingdom Border Agency.*
Internet link:
www.ukba.homeoffice.gov.uk/sitecontent/documents/policyandlaw/legislation/bci-act1/
and www.dcsf.gov.uk/everychildmatters/12870

*Information Sharing: Guidance for practitioners and managers.*
Internet link:
www.dcsf.gov.uk/ecm/informationsharing

The *Embedding information sharing toolkit.*
Internet link:
www.dcsf.gov.uk/ecm/informationsharing

The Children Act 2004 Information Database (England) Regulations 2007.
Internet link:
www.opsi.gov.uk/si/si2007/uksi_20072182_en_1

*National Service Framework for Children Young People and Maternity Services.*
Internet link:
www.dh.gov.uk/en/Publicationsandstatistics/Publications/
PublicationsPolicyAndGuidance/DH_4089101

*Building a safe, confident future: the final report of the Social Work Task Force.*
Internet link:
www.dcsf.gov.uk/swtf

Government Response to the Social Work Task Force.
Internet link:
www.dcsf.gov.uk/swtf

*Statutory guidance on making arrangements to safeguard and promote the welfare of children under section 11 of the Children Act 2004.*
Internet link:
www.everychildmatters.gov.uk/resources-and-practice/IG00042/

*Staying Safe: Action Plan.*
Internet link:
www.dcsf.gov.uk/everychildmatters/_download/?id=443

*When to suspect child maltreatment.*
Internet link:
www.nice.org.uk/nicemedia/pdf/CG89FullGuideline.pdf

*What to do if you're worried a child is being abused.*
Internet link:
www.dcsf.gov.uk/everychildmatters/_download/?id=760

*Responding to domestic abuse: A handbook for health professionals.*
Internet link:
www.dh.gov.uk/prod_consum_dh/groups/dh_digitalassets/@dh/@en/documents/
digitalasset/dh_4126619.pdf

*Improving safety, Reducing Harm: Children, young people and domestic violence; a practical toolkit for front line practitioners.*
Internet link:
www.dh.gov.uk/en/Publicationsandstatistics/Publications/
PublicationsPolicyAndGuidance/DH_108697

*Safeguarding Children and Young People: Roles and competencies for Health Care Staff.*
Internet link:
www.rcpch.ac.uk/doc.aspx?id_Resource=1535

*Local Safeguarding Children Boards: A Review of Progress* report.
Internet link:
www.dcsf.gov.uk/everychildmatters/_download/?id=3082

The Healthy Child Programme.
Internet link:
www.dh.gov.uk/en/Healthcare/Children/Maternity/index.htm

*Good Medical Practice* (GMC).
Internet link:
www.gmc-uk.org/GMC_Good_Medical_Practise_1209.pdf_30373048.pdf

*Patients as Parents.*
Internet link:
www.rcpsych.ac.uk/files/pdfversion/cr105.pdf

*Child Abuse and Neglect: the Role of Mental Health Services.*
Internet link:
www.rcpsych.ac.uk/files/pdfversion/cr120.pdf

*Think child, think parent, think family: a guide to parental mental health and child welfare*
(SCIE Guide 30).
Internet link:
www.scie.org.uk/publications/guides/guide30/index.asp

*Guidance on the Visiting of Psychiatric Patients by Children.*
Internet link:
www.dh.gov.uk/prod_consum_dh/groups/dh_digitalassets/@dh/@en/documents/
digitalasset/dh_4012658.pdf

*Guidance on Development of Local Protocols between Drug and Alcohol Treatment Services
and Local Safeguarding and Family Services.*
Internet link:
www.nta.nhs.uk/publications/documents/yp_drug_alcohol_treatment_protocol_1109.pdf

*Safeguarding Children and Young People: Roles and Competencies for Health Care Staff.*
Internet link:
www.rcpch.ac.uk/doc.aspx?id_Resource=1535

*Guidance on Paediatric Forensic Examinations in Relation to Possible Child Sexual Abuse.*
Internet link:
www.rcpch.ac.uk/doc.aspx?id_Resource=1750

*Acting as an expert witness* (GMC).
Internet link:
www.gmc-uk.org/guidance/ethical_guidance/expert_witness_guidance.asp

*Medical Expert Witness: Guidance from the Academy of Medical Royal Colleges.*
Internet link:
www.aomrc.org.uk

*Child protection and the Dental Team – an introduction to safeguarding children in dental practice.*
Internet link:
www.cpdt.org.uk/

*Investigating Child Abuse and Safeguarding Children 2nd Edition.*
Internet link:
www.npia.police.uk/en/14532.htm

Home Office Circular 017/2008.
Internet link:
www.homeoffice.gov.uk/about-us/publications/home-office-circulars/
circulars-2008/017-2008/

*The Use of Force to Control or Restrain Pupils.*
Internet link:
www.teachernet.gov.uk/_doc/12187/ACFD89B.pdf

*Statutory Framework for the Early Years Foundation Stage (EYFS).*
Internet link:
http://nationalstrategies.standards.dcsf.gov.uk/earlyyears

*Recruiting safely: Safer recruitment guidance helping to keep children and young people safe* and associated materials.
Internet link:
www.cwdcouncil.org.uk/safeguarding/safer-recruitment/resources

## Chapter 3

Children Act 2004.
Internet link:
www.opsi.gov.uk/acts/acts2004/ukpga_20040031_en_1

The Local Safeguarding Children Boards Regulations 2006, SI 2006/90.
Internet link:
www.opsi.gov.uk/SI/si2006/20060090.htm

## Chapter 4

Carpenter et al. (2009) *The Organisation, Outcomes and Costs of Inter-agency Training to safeguard and promote the welfare of children*. London: Department for Children, Schools and Families

Induction guidance and supporting materials (CWDC).
Internet link:
www.cwdcouncil.org.uk/induction-standards

Training in relation to the child death review processes and Serious Case Reviews.
Internet link:
http://childdeath.ocbmedia.com/

*The Common Core of Skills and Knowledge for the Children's Workforce.*
Internet link:
www.dcsf.gov.uk/everychildmatters/strategy/deliveringservices1/commoncore/
commoncoreofskillsandknowledge/

Department of Children, Schools and Families et al. (2008) *The Developing World of the Child*. Resource Pack. London: NSPCC.

Department for Education and Skills (2007) *Safeguarding Children – a shared responsibility*. London: NSPCC.

Department of Children, Schools and Families (2009) *Incredibly Caring*. Oxford: Radcliffe Publishing.

Department of Children, Schools and Families (2010) *The Child's World*. Training Resource. Second Edition. London, DCSF.

*When to suspect child maltreatment* (NICE).
Internet link:
www.nice.org.uk/nicemedia/pdf/CG89FullGuideline.pdf

*Guidance on Investigating Child Abuse and Safeguarding Children* (NPIA and ACPO).
Internet link:
www.npia.police.uk/en/14532.htm

Morrison, T. (2005) *Staff Supervision in Social Care*. Third edition. Brighton: Pavilion.

*Building a safe, confident future: the final report of the Social Work Task Force*.
Internet link:
www.dcsf.gov.uk/swtf

Bools, C. (2007) *Fabricated or induced illness in a child by a carer: A reader*. Oxford: Radcliffe Publishing.

Aldgate, J., Jones, J., Rose, W. and Jeffery, C. (Eds) (2006) *The Developing World of the Child*.
London: Jessica Kingsley Publishers.

Cleaver, H., Cawson, P., Gorin, S. and Waller, S. (Eds) (2009): *Safeguarding Children: A Shared Responsibility*. Chichester: Wiley-Blackwell.

Horwath, J. (2009) *The Child's World: The Comprehensive Guide to Assessing Children in Need*.
2nd edition. London: Jessica Kingsley Publishers.

*Providing Effective Supervision* (Skills for Care/CWDC).
Internet link:
www.cwdcouncil.org.uk/providing-effective-supervision

## Chapter 5

*What to do if you are worried a child is being abused*.
Internet link:
www.dcsf.gov.uk/everychildmatters/resources-and-practice/IG00182/

National Minimum Standards and regulations.
Internet link:
www.dcsf.gov.uk/everychildmatters/safeguardingandsocialcare/childrenincare/
childrenincare/

*Information Sharing: Guidance for practitioners and managers*.
Internet link:
http://publications.everychildmatters.gov.uk/default.aspx?PageFunction=productdetails&
PageMode=publications&ProductId=DCSF-00807-2008&

*Framework for the Assessment of Children in Need and their Families*.
Internet link:
www.dh.gov.uk/en/Publicationsandstatistics/Publications/
PublicationsPolicyAndGuidance/DH_4003256

*Volume 1 of the Children Act 1989 Guidance and Regulations, Court Orders.*
Internet link:
www.dcsf.gov.uk/everychildmatters/publications/documents/
childrenactguidanceregulations/

Recent research evidence on effective interventions in safeguarding children.
Internet link:
www.dcsf.gov.uk/cgi-bin/rsgateway/search.pl?cat=3&subcat=3_1&q1=Search

Bentovim, A., Cox A., Bingley Miller, L., and Pizzey, S (2009) *Safeguarding Children Living with Trauma and Family Violence. Evidence-Based Assessment, Analysis and Planning Interventions.* London, Jessica Kingsley Publishers.

## Chapter 6

*Safeguarding Children and Young People from Sexual Exploitation.*
Internet link:
www.dcsf.gov.uk/everychildmatters/_download/?id=6021

*Safeguarding Children in whom Illness is fabricated or induced.*
Internet link:
www.dcsf.gov.uk/everychildmatters/_download/?id=3161

*Complex Child Abuse Investigations: Inter-agency issues.*
Internet link:
www.dh.gov.uk/PublicationsAndStatistics/Publications/PublicationsPolicyAndGuidance/
fs/en

The Female Genital Mutilation Act 2003.
Internet link:
www.opsi.gov.uk/acts/acts2003/ukpga_20030031_en_1

Home Office Circular 10/2004.
Internet link:
www.homeoffice.gov.uk/about-us/publications/home-office-circulars/
circulars-2004/010-2004/index.html

Dorkenoo et al. (2007). *A Statistical Study to Estimate the Prevalence of Female Genital Mutilation in England and Wales.* Available from FORWARD UK.

*Local Authority Social Services Letter LASSL (2004)4.*
Internet link:
www.dh.gov.uk/en/Publicationsandstatistics/Lettersandcirculars/
Localauthoritysocialservicesletters/AllLASSLs/DH_4074779

*The Right to Choose: Multi-agency statutory guidance for dealing with forced marriage.*
Internet link:
www.fco.gov.uk/resources/en/pdf/3849543/forced-marriage-right-to-choose

*Multi-agency practice guidelines: Handling cases of Forced Marriage.*
Internet link:
www.fco.gov.uk/resources/en/pdf/3849543/forced-marriage-guidelines09.pdf

*Forced marriage guidance for local authorities and relevant third parties.*
Internet link:
www.justice.gov.uk/guidance/forced-marriage.htm.

*Safeguarding Disabled Children – Practice Guidance.*
Internet link:
www.dcsf.gov.uk/everychildmatters/_download/?id=6195

The Youth Justice and Criminal Evidence Act 1999.
Internet link:
www.opsi.gov.uk/Acts/acts1999/ukpga_19990023_en_1

*Achieving Best Evidence in Criminal Proceedings: Guidance on vulnerable and intimidated witnesses including children.*
Internet link:
www.homeoffice.gov.uk/documents/ach-bect-evidence/

*Safeguarding Children from Abuse Linked to a Belief in Spirit Possession.*
Internet link:
www.dcsf.gov.uk/everychildmatters/_download/?id=661

*Safeguarding Children who may have been trafficked.*
Internet link:
http://publications.everychildmatters.gov.uk/default.aspx?PageFunction=productdetails&PageMode=publications&ProductId=HMG-00994-2007&

Child Trafficking Strategic Threat Assessment (CEOP).
Internet link:
www.ceop.police.uk/publications

*Safeguarding children and young people who may be affected by gang activity.*
Internet link:
publications.everychildmatters.gov.uk/default.aspx?PageFunction=productdetails&PageMode=publications&ProductId=DCSF-00064-2010

## Chapter 7

*Guidance about Compliance Essential Standards of Quality and Safety* (CQC).
Internet link:
www.cqc.org.uk/publications.cfm?fde_id=13512

Children and Young Persons Act 2008.
Internet link:
www.opsi.gov.uk/acts/acts2008/ukpga_20080023_en_1

*Responding when a child dies. Training resources.*
Internet link:
www.dcsf.gov.uk/everychildmatters/safeguardingandsocialcare/safeguardingchildren/
childdeathreviewprocedures/trainingmaterials/trainingmaterials/

*National templates for LSCBs to use when collecting information about child deaths.*
Internet link:
www.dcsf.gov.uk/everychildmatters/safeguardingandsocialcare/safeguardingchildren/
childdeathreviewprocedures/nationaltemplatesforlscbs/lscbtemplates/

*Framework for the assessment of children in need and their families.*
Internet link:
www.dh.gov.uk/en/Publicationsandstatistics/Publications/PublicationsPolicyandGuidance/
DH_4003256

Foundation for Sudden Infant Deaths (2010) *The child death review:
A guide for parents and carers.* Available to order from DCSF Publications, 00180-2010LEF-EN

Human Tissue Act 2004.
Internet link:
www.opsi.gov.uk/acts/acts2004/ukpga_20040030_en_1

*LSCB designated person to whom child notifications should be sent by the DCSF.*
Internet link:
www.everychildmatters.gov.uk/resources-and-practice/IG00351/

*Guidance for coroners and Local Safeguarding Children Boards on the supply of information
concerning the death of children.*
Internet link:
www.justice.gov.uk/guidance/coroners-guidance.htm

Fleming P. J., Blair P. S., Bacon C., and Berry P. J. (2000) *Sudden Unexpected Death In Infancy.
The CESDI SUDI Studies 1993-1996.* London: The Stationery Office.

Resuscitation Council (UK) (2005) *UK Resuscitation Guidelines.*
Internet link:
www.resus.org.uk/pages/guide.htm

*Sudden unexpected death in infancy. A multi-agency protocol for care and investigation.*
Internet link:
www.rcpath.org

*The Report of a working group convened by the Royal College of Pathologists and the Royal College of Paediatrics and Child Health.*
Internet link:
www.rcpath.org

The Coroners (Amendment) Rules 2008.
Internet link:
www.opsi.gov.uk/si/si2008/uksi_20081652_en_1

## Chapter 8

The Local Safeguarding Children Boards Regulations 2006, Statutory Instrument no. 2006/90.
Internet link:
www.opsi.gov.uk/SI/si2006/20060090.htm

*Safeguarding Disabled Children: Practice guidance* (2009). London: Department for Children, Schools and Families.
Internet link:
www.dcsf.gov.uk/everychildmatters/_download/?id=6195

Fish S., Munro E. and Bairstow S. (2008) *SCIE Report 19: Learning together to safeguard children: developing a multi-agency systems approach for case reviews*. London: Social Care Institute for Excellence.
Internet link:
www.scie.org.uk/publications/reports/report19.asp

Prisons and Probation Ombudsman (PPO) Fatal Incidents Investigation
Internet link:
www.ppo.gov.uk/investigating-fatal-accidents.html

Serious Further Offence (SFO) Probation Circular 22/2008 – Revised Notification and Review Procedures for Serious Further offences
Internet link:
www.probation.homeoffice.gov.uk/output/page31.asp

MAPPA Serious Case Review (MSCR).
Internet link:
www.probation.homeoffice.gov.uk/output/page30.asp

How best to liaise with the coroner. See guidance for coroners on reports to prevent future deaths and on the supply of information concerning the death of children
Internet link:
www.justice.gov.uk/guidance/coroners-guidance.htm

## Chapter 9

Brandon, M., Bailey, S., Belderson, P., Gardner, R., Sidebottom, P., Dodsworth, J., Warren, C. and Black, J. (2009) *Understanding Serious Case Reviews and their Impact: A Biennial Analysis of Serious Case Reviews 2005-7*. London: Department for Children Schools and Families.

Montgomery, P., Ramchandani, P., Gardner, F., and Bjornstad, G. (2009) *Systematic reviews of interventions following physical abuse: helping practitioners and expert witnesses improve the outcomes of child abuse*. London: Department for Children, Schools and Families.

Barlow, J., and Schrader-MacMillan, A. (2009) *Safeguarding Children From Emotional Abuse – What Works?* London: Department for Children Schools and Families. DCSF-RBX-09-09.

Jones, D. P. H. and Ramchandani, P. (1999) *Child Sexual Abuse. Informing Practice from Research*. Abingdon: Radcliffe Medical Press Ltd.

Daniel, B., Taylor, J., and Scott, J. (2009) *Noticing and helping the neglected child*. London: Department for Children, Schools and Families. DCSF – RBX-09-03.

Stein, M., Rees, G., Hicks, L. and Gorin, S. (2009) *Neglected adolescents: a review of the research and the preparation of guidance for multi-disciplinary teams and a guide for young people*. London: Department for Children, Schools and Families. DCSF-RBX-09-04.

Home Office (2009) *What is Domestic Violence?* London: Home Office.

Cleaver, H., Unell, I. and Aldgate, A. (2010) *Children's Needs – Parenting Capacity: The impact of parental mental illness, learning disability, problem alcohol and drug use, and domestic violence on children's safety and development. 2nd Edition*. London: The Stationery Office.

*The Protection of Children in England: A Progress Report.*
Internet link:
http://publications.everychildmatters.gov.uk/eOrderingDownload/HC-330.pdf

Humphreys, C. and Stanley, N. (eds) (2006) *Domestic Violence and Child Protection*. London: Jessica Kingsley Publishers.

Hester, M., Pearson, C. and Harwin, N. with Abrahams, H. (2007) *Making an impact: children and domestic violence*: *A reader. 2nd Edition*. London: Jessica Kingsley Publishers.

Onyskiw, J. E. (2003) 'Domestic Violence and Children's Adjustment: A Review of Research.' *Journal of Emotional Abuse 3*, 1/2, 11-45.

Mental Health Act 2007.
Internet link:
www.opsi.gov.uk/acts/acts2007/ukpga_20070012_en_1

Office for National Statistics (2006) *Labour Force Survey*. London: The Stationary Office.

Melzer, D. (2003) 'Inequalities in mental health: A systematic review.' *The research findings register, Summary No. 1063*. London: Department of Health.

Reupert, A. and Maybery, D. (2007) 'Families Affected by Parental Mental Illness; A Multiperspective Account of Issues and Interventions.' *American Journal of Orthopsychiatry 77*, 3, 362-369.

Egeland, B. (2009) 'Taking stock: Childhood emotional maltreatment and developmental psychopathology.' *Child Abuse & Neglect 33*, 1, 22-27.

Tunnard, J. (2004) *Parental Mental Health Problems: Key Messages from Research, Policy and Practice*. Dartington: Research in Practice.

Klein, D., Clark, D., Dansky, L. and Margolis, E.T. (1988) 'Dysthymia in the offspring of parents with primary unipolar affective disorder.' *Journal of Abnormal Psychology 94*, 1155-1127.

Green, H., McGinnity, A., Meltzer, H., Ford, T. and Goodman, R. (2005) *Mental health of children and young people in Great Britain, 2004*. London: Office for National Statistics.

Weissman, M. M., John, K., Merikangas, K. R., Prusoff, B. A., Wickramaratne, P., Gammon, G. D., Angold, A. and Warner, V. (1986) 'Depressed parents and their children: General health, social and psychiatric problems.' *American Journal of Diseases of Children 140*, 801-805.

Somers, V. (2007) 'Schizophrenia: The Impact of Parental Illness on Children.' *British Journal of Social Work 37*, 8, 1319-1334.

Hoare, J. and Flatley, J. (2008) *Drug Misuse Declared: Finding from the 2007/08 British Crime Survey, England and Wales*. London: Home Office Statistical Bulletin.

Advisory Council on the Misuse of Drugs (2003) *Hidden harm: Responding to the needs of children of problem drug users*. London: Home Office.

Hogan, D. and Higgins, L. (2001) *When Parents Use Drugs: Key Findings from a Study of Children in the Care of Drug-using Parents*. Dublin: The Children's Research Centre.

Cleaver, H., Nicholson, D., Tarr, S. and Cleaver, D. (2007) *Child Protection, Domestic Violence and Parental Substance Misuse: Family Experiences and Effective Practice*. London: Jessica Kingsley Publishers.

Velleman, R. and Templeton, L. (2007) 'Understanding and modifying the impact of parental substance misuse on children.' *Advances in Psychiatric Treatment 13*, 79-89.

Cleaver, H. and Nicholson, D. (2007) *Parental Learning Disability and Children's Needs: Family Experiences and Effective Practice*. London: Jessica Kingsley Publishers.

Julien, R. M. (1995) *A Primer of Drug Action: A Concise, Non-Technical Guide to the Actions, Uses, and Side Effects of Psychoactive Drugs. 7th Edition*. New York: W.H. Freeman and Co.

Standing Conference on Drug Misuse (SCODA) (1997) *Working with Children and Families Affected by Parental Substance Misuse*. London: Local Government Association Publications.

Powell, J. and Hart, D. (2001) 'Working with Parents who Use Drugs.' In R. Gordon and E. Harran (eds) *Fragile handle with care: protecting babies from harm: Reader*. Leicester: NSPCC.

Barnard, M. (2007) *Drug Addiction and Families*. London: Jessica Kingsley Publishers.

Covell, K. and Howe, R. B. (2009) *Children, families and violence: Challenges for children's rights*. London: Jessica Kingsley Publishers.

*Safe. Sensible. Social. The next steps in the National Alcohol Strategy.*
Internet link:
www.dh.gov.uk/en/Publicationsandstatistics/Publications/
PublicationsPolicyAndGuidance/DH_075218

General Lifestyle Survey 2008 (2010) *Smoking and Drinking among adults 2008*. London: Office of National Statistics.

ChildLine (1997) *Beyond the limit: children who live with parental alcohol misuse*. London: ChildLine.

*Updated NICE guideline on care and support that women should receive during pregnancy.*
Internet link:
www.nice.org.uk/media/E5D/8B/2008022AntenatalCare.pdf

Abel, E. L. (1998) 'Fetal Alcohol Syndrome: The American Paradox.' *Alcohol and Alcoholism 33,* 3, 195-201.

Macleod, J., Hickman, M., Bowen, E., Alati, R., Tilling, K. and Davey Smith, G. (2008) 'Parental drug use, early adversities, later childhood problems and children's use of tobacco and alcohol at age 10: birth cohort study.' *Addiction 103,* 1731-43.

Li, C., Pentz, A. and Chou, C-P. (2002) 'Parental substance use as a modifier of adolescent substance use risk.' *Addiction 97,* 1537-50.

Velleman, R. and Orford, J. (2001) *Risk and Resilience: Adults who were the children of problem drinkers.* Amsterdam: Harwood Academic Publishers.

Quilgars, D., Johnsen, S. and Pleace, N. (2008) *Youth homelessness in the UK. A decade of progress?* York: Joseph Rowntree Foundation.

Cm 5086 (2001) *Valuing People: A New Strategy for Learning Disability for the 21st Century.* London: The Stationery Office. Cm 5086 2001, p.14, paragraph 1.5

Emerson E. and Hatton, C. (2008) *People with Learning Disabilities in England.* Lancaster: Centre for Disability Research.

Department of Health and Department for Education and Skills (2007) *Good practice guidance on working with parents with a learning disability.* London: Department of Health.

Booth, T. and Booth, W. (2002) 'Men in the Lives of Mothers with Intellectual Disabilities'. *Journal of Applied Research in Intellectual Disabilities 15,* 187-199.

James, H. (2004) 'Promoting Effective Working with Parents with Learning Disabilities.' *Child Abuse Review 13,* 1, 31-41.

*Framework for the Assessment of Children in Need and their Families.*
Internet link:
www.dh.gov.uk/en/Publicationsandstatistics/Publications/
PublicationsPolicyAndGuidance/DH_4003256

Social Services Inspectorate (2000) *A Jigsaw of Services: Supporting disabled adults in their parenting role.* London: Department of Health.

Working Together with Parents Network (2009). Supporting parents with learning disabilities and difficulties: stories of positive practice Norah Fry Research Centre. DH/DCSF Joint Good Practice Guidance on Supporting Parents with a Learning Disability
Internet link:
www.dh.gov.uk/en/Publicationsandstatistics/Publications/
PublicationsPolicyAndGuidance/DH_075119

*Supporting disabled parents and parents with additional support needs* (SCIE).
Internet link:
www.scie.org.uk/publications/knowledgereviews/kr11.pdf

James, H. (2004) 'Promoting Effective Working with Parents with Learning Disabilities.'
*Child Abuse Review 13*, 1, 31-41.

McGaw, S. and Newman, T. (2005) *What works for parents with learning disabilities.* Essex: Barnardo's.

McGaw, S., Ball, K. and Clark, A. (2002) 'The effect of group intervention on the relationships of parents with intellectual disabilities'. *Journal of Applied Research in Intellectual Disabilities 15*, 4, 354-366.

Tarleton, B., Ward, L. and Howarth, J. (2006) *Finding the right support? A review of issues and positive practice to support parents with learning difficulties and their children.* London: The Baring Foundation.

C4EO (2010) *Knowledge Review – Effective practice to protect children living in 'highly resistant' families.*
Internet link:
www.c4eo.org.uk/themes/safeguarding/default.aspx?themeid=11&accesstypeid=1

## Chapter 10

*Statutory guidance on making arrangements to safeguard and promote the welfare of children under section 11 of the Children Act 2004.*
Internet link:
www.dcsf.gov.uk/everychildmatters/resources-and-practice/IG00042/

Families at Risk Review.
Internet link:
www.cabinetoffice.gov.uk/social_exclusion_task_force/families_at_risk.aspx

Farrington and Welsch (2007) Saving children from a life of crime; Farrington and Welsh (2003). Meta analysis in ANZJC.

NICE (2006) *Parent – Training/education programmes in the management of children with conduct disorders.* In NICE Technology appraisal guidance 102.

Friedli and Parsonage (2007) *Mental Health Promotion: Building an Economic Case.* Northern Ireland Association for Mental Health.

*The Dad Test*
Internet link:
www.think-fathers.org

## Chapter 11

Fostering Services: National Minimum Standards – 9.8

Children Act 1989 guidance on private fostering (2005).
Internet link:
www.dcsf.gov.uk/everychildmatters/safeguardingandsocialcare/safeguardingchildren/
privatefostering/fostering

Department of Health and the Department for Education and Skills (2004) *The National Service Framework for Children, Young People and Maternity Services.* London: Department of Health

The Healthcare Commission undertook an improvement review of the NHS implementation of the hospital standard in 2006.
Internet link:
www.cqc.org.uk/_db/_documents/children_improving_services_Tagged.pdf

*When to share information: best practice guidance for everyone working in the youth justice system.*
Internet link:
www.dh.gov.uk/en/Publicationsandstatistics/Publications/
PublicationsPolicyAndGuidance/DH_084703

*Healthy Children, Safer Communities: a strategy and action plan to promote the health and well being of those in contact with the youth justice system.*
Internet link:
www.dh.gov.uk/en/Publicationsandstatistics/Publications/
PublicationsPolicyAndGuidance/DH_109771

*Review of people with mental health problems or learning disabilities in the criminal justice system* (the Bradley report).
Internet link:
www.dh.gov.uk/en/Publicationsandstatistics/Publications/
PublicationsPolicyAndGuidance/DH_098694

*The law, policy and guidance for schools and the tackling school bullying guidance.*
Internet link:
http://publications.teachernet.gov.uk/default.aspx?PageFunction=productdetails&PageM
ode=publications&ProductId=DCSF-00668-2007

*Safe to Learn: Embedding Anti-bullying Work in Schools.*
Internet link:
www.teachernet.gov.uk/wholeschool/behaviour/tacklingbullying/racistbullying/

*New guidance for schools on preventing and tackling sexist, sexual and transphobic bullying.*
Internet link:
www.teachernet.gov.uk/wholeschool/behaviour/tacklingbullying/
sexistsexualandtransphobicbullying/

DVD Resource pack on bullying related to SEN and disabilities.
Internet link:
www.teachernet.gov.uk/wholeschool/behaviour/tacklingbullying/sendisab/

Prevent Strategy.
Internet link:
www.dcsf.gov.uk/violentextremism

*Framework for the Assessment of Children in Need and their Families.*
Internet link:
www.dh.gov.uk/en/Publicationsandstatistics/Publications/
PublicationsPolicyAndGuidance/DH_4003256

*Improving safety, Reducing harm: Children, young people and domestic violence – A practical toolkit for front line practitioners.*
Internet link:
www.dh.gov.uk/prod_consum_dh/groups/dh_digitalassets/documents/digitalasset/
dh_108704.pdf

*A vision for services for children and young people affected by domestic violence*
(LGA, ADSS, Women's Aid and Cafcass, 2005).
Internet link:
http://new.lga.gov.uk/lga/aio/1224298

*Statutory guidance setting how local authorities and agencies should respond when a child or young person goes missing from home or care.*
Internet link:
www.dcsf.gov.uk/everychildmatters/_download/?id=6178

*Identifying and maintaining contact with children missing, or at risk of going missing, from education.*
Internet link:
http://publications.everychildmatters.gov.uk/default.aspx?PageFunction=productdetails&
PageMode=publications&ProductId=LEA%2F0225%2F2004&

## Chapter 12

*Guidance on offences against children* (Home Office Circular 16/2005)
Internet link:
www.homeoffice.gov.uk/about-us/publications/home-office-circulars/
circulars-2005/016-2005/

National MAPPA Guidance.
Internet link:
www.probation.homeoffice.gov.uk/output/page30.asp

Risk Identification tool.
Internet link:
www.caada.org.uk/searchresult.html?sw?risk%20identification%20checklist

*Managing Sexual Offenders and Violent Offenders* (ACPO).
Internet link:
www.homeoffice.gov.uk/about-us/publications/home-office-circulars.

## Appendix 3

Bentovim, A. and Bingley Miller, L. (2001) *The Family Assessment*. Brighton: Pavilion Publishers.

Birleson, P. (1980) The validity of depressive disorder in childhood and the development of a self-rating scale: A research report. *Journal of Child Psychology & Psychiatry 22*, 73-88.

Brugha, T., Bebington, P., Tennant, C. and Hurry, J. (1985) The list of threatening experiences: A subset of 12 life event categories with considerable long-term contextual threat. *Psychological Medicine 15*, 189-194.

Cox, A. and Walker, S. (2002) *The Home Inventory*. Brighton: Pavilion Publishers.

Crnic, K. A. & Greenberg, M. T. (1990) Minor parenting stresses with young children. *Child Development 61*, 1628 – 1637.

Crnic, K. A. & Booth, C. L. (1991) Mothers' and fathers' perceptions of daily hassles of parenting across early childhood. *Journal of Marriage and the Family 53*, 1043 – 1050.

Davie, C. E., Hurt, S. J., Vincent, E. and Mason, M. (1984) *The young child at home.* Windsor: NFER-Nelson.

Department of Health (2000) *The Family Pack of Questionnaires and Scales.* London: The Stationery Office.

Goodman, R. (1997) The Strengths and Difficulties Questionnaire: A Research Note. *Journal of Child Psychology and Psychiatry 38*, 581 – 586.

Goodman, R., Meltzer, H. and Bailey, V. (1998) The strengths and difficulties questionnaire: A pilot study on the validity of the self-report version. *European Child and Adolescent Psychiatry 7*, 125 – 130.

Piccinelli, M., Tessari, E., Bortolomasi, M., Piasere, O., Semenzin, M., Garzotto, N. and Tansella, M. (1997) Efficacy of the alcohol use disorders identification test as a screening tool for hazardous alcohol intake and related disorders in primary care: A validity study. *British Medical Journal 514*, 420 – 424.

Smith, M. A. (1985) *The Effects of Low Levels of Lead on Urban Children: The relevance of social factors.* Ph.D. Psychology, University of London.

Snaith, R. P., Constantopoulos, A. A., Jardine, M. Y. and McGuffin, P. (1978) a clinical scale for the self-assessment for irritability. *British Journal of Psychiatry 132*, 164 – 171.